DISCOVERIES IN THE JUDAEAN DESERT · XX

QUMRAN CAVE 4

XV

DISCOVERIES IN THE JUDAEAN DESERT

EMANUEL TOV, EDITOR-IN-CHIEF

DISCOVERIES IN THE JUDAEAN DESERT · XX

QUMRAN CAVE 4

XV

SAPIENTIAL TEXTS, PART 1

BY

TORLEIF ELGVIN, MENACHEM KISTER,
TIMOTHY LIM, BILHAH NITZAN,
STEPHEN PFANN, ELISHA QIMRON,
LAWRENCE H. SCHIFFMAN,
and ANNETTE STEUDEL

IN CONSULTATION WITH

JOSEPH A. FITZMYER, S.J.

PARTIALLY BASED ON EARLIER TRANSCRIPTIONS BY
JOZEF T. MILIK AND JOHN STRUGNELL

CLARENDON PRESS · OXFORD

1997

Oxford University Press, Great Clarendon Street, Oxford OX2 6DP
Oxford New York
Athens Auckland Bangkok Bogota Bombay
Buenos Aires Calcutta Cape Town Dar es Salaam
Delhi Florence Hong Kong Istanbul Karachi
Kuala Lumpur Madras Madrid Melbourne
Mexico City Nairobi Paris Singapore
Taipei Tokyo Toronto Warsaw
and associated companies in
Berlin Ibadan

Oxford is a trade mark of Oxford University Press

Published in the United States
by Oxford University Press Inc., New York

British Library Cataloguing in Publication Data
Data available

Library of Congress Cataloging in Publication Date
Data available

ISBN 0–19–826938–2

1 3 5 7 9 10 8 6 4 2

Printed in Great Britain on acid-free paper by
St Edmundsbury Press, Bury St Edmunds

This volume is dedicated to individuals and organizations who have graciously supported its publication

The Ashton Family Foundation, Orem, Utah
The Edith C. Blum Foundation, New York
The Catholic Biblical Association, Washington, D.C.
Martha Frey, Rochester, Minnesota
Steven J. and Kalleen Lund, Provo, Utah
The Royal Academy of Letters, History and Antiquities, Sweden
Martin Schøyen, Oslo, Norway

CONTENTS

TABLE OF PLATES

FOREWORD

THE sapiential texts from Qumran are presented in two volumes in this series. The present volume contains a collection of previously unknown sapiential compositions from the Second Temple period. Didactic in character, they include admonitions, instructions, and meditations. They are part of the larger genre of 'wisdom literature', common in the ancient Near East, which includes other collections of sayings and instruction such as the Book of Proverbs, Ben Sira and the Epistle of James.

Volume XXXIV, the second of the sapiential volumes, will contain the text edition of the five manuscripts from cave 4 of a previously unknown composition, originally dubbed 'Sapiential Work A' and now known as 'Instruction.' The numerous copies of this composition, and its presence in cave 1, attest to its importance for the community at Qumran.

Professor Joseph A. Fitzmyer, S.J. of Georgetown University served as the consulting editor for this volume. Our sincere appreciation is expressed to him for his careful editing and judicious remarks.

The volume was typeset in Jerusalem by Eva Ben-David, Miriam Berg, and Janice Karnis, and copy-edited by Valerie Carr Zakovitch. The production was co-ordinated by Claire Pfann.

As in the past, we are grateful to the Oxford University Press for its professional production of the text and plates.

The in-context concordances were prepared by Stephen Pfann of the Center for the Study of Early Christianity, Jerusalem. The corrections and formatting of the concordances for this volume have been supported by the Foundation for Ancient Research and Mormon Studies in Provo, Utah.

As in the past, we are indebted to the Israel Antiquities Authority for its constant encouragement and for the network of support services it supplies, including public relations, access to archival materials, production of photographic plates, and the on-going task of preservation of the scrolls. In particular we wish to thank the Director, General (ret.) Amir Drori, Ayala Sussmann, Director of Publications, Tsila Sagiv, photographer, and Lena Libman, conservator. By the same token, we owe a debt of gratitude to the Advisory Committee of the Israel Antiquities Authority for its active involvement in the reorganization of the Dead Sea Scrolls Publication Project over the past six years, which has contributed to the present accelerated rate of progress in the publication of the *DJD* volumes.

The Qumran Project of the Oxford Centre for Hebrew and Jewish Studies is to be thanked for its support for the typesetting of this volume and for the work of the international Dead Sea Scrolls Publication Project as a whole.

Jerusalem
March 1997

EMANUEL TOV
EDITOR-IN-CHIEF

298. 4QcryptA Words of the Maskil to All Sons of Dawn

(PLATES I–II)

Preliminary publication: S. Pfann, '4Q298: The Maskil's Address to All Sons of Dawn', *JQR* 85 (1994) 203–35; M. Kister, 'Commentary to 4Q298', *JQR* 85 (1994) 237–49.

4Q**298** is a small, fragmentary scroll consisting of eight separate fragments.[1] To date this manuscript is unique—no other copies of this composition have been discovered among the manuscripts deriving from the Judaean wilderness.

The history of the previous work on this scroll can be derived from the PAM photographs (for the reconstruction of the scroll) and the *Preliminary Concordance* (*PC*; for the transcription of J. T. Milik). The fact that fragments of this manuscript appear on PAM 40.581 ('G' or Government series) indicates that it was represented among the first fragments of probable provenience from Qumran cave 4 to be offered for sale by the Bedouin.[2] PAM 41.776, taken during August 1955,[3] represents the reconstruction of the scroll suggested by J. T. Milik at that time.[4] This photograph was taken before the museum plates were changed from a horizontal to a vertical format.[5] At that stage all of the larger fragments had been identified and were reconstructed (including frg. 5) to represent the first three columns of the scroll. PAM 43.384 represents the arrangement of the fragments in a vertical format for the final photograph as of April 1960.[6] At this point frg. 5 appears among other small unplaced fragments at the bottom of the photograph.

4Q**298** was the first of the scrolls written in Cryptic A to be deciphered. This script, though originally dubbed 'cryptic' (a term retained here for convention), is actually an

---

[1] All sections of this treatment of 4Q**298** were prepared by S. Pfann except for the sections labelled COMMENTS, following each transcribed fragment, which were contributed by M. Kister.

[2] The fact that two non-adjacent fragments alone were found among the original acquisitions confirms that the fragments did not arrive at the museum as a wad but must have been separated sometime before their arrival. PAM 40.962–985 represent what was dubbed the 'E series' which were photographs taken of the manuscript fragments obtained in the official excavation of the cave in September 1952. The 'G series' (PAM 40.575–637, 986–992) were photographs taken of the first groups of fragments said to have derived from the earlier clandestine excavation of cave 4 by the Bedouin and were purchased with funds provided by the Jordanian Government. Thus only the provenience of those manuscripts in the 'E series' photographs can be proven conclusively.

[3] S. Pfann, 'Chronological List of the Negatives of the PAM, IAA, and Shrine of the Book', *The Dead Sea Scrolls on Microfiche: Companion Volume* (Leiden: E. J. Brill & IDC, 1995) 84 (hereafter: *Companion Volume*). We are indebted to J. T. Milik for his expert care in both restoring the fragments of this scroll as well as deciphering its text.

[4] On the assignment of the manuscripts written in esoteric scripts to J. T. Milik, cf. F. M. Cross, *The Ancient Library of Qumran and Modern Biblical Studies* (Garden City, NY: Doubleday, 1958).

[5] For the reasons for this change cf. J. Strugnell, 'On the History of the Photographing of the Discoveries in the Judean Desert for the International Team', *Companion Volume,* 125.

[6] S. Pfann, 'Chronological List', 91.

Essene esoteric script, written for the internal purposes of the Qumran community. **4Q298** is the only one of the ten manuscripts written in an Essene esoteric script to be included in the *Preliminary Concordance* (under the siglum 'DS')[7]. *The Preliminary Concordance* relied upon Milik's transcriptions made during the period 1958–1959 (recorded in R. Brown's hand). Already at that time, frg. 5 had been excluded by Milik from the first three columns of his reconstruction. The first three columns of the scroll (comprising frgs. 1–4) were then dubbed DS 1 i–iii and frg. 5, DS 2 i–ii.

Physical Description

Skin Preparation

The collection of fragments represents the remains from two sheets of fine parchment from a single scroll. The colour of both sheets is light brown (7.5YR 6/3) to very dark brown (7.5YR 2.5/2).[8] The scribe wrote on the hair side according to customary practice.

The grain and pores which are normally visible after the dehairing of the skin are more noticeable on the second sheet than on the first. A more thorough smoothing of the surface seems to have been applied to the first sheet than to the second (normally done using a pumice stone). This could also explain why the first sheet is slightly thinner than the second sheet.[9] Microscopic examination of the hair follicle pattern reveals that the sheet was taken from the right half of the skin of an animal, from along its back. The line of the back runs along the top edge; cf. fig. 2.

The second sheet was more susceptible to cracking. The largest fragment is actually a composite of twelve smaller fragments joined together during the 1950s. The repair work was not always successful, leaving some cases where the joins are not flush or the fragments are misaligned up to a millimetre. Care must be taken in the decipherment of letters which are split at a join between two fragments.[10] The hair follicle pattern indicates that this sheet was also taken from the right side of an animal but the back runs along the leading (sewn) edge of the sheet (cf. fig. 2), resulting in a different orientation of the hair follicles, which in turn has aided in the assignment of the fragments to a particular sheet.

Sewing

Sewing of the one extant seam was performed from the back of the skin with flax thread. Stitching was made at 3 to 5 mm intervals along the seam.

---

[7] Cf. *A Preliminary Concordance to the Hebrew and Aramaic Fragments From Qumrân Caves II-X* (Göttingen: printed privately, 1988). According to J. Fitzmyer the three main compilers of the concordance (Fitzmyer, Brown and Oxtoby) worked in one year shifts beginning in the summer of 1957.

[8] The colour scale used here is that of the *Munsell Soil Color Charts* (Baltimore, MD: Macbeth Division of Kollmorgen Corp., 1991).

[9] However the first stages of gelatination will often achieve similar results.

[10] There also seems to be one fragment involving lines 8 and 9 that is out of place.

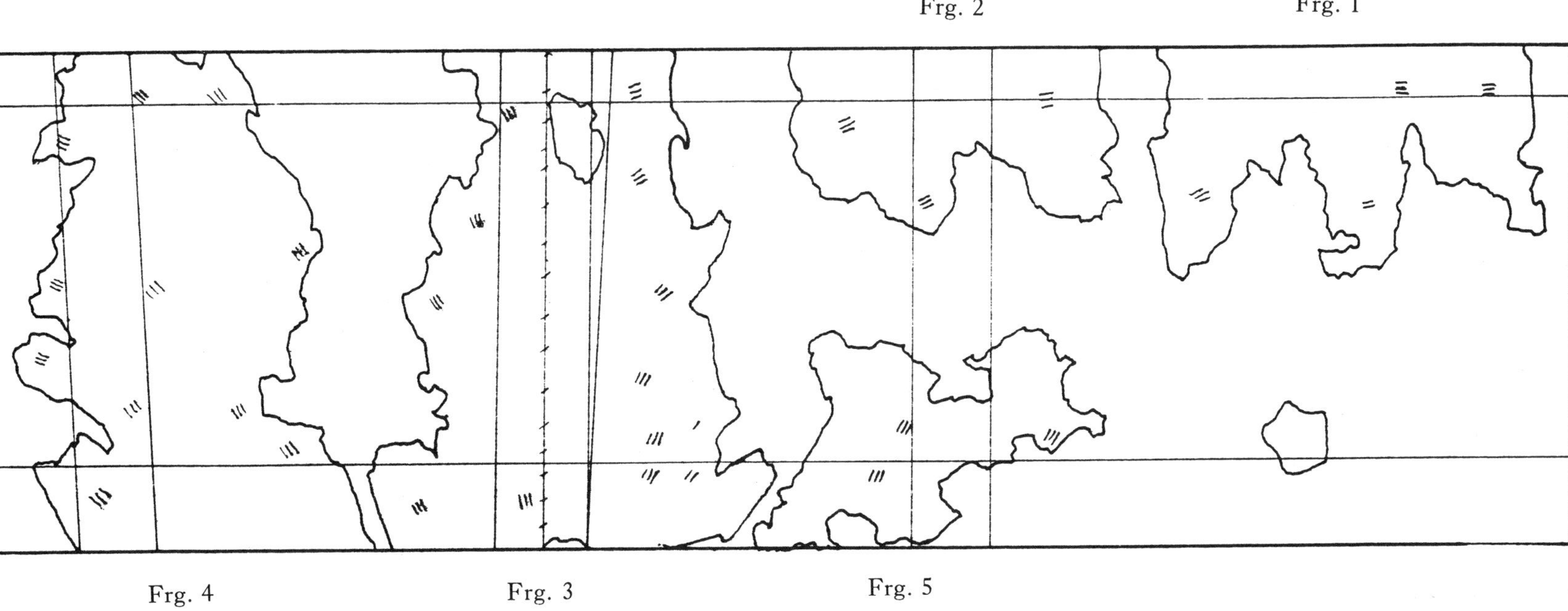

Figure 1. Fragments of 4Q**298** arranged according to lines, patterns of deterioration, and hair follicle patterns (the configuration of fragments follows that of PAM 41.776). The orientation of the hair follicles are represented by parallel strokes (which also indicate the areas examined under the microscope). In several cases, hairs were still visible protruding from their follicles.

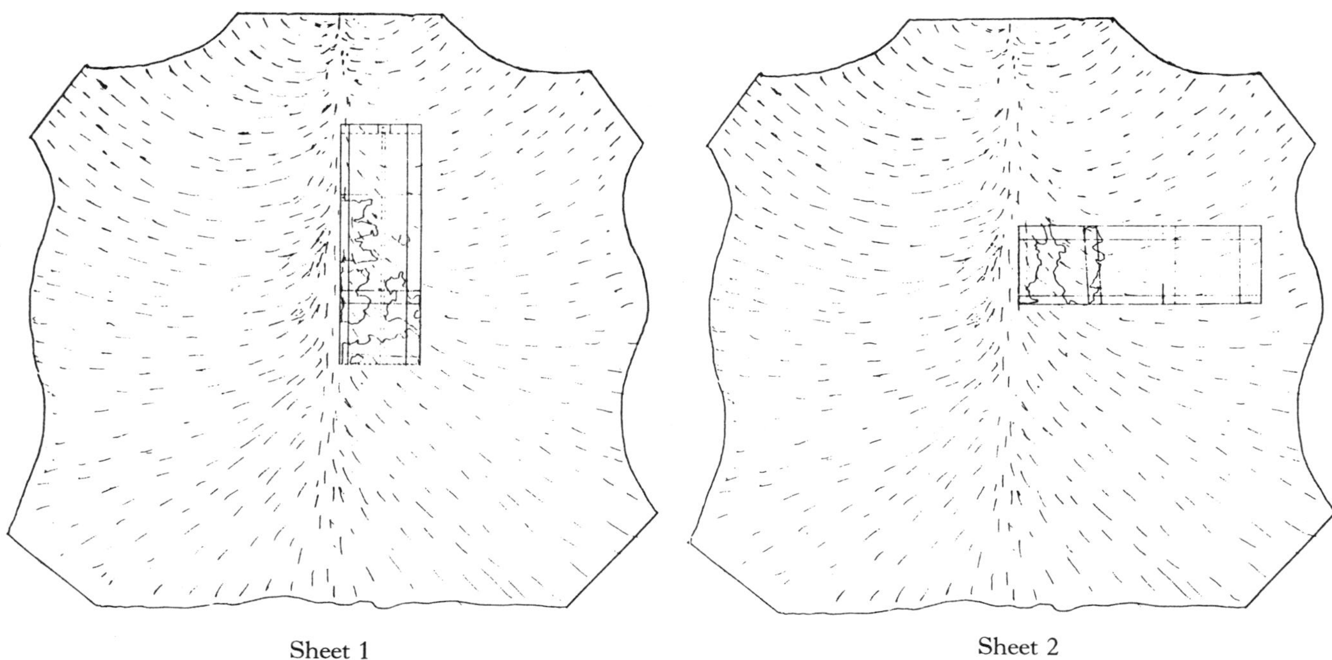

Figure 2. Depiction of the origin of sheets 1 and 2 based upon hair follicle patterns and the skin of an average-sized adult sheep.

Ruling

Ruling of the parchment was made by a dull point with ten horizontal lines on each sheet. Although the height remains consistent for the entire length of each line, the height of each of the ten lines varies from 6 to 8 mm. It is likely that the sheets of parchment were supplied to the scribe both sewn and ruled horizontally.

More attention seems to have been given to maintaining consistent internal margins (approximately 13 mm) through the use of vertical lines marking off the columns, than to maintaining consistent column widths. The left line of each column was drawn rather carelessly, lacking exact perpendicular intersections with the horizontal lines. In fact one of these lines was redrawn to more closely parallel the left edge of the sheet (frg. 3). Due to these factors and the variable column widths it would seem that the scribe himself must have made the vertical ruling as he copied the text from the *Vorlage*.

Column Width

The extra width of the first column may in fact reflect the actual width of the first column of the *Vorlage*.

Ink

The ink used by the first hand is black to gray; that of the second hand is black.

Tying

There is evidence that there was at one time an affixed thong used for tying the scroll closed while it was not being used. The clearest evidence can be seen on the verso of frg. 3 where the presence of the thong left a pale horizontal line stretched across it midway between the top and bottom edges.[11] At the left end of the pale line an indentation was left by the pressure of the thong's knot and reinforcing tab by which it was attached to the leading edge of the scroll. There is also a corresponding wrinkled, darkened, horizontal indentation on the recto of this fragment to the right of the seam. The gap between the upper and lower fragments of sheet 1 (if frg. 5 should be included there) seems to have been created initially by the cracking and ensuing oxidation produced by the pressure of the leather tie (cf. fig. 3).[12]

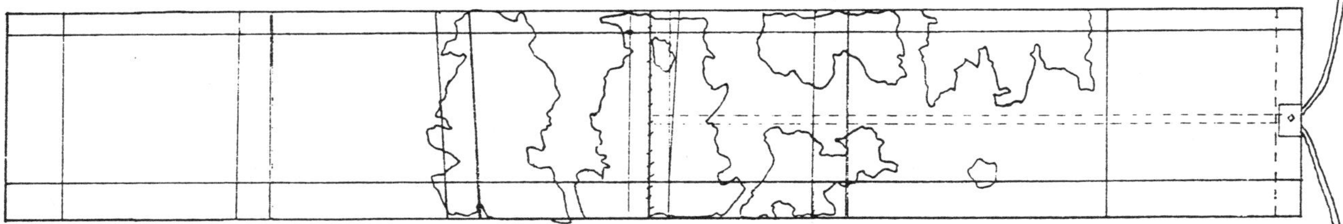

Figure 3. 4Q**298**: Reconstructed Scroll

Patterns of Deterioration

The skin exhibits three forms of deterioration, in both horizontal and vertical patterns, due to three causes: cracking, oxidation, and worms. There is a repetition of a vertical gap which can be reconstructed to have occurred at regular intervals between fragments for four or five turns of the scroll.[13] The scroll seems to have lain on its side on the floor of the cave, which transferred moisture along this line.

There is also a pattern of deterioration involving the first sheet of the scroll which can be traced along a horizontal line drawn midway between its top and bottom. This line represents the line of pressure from tying the scroll closed with a leather thong when the scroll was not in use. The pressure created indentations, wrinkles and cracks in the surface of the skin for approximately three or four turns of the scroll arrested only by the hardened line of the first seam which proved to be less susceptible to its pressure.[14] It is still possible to see this line of pressure just before the seam in pl. II

[11] Cf. pl. II. Special thanks are due to Lena Libman of the IAA and Jan Karnis of CSEC who aided the editor during the process of photographing the fragments.

[12] Cf. 1QSb where the gap between the upper and lower fragments was created by the pressure of a tie.

[13] The original edges of each fragment should be distinguished by tracing the outline of each to include only (1) the original top and bottom edges of the manuscript, (2) the darkened, deteriorated edges surviving the gelatination of the skin resulting from oxidation and moisture, (3) the worm-eaten edge of the fragments (characterized by irregular edges with cupped chewing patterns), especially where there once was a darkened edge. All other edges formed from cracking or tears are potential joins for missing or unidentified fragments.

[14] If the leather thong had become damp while in the cave, its resulting shrinkage may have caused it to cut entirely through the first 2–3 turns of the scroll. In 1QIsa[a] this line of pressure from the tie is represented by a darkened line on the skin which can be traced through the first nine sheets (twenty-six columns) of the scroll ending at the seam concluding the ninth sheet. In 1QS the tie caused a crack at the original beginning of the scroll for at least the first two columns. It may be that this crack necessitated that the scroll be stored rolled in the opposite direction in order to protect the fragile beginning. The reconstructed scroll adding 1QSa and1QSb to the end of 1QS exhibits a gap between upper and lower fragments of 1QSb and a crack extending across 1QSa. It seems that

(and cf. figs. 1 and 3). The constant constriction by the tie pulled the upper and bottom portions of the sheet in toward the tie resulting in (1) the relative shortening of the height of the sheet (by 3 mm) and (2) diagonal wrinkles at the end of the first sheet resulting from the resistance of the hardened seam against this constriction. It is along this worn line that gelatination set in. It seems that the knot and reinforcing tab which was used in securing the thong to the leading edge of the scroll were responsible for the additional pressure that created the deep indentation at the left edge on the back of frg. 3 and, in part, the wavelike pattern along the bottom of frgs. 1 and 2, as well as along the top of frg. 5.[15]

The worms were drawn to the darkened areas on the scroll which were in the process of gelatination. Gelatination of the skin takes place at points along the edges, cracks and holes in the manuscript exposed to moisture and oxidation. A worm was also responsible for eating a small hole through the first two layers of the scroll and in the third layer expanded the hole to about one square cm. At that point the worm stopped and left only a lightened area on the back of the fourth layer at the same spot where it failed to penetrate. This set of holes (and the lightened spot) proved to be helpful for the placement of the fragments and for the calculations necessary for the reconstuction of the scroll.

With the exception of frg. 2, which survives with a single crack, all other cracking occurred on the remains of the second sheet of the scroll (frgs. 3 and 4).

Measurements

The following measurements are based upon the configuration of fragments presented in PAM 41.770. Although the physical evidence clearly supports this reconstruction, the resulting column of text remains difficult to reconstruct.

Height: 8.4 cm

Length: *c*.50 cm (based on the assumption that the estimate of the size of the first sheet and that of the second sheet would be the same)

Sheet I: *c*.25 cm (taking into account a fly leaf)

Sheet II: *c*.25 cm (based upon the calculation of the remaining turns of the scroll until a final turn of an estimated 5 cm and each successive turn decreasing by 0.5 cm from an initial turn estimated at 8 cm yielding seven turns in all)[16]

Col. i: *c*.10.1 cm wide

Col. ii: *c*.5.8 cm wide (based upon physical evidence only)

Col. iii: *c*.6.7 cm wide

---

this horizontal line of deterioration resulted from the pressure of the tie which bound the scroll over the last 2,000 years. This is similar to the pattern of deterioration at the beginning of 4Q**298**.

15 The placement of frg. 5 is somewhat strengthened by the similarity between its outline and the light patches in the lower part on the back of frg. 3, cf. pl. II. However a reconstruction of the text of col. ii based upon this placement remains problematic.

16 Cf. H. Stegemann, 'Methods for the Reconstruction of Scrolls from Scattered Fragments', in *Archaeology and History in the Dead Sea Scrolls* (JSPSup 8; ed. L. H. Schiffman) 188–220. I would like thank Prof. Stegemann for his suggestions during the initial stages of my work. A third sheet might be proposed if a decrease of 0.25 cm per turn could be established.

[Col. iv (only right margin preserved): *c*.6.7 cm]
[Col. v (not preserved): *c*.6.7 cm?]
Intercolumnar space: *c*.1.3 cm; at the seam itself, *c*.1.6 cm including the seam.

The unusually small height of the scroll (8.4 cm; 10 lines) places it among the portable scrolls intended to be carried during feasts or carried for a distance concealed (e.g. in a purse or belt).[17]

Palaeography

With the exception of the title, the scribe utilized for this small scroll a script dubbed by the original editor 'Cryptic A'.[18] Since no chronology has been set up for the esoteric scripts from Qumran, we are forced to rely upon indirect evidence in order to determine its dating. The fact that the title (and first sentence) of this manuscript was written in Jewish 'square' script provides us with a possibility of determining a relative date for the esoteric script utilized in the remainder of the manuscript.

A. The Jewish 'Square' Script

ʾAlep The slightly curved left leg connects near the top of the diagonal axis close to the inverted 'v' typical of the Herodian period. However there is no serif on the right arm which would be expected in the middle to late Herodian periods.

א

Bet The upper right-hand tick is not prominent and the bottom line is drawn from right to left. Both features begin in formal script at the time of transition between the Hasmonaean and Herodian periods.

בב

Dalet The head is wider than that used in the archaic period but is still drawn by a single stroke leaving a 'v' or 'u'-shaped notch between the two points of the head. This is in contrast to the two-stroke form with a still wider head and squared notch typical of the middle to late Herodian periods.

[17] Most portable scrolls were owned by individuals and were intended to be carried about and read during certain feasts. Typically these scrolls contain 7–10 (and not more than 15) lines. Many of those included in this category comprised the biblical *Megillot* (Ruth, Song of Songs, Ecclesiastes, Lamentations, and Esther) including 2QRuth^{a} (8 lines), 4QCant^{a} (9 lines), 4QCant^{b} (15 lines), 4QQoh^{a}, 4QLam (10 lines), 5QLam^{a} (7 lines), and 6QCant (7 lines). A few liturgical texts are also portable scrolls: 4Q**501** (4QapocrLam B, 9 lines), 4QShir^{a} (9 lines), 5QCurses (5 lines). To these should be added several texts in Aramaic: 4Q**246** (4QApocDan, 9 lines), 4Q**318** (4QZodiology and Brontology, 9 lines), 4Q**542** (4QTQahat, 13 lines), 4Q**550** (4QPrEsther^{a-f} ar, 7 lines). Perhaps to be added to these are 4Q**180** (4QAgesCreat^{a}, 10 lines) and 4Q**181** (4QAgesCreat^{b}, 12 lines).

[18] Seven manuscripts from cave 4 were written in this script: 4Q**186** (mixed), 4Q**249**, 4Q**250**, 4Q**298**, 4Q**313**, 4Q**317**, and 4Q**324c**. Cryptic A letters were also used as signs in 1QIs^{a}, 1QS, 1QH^{a}, and in several manuscripts from cave 4; see Pfann, '4Q298', 234–6. Three distinct scripts were termed 'cryptic' by J. T. Milik in earlier inventory lists: Cryptic A, Cryptic B, and Cryptic C. In publications he distinguished only two, cf. *Ten Years of Discovery in the Wilderness of Judea* (London: SCM Press, 1959) 115, 133. The circumstances surrounding the decipherment of Cryptic A are recounted by F. M. Cross in *The Ancient Library from Qumran and Modern Biblical Studies* (New York: Doubleday, 1958) 35–6.

Waw The angular hook form begins to appear in the late Hasmonaean period and continues into the Herodian period.

Ḥet The letter is relatively narrow and the join between the two uprights and the cross-member form a 'v'-shaped profile along the upper edge similar to forms from the late Hasmonaean and early Herodian periods.

Yod The angular hook profile appears here in both shaded and unshaded forms, such as are attested in the late Hasmonaean and early Herodian periods. Both examples are ligatured, connected to the letter on the right by means of a lengthened right leg.

Kap These two examples have a sharp bend at the juncture between the right member and the bottom line. This feature develops in the late Hasmonaean period and becomes a typical feature during the Herodian period. The first example has a narrow head similar to exemplars from the late Hasmonaean period. The second example, however, features a broader head which developed as a standard feature during the early Herodian period.

Lamed The particularly long hook at the base of each example provides the best argument for assigning the script to the Herodian period. However, the curved join at the base of the upright and its unornamented top are reminiscent of earlier periods.

Mem Close examination of the manuscript under a high power microscope indicates that the first stroke of the letter was formed starting at the upper left to form a 'u' and then bending sharply downward and turning suddenly to the left near the base. The second stroke begins at the base of the 'u' and descends diagonally to the left. These combined features are at home in both the late Hasmonaean and early Herodian periods.

Nun The letter is connected to the left and to the right and is uniform in height with most of the letters in the title. The top is bent slightly to the right. The combination of these features begins in the late Hasmonaean period and proceeds into the early Herodian period when a shaded head (and thus a serif) begins to develop from the bent top.

Reš The forms are mixed varying from a form reminiscent of the Archaic period (narrow with sloping right shoulder) to one typical of the middle Herodian period (wide and heavily ticked and wide head descending sharply at the right shoulder). The latter form has a tick at the foot of the upright which seems to be due to an unintended slip of the scribe's hand.

Śin The thickening of the top of the right arm develops in the late Hasmonaean period and eventually bends or forms a serif particularly during the middle to late Herodian periods.

Most of the features exhibited by the few letters occurring in this title would indicate that the script was a formal script to be dated somewhere between the late Hasmonaean and early Herodian periods (50–1 BCE). The early features exhibited in the single exemplars of *kap* and *reš* are offset by others of the same letters with rather late features and so must be considered archaisms. With the strong presence of late Hasmonaean and early Herodian features, the rather late features of the *lamed* and the one example of *reš* should not influence the dating of the script. These late features may be due to the scribe periodically allowing some features of the current semi-formal script to slip in.

B. Cryptic A

The development of the script of 4Q**298** will be traced relative to the scripts of two earlier manuscripts, 4Q**249** (4QMidrash Sefer Moshe)[19] and 4Q**317** (4QPhases of the Moon).[20] The scripts of these two manuscripts are very close in style to that of 4Q**298** and thus seem to be roughly contemporary. Four general tendencies governed the developments which took place between the early period and the first century BCE:

1. A rotation of the letter ranging from 15 to 70 degrees counterclockwise.
2. The development of a tendency toward horizontal instead of vertical shading.[21]
3. Extended lines which give the letter extra width are shortened.
4. Hooked lines at the tops of letters in the early period are reduced to a single line with an upturned end in the later period (similar reduction is found in the development of the Aramaic alphabet).

Several letter forms bear a striking resemblance to their corresponding forms in the Late Phoenician alphabets, including *bet, zayin, lamed* and *ṣade*.[22] Also there is a noteworthy resemblance in the letters *waw, nun, qop, reš, šin* and *taw*. There are also

[19] The title added to the back of this manuscript in 'square' Jewish script was dated to the late second century BCE by J. T. Milik. This title may have been added to the outside of the scroll some time after it was written and therefore merely indicates the latest point in time when the scroll may have been written.

The top line in each of the following examples is taken from 4Q**317** unless a well-preserved example was lacking, in which case an example from 4Q**249** was used. The second line is from 4Q**298**.

[20] Carbon-14 tests date both of these manuscripts to the early period (before 92 BCE), and likely to the second century BCE. The date of 4Q**249** may be slightly earlier than that of 4Q**317**. See A. J. T. Jull, D. J. Donahue, M. Broshi, and E. Tov, 'Radiocarbon Dating of Scrolls and Linen Fragments from the Judean Desert', *ʿAtiqot* 28 (1996) 1–7.

[21] Vertical shading was typical of most scripts derived from the Phoenician script during the early first millenium BCE. However, already in the eighth century Aramean scribes began using horizontal shading. J. Naveh, *The Early History of the Alphabet* (Jerusalem: Magnes Press, 1982) 174. This form of shading prevailed among the Jewish Formal Scripts from the fifth century BCE on. The tip of the reed was cut to be rectangular in shape and the widest part of the tip positioned more or less vertically during use (as opposed to the horizontal to diagonal positioning of the earlier period).

[22] Cf. J. Brian Peckham, *The Development of the Late Phoenician Scripts* (Cambridge, MA: Harvard University Press, 1968) pls. I–VI, IX.

marked dissimilarities which bring into doubt any direct descent from the Late Phoenician alphabets.

ʾAlep The leg of the *ʾalep* turns from a nearly horizontal trajectory to a vertical stance. The top of the loop is on the same plane as the tip of the upper arm.

Bet The fully hooked head of the *bet* degenerates to a single line slightly upturned at the left.

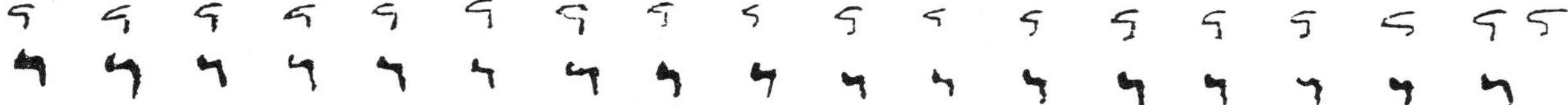

Gimel The oval head of the *gimel* degenerates to a single line descending leftward, the vertical upright tilting to the left. This may be due to assimilation to the *gimel* found in the square script of this period.

Dalet The axis of the *dalet* rotates, changing the letter from a tilt towards the right to a leftward tilt; the hooked head and the extended tail are both shortened.

He The widened foot of the *he* is tapered and the axis of the leg usually turns slightly counterclockwise; earlier the leg is shorter than the horizontal, later the leg is as long or longer than the horizontal. Final *he* is peculiar to 4Q**298** and is merely an optional biform of the letter *he* used at the end of words (often at the end of a clause or sentence).[23]

Waw The top line of the 'S-shaped' head of the *waw* degenerates to a slight upturned end at the upper left; there is a slight counterclockwise rotation.

[23] The use of the final *he* form is here indicated by the use of a 2-pt. larger *he*, e.g. גבולה.

Zayin The *zayin* is not found in the other manuscripts in this script. The form resembles the same letter in certain forms of the Phoenician script.[24]

Ḥet The oval of the *ḥet* becomes round; earlier there is a 90-degree join between the horizontal and vertical but later the horizontal turns upward at the upper right and then makes a radical turn downward, hooking back under and to the left, resembling a claw.

Ṭet The *ṭet* has no certain counterpart extant from the earlier forms of the alphabet. The letter resembles its contemporary *reš* with the main exception that the *ṭet* adds a foot extending to the left from the base of the upright member.

Yod The *yod* decreases its width leaving the horizontal and diagonal lines at about the same length. A trace of the trail from turn of the pen as the scribe moved his pen in the direction of the next letter to the left is sometimes visible at right end of the horizontal.

Kap The *kap* rotates and becomes rounder but retains a rather distinctive point at the top of the letter.

Lamed The *lamed* is rotated about 70 degrees counterclockwise and is formed by two distinct strokes of the pen instead of one continuous stroke. It seems to be assimilating toward the *lamed* of the Jewish square script of that period.

Mem The later *mem* tends to have horizontal shading instead of vertical shading. The entire letter is usually rotated slightly counterclockwise. In the later form the lower of

[24] Cf. Peckham, *The Development of the Late Phoenician Scripts*, pls. I–VI, IX.

the two crescents which form the right side of the letter is generally drawn further to the right of the upper crescent (a result of the preceding feature).

Nun The *nun* is made from three strokes instead of two. The earlier form's horizontal member ends at times with an accidental tick, trailing down and to the left. In this text an additonal stroke is intentionally added starting above the right end of the horizontal and ending at that point. The vertical line on the left is often rotated clockwise, creating a diagonal.

Samek The earlier *samek* is formed by four separate strokes: two vertical and two horizontal with a trailing tail. The left vertical extends above the upper horizontal and below the lower one. The other vertical connects the two horizontals at midpoint. The *samek* of 4Q**298** is formed by two strokes. The vertical on the left is formed along with the lower horizontal without lifting the pen. A remnant of the second vertical is found in only one example.

ʿAyin The *ʿayin* is later formed by two strokes rather than one. The ratio of height to width in the letter becomes less pronounced in the later form.

Pe The *pe* of the earlier period does not resemble that used in this text. The form in 4Q**298** can be distinguished from its contemporary *mem* only by the rather pronounced extended foot extending leftward from the base of the left vertical.

Ṣade The z-shaped head of the *ṣade* is now formed along with the upright without lifting the pen. The upright is rotated slightly counterclockwise. The bottom line of the 'z' is drawn further down along the upright.

Qop The *qop* in the early period is distinguished from the *mem* by the closure of the letter at the bottom and in several examples the extension of the top horizontal to the left of the left vertical. The later form is rounded off somewhat, creating the appearance of a figure-eight.

Reš In 4Q**317**, the top of the earlier *reš* is composed of two complete loops which were formed independently. In some cases the right loop is open at the top. The later form is always open at the upper right and is formed with a single unbroken line.

Śin/Šin The horizontal of the *śin/šin* is uneven since it is now formed along with the downstrokes instead of a single stroke. The downstrokes are slanted in the opposite direction.

Taw The earlier *taw* is a simple 't' formed by the crossing of a horizontal and vertical line, often with an accidental tick extending downward and to the left. The later form incorporated the tick and developed it as part of the actual letter form. The horizontal also developed an upturned tip on the left side. There may be some assimilation to the contemporary form in the square script.

It should be noted that the height and width of the letters is smaller in frgs. 3–4 ii, perhaps due to the rougher finish of the vellum in this section.

The Script of the Vorlage

It is possible that the *Vorlage* of this scroll was written in square script as suggested by a possible *waw/yod* confusion in frgs. 3–4 ii 7 ואׄהבו חסד[(from ואׄהבי חסד? see NOTES ON READINGS) and frg. 1 3 וׄשיבׄו] (from ושובׄו?)

Scribal Corrections

Scribal corrections in 4Q**298** include the following features: the addition of the word לבב in the margin of frg. 2 i 1; the insertion of letters: supralinear *he* in frg. 1 3 וׄשיבׄו] and supralinear *taw* in frg. 6 3]◦ת[; the substitution of a letter in frgs. 3–4 ii 3 גבולה, where *gimel* was overwritten by another, better formed, *gimel*. Only the first example is likely the work of a second hand, cf. NOTES ON READINGS.

Orthography

The scribe of 4Q**298** exhibited a decided preference for *plene* spellings with the single example of a defective spelling being found in frgs. 3–4 ii 4 וידעים. Examples of *plene* spellings include the following:

1. *Waw* for *o* (Tiberian *qamets ḥatup*): frg. 1 1 לכול; frg. 2 i 1 כ]ול; frgs. 3–4 i 5]בֿכול; *ŏ* without *waw* frgs. 3–4 ii 10 ובקד̊[מ]וניות;

2. *Waw* for *ô* (Tiberian *ḥolem*): frg. 1 4]עולמ̊י̊ם; frg. 2 ii 1 שורשיה; frg. 2 ii 2 בתהום; frg. 2 ii 3 התבֿו̊ננ[; frgs. 3–4 i 9 אוצר, בינות; frgs. 3–4 ii 1 גבלותיה; frgs. 3–4 ii 5 ודורש[י]; frgs. 3–4 ii 6 אומץ; frgs. 3–4 ii 10 עולמ̊ות, ובקד̊[מ]וניות; frg. 5 i 9 לדרוך; frg. 5 ii 9 גבולותיו[; frg. 5 ii 10 גבולות̊[; frg. 6 2]ותיה; frg. 7 1]ות̊י̊ו/ה[.

3. *Ō* without *waw*: frgs. 3–4 ii 4 וידעים.

4. *Waw* for original *aw*: frgs. 3–4 ii 6]ה̊וסיפו; frgs. 3–4 ii 7 הוסיפו. There are no occurrences of original *aw* without *waw*.

5. *Waw* for *û* (Tiberian *šureq*): frg. 1 2 אמונה; frgs. 3–4 i 1]זבול; frgs. 3–4 i 6 תכונם; frg. 3–4 i 8 ת]כונם; frgs. 3–4 ii 1 גבלותיה; frgs. 3–4 ii 2 רום; frgs. 3–4 ii 3 ג̊בולה; frgs. 3–4 ii 4 שמעו; frgs. 3–4 ii 6]ה̊וסיפו; frgs. 3–4 ii 7]ו̊אהבו, הוסיפו; frgs. 3–4 ii 8 תעודה; frgs. 3–4 ii 9 בֿעֿבור; frgs. 3–4 ii 9 תבֿינו; frgs. 3–4 ii 10 תביטו; frg. 5 ii 9 גבולותיו[; frg. 5 ii 10 גבולות̊[. There are no occurrences of *û* without *waw*.

6. *Yod* for *î*: frg. 1 1 משכיל, האזי]נו; frg. 1 2 הבי[נ]ו̊; frg. 1 3 וי[ד̊עים, ו̊שיב̊[ו; frg. 1 4]עולמ̊י̊ם; frg. 2 i 3]חיים; frgs. 3–4 i 9 בינות; frgs. 3–4 i 10 מ]לתי(?); frgs. 3–4 ii 2 לבלתי; frg. 3–4 ii 4 וידעים, האזי̊[נו; frgs. 3–4 ii 5 בינה, הצניע; frgs. 3–4 ii 6]ה̊וסיפו; frgs. 3–4 ii 7 הוסיפו; frgs. 3–4 ii 9 תבֿינו; frgs. 3–4 ii 10 תביטו, ובקד̊[מ]וניות; frg. 5 i 8 תכלית. There are no occurrences of *î* without *yod* or of *yod* for *i*.

7. *Ī* without *yod*: frgs. 3–4 i 6 תכונם; frg. 1 1 דבר.

8. *Yod* for *ê*: frg. 1 1 בני; frg. 1 2 [ורוד]פ̊י; frg. 2 i 1 אנשי; frg. 2 ii 1 שורשיה; frgs. 3–4 ii 1 גבלותיה; frgs. 3–4 ii 4 ואנשי; frgs. 3–4 ii 6 ואנשי.

9. Defective spelling:[25] frgs. 3–4 ii 4 וידעים; frgs. 3–4 ii 7]ו̊אהבו חסד.

Phonology

Assimilation of Nun

As in Biblical Hebrew the *nun* of *Pe-nun* verbs assimilates to the following consonant if it closes a syllable, e.g., נבט in frgs. 3–4 ii 10 תביטו and possibly frg. 1 5 ◦י̊בֿט̊; נתן in frgs. 3–4 i 4 נ]תן; and possibly נשג in frg. 1 3 ו̊שיגֿו.

The assimilation or ellision of the *nun* of מן is not uncommon in Qumran. There is only one possible example in 4Q**298**, frg. 2 ii 2 מת̊]חת in place of מן ת̊]חת, yet this reading is uncertain.

[25] Cf. also frgs. 3–4 i 5 תבל; frgs. 3–4 ii 9 בקץ.

Morphology

The Verb

The following verbal conjugations are represented:

1. *Hitpaᶜel*: frgs. 3–4 i 8 להתהלך.
2. *Hitpolel*: frg. 2 ii 3 התבֿוננ.
3. *Hipᶜil*: frg. 1 1 משכיל, האזי]נו; frg. 1 2 הבי]נ[ו; frg. 1 3 ו]שיבֿו ה (or ו]שיגו ה); frgs. 3–4 ii 4 האזינ]ו; frgs. 3–4 ii 5 הצניע; frgs. 3–4 ii 6]הוסיפו; frgs. 3–4 ii 7 הוסיפו; frgs. 3–4 ii 9 תבֿינו; frgs. 3–4 ii 10 תביטו.
4. *Piᶜel*: frg. 1 1 דבר; frg. 1 2 ומבֿקשי.

The following weak stem forms are represented:

1. *Pe-nun*: נבט, frgs. 3–4 ii 10 תביטו and possibly frg. 1 5 °יבֿט°; נתן, frgs. 3–4 i 4 נת]ן[; possibly נשג, frg. 1 3 ו]שיג ה ו.
2. *Pe-yod*: יסף, frgs. 3–4 ii 6]הוסיפו, frgs. 3–4 ii 7 הוסיפו, frgs. 3–4 ii 8 והו]סיפו; ידע, frg. 1 3 וי]דעים, frgs. 3–4 ii 4 וידעים, frgs. 3–4 ii 10 לדעת.
3. *ᶜAyin-waw*: בון, frg. 1 2 הבי]נ[ו, frg. 2 ii 3 התבֿוננ, frgs. 3–4 ii 9 תבֿינו; שוב, frg. 1 3 ו]שיבֿו ה; שום, frgs. 3–4 i 7 שם, frg. 5 ii 10 שם; רום, frgs. 3–4 ii 2 רום.

The Pronoun

Pronominal suffixes occur in the following words: frg. 1 2 במלי, 2 i 2 למלי; frg. 2 ii 1 שורשיה; frgs. 3–4 i 2 ובמה; frgs. 3–4 i 6 תכונם; frgs. 3–4 i 8 ת]כונם;[26] frgs. 3–4 ii 1 גבלותיה; frg. 3–4 ii 3 גבולה; frg. 5 ii 9 גבולותיו]; frg. 6 2]ותיה.

The Noun

The construct state is attested in the following: frg. 1 1 משכיל [דבר], לכול בני שחר, frg. 1 2 ומבֿקשי אמונה, [ורוד]פי צדק; frg. 1 3 [מ]וצא שפתי; frg. 2 i 1 כ]ול אנשי לבב; frgs. 3–4 i 5]בכול תבל; frgs. 3–4 i 9 אוצר בינות; frgs. 3–4 ii 1 ומספר גבולותיה; frgs. 3–4 ii 4–5 ואנשי בינה; frgs. 3–4 ii 5 ודורש[י] משפט; frgs. 3–4 ii 5–6 הצניע לכת; frgs. 3–4 ii 6–7 ואנשי אמת; frgs. 3–4 ii 7]ואהבו חסד; frgs. 3–4 ii 9–10 בקץ עולמות.

Syntax

The fragmentary condition of the scroll greatly limits our ability to determine its syntax. Of interest, however, is the negation of the infinitive by לבלתי in frgs. 3–4 ii 2 לבלתי רום (cf. Qimron, *HDSS* §400.12).

Vocabulary

Semantic Ranges

In common with other sectarian scrolls, 4Q**298** uses Hebrew Bible terminology with some modification. In some cases the scroll shows a preference—consistent with usage

---

[26] The so-called Qumran spelling -המה is not attested here.

in the other sectarian scrolls—for one of two synonymous terms found in Biblical Hebrew, e.g., בינה (vs. תבונה): understanding, insight.

Sectarian or restricted usages include the following: משכיל: *maskil*, sage, teacher, mentor (frg. 1 1); תעודה: appointed time; assembly; destination (frgs. 3–4 ii 8; not 'testimony' as in BH); אמון, אמונה: faith, truth (frg. 1 2 אמונה); תכון: measure i.e. place, rank (frgs. 3–4 i 6 תכונם; frgs. 3–4 i 8 [ת]כונם).

A list of virtues required of members of the community had achieved a fixed order in other community writings (e.g. 1QS V and IX, and 4QBarki Nafshi; see Table 1)—an order determined in part by Mic 6:8, where three of them already occurred. These are encouraged among the audience of 4Q**298**. The idea of 'adding' (הוסיפו) one virtue to another, which is frequent in frgs. 3–4 of this passage, is found sporadically elsewhere in the scrolls. In those passages, where it is used to encourage virtuousness, the virtues are clustered in a group as in this text.[27]

TABLE 1: *List of Essene Virtues*

Virtue	1QS V	= 4QS^{d}	= 4QS^{b}	1QS VIII	= 4QS^{e}	4QBN^{e} 5 2	4Q**298** 3-4
	Relating to Members			*Relating to Council*			*To Novices*
לעשות אמת	•	–	[ ]	•	•	[ ]	•
וענוה	•	•	[ ]	–	–	[ ]	•
צדקה	•	•	[ ]	•	•	צדק	•
ומשפט	•	•	[ ]	•	•	•	•
ואהבת חסד	•	•	•	•	[ ]	•	•
והצנע לכת	•	•	•	•	[ ]	•	•

Terms which seem to have a sectarian character but are unattested elsewhere in the scrolls include: בני שחר: Sons of Dawn, i.e. novices, catechumens (frg. 1 1)[28]; אנשי לבב: men of understanding (lit., men of heart; frg. 2 i 1); אוצר בינות: treasury of insights (frgs. 3–4 i 9); גבול(ות): border(s) (frgs. 3–4 ii 1 גבלותיה; frgs. 3–4 ii 3 גבולה; frg. 5 ii 9 גבולותי֯ו[; frg. 5 ii 10 גבולות֯[).

---

[27] A similar use of the command to 'add' one virtue to another in a list of virtues is otherwise unattested in classical Hebrew sources. However, cf. 2 Peter 1:5-7: 'For this very reason make every effort to supplement your faith with virtue, and virtue with knowledge, and knowledge with self-control, and self-control with steadfastness and steadfastness with godliness, and godliness with brotherly affection and brotherly affection with love'. Cf. also 1 Macc 2:29 where the multitudes descended to the desert ζητοῦντες δικαιοσύνην καὶ κρίμα 'seeking righteousness (צדק) and justice (משפט)', perhaps following Zeph 2:3: 'Seek the Lord, all you humble (ענוי) of the land, who do his justice (משפטו), seek righteousness (צדק), seek humility (ענוה); perhaps you may be concealed during the day of the Lord's wrath'.

[28] Cf. *IEJ* 33 (1983) 81–5, where J. Baumgarten would read בני השחר in place of בני השחת in CD XIII 14–15. If this reading were correct, the text would imply that certain limitations were placed upon full members of the community concerning business procedures with novices who still hold a probationary status. Similar limitations upon mingling the novices' goods and finances with those of full members are found in 1QS VI 17–20. However, personal examination of the manuscript of CD by the author would seem to confirm the reading בני השחת rather than בני השחר, though the left leg of the *taw* is very faint.

Function and Content

The reasons which make both the portability and the use of an esoteric script in this scroll essential may be explained by examining the nature of the relationship between the speaker and his audience. The curious term בני שחר ('Sons of Dawn'), not paralleled elsewhere, should be understood in the light of the content of the *Maskil*'s message that follows. Since this composition seems to be an introductory address, it is probable that he is speaking to novices and that the term 'Sons of Dawn' implies that these individuals are 'dawning' out of the darkness and into the light, and are thus on the verge of becoming 'Sons of Light'. These are most likely those who are described in 1QS VI as serving a two-year preparatory and probationary period before induction into the community. Since it is the responsibility of the *Maskil* to teach all members of the community,[29] and the novices have not yet been fully inducted,[30] he must leave the community premises in order to teach them. The size of the scroll permitted it to be safely carried (or hidden) while travelling. The use of the esoteric script (aside from the title) protected the scroll's contents from being read by anyone except the *Maskil* and other elite members of the group. In case the scroll was stolen or lost, the legible title made it possible for the scroll to be returned to its rightful owner(s).

At first glance, the contents of this short scroll would not seem to warrant such careful protection. However, a closer look at the contents reveals that the words of the *Maskil* are the novices' key to truth, knowledge, understanding, righteousness, and life. Thus all Essene teaching, even the foundational principles, was treated as crucial, even mystical knowledge, and hence was worthy of concealment from non-members.

Form and Structure

1. Title (1 1)

2. Exhortation to listen (1–2 i 1-3)

The בני שחר ('Sons of Dawn') are beckoned to listen to and heed the words of the *Maskil*. This group is further called 'men of heart', 'pursuers of righteousness', and 'seekers of faith'. It seems that the requirement to be included in this group is merely that the individual recognize his need to hear and that he actively seek to learn the doctrine of the master.

3. Statement concerning the fruits of listening (1–2 i 3-8)

The words of the *Maskil*, if heeded, become to the disciple 'who knows', a source of life and peace beyond comprehension. This not only gives the promise of life and peace to the novice who, by becoming an attentive student, will know the way, but it also identifies the *Maskil* as the sole legitimate source of this knowledge.

---

[29] Cf. 1QS I 1, III 13.

[30] Cf. 1QS VI 13b–23.

4. The order and limits of the created universe (1-2 i 9–3-4 ii 3)
Most of this section is made up of disjointed fragments. However, enough has been preserved to enable a determination of the general content. Creation's design (especially its categories and borders) is a key to understanding. It is 'a treasure trove of insights' from which the *Maskil* draws his wisdom and teaching. It is within this naturalistic view that the position and rules governing each member are defined and justified.

The term תכונם 'their measurement' is found twice; once alongside the verb ממד 'to measure'. The terms לדרוך and להתהלך are found at least twice, referring to movement within a domain or along a path. The term גבלות 'borders, limits, boundaries' is found at least four times in this section, defining the limits of the domain or path. The use of these terms seems to imply that, just as the Divine has imposed certain measures and limits on each entity within His creation, He has also assigned varying statuses and rules among men and they must walk and live accordingly. Therefore, in this section the *Maskil* teaches the novice: (1) to accept the status assigned to him within the community and (2) to learn the rules which govern him, which the *Maskil* himself has discerned within nature.

This section echoes in both style and content other sectarian works such as 1 and 4QMysteries, 1 and 4QInstruction, and 4QSapiential Works B–C, as well as several hymns in 1 and 4QHodayot. The status and rules which are intended to govern the life of each member are defined more specifically in the various *serekh*'s, or rule books, which were found in most of the caves.

5. The *Maskil* addresses those who 'know' (3–4 ii 3-4)
As in frgs. 1–2 i 1-2, the *Maskil* begins his address with two standard terms האזינו ושמעו.[31] The addressees probably do not represent a group separate from that addressed earlier. They are possibly a subgroup within the בני שחר, perhaps those who have already learned the principles and rules referred to in the previous exhortation. They may even be those who are serving the second year of their novitiate. In any case, the *Maskil* now encourages the hearer to go beyond mere knowledge.

6. Exhortation to a virtuous life (3–4 ii 4-8)
The listener is enjoined to embrace all the Essene virtues. Those who have developed certain virtues are encouraged to add to those yet other virtues. The terms 'understand', or 'seek justice', or 'men of truth', seem to describe individuals who have achieved a certain degree of legal righteousness (i.e. fulfilling the letter of the law). These are further encouraged to embrace other virtues which might be said to reflect the spirit of the law.

---

[31] Elsewhere in Hebrew literature, the two parallel commands שמעו ('listen') and האזינו ('give ear to') are often found, as here, at the beginning of an address or a sapiential teaching (seventeen times in 𝔐). However, in 4Q**298** here (as well as in frgs. 1–2 i 1-3 where the formula is expanded to incude הבינו), the order is reversed. The order is also reversed in one example of 𝔐 (Isa 28:23).

7. Teaching concerning the ages of the world (3–4 ii 8-10)
This seems to be the beginning of a teaching stressing the importance of the new member heeding the *Maskil*'s interpretation of the community's sacred writings. He will become the sole source for lessons to be learned from past events (especially those recorded in the Bible and related texts) as well as for interpreting the fulfillment of prophecies concerning the community—past, present and future.

Mus. Inv. 898
PAM 40.581, 41.776, 43.384*

Frg. 1

1 [דבר]יׄ משכיל אשר דבר לכול בני שחר האזי[נו לי
2 [ורוד]פׄי צדק הבי[נ]וׄ במלי ומבׄקׄשי אמונה ◦[
3 [מ]וצׄא שפׄתׄ[י וי]דׄעים דרׄ[ש]וׄ[א]לׄהׄ וׄ^השיבׄ[ו
4 רצו]נׄו וׄ[אור]עולמׄיׄ[ם לאין] חקר בׄ[
5]◦יבׄטׄ ע[ ]יהׄ[

NOTES ON READINGS

L. 1 משכיל [דבר]יׄ. Traces of ink are visible before the *mem* of משכיל on the parchment and on PAM 40.581. The reconstruction [דבר]יׄ is tentative.

L. 2 הבי[נ]וׄ. The leg and upturned tip of the head of the *waw* are clearly visible.

L. 2 אמונה. A two-point larger *he* is used in the transcriptions to indicate the biform final *he* (see above).

L. 3 The top of a letter is visible before the *he* in א]לׄהׄ which is most likely a *lamed* although it may also be an unusually high upturned tip of a *bet*.

L. 3 וׄ^השיבׄ[ו. The reason for the supralinear *he* may be explained if the *Vorlage* to this manuscript was in square script and read ושבו. The descending line of the *bet* is straight and long which makes it a more likely choice than *gimel* (והשיגׄ[ו, so Milik, *PC*). However both readings remain viable.

L. 4 רצו]נׄו All but the upper right tip of the *nun* is preserved. If the word is to be taken as following אנשי then the root must be a noun ending in *nun*. Its restoration as רצו]נׄו (so Milik) is conjectural but credible.

L. 4 וׄ[אור]עולמׄיׄ[ם. The restoration is based upon similarities in idiom with אור לאין חקר (4Q**392**) and אור עולמים (1QS IV 8; 1QM XIII 6, XVII 6; and 4Q**369** [4QPrayer of Enosh] 1 ii 6).

L. 5 Only the top of the *ṭet* of יבׄטׄ is visible. It might also be read as *reš* but that reading is less likely.

Frg. 2 i

1 כ]ול אנשי לבב

2]° לׄמלי בכול

3]חׄיים אׄ[נשי]

NOTES ON READINGS

L. 1 לבב. The word לבב seems to have been added by a second hand based on the following evidence: (1) Three-fourths of the word extends beyond the margin guide (which is not usual for this scribe and is contrary to normal scribal practice at Qumran and elsewhere).[32] (2) The script is irregular in that the lettering is disproportionally large, the *lamed* was formed by three separate strokes, and the *bet's* have a rounder form than found elsewhere in the manuscript. (3) The tip of the reed used to form this word was wider than that used elsewhere. (4) The ink is darker than that of the preceding and following words.

L. 3 The loop of the *ʾalep* is clear after the word חיים. No other letter has a single loop on the right side. The reconstruction as אׄ[נשי is conjectural (so Milik) although a vocative might be expected at this point.

The following reconstruction of frgs. 1–2 i can be proposed, although the combination is not certain:

Frgs. 1–2 i

1 *[דבר]ׄ משכיל* אשר *דבר לכול בני שחר* האזי[נו לי כ]ול אנשי לבב

2 [ורוד]פׄי צדק הבי[נ]ו במלי ומבׄקׄשי אמונה שׄ[מע]וׄ לׄמלי בכול

3 [מ]וצׄא שפׄתׄ[י וי]דׄעים דרׄ[ש]וׄ[א]לׄהׄ וׄ‏ׄשיבׄ[ו לאורח]חׄיים אׄ[נשי]

4 רצו[נו וׄ[אור]עולמׄיׄ[ם לאין] חקר בׄ[

5]°יבׄטׄ ע[ ]יׄהׄ[

NOTES ON READINGS

L. 1 [דבר]ׄ משכיל אשר דבר לכול בני שחר. This phrase, written in Jewish square script, identifies it as the title of the composition.

L. 3 Alternatively, והשיגׄ[ו, 'have taken hold of'.

L. 3 לאורח]חׄיים. This tentative restoration is based on 4Q**437** (4QBarki Nafshi[d]) 3 2 and 4Q**525** (4QBeatitudes) 15 8]לוא [ו]השיגו לאורחות חיים.

[32] According to the minor tractate *Soferim* 2.3 the majority of the letters of a word must stand within the column and not in the margin.

Translation

1. *[Word]s of a Maskil which he spoke to all Sons of Dawn.*
   Lend your ea[r to me, a]ll men of understanding;
2. [and you who pur]sue righteousness, do understa[n]d my words;
   and you who seek truth, li[st]en to my words in all
3. that [is]sues from [my] lips. [And those who k]now, have pur[s]ued [the]se things
   and have turn[ed[33] to the way] of life. O m[en of]
4. His [wi]ll, and etern[al light beyond] comprehension [
5.] [

Comments

L. 1 משכיל. This position is mentioned several times in the Dead Sea scrolls (1QS III 13, IX 12, 21; 1QSb I 1; 4Q**511** [DJD VII, 221]). Cf. also CD XIII 7–8: 'And this is the order of the camp overseer: He shall instruct (ישכיל) the 'Many' (הרבים) in the works of God and make them understand (ויבינם) His wonderful mighty deeds, and he shall recount before them the events of eternity with their [religious] interpretations (בפתריהם)'.[34] This listing is not far removed from the content of the fragment before us, which tells of the mighty acts of God in nature and history, perhaps even using the root פתר (frgs. 3–4 ii 9). There are clear stylistic parallels between the fragment before us and CD I 1, II 2, and 4QD^e (4Q**270** 2 ii 18–20), which opens with a similar line: 'And now hearken to me, you who know righteousness [. . .] for you the ways of life and the paths of perdition'. It may be suggested that the Damascus Covenant, too, is a product of a *maskil* just as the parallel passage in 1QS III 13ff is exposed by the *maskil*.[35] (Another section in the *Manual of Discipline*, found in both in 4QS^b and 4QS^d, is entitled מדרש למשכיל).[36]

L. 1 בני שחר. This term is discussed by Baumgarten. The term in the present fragment was compared by him to CD XIII 14, where he reads: ואיש מכל באי ברית אל ישא ואל יתן לבני השחר כי אם כף לכף ('And let no man of all the members of the covenant of God trade with the Sons of Dawn except for cash'). The term בני שחר ('Sons of Dawn') is understood by Baumgarten as a synonym of the term בני אור ('Sons of Light').[37] The reading שחר (rather than שחת 'perdition') in the Damascus Covenant is open to question, but it seems materially preferable. If we are in fact to read בני שחר in the Damascus Covenant, then it seems that this term refers to people who are not 'members of the covenant'. In this text, and in the Damascus Covenant as well, the term בני שחר is a *terminus technicus* (not a poetic turn of phrase), and it is difficult to understand why 'the Sons of Light' should also be called in such a context 'the Sons of Dawn'. We have no clear answer to these questions, but we might surmise that the 'Sons of Dawn' are *catechumens*, candidates for admission to the sect.[38] In that case, the term 'the Sons of Dawn' was created after the basic typological division of 'Sons of Light' and 'Sons of Darkness', and the term 'Sons of Dawn' reflects a relatively advanced stage of the sect's terminology. It should be recalled, however, that even this is tentative.

---

33 Alternatively, והשיג[ו] 'have taken hold of'.

34 The reading בפתריהם is according to 4QD^b (4Q**267** 9 iv 6); cf. E. Qimron, *The Damascus Document Reconsidered*, ed. M. Broshi (Jerusalem: IES, 1992) 35.

35 For the relationship between the doctrine of the two spirits and the doctrine of the two ways, alluded to in the Damascus Document, cf. D. Flusser, 'Which is the Right Way that a Man Should Choose for Himself?', *Tarbiz* 60 (1991) 165–8 [Heb].

36 G. Vermes, 'Preliminary Remarks on Unpublished Fragments of the Community Rule from Qumran Cave 4', *JJS* 42 (1991) 251.

37 J. Baumgarten, 'The "Sons of Dawn" in *CDC* 13:14–15 and the Ban on Commerce among the Essenes', *IEJ* 33 (1983) 81–5. This reading was preferred by E. Qimron in his edition of the Damascus Document (above, n. 33).

38 Cf. Pfann, '4Q298', 224–5.

L. 1 האזי[נו לי כ]ול אנשי לבב. Cf. Job 34:10 לכן אנשי לבב שמעו לי (𝔊: συνετοὶ καρδίας; ℭ: אנשי חכימי). See in particular האזינו לי [אנשי] לבב (4Q**525** [4QBeatitudes] 23 2).

L. 2 [ורוד]פי צדק. Cf. Isa 51:1: שמעו אלי רדפי צדק מבקשי ה' ('Hearken to me, you who pursue righteousness, you who seek the Lord') and cf. CD I 1: 'And now hearken to me, all of you who know righteousness (ידעי צדק) and understand the works of God' (for ידעי צדק cf. Isa 51:7!). A similar opening formula is found in another section of the Damascus Covenant as well, in 4QD[e] (4Q**270** 2 ii 18–20, cf. above). Mention is made there of teaching 'the Ways of Life' (cf. below, line 3), which become known through 'the understanding of the works of every generation' (cf. below, frgs. 3–4, lines 9–10). It is clear that these verses were taken to refer to members of the sect. Perhaps רודפי צדק is understood as the *catechumens* (in contradistinction to יודעי צדק). It has been argued elsewhere that a statement of John the Baptist directed to those who came to him may have its origins in a midrash on Isa 51:1-2.[39]

L. 2 הבי[נ]ו֯ במלי. The verbal phrase הבין ב is common in late BH and the language of the Dead Sea scrolls.[40]

L. 2 ומב֯ק֯שי אמונה. Cf. Jer 5:1.

L. 3 וי[ד֯עים. The word (probably to be pronounced *yaddaʿim*) is not uncommon in the writings of the sect. E. Qimron has shown that elsewhere it is based on a reading and exegesis of Deut 1:13.[41] Here it may be based on Job 34:2 (cf. COMMENTS on line 1).

L. 3 ו^ה^שיב֯[ו לאורח]חיים. Perhaps השיבו should be understood as semantically equivalent to שובו. 1QS V 1 reads לשוב מכול רע, while another manuscript (4QS[d]) reads in the same text להשיב מכל רע. The use of the *Hipʿil* conjugation in place of the *Qal* is not uncommon in the Dead Sea scrolls.[42] However, it may be that the proper reading here is והשיגו [אורח?] חיים, perhaps following Prov 2:19. Cf. COMMENTS on line 1, משכיל.

---

[39] M. Kister, 'Plucking on the Sabbath and Christian-Jewish Polemic', *Immanuel* 24/25 (1990) 35 n. 1.

[40] Cf. Ch. Rabin, *The Zadokite Document* (Oxford: Clarendon, 1958) 34 n. 1; A. Hurvitz, *The Transition Period in Biblical Hebrew* (Jerusalem: Bialik Institute, 1972) 136 n. 181. Hurvitz argues, following Bacher, that the meaning of this verb in Neh 8:8 and Dan 9:2 is similar to that of the root דרש. For this point add also Sir 4:11, where the Hebrew has לכל מבינים בה, whereas the Greek has τῶν ζητούντων αὐτήν (although there are considerable differences between the Hebrew and the Greek in this verse). The usage of מבין in late BH and writings of the Second Temple Period as meaning 'make <somebody> understand <something>' might contribute to the addition of the prepositions -ב ('something') and -ל ('somebody') after this verb.

[41] E. Qimron, 'Biblical Philology and Dead Sea Scrolls', *Tarbiz* 54 (1989) 303–4 [Heb].

[42] Cf. E. Qimron, *The Hebrew of the Dead Sea Scrolls* (Atlanta: Scholars Press, 1986) 49; M. Moreshet, 'The *Hifʿil* in Mishnaic Hebrew as Equivalent to the *Qal*', *Bar-Ilan* (Annual of Bar-Ilan University) 13 (1976) 249–81 [Heb]; cf. also שובו והשיבו (Ezek 18:30, 32): the verb was repeated in a derived conjugation for emphasis (cf. H. Yalon, *Introduction to the Vocalization of the Mishnah* [Jerusalem: Bialik Institute, 1964; Heb] 95–8 for stylistic repetition of *Qal* and *Piʿel*). The interchange between כתב and הכתיב in *Jubilees* (J. C. VanderKam, 'The Putative Author of the Book of Jubilees', *JSS* 26 [1981] 209–17; idem, 'The Jubilees Fragments from Qumran Cave 4', *The Madrid Qumran Congress* (Leiden: Brill] 646–7) may be caused by the double meaning of הכתיב: 'to make <somebody> write', but also 'to write' (cf. אכתב in Syriac [Payne-Smith, *Thesaurus Syriacus*, 1850; F. Schulthess, *Lexicon Syropalestinum* (Berlin, 1903) 99]; שהכתבתם בתורתכם [PT *Sotah* 7.3 21c] = שכתבתם [*Sifre Deut* 56, ed. Finkelstein, 123]).

Frg. 2 ii

1 שורשיה יצ[או

2 בתהום מת[חת

3 התבוננ ◦[

Notes on Readings

L. 1 יצ[או. A short horizontal line of ink after and slightly below the level of the *yod* is almost certainly the end of a *ṣade*.

Translation

1. its roots went for[th
2. in the abyss be[low
3. Consider [

Frgs. 3–4 i

1]זבול

2]ל ובמה

3] עפר

4]נתן אל

5]בכול תבל

6] מדד תכונם

7 מת]חת שם

8 ת]כונם להתהלך

9]◦ אוצר בינות

10]מ[מ]לתי ואשר

Notes on Readings

L. 2]ל ובמה. Nearly the entire *lamed* is visible on PAM 40.581.

L. 7 מת]חת. A circle of ink is left along the edge of the parchment. The height and shape of the circle suggest a *ḥet*. However it may also be a poorly formed *kap* (if so then perhaps the reconstruction should be [לל]כת).

TRANSLATION

1.]habitation
2.] and by what
3.]dust
4.]God gave
5.] in all the world
6.] he meted out their portion[43]
7. bel]ow he placed
8. their [p]ortion to go about
9.] a treasury of insights
10. my [w]ord and which

COMMENTS

L. 1 [זבול. In other sources from Qumran, this word indicates heavenly abodes (1QS X 3; 1QM XII 1f.; 1QH^a III 34; the Song of the Sabbath Sacrifices, e.g. 4Q**403** 1 i 41. The word recurs below as well (frgs. 3–4 ii 3). Perhaps it refers to the abode of the heavenly bodies (as in the verse referred to in 1QS).[44]

L. 6 מדד תכונם. The lines in question are highly fragmentary, but from the repetition of the word תכון here and in line 8 and from the word גבולותיה in frgs. 3–4 ii 1, we can infer that the central topic of these lines is the measure and limits fixed by God. The word תכון[45] is used to refer to a defined measure of time in nature (1QS X 6–7), to a defined measure of eschatological time (1QpHab VII 12–14), and to the proper, legal measure of what should be done (1QS V 7). In all its meanings, תכון is related to law, whether the law of nature, the law of history, or halakha—all of which are equally the law of God. This is also true of the term גבול, which appears less frequently: it certainly refers to a border between God's creations, but it refers to God's law as well (cf. e.g. 1QS X 10–11 ובהיותם אשים גבולי לבלתי שוב;[46] and 4Q**266** 11 13 וגבולות הגבלתה לנו אשר את עובריהם ארותה, 'You have set boundaries for us and cursed those who transgressed them').[47] The multiplicity of meanings of the term תכון does not indicate any vagueness of terminology, but rather that this concept—divinely ordained measure—is a basic concept in the sect's thought, and its uses indicate that the sect perceived no distinction between law ordained by God for humanity in the Torah and His law or commands in nature and in history.[48] In fact, they

---

43 Lit., 'measure'.

44 𝔊 translates Hab 3:11 by τάξις, which suits the context in this fragment; but this seems to be an ad hoc translation of a difficult verse, and it seems that in Qumran the biblical verse was interpreted differently.

45 For the pattern of this word see E. Qimron, *HDSS* §330.1b n. 1.

46 גבול סמוך לשמור אמונים (ibid., line 25) is irrelevant: the expression גבול סמוך is based on the biblical expression יצר סמוך (Isa 26:2-3; for יצר in this verse meaning 'creature' cf. Qimron, 'Biblical Philology', 307–8; R. E. Murphy, 'Yēṣer in the Qumran Literature', *Biblica* 39 (1958) 339–43. It is difficult to account for the substitution of the verb יצר in the biblical verse by גבול assuming that גבול means 'boundary' (or something similar). Therefore גבול here seems to be a synonym to יצר, meaning a creature created from wet clay, as in other passages in the Qumran scrolls (cf. יצר החמר ומגבל המים [1QH^a I 21]; והואה מעפר מגבלו [1QS XI 21]). On the root גבל see J. C. Greenfield, *RevQ* 2 (1960) 155–62.

47 M. Kister, 'Some Aspects of Qumranic Halakha', *The Madrid Qumran Congress* (Leiden: Brill, 1992) 575 n. 14.

48 For the relation between God's commandments observed by Nature (as proven by the natural order) and the order of God as represented in the Torah, see M. Kister, 'Metamorphoses of Aggadic Tradition', *Tarbiz* 60 (1991) 196–9 [Heb.]. Cf. also M. E. Stone, 'The Parabolic Use of Natural Order in Judaism of the Second Temple Age', *Gilgul* [= Numen Supplement 50] (Leiden: Brill, 1987) 298–308. The lack of distinction between the commandments of God to human beings in the Torah and to nature, and the concept that both of them are eternal and universal rules, illustrate a possible Jewish Palestinian heritage and philosophical thought (Stoic concepts, in this case). Cf. M. Koester, 'Nomos Physicos: The Concept of Natural Law in Greek Thought', *Religions in*

perceived a congruity between God's laws in nature and history and in the products of human activity (1QS IX 12 לתכון עת ועת ולמשקל איש ואיש).[49] This is one of the cornerstones of the sect's ideology of predestination and of the hierarchy of its members (which is also described with the term תכון—e.g. 1QS VI 4).[50] The term תכון appears several times in Qumran wisdom texts yet to be published, e.g. 4Q**418** 127 6, במוזני צדק שקל כול תכונם ('for in righteous balance He weighed all their measures'); cf. *Enoch* 43:2: 'And I saw how they [the lightnings] are weighed in a righteous balance according to their properties of light; לו[א ישבות אחד מכול צבאם . . . בא — אמת ומשקל צדק תכן אל כול מ[('[n]ot one of their multitude ceases . . . with just [ ] and righteous balance God measured all their . . .' 4Q**418**) and others. These texts too are fragmentary, but they too appear to view God's measure and order (*tikkūn*) in nature as a model for His 'measure' and order for human beings.

Frgs. 3–4 ii

1 י֯[ ]ומספר גבלותיה

2]ךׄ לבלתי רום

3 מׄתׄ[כונה ול. . .]וׄת את ג֯בולה ועתה

4 האזׄינׄ[ו חכמים] וידעים שמעו ואנשי

5 בינה ה֯[וסיפו לק]ח֯ ודורש[י] משפט הצניע

6 לכת יוׄ[דעי הדרך]ה֯וסיפו אומץ ואנשי

7 אמת רד֯פׄ[ו צדק]וׄאהבו חסד הוסיפו

8 ענוה וה֯וׄ[סיפו ד]עׄתׄ[י]מׄי תעודה אשר

9 פתׄר֯[י]המׄ[אספ]רׄ בׄעׄבור תב֯ינו בקץ

10 עולמׄות ובקדׄ[מ]וניות תביטו לדעת

Notes on Readings

L. 3 ג֯בולה. Milik's transcription in *PC* reads זבולה. The parchment is broken at this point and the restoration left the ceiling lines of the left fragment 1 mm higher than the right. The character is thus split and shifted vertically at its extreme left. The character is composed of two angled strokes which were each formed without lifting the pen. The upper stroke rises to the ceiling line from the bottom of the character diagonally upward and to the left and then turns downward and to the left. The left tip of this upper stroke terminates at the break. The lower stroke begins further to the right and rises diagonally to the left in a lower trajectory peaking just below the midpoint between the theoretical base line and the ceiling line. The lower stroke terminates further to the left than its upper counterpart and

---

Antiquity: Essays in Memory of E. R. Goodenough (Leiden: Brill, 1968) 530–41; R. A. Horsley, 'The Law of Nature in Philo and Cicero', *HTR* 71 (1978) 35–59.

[49] Cf. CD XII 20, in which the same sentence occurs, ending with למשפט עת ועת: משפט replaces תכון in 1QS.

[50] 4Q**215a** (4QTime of Righteousness) 1 2–4.

the left tip is visible on the left fragment. The ink of the upper stroke is gray which is not consistent with the surrounding letters. However the darkness of the lower stroke is. It seems then that the lower stroke which was meant to represent a *gimel* was not well formed. A scribe later penned in a more nicely formed *gimel* but did not remove the original.

L. 4 האזי֯נ֯[ו. On PAM 40.581 the form of the *yod* is distinct and clear. However the form is somewhat anomalous since the turn of the diagonal line to the horizontal is rounded. Most of the top of the *nun* with its upturned end is discernible in the early photographs. חכמים is restored upon an expected parallelism in terminology with the following phrase ידעים שמעו. Cf. also שמעו חכמים 1QH^a I 34f.

L. 5 ה֯[וסיפו. All but the left arm of the *he* has been preserved. The remainder of the restoration has been derived from the context. The reconstruction is suggested since this seems to be the beginning of a string of imperatives, often beginning with הוסיפו; cf. lines 6, 7, and 8.

L. 5 לק[ח֯. The left part of the top of a letter with a circular end makes the *ḥet* unmistakable. The idiom להוסיף לקח is common in Qumran literature; cf. 4Q**418** 81 7; 4Q**221** 3; 4Q**436** (4QBarki Nafshi^c) 1 i 2; and possibly 4Q**299** (4QMyst^a) 6 ii 18. No other word ending in *ḥet* follows the verb להוסיף, making other constructions such as להוסיף כוח unlikely.

L. 7 רדפ[ו צדק. In Qumran literature, the verb רדף is found coupled with two virtues: צדק (two times, 4Q**298** 1 2; 11QT^a LI 15) and דעת (three times: 4QMyst^a 8 7; 4Q**418** 69 ii 11; 4Q**424** 3 2). In 𝔐 it occurs with צדקה/צדק (four times: Deut 16:20; Is 51:1; Prov 11:19, 15:9) and once with לדעת (Hos 6:3). Either term could be restored here but the context favours צדק or צדקה.

L. 7 ו֯אהבו חסד. As the text stands, אהבו is one in a chain of imperatives, which is not uncommon in hortatory texts. Alternatively, one could correct the text to read instead ו֯אהבי חסד in order to remain consistent with the masc. pl. constructs of the addressees in the preceding lines. If so, the scribe confused the *yod* for a *waw* in a *Vorlage* written in Jewish square script.[51] Otherwise the word must be read as an imperative 'love kindness', creating a string of three imperatives. There would be no confusion between *yod* and *waw* if the *Vorlage* had been written in the same script as this manuscript.

L. 8 וה֯ו֯[סיפו ד]ע֯ת֯ י֯[מ֯י. The length, thickness and angle of the downstroke of the second letter (besides a trace of the horizontal to the right) suggest the bottom of the letter *he*. In PAM 40.581 the third letter is survived by a crescent of ink which resembles the right side of a *waw, lamed, ʿayin,* or *taw*.

The placement of the lower fragment which forms the lower half of the first word of this line and the first word of the next line is tentative, placed by Milik in this position only in the final photo. The join on the upper edge is not flush.

The *ʿayin* of ד]ע֯ת֯ י֯[מ֯י is missing only the tail; the following letter retains its upper right arm and traces of a line of ink which ascend to the left which seem to imply the existence of a head. This combination of lines implies either a *reš*, a *tet*, or a *taw*. *Taw* has been selected on philological grounds. הוכיחו דעת would be expected here instead of הוסיפו דעת since דעת is attested with the former and not the latter; cf. e.g. 1QS IX 17 להוכיח דעת אמת ומשעט צדק. The following letter has a left leg below the crack and above the crack and to the right the traces of a line of ink which is tent-shaped. This combination could form part of a *mem* or a *šin* with preference for the former.

L. 9 פת֯ר֯[י]ה֯ם֯. A worm hole has removed enough of this word to force the second letter to be pure conjecture while the remaining circle of the third letter could survive from a *ḥet*, *ṭet*, *kap,* or *reš*. The shape of the circle suggests a *reš*. For the reconstruction פתריהם אספר cf. CD XIII 8 concerning the role of the overseer ויספר לפניהם נהיות עולם בפתריהם.

L. 9 אספ[ר֯ בׄע֯בור. A trace of the left tip of the top of a letter can be seen to the right of the *bet*. A small triangular fragment from the earlier photo is missing in the final photo and contains the tips of two downstokes. Milik's reconstruction (joining frg. 8) which reads בׄע֯בור is theoretically still possible.

L. 9 תבׄינו. Only the upturned tip of the *bet* has survived. The dark diagonal descending from that tip in the photograph is merely the shadow of a hole in the join.

---

[51] Cf. Kister, '4Q298', 242-3.

Translation

1.]and the number of its boundaries
2. with[out raising itself up
3. from [its] po[sition,[52] and to] its boundary. And now
4. give ea[r, O wise ones]; and you who know, listen! And men of
5. understanding, in[crease learning[53]]; and you who seek justice, (add) modesty;[54]
6. you who kn[ow the way], add strength; and men of
7. truth,[55] pur[sue righteousness]; and you who love kindness, add
8. humility; and a[dd kn]owledge of the appointed [t]imes,[56] whose
9. interpre[ta]tion [I will recou]nt, in order that you may give heed to the end
10. of the ages and that you may look upon for[m]er things in order to know

Comments

L. 1–2 Cf. 4Q**405** 23 i 11–12: מגבולו לא ירומו ממשלוחתו לא ישפלו.[57]

L. 3–8

ועתה האזינ֯]ו [	וידעים שמעו
ואנשי בינה ה֯[ ]ח֯	ודורש[י] משפט הצניע לכת
[ ]הוסיפו אומץ	ואנשי אמת רד֯פ֯[ ]
ואהבי חסד הוסיפו ענוה	וה֯ו֯[סיפו

This arrangement of the verses makes it clear that the correct reading is ואהבי חסד (rather than ואהבו חסד), but since in the esoteric script there is no graphic similarity between the letters *waw* and *yod*, we must conclude that the *Vorlage* to this scroll was written in the usual square letters, in which it is often impossible to distinguish between those two letters. On the basis of parallelism, we might attempt to restore האזינו [חכמים]; ואנשי בינה ה[וסיפו לק]ח; ואנשי אמת רד[פו צדק]. These restorations, however, are not certain. הוסיפו אומץ (line 6) is based upon Job 17:9,[58] hence the restoration יו[דעי הדרך] (which is, however, tentative).

Despite the fragmentary nature of the text, it seems that we have here a poetic rendering of the common formula for defining the sect, which appears several times in the writings of the sect; cf., e.g. 1QS V 4–5 לעשות אמת יחד וענוה צדקה ומשפט ואהבת חסד והצנע לכת בכול דרכיהם ('to do together truth and humility and righteousness and justice and love of kindness and modesty [or: wisdom] in all their ways'). The expression אהבי חסד shows that אהבת חסד in this formula should not be translated 'affectionate love' or 'love and affection'.[59] For the development of this formula and its parallels, see Kister, '4Q298', 245–9.

The phrase הצנע לכת in this formula is based on Mic 6:8. Its meaning there is unclear. In 1QS IV 5, it appears that this expression serves to express a religious ideal of relations between humans and the Deity. Its meaning in 1QS V 5 is uncertain. It seems there to refer to wisdom (supported by uses of the root צנע in a number of unpublished Qumran texts) and proper religious behaviour.[60] That meaning is

---

[52] If זבולה, then perhaps 'its habitation'.

[53] If כו[ח, then perhaps 'a[dd strength/stamina]'.

[54] Or 'cautiousness'. See comments.

[55] Or 'integrity'.

[56] The author would like to thank Claire Pfann for suggesting this reconstruction.

[57] C. Newsom, *Songs of the Sabbath Sacrifice* (Atlanta, 1985) 322.

[58] The original meaning of אמץ in the biblical verse is probably 'to girdle' one's loins for travel; in our text, however, the meaning may be 'to endure' the persecution of the sect because of its special 'way' (cf. 1QH^a II 8; 1QM XIV 7).

[59] Unlike Licht's suggestion in his commentary (J. Licht, *The Rule Scroll* [Jerusalem: Bialik Institute, 1965] 73).

[60] See P. Wernberg-Møller, *The Manual of Discipline* (Leiden: Brill, 1957) 77–8; E. Y. Kutscher, *Archive of the New Dictionary of Rabbinic Literature* I (Ramat-Gan: Bar-Ilan University, 1972) 103 [Heb]; M. Kister, 'A Contri-

appropriate to the context of the verse in Micah (והצנע לכת עם אלהיך, 'with your God'). But 1QS VIII 2 would seem to indicate that this expression refers to interpersonal relations[61] והצנע לכת איש אם [= עם] רעהו. Indeed, such an understanding of this biblical phrase as referring to interpersonal relations appears in *b. Sukkah* 49b (and see Rashi's commentary ad loc.). Cf. also *Tanḥuma* to Genesis (*Miqqeṣ*, sections 8, 97a; ed. Buber).[62] It seems, however, that the original formula in 1QS read: 'To enact truth, and righteousness, and justice <each one to his neighbour> on the earth'. The words והצנע לכת seem to be a later insertion into the original formula. The words איש אם רעהו ('each one to his neighbour') in 1QS modify not the words והצנע לכת, but the entire formula.[63] The present text is not decisive for the meaning of הצנע לכת, but it should be noted that it is what דורשי משפט should do, according to this text. The expression דרש משפט means in the sect 'to judge members' (see 1QS VI 24, and also VI 7 and VIII 24), so it may be that here too the expression הצנע לכת is related to interpersonal matters.

L. 8 תעודה. This word should be understood as an abstract noun from the root יעד, meaning that which has been determined,[64] which is naturally related to מועד and קץ ('fixed, appointed time'; see 1QM XI 8, and cf. below, line 9).

L. 9 פת֯ר֯[י]ה֯ם֯. See COMMENTS to frg. 1–2 i 1.

L. 9–10 ב֯ע֯בור תב֯ינו בקץ עולמ֯ות ובקד֯[מ]וניות תביטו לדעת. Cf. Isa 43:18 אל תזכרו ראשנות וקדמניות אל תתבננו. These words are the opening of a historical speech, which projects from the past onto the (eschatological?) future. Cf. CD I 1ff; II 14ff. Here too it seems that קץ עולמות refers to the eschaton, standing in opposition to ('ancient times'). The ostensible contradiction between the verse in Isaiah and the formulation in this text is the result of the interpretation of the negatives in the Isaiah verse as merely rhetorical. In an as yet unpublished Qumran wisdom text we find an imperative בינה לקדמוניות (4Q**418**; 4Q**413** 4 reads]ר֯א֯ישונים ובינו ב֯שני ד[ור ו]דור [see below]). While the preceding lines perhaps dealt with the laws of nature (as it would seem from several words that have been preserved: זבול, גבולות, תכון, עפר, בכול תבל), these lines seem to deal with the historical laws, reaching its climax in a preordained eschatological period.[65]

---

bution to the Interpretation of Ben Sira', *Tarbiz* 59 (1990) 352–3 [Heb]; Z. Ben-Hayyim, 'Forgotten Senses of צנוע and ענו', *Leshonenu* 57 (1993) 51–4 [Heb].

[61] See Licht's commentary (*The Rule Scroll*, 178): 'איש עם רעהו instead of עם אלהיך in the alluded biblical verse. The same attitude—transforming the formula from its biblical meaning into a meaning concerning the principle of "brotherhood" among the sect's members—may be recognized also in the other usages of this formula [in the Rule Scroll—M. K.]'. As we shall see, Licht's statement needs some modification.

[62] See also *Midrash ha-Gadol Deut* 23:15 (p. 323, line 11); *Tana de-Be Eliyahu Rabba* (ed. M. Friedmann) 143.

[63] Cf. Kister, '4Q298', 247–8.

[64] See Qimron, *HDSS*, 115 §500.3. Cf. also a similar usage of תעודה as derived from יעד in medieval Hebrew (Ben-Yehuda's Dictionary, s.v. תעודה).

[65] The notes of Eisenman and Wise (R. Eisenman and M. Wise, *The Dead Sea Scrolls Uncovered* [Shaftesbury: Element, 1992] 161–4) to this fragment are inaccurate and partially misleading: the term משכיל does not have a specific eschatological aspect (although every doctrine of the sect may be considered eschatological). CD XIV 19 does not imply that the Messiah 'will (or: did) atone for their sins'; the text was rightly restored (with the help of 4QD^a (4Q**266** 10 i 13); cf. Qimron, *The Damascus Document Reconsidered*: ויכפר עונם מ[נחה וחטאת] ('and their sins will be atoned [in the Messianic era—M. K.] by cereal offering and sin offering [defiled in the present era—M. K.]) It seems rather unlikely to interpret בני שחר as 'some kind of all-night community vigils', and it has nothing to do with Qumranic verses (ibid., 162–3); the alternative explanation of the term בני שחר has been already suggested by Baumgarten (not mentioned by Eisenman and Wise). אמונה in frg. 1–2 i 3 is based (as shown above) on Jer 5:1, and therefore it should not be interpreted as 'faith' (with its Christian connotations; ibid. 161). Eisenman and Wise's comment to frgs. 3–4 ii 7 ('Once again . . . we have an allusion to the Righteousness/Piety dichotomy so much a part of the consciousness of this group') is untenable. Frgs. 3–4 ii 10 have nothing to do with *m. Ḥag* 2.1 (ibid., 162).

Frgs. 3–4 iii

1–4]
5]◦
6]תׄ
7]הטׄ
8]להׄ
9]
10]משׄ

Frg. 5 i

7]]צׄיה
8]] תכלית
9]]תׄ לדרוך
10]]◦ ◦[

Translation
8.] uttermost
9.] to tread

Frg. 5 ii

7 ◦◦◦◦ךׄ ואׄ]
8 השחר וקׄ]
9 גבולותיו]
10 שם גבולותׄ]

NOTES ON READINGS

L. 7 ךֺ∘∘∘∘. Sufficient space exists for 4–5 letters. Milik proposed לדורך; an alternative reading might be להתהלך.

TRANSLATION

7. and [
8. the dawn and [
9. its boundaries[
10. he placed boundaries[

Frg. 6

]∘∘[1

]ותיה פ∘[2

]∘ת[3

Frg. 7

]ותי[ו/ה 1

Frg. 8

]מׄ∘דׄמׄ[1

]בׄ∘[2

NOTES ON READINGS

L. 1]מׄ∘דׄמׄ[. Both the first and last letters contain enough of the inner outline of the letter *mem* to identify them securely. Of the second letter, only the tail remains, which descends and then turns immediately to the left at about midpoint down the length of the *mem*. There are three letters which have this type of tail: *ḥet, lamed* and *ʿayin*. The third letter only provides a crescent-shaped piece from its bottom whose tail terminates vertically. Considering the height of the crescent and the narrow width, it best resembles the bottom of a *dalet*.

L. 2]בׄ∘[. The size and the height of the upturned tip makes the identification of the first letter as a *bet* secure. Only a spot of ink at about the height of the tip of *bet* betrays the presence of the second letter.

299–301. 4QMysteries[a–b, c?]

(PLATES III–IX)

Preliminary publication: L. Schiffman, '4QMysteries[a]: A Preliminary Edition and Translation', in *Solving Riddles and Untying Knots, Biblical, Epigraphic, and Semitic Studies in Honor of Jonas C. Greenfield*, ed. Z. Zevit, S. Gitin, M. Sokoloff (Winona Lake, IN: Eisenbrauns, 1995) 207–60; idem, '4Q Mysteries[b], A Preliminary Edition', *RevQ* 16 (1993) 203–23. B. Z. Wacholder and M. G. Abegg, *A Preliminary Edition of the Unpublished Dead Sea Scrolls, The Hebrew and Aramaic Texts from Cave Four*, Fascicle Two (Washington, D.C.: Biblical Archaeology Society, 1992) 1–37.

THE texts entitled 'Mysteries' consist of four manuscripts.[1] Three of these, 1Q**27**, 4Q**299** (4QMyst[a]), and 4Q**300** (4QMyst[b]), can definitely be shown to constitute one and the same composition. The fourth, 4Q**301** (4QMyst[c]), was classified as part of this composition by J. T. Milik, although no definite overlap in text exists. This lack of overlap, coupled with the close parallels between 4Q**301** and hekhalot literature, parallels not found in 1Q**27**, 4Q**299**, and 4Q**300**, makes such an identification uncertain.

It is certain that 'Mysteries' is of similar genre and content to the so-called sapiential works, especially 4Q**415–418**.[2] Terms such as רז נהיה, הבט, התבונן, and numerous others, tie these texts together. At the same time, considering the extent of the material preserved in both sets of manuscripts, the lack of any textual overlap makes it extremely unlikely that the 'Mysteries' texts constitute part of the same composition as 4Q**415–418**.

The title 'Mysteries' is derived from the occurrence in these texts of the term רזים. Numerous studies of the use of this term in Qumran literature have been undertaken.[3] In this composition it refers to the mysteries of creation, i.e. the natural order of things which depends on God's wisdom, and to the mysteries of the divine role in the processes of history. Wisdom is another motif which occurs in these documents, and its

---

[1] Thank are due E. Larson and S. Berrin for supplying the technical information on which the physical descriptions of the manuscripts are based, E. Qimron for reviewing the transcriptions and for making valuable suggestions and corrections, and J. Fitzmyer for providing numerous suggestions which helped to improve this work. P. Torijano assisted in the preparation of the material for publication. Most of this study was completed while a Fellow of the Annenberg Research Institute in 1992–3.

[2] On this genre, see T. Elgvin, 'Admonition Texts from Qumran Cave 4', in *Methods of Investigation of the Dead Sea Scrolls and the Khirbet Qumran Site, Present Realities and Future Prospects, Annals of the New York Academy of Sciences* 722, ed. by M. O. Wise, et al. (New York: New York Academy of Sciences, 1994) 179–96, and D. Harrington, 'Wisdom at Qumran', in *The Community of the Renewed Covenant, The Notre Dame Symposium on the Dead Sea Scrolls*, eds. E. Ulrich and J. C. VanderKam (Notre Dame, IN: University of Notre Dame Press, 1994) 137–52.

[3] See, e.g. R. E. Brown, *The Semitic Background of the Term 'Mystery' in the New Testament* (Philadelphia: Fortress Press, 1968) esp. 22–30; B. Rigaux, 'Révélation des mystères et perfection à Qumran et dans le Nouveau Testament', *NTS* 4 (1957–8) 237–62.

importance lies in its being the source from which the divine mysteries emerge. All the natural phenomena and events of history are seen here as part of the divine wisdom.

The first exemplar of this composition (1Q**27**) was published by R. de Vaux in a very preliminary manner with little analysis[4] even before the formal publication by J. T. Milik in 1955.[5] An important study by I. Rabinowitz set forth the basic interpretation of the work and its poetic structure.[6] The composition which is represented in 1Q**27**, 4Q**299**, and 4Q**300** is definitely poetic and is part of a type of reflective (i.e. non-liturgical) poetry to which many Qumran compositions belong.

The present edition employs fragment numbers which are different from those used by Milik in the *Preliminary Concordance*. Many improvements in the readings and restorations have been possible. It is impossible to determine, in the opinion of this editor, the order in which the material stood in the original composition.

---

[4] R. de Vaux, *RB* 56 (1949) 605–9, pl XVII; cf. J. T. Milik, *Verbum Domini* 30 (1952) 42–3.

[5] D. Barthélemy, J. T. Milik, et al., *Qumran Cave I* (DJD I; Oxford: Clarendon Press, 1955) 102–7, pls XXI–XXII. English translation of col. I is available in G. Vermes, *The Dead Sea Scrolls in English* (London: Penguin Books, 1995) 272. A complete English translation is found in F. García Martínez, *The Dead Sea Scrolls Translated, The Qumran Texts in English*, tr. W. G. E. Watson (Leiden: E. J. Brill, 1994) 399–400. Parts of 1Q**27** were republished by J. Licht in his edition and commentary on the *Hodayot Scroll*; J. Licht, מגילת ההודיות (Jerusalem: Bialik Institute, 1957) 242.

[6] I. Rabinowitz, 'The Authorship, Audience and Date of the de Vaux Fragment of an Unknown Work', *JBL* 71 (1952) 19–32.

299. 4QMysteries[a]

(PLATES III–VII)

Preliminary publication: L. Schiffman, '4QMysteries[a]: A Preliminary Edition and Translation', in *Solving Riddles and Untying Knots: Biblical, Epigraphic, and Semitic Studies in Honor of Jonas C. Greenfield*, ed. Z. Zevit, S. Gitin, M. Sokoloff (Winona Lake, IN: Eisenbrauns, 1995) 207–60. B. Z. Wacholder and M. G. Abegg, *A Preliminary Edition of the Unpublished Dead Sea Scrolls, The Hebrew and Aramaic Texts from Cave Four*, Fascicle Two (Washington, D.C.: Biblical Archaeology Society, 1992) 1–37.

Physical Description

THE manuscript is tannish-brown in colour, becoming dark brown where stained (as on the two top fragments in PAM 43.389; the fragments themselves are now almost illegible to the naked eye). The skin is of medium thickness and the writing is on the hair side, as is usual in Qumran manuscripts. Parts of the surface have flaked off on some of the fragments, resulting in the loss of letters or parts of letters.

The average line height measures 0.6–0.7 cm, with extremes of 0.4 and 1 cm. The average letter height is 0.2 cm, but letters of 0.3 cm are not uncommon. Dry lines, both horizontal and vertical, are visible on several fragments and the writing is suspended from them. Dry lines are extremely difficult to make out on the material preserved on other plates. Intercolumnar margins are 0.8 cm and the bottom margin is 1.7 cm.

F. M. Cross has identified the script as developed Herodian semi-formal hand.

Orthography and Morphology

The orthography of the fragments is rather consistent. The scribe made abundant use of *matres lectionis*, spelling, e.g. לוא, כול throughout the fragments. (It should be noted that 1Q27 which was used to supply restorations, exhibits an alternation of כל/כול, לא/לוא). In 4Q299, *yod* serves to indicate *ī*, *ê<ay* in plural constructs, plural suffixed forms and other internal diphthongs. Qumranic spellings like חוכמת are rather common (e.g. frg. 3a ii-b 5). The pronouns appear always in the short form (except in frg. 24 2, היאה[, and in frg. 65 2,]הואה). Pronominal suffixes are almost always of the short form (e.g. frg. 6 ii 2 ועליכם; but notice again that 1Q27 exhibits an alternation between long and short forms). In frg. 1 1 the form כולמה appears for כלם. The particle כי is spelled with א (e.g. frg. 6 ii 6 כיא).

Though forms similar to those of 𝔐 are in the majority, nevertheless, the two long forms of the pronoun, the case of the long pronominal suffix, spellings like חוכמה, and the tendency towards *scriptio plena* warrant the inclusion of the manuscript within the orthographic system of Qumran Hebrew.

Mus. Inv. 594, 595, 604, 605
PAM 40.592, 40.612, 40.614*, 41.208, 41.211, 41.321*, 41.389, 41.422, 41.423, 41.515, 41.694, 41.695, 42.181, 43.389*, 43.390*, 43.391*, 43.392*, 43.393*

Frg. 1

1 [ ]ם֯ שנאו עול
2 [ ] ה֯אמת היש שפה ולשון
3 [ ]מ֯י גוי אשר לוא גזל֯
4 [ ]ב֯ית מולדים נשט֯ר֯ה֯ ∘
5 [ ]אנשי מחשבת לכול
6 [ ]∘∘ם֯ נ֯בחנה דברים
7 [ ]ל֯[תו]צ֯אותם
8 [ ]ולכ֯[ול]
9 [ ]∘[

PAM 43.389

NOTES ON READINGS

L. 4 ∘ נשט֯ר֯ה֯. The reading is extremely doubtful as no interpretation can be suggested. It is unclear whether the indicated last letter belongs to this word or starts a new one.

L. 7]ל֯[. Reading with Wacholder-Abegg.

TRANSLATION

1. [ ] hate iniquity?
2. [ ] truthful [report]. Is there a language or a tongue
3. [ ] What nation (is there) which has not stolen
4. [ ] time of birth . . .
5. [ ] men of (evil) devices for all
6. [ ] it has been tested, the words
7. [ ] according to [that which re]sults from them
8. [ ] and for a[ll]

Variants

(2) כולמה] 1Q27 כולמ[ה]

(2) ולשן] 1Q27 ולשון

(3–4) מי גוי אשר לוא גזל [הון] 1Q27 has a longer text: מי יחפץ כי יגזל ברשע הונו מי גוי אשר לוא עשק רעה[ו] איפה עם אשר לוא גזל הון, ‘Who would desire to be wickedly robbed of his property? Which is the nation that has not extorted from [its] neighbour an ephah, the people that has not stolen [property]?’

(4) [הון] In 1Q27 there follows ל[אחר as restored by Milik.

(7) תו[צ̇אותם] Cf. 1Q27 line 12 as read by Milik: הו ותוצאות ית . . . [.

Reconstructed Text

1Q**27** contains text preserved in both 4Q**299** and 4Q**300**. On this basis, the text preceding 4Q**299** 1 1–3 can be restored, as can the text following 4Q**300** 3 1–6. It is not certain that this restored text appeared in the same column as fragment 1 of 4Q**299**; some or all of it may have appeared in the preceding column. An approximate line length of 55–59 letter-spaces, based on the lengths of 4Q**299** 1–3, has been used in this restoration. The following sigla are used:

1Q27 1 i 1–12: underline
4Q**299** 1 1–9: dotted underline
4Q**300** 3 1–6: overbar

[ ]כול ◦[ ] 01

[ ]בעבור ידעו בין טוב ובין רע ובין שקר לא[מ̇ת̇]] 02

]ויבינו[רזי פשע כל חוכמתם ולא ידעו רז נהיה ובקדמוניות לוא 03

התבוננו ולא ידעו מה אשר יבוא עליהם ונפשם לא מלטו מרז נהיה 04

ו̇זה לכם האות כי יהיה בהסגר מולדי עולה וגלה הרשע מפני הצדק 05

כגלות [ח]ושך מפני אור וכתום עשן וא[יננ]ו עוד כן יתם הרשע לעד 06

והצדק יגלה כשמש תכון תבל וכול תומכי רזי [בליעל] אינמה עוד 07

ודעה תמלא תבל ואין שם לע̇[ד] אולת נכון הדבר לבוא ואמת המשא 08

]ומזה יודע לכמה כי לוא ישוב אחור הלוא כול העמי[ם̇ שנאו עול 1

]וביד כולמ[ה] יתהלך הלוא מפי כול לאומים שמע[ה̇אמת היש שפה ולשן 2

]מחזקת בה מי גוי חפץ אשר יעושקנו חזק ממנו[מ̇י גוי אשר לוא גזל̇ 3

]ה̇ו̇[ן]ב̇ית מולדים נשט̇ר̇ה̇ ◦ 4

5 [אנשי מחשבת לכול]

6 [°°ם̊ נׄבחנה דברים]

7 [לׄ[תו]צׄאותם]

8 [ולכׄ[ו]ל]]

9 [°[ ]

Translation[1]

01.] everything [
02. [in order that they might know (the difference) between good and evil, and between falsehood and truth,]
03. [and that they might understand] the mysteries of transgression, (with) all their wisdom. But they did not know the mystery of that which was coming into being, and the former things they did not consider.
04. Nor did they know what shall befall them. And they did not save their lives from the mystery that was coming into being.
05. And this shall be the sign to you that it is taking place: When the begotten of unrighteousness are delivered up, and wickedness is removed from before righteousness,
06. as darkness is removed from before light. (Then,) just as smoke wholly ceases and is no more, so shall wickedness cease forever,
07. and righteousness shall be revealed as the sun (throughout) the full measure of the world. And all the adherents of the mysteries of [Belial] will be no more.
08. But knowledge shall fill the world, and folly shall nevermore be there. The thing is certain to come, and the oracle is true.
1. [And from this you will know that it will not be reversed: Do not all the people]s hate iniquity?
2. [But it goes on at the hands of all of them. Does not the] truthful [report (issue) from the mouth of all the nations?] Is there a language or a tongue
3. [which upholds it? What nation (is there which) desires that (a) stronger one should oppress it?] Yet what nation (is there) which has not stolen
4. [property] time of birth
5. [ ] men of (evil) devices for all
6. [ ] it has been tested, the words
7. [ ] according to [that which re]sults from them
8. [ ] and for a[ll]

Comments

Man was given wisdom in order that he should discern the difference between good and evil, and truth and falsehood. Despite this wisdom, which should have been sufficient, mankind failed to realize that which would happen in the future, since they did not properly grasp the significance of the events of the past. Yet there is a sign from God that the end of days is about to dawn. For at that time all the wicked and

---

[1] Lines 01–08 of the translation have been supplied from 1Q**27** in order to supply a context for this fragment.

evil itself will be eliminated and will cease forever. Then knowledge of God will fill the earth. How can one be certain that the end of days is really at hand? It is because of the hypocrisy of all the nations. All nations claim to revile evil but commit it themselves against their neighbours. This passage is reminiscent of tannaitic teachings that on the eve of the messianic era, חצפא יסגי, 'impudence will be abundant' (*m. Soṭa* 9.15).

L. 01 The motif of distinguishing between good and evil is common in this literature.

L. 03 The term רז נהיה, found throughout the wisdom texts and mysteries from Qumran and in the sectarian corpus as well, is discussed by T. Elgvin, 'The Mystery to Come: Early Essene Theology of Revelation', *Qumran Between the Old and New Testament*, ed. T. L. Thompson, N. P. Lemche (Sheffield, forthcoming). This term, as can be seen from 4Q**418** 123 3 and such sectarian texts as 1QS III 15 and XI 3–4, takes in the entire past, present, and future. Accordingly, נִהְיֶה is understood as a participle and translated accordingly. Cf. Sir 42:19 (נהיות) and ℭ τὰ ἐσόμενα.

L. 07 Although the text of 1Q**27** has פלא it is obvious from the context that it must be emended to בליעל or some synonym.

L. 1 [יודע לכמה]. The verb is a *Nipᶜal*. The expression יודע לכם occurs only in Ezek 36:32.

L. 1 [ישוב אחור]. For the *Qal* of שוב + this adverb, see Ps 9:4; 56:10; Lam 1:8. This same expression occurs in the sapiential texts. See 4Q**520** 1 ii 4, 4Q**421** 1 ii 15, and 1QH[a] XIII 19. Cf. also the benedictions after the reading of the haftarah (*Sop.* 13.10 [ed. Higger, 246–7] אחור לא ישוב ריקם '(Your word) will not return unfulfilled' (cf. Isa 55:11 where אחור does not occur).

L. 1 שנאו עול. Cf. Isa 61:8 שנא גזל בעולה speaking of God (Rabinowitz, 'Authorship, Audience, and Date', 29). If instead of *ᶜôlāh* the text is vocalized *ᶜawlāh,* it may be translated, 'hates iniquitous theft'.

Ll. 1–4 The text seeks to point to the hypocrisy of man who claims to seek to do good but instead does evil (cf. Milik, 105).

L. 2 שפה ולשון. Rabinowitz (p. 29) notes that the author has blended both the literal and figurative meaning of the words which can designate 'peoples'. Cf. Isa 28:11; Ezek 3:5, 6.

L. 3 יעושקנו. See E. Qimron, *The Hebrew of the Dead Sea Scrolls*. HSS 29 (Atlanta: Scholars Press, 1986) §311.13g.

L. 3 חזק ממנו. Cf. 2 Kgs 3:26; Jer 31:11; Ps 35:10.

L. 4]בׄית מולדים. This enigmatic phrase, which occurs again in frg. 3a ii–b, must be taken as referring to the time of birth which is seen to affect the future and nature of the individual. Cf. *Tg. Onq.* Gen 40:20 בית ולדא paralleled by *Tg. Ps-J.* יום גנוסא, translating יום הלדת. Note also מולדי עת in 1QH[a] XII 8. The same sense of מולד as the 'time of birth' is behind the regular use of this word for the onset ('birth') of the new moon in rabbinic parlance. While it cannot be proven that this is the correct interpretation, other possibilities do not seem preferable. In 4Q**418** and **416** (4QInstruction[a,b], two manuscripts of the same text, an identical passage states דרוש מולדיו (4Q**418**: מולדו) ואז תדע נחלתו, 'investigate his time of birth and then you will know his lot' (i.e. his nature; 4Q**416** 2 iii 9–10 ; 4Q**418** 9 8–9). This seems to be the same usage. The phrase בית מולדים occurs several times in the sapiential and Mysteries texts; cf. 4Q**415** 2 ii 9.

L. 7 תו]צׄאותם. Milik suggests 'expenses' (p. 105), but such an interpretation is refuted by the usage of this word in the sapiential texts.

Poetic Rendering

[in order that they might know (the difference)
between good and evil,
and between falsehood and truth,

and that they might understand the mysteries of transgression,
(with) all their wisdom.

But they did not know the mystery of that which was coming into being,
and the former things they did not consider.

Nor did they know what is to come upon them.
And they did not save their lives from the mystery that was coming into being.

And this shall be the sign to you that it is taking place:

When the begotten of unrighteousness are delivered up,
and wickedness is removed from before righteousness,
as darkness is removed from before light.

(Then,) just as smoke wholly ceases and is no more,
so shall wickedness cease forever,
and righteousness shall be revealed as the sun
(throughout) the full measure of the world.
And all the adherents of the mysteries of Belial will be no more.

But knowledge shall fill the world,
and folly shall nevermore be there.

The thing is certain to come,
and the oracle is true.]

[And from this you will know that it will not be reversed:

Do not all the people]s hate iniquity?
[But it goes on at the hands of all of them.

Does not the] truthful [report (issue) from the mouth of all the nations?]
Is there a language or a tongue [which upholds it?

What nation desires that a stronger one should oppress it?]
(Yet) what nation (is there) which has not stolen [property (of another)]

. . . time of birth

. . . men of (evil) devices for all

. . . it has been tested, the words

. . . according to [that which re]sults from them

. . . and for a[ll . . .

Frg. 2

Parallel: **1Q27** 1 ii 5–7 (underline)

01 ו◦◦[ ]לו שוו חשבונו[ת]

02 [ ]מנכ◦[ ]◦נׄוׄ מה הוא היותר לׄ[ ]

03 [ ]כי אם המטיב והמרע אם יוׄ◦[ ]

1 [ ]לׄא יׄצׄלׄחׄ[לכול כן כול טוב ממונו ברוׄ]

2 [ו]יגל בלוא ה[ון ונמכר בלוא מחיר כי ◦ת]

3 [יש]וׄה בה מהׄ[מ מׄחים כי אם כול]

4 [ ]◦◦◦◦[ ]

(5) [ ]דמי וכו[ל מח]יר לוא ישוה ב◦[ ]

(6) [ ]לכול העמים ונס◦[ ]

(7) [ ]אל ידע כול מׄ[ ]

(8) [ ]◦ל[ ]

PAM 43.389

It appears that the order originally proposed for frgs. 2 and 3a-b of 4Q**299** is incorrect. 1Q**27** II preserves a text which continues after 4Q**299** 1 4–8 (which is not paralleled in 1Q**27** I but which follows it). No proposed line length would allow the placement of the substantial 4Q**299** 3a-b (*olim* frg. 2) between the end of frg. 1 and of 1Q**27** II. Frg. 2 (*olim* frg. 3) is thus placed here, with the preceding and following text restored on the basis of 1Q**27** II. Since the right margin of 1Q**27** II is preserved, the relative position of the words as they would have appeared in 4Q**299** can be calculated in accordance with a line length of 55–58 letter-spaces in 4Q**299** and 56–65 letter-spaces in 1Q**27**. Lines restored above line 1 are numbered 01–03, and those restored below appear in parentheses (5)–(8).

TRANSLATION

01. [ ] And [ ] they set up (?) the calculation[s]
02. [ ] what advantage is there to [ ]
03. [ ] except one who does good and one who does evil, if [ ]
1. [ ] he will not succeed [in anything; thus, all good is his wealth (?)]
2. [and]he will be exiled without pro[perty (i.e. payment) and sold without a price, because it]
3. [will be wo]rth it. How [except every]
4. [ ] [ ]
(5). [ ]amount and it will not be worth any price [

(6). [ ]for all the nations and [
(7). [ ]God knew every [
(8). [ ] [ ]

COMMENTS

The passage appears to concentrate on the fate of the evildoer who will be sold into slavery and exiled, in fulfillment of the Torah's prophecy.

L. 02 Milik: 'les comptes sont satisfaisants' (p. 105).

L. 1]לֹא יִצְלָח[לכול. See Jer 13:7. Perhaps translate 'it will not be good [for anything . . . '.

L. 2 [בלוא מחיר]. Cf. Isa 55:1; Jer 15:13. Deut 28:68 may lie behind this line from a conceptual point of view, as it describes the exile to Egypt where the Israelites will be sold into slavery to their enemies, but no one will purchase them.

Frg. 3

Frg. 3 comprises three fragments: frgs. 3a, 3b, and 3c. Frg. 3a preserves a few remnants of col. i. Frg. 3a ii is parallel to and may be restored from 4Q**300** 5. On the basis of this parallel, the placement of frg. 3b at the upper left-hand corner of frg. 3a is certain, as is the restoration of the text preceding frg. 3a ii-b. (The continuation of 4Q**300** 5 can, in turn, be reconstructed from 4Q**299** 3a-b ii). The restoration of the text immediately preceding 4Q**299** 3a ii maintains the line position of 4Q**300** 5.

Frg. 3c preserves the leftmost part of a column, which Milik in the *Preliminary Concordance* took to be part of frg. 3a i 13–18. It also preserves the intercolumnar space and two letters of a second column. These two letters cannot be successfully placed in frg. 3a ii based on the parallel in 4Q**300** 5. Thus the fragment does not belong with frg. 3a-b ii.[2] Frg. 3c does have a small overlap with 4Q**300** 1 ii which allows the restoration of portions of the preceding text and additional words below, difficult as they are to place.

Frg. 3a i

3] °[
4] הוא[
5] מֹה[

PAM 41.211, 41.423, 41.694, 43.389*

[2] The plate reproduced here, PAM 43.389, reflects Milik's original placement of these fragments, a join which can no longer be accepted on textual grounds.

Notes on Readings

L. 3 The surviving letter was read as a possible *he* by Milik.

Ll. 3–5 The leftmost portion of this column is preserved on frg. 3a as is the narrow margin separating the columns.

Translation

3. [ ]
4. [ ]he
5. [ ]what (?)

Frg. 3a ii-b

Parallel: 4Q**300** 5 (underline)

01 מחשבת בי]נה

02 מ]שפט בגלל הון[

1]]◦ הא◦[אביון[

2 מה נקרא ה[ ]הו ומעש]יו

3 וכול מעשה צדיק הטמ]אה ומה [נקרא לאד]ם

4 חכם וצדיק כי לוא לאיש[ ]ה ולו]א ה חכמה נכחדת כי[

5 אם חוכמת עורמת רוע ומ]חשבת בליעל

6 מעשה אשר לוא יעשה עוד כיא אם [

7 דבר עושו ומה (ו)הוא אשר יעשה ג]בר

8 המרה את דבר עושו ימחה שמו מפי כול[

9 { } שמעו תומכי ◦[

10 עולם ומזמות כול מעשה ומח]שבות

11 כול רז ומכין כול מחשבת עושה כול[הנהיות

12 הו]אה מק]דם עולם הואה שמו ולע]ולם

13 ותש[ ]ל [מ]חשבת בית מולדים פתח לפ]ניהם

14 [ ]◦שבו כי לבנו בחן וינחילנו[

15 [ ]כול רז וחבלי כול מעשה ומה [

16 [ומה]עמים כ[י] בראם ומעש]יהמה

NOTES ON READINGS

L. 11 הנהיות. An alternative restoration is הבריאות.

L. 12 The restoration in Wacholder-Abegg, taken from Milik's reading, is too short to fill the lacuna.

TRANSLATION

01.] a thought of discern[ment
02. ju]dgement because of property[
1.] [poor]
2. What shall we call the[ ] his [ ] and [his?] deeds [ ]
3. and every action of the righteous is imp[ure. And what] shall we call a per[son]
4. wise and righteous, for it is not to a person[ ] and no[t hidden wisdom, ex-]
5. cept the wisdom of evil cunning and the de[vices of Belial.
6. a deed which should not be done again, except[
7. the command of his Creator. But what is it which a m[an] shall do[
8. violated the command of his Creator, his name shall be erased from the mouth of every [
9. [ ] Listen O you who hold fast [
10. eternity, and the schemes of every creature. And the de[vices
11. every mystery and preordains every plan. He causes everything [which comes into being.
12. H[e is from bef]ore eternity; the Lord is His name, and for e[ternity
13. [ ] [p]lan of the time of birth He opened be[fore them
14. [ ] for He tested our heart, and He caused us to inherit [
15. [ ] every mystery and the tribulations of every creature. And how [
16. [and what are] the peoples th[at] He created them, and [their] deed[s

COMMENTS

This passage begins with a set of rhetorical questions. Such questions, beginning with מה, 'what' or 'how', are typical of the rhetoric of the Qumran sapiential literature. 4Q**301** also has a series of such questions. In this passage, they are intended to bemoan the person whose wisdom serves only his wickedness. From line 8 on, there is a hortatory speech addressed to the righteous who hold fast to eternity. It emphasizes the all-knowing quality of God who sets forth the fate of all humanity. Here the reader encounters the familiar concept of predestination found in the Qumran sectarian corpus.

L. 3 מעשה צׄדׄיׄקׄ. Cf. Eccl 8:14.

L. 4 חכם וצדיק. Cf. Eccl 9:1.

L. 4 Restore after לאיׄשׄ[either חוכמ]ה, תושי]ה, or תבונ]ה, meaning 'wisdom', 'sound wisdom', 'understanding'.

L. 5 ומׄ]חשבת. An alternative restoration is ומ]זמת. Cf. 1QH[a] II 16–17.

L. 6 מעשה אשר לוא יעשה. Cf. Gen 20:9; Isa 19:15.

L. 7 <ו>הוא. The first *waw* is clearly a scribal error.

L. 7 The end of line 7 must have contained a word meaning either 'since he' or 'whoever'.

L. 8 ימחה שמו. See Deut 25:6; cf. 29:19.

L. 8 Perhaps restore at the end בשר] or a similar word.

L. 9 There is an erasure at the beginning of the line.

L. 9 שמעו. This is a regular form of address in hortatory and wisdom texts known from the Qumran sect. This formula is used in CD I 1; II 2, 14; 1QH[a] I 35; it is used often with (ו)עתה which also figures prominently in this text.

L. 10 The line must have ended with a verb with the sense, 'He sets out'.

L. 12 Cf. Exod 15:3. הואה here serves as a substitute for the tetragrammaton (cf. L. H. Schiffman, *Sectarian Law in the Dead Sea Scrolls, Courts, Testimony and the Penal Code*, Brown Judaic Studies 33 [Chico, CA: Scholars Press, 1983] 100–101 n. 16).

L. 14 לבנו בחן. Cf. Jer 12:3; Ps 7:10; 17:3; Prov 17:3.

L. 15]כ֯ול רז. Cf. Dan 4:6.

Frg. 3c

Parallel: 4Q**300** 1a ii-b (underline)

01 [ ]ת֯◦[החר]טמים מלמדי פשע אמרו ה֯משל והגידו ה֯חידה בטרם נדבר ואז תדעו אם הבטתם֯

02 ותע֯ודות הש֯מ֯[ים]כסלכמה כי חתום מכם[ח]ת֯ם החזון וברזי עד לא הבטתם ובבינה לא השכלתם

03 א֯[ז]ת֯אמרו ל[ ]◦ה והמ֯י֯[ ]כי לא הבטתם בשורש חוכמה ואם תפתחו החזון

1 [ ]יה◦◦◦◦ם

2 [ ]תסתם מ֯כם

3 [כל חוכמתכם כי לכם המשל]◦ שמעו כי מה

4]היא חכמה נכחדת]◦◦א שמה

5 [עוד לא תהיה]ש֯ו ◦◦ר֯זי עד

6 [חזון]◦ מ֯עשו יהו[

PAM 41.211, 41.423, 41.694, 43.389*

TRANSLATION

01. [mag]icians, who teach transgression, utter the parable and relate the riddle before it is discussed. And then you will know whether you have considered

02. and the testimonies (?) of hea[ven] your foolishness, for the [se]al of the vision is sealed from you. [Se]aled is the vision. And you did not look at the eternal secrets, and you did not contemplate with understanding.

03. Th[en] you shall say [ ] for you did not look at the root of wisdom. And if you should open the vision,

1. [ ]
2. [ ] it will be kept secret from you
3. [all your wisdom, for yours is the parable] listen for what
4. [is hidden wisdom(?)] there
5. [still you will not be] eternal secrets
6. [vision] His deeds [

COMMENTS

Frg. 3c relates further evidence of the signs of the impending end. It may therefore eventually have to be placed with the restored frg. 1. It asserts that the signs are in the heavens, but that they are not comprehended. They are unavailable even if one tries to understand the 'vision', for it is hidden wisdom.

L. 2]סתם. Cf. Dan 8:26; 12:4, 9; Ps 51:8.

Frg. 4

1 לב]לתי המ֯ו[
2 [◦מו בת֯]
3]א֯ר֯ץ֯ וכמה֯ו֯ ל[
4 י]ד֯ע ונספר֯ו֯ ריש֯]ונות
5]אינה לש֯ל֯ם֯[

PAM 41.695, 43.389*

TRANSLATION

1. so as] not to [
2.] [
3.]land, and like it [
4. k]new, and the fir[st things] were related (?) [
5.] is not to pay (?)[

COMMENTS

L. 4 ריש]ונות. Cf. Isa 41:22; 43:9, 18; 46:9; 48:3; where this term refers to the events of the past. In BDB (911a), the term is understood in Isa 42:9 as referring to 'earlier predictions'.

Frg. 5

1 מאור]ות כוכבים ל֯ז֯[כר]ו֯ן שמ֯[ו
2 גב]ו֯רות רזי אור ודרכי חוש֯[ך

3]בֿדין מועדי חֿום עֿם קֿצֿ[י

4 מבוא יום]ומוצא לילהֿ[ ]ל[

5]ובית מולדיםֿ[

PAM 43.389

TRANSLATION

1. light]s of the stars for the re[membr]ance of [His] name[
2. migh]ty mysteries of light and the ways of dark[ness
3.] seasons of warmth as well as period[s of
4. the coming in of day] and the going out of night[
5.]and the times of birth of the creatures[

COMMENTS

That God's wonders are beyond the ken of humanity is asserted here. The heavenly bodies and the seasons are called forth as evidence of God's hidden wisdom.

L. 1 מאור]ות כוכבים. The restoration עבו]דת כוכבים ('star worship') in Wacholder-Abegg, originally suggested by Milik, does not fit the context, as the text is dealing here with the wonders of creation.

L. 1 לזֿ[כר]ון שמֿו. Cf. Mal 3:16.

L. 2 ודרכי חושֿ[ך. Cf. Prov 2:13. This same phrase is found in 1QS III 21 and IV 11.

L. 3 Cf. Gen 8:22.

L. 4 [מבוא יום]. The restoration is conjectural but this must be the sense of the text.

L. 4 Cf. Ps 19:7; 4Q**418** 123 ii 2; 1QS X 10; 1QH[a] XII 4, 7.

Frg. 6 i

1]מים

2]מרותם

3]◦םֿ עבוֿדתם יחזקו

4 ברק]ים עשה לנצח גשמים

5 מי]םֿ ובֿמשורה ישקו

6]יֿאמר להם ויתנו

7] בגברתו ברא

8]אֿ[ ]◦ל [ה]ריה כול

ה
9]◦◦ כֿל צאצאי

10]מֿטֿברו פרש

]○○○דׄם עת בעת 11

]וׄ להרות לכול 12

]כׄיׄ מעפר מבניתם 13

]○כול מקויהם וחדר 14

]נׄתׄן ממשל לחזק 15

]○ת כול גבורה 16

] וׄמׄחׄזק כול 17

]○ עׄבׄוׄדת גבר 18

עב]וׄדׄתׄוׄ 19

PAM 41.422, 41.515, 43.390*

NOTES ON READINGS

L. 9 The *he* was written above the *yod* due to lack of space at the end of the line.

TRANSLATION

1.]water (?)
2.]their (?)[
3.] their task. They will strengthen
4. lightning bolt]s He made for eternal rain
5. wat]er, and according to measure they shall drink.
6.]He will say to them, and they will give
7.] in His might He created
8.]its [moun]tains, all
9.] all its descendants
10.]it spread out from its *omphalos* (?)
11.] for each and every time
12.] to water all
13.] for they are constructed of dust
14.] all their hopes (?) and the chamber (?)
15.] He gave dominion to the strong
16.]s of all might
17.] He held fast to all
18.] the work of a man
19.]his [wo]rk

COMMENTS

L. 4 ברק]ים עשה. Cf. Jer 10:13; 51:16; Ps 135:7.

L. 5 מי]םׄ וׄבׄמשורה. Cf. Ezek 4:11, 16 (where שתה appears instead of שקה as in our text). Cf. also the *Baraita Qinyan Torah*, preserved as *ʾAbot* 6.4, ומים במשורה תשתה 'you will drink water by measure', describing the hard life of a sage of the Torah.

L. 11 Similar phrasing occurs in CD XII 19–21 (עת ועת) as referring to the progression or evolution of the law with the times. Cf. also 1QS IX 13–14 (L. H. Schiffman, *The Halakhah at Qumran* [Leiden: E. J. Brill, 1975] 25, 43–4).

L. 13 מבניתם. The noun מבנית, 'construction', is found in 1QH[a] VII 4, 9 and 1QS XI 8, and three times in the Songs of the Sabbath Sacrifice: 4Q**403** 1 i 41; 4Q**405** 14–15 i 6; 11QShirShabb 2–1–9 9.

L. 14 מקוידם. Or: 'their cisterns'.

L. 15]נתן ממשל לחזק. 'He gave dominion to the strong'. For ממשל as dominion cf. 1QS IX 24; 1QM I 5. For חזק, cf. 1QH[a] II 33.

Frg. 6 ii

ל]וא ◦◦◦[
ועליכם החי ◦[
אוילי כסה ◦[
נסתרה מכול תומכ[י
מה אב לבנים מאיש[
כיא אם ארץ להדר ◦[
ממנו כי אם רוח ◦ע[
עמים מהיא אשר[
אשר אין ל◦◦[
חוש[ך] וא]ור
כן יהיה כ[
לב רעו ואורב מ◦[
מאיש נואל הון הון ◦[
לפי תבאות ומה ב◦[
מודה או תכלית י[
תכון אחד ולוא יש]בע
משפט כן ירד המ[
ואם דש יוסיף ל[
הוא י◦[ ]ל[ ]מ[
◦◦ל[

PAM 41.422, 41.515, 43.390*

TRANSLATION

1. n]ot [
2. and upon you, the live (?)[
3. the fools of [
4. hidden from all who hold fast [to
5. Why is a father (better) for children than (another) man[
6. except land to beautify (?) [
7. from it, except the spirit of [
8. peoples. What is it that [
9. which has not [
10. dar[kness] and li[ght
11. thus may it be like [
12. the heart of his neighbour, and he ambushes [
13. from a foolish man property, property [
14. according to the crops. And how [
15. its abundance, or the end of [
16. one measure and it will not be s[ated
17. judgement, thus may the[ ]go down [
18. and if he threshed, he shall add to [
19. he [
20. [ ]

COMMENTS

Col. i evokes as evidence of God's mysteries His creation of the irrigation of the earth, based on rain and flowing streams. The end of the column seems to discuss God's endowing man with the arts of civilization.

Col. ii is illusive. It is a series of questions which rhetorically emphasize aspects of God's creation, such as parent-child relationships, which cannot be thoroughly fathomed by human beings. The second part (lines 12–19) seems to discuss the ability of man to grow crops, but the context is insufficient for further explication.

L. 3 אוילי כסה. Cf. Prov 12:16.

L. 5 אב לבנים. See Isa 38:19.

L. 7 Perhaps restore at the end רוח [ה]ע[ול.

L. 8 מ֯היׄא = מה היא.

L. 13 נואׄל. This word for a 'fool' appears in some readings in the genizah manuscripts of Sir 37:19. Only the verbal usage of this root יאל occurs in the Bible.

L. 14 לפי תׄבאוׄת. Cf. Lev 25:15-16.

L. 15 מׄודה. This is a Qumran form for biblical מאד.

L. 16 Or 'he will not'.

L. 16 תכון. In the sectarian texts, תכון has the complex meaning of 'that which God has apportioned', 'measure', or 'lot'. Here it no doubt refers to the allotted fates of God's people, according to the lots He has placed them in.

L. 17 מׄשפט. For the use of this word in the sectarian scrolls, see Schiffman, *Halakhah at Qumran*, 42–7.

Frg. 7

Parallels: 4Q**300** 6 4–5 (underline)
4Q**300** 7 2 (overbar)

[ ]הׄוא אׄ[1

[ ]קרוב [2

[מה הוא רחו]ק לאיש ממעשׂ[ה 3

מׄוׄלׄ איׄשׂ והוא רׄחׄוק מ◦[ואין לענה] 4

לנגדו מנוטׄר [לנ]קׄ[ו]ם בלוא מׄשׂ[פט 5

אשׂ[ר מ]עׄל ועשׂהׄ[6

PAM 40.592, 41.694, 43.390*

This fragment may be further reconstructed in light of 4Q**300** 6–7 which has definite overlaps with it. Their exact relationship, however, is difficult to determine.

TRANSLATION

1. [ ]he [
2. [ ]close [
3. [What is furth]er from a person than an ac[t of
4. to a(nother) person and he is far from [and there is no (greater) poison]
5. before him than the one who bears a grudge [to a]ve[n]ge unju[stly
6. wh[o tr]espassed and did [

COMMENTS

This fragment also contains rhetorical questions. It clearly castigates one who bears a grudge. It is in accord with the biblical tradition, while emphasizing a principle stressed in the *Zadokite Fragments* as well.

L. 5 Such grudges are prohibited by the law of reproof of CD IX 2–8 as well as by CD VII 2–3 and XIV 22. (See Schiffman, *Sectarian Law*, 90–98.)

L. 5 מנוטׄר [לנ]קׄ[ו]ם. Cf. Lev 19:18; Nah 1:2.

L. 5 בלוא מׄשׂ[פט. Cf. Jer 22:13; Ezek 22:29; Prov 13:23; 16:8.

L. 6 מ]עׄל ועשׂהׄ[. Cf. Ezek 18:24.

Frg. 8

1]ה֯וא הכין ע[

2]◦ פלג שכל֯ם[

3]ן֯ הוא ◦[

4]בה מ[

5]◦◦ ר מה יתבונן גב֯[ר] בלוא יד֯ע ולוא שמע [

6 ה]ב֯ינה יצר לב֯נ֯[ו] ברוב שכל גלה אוזננו ונש֯[מעה

7]י֯צ֯ר בינה ל֯כ֯ול רודפי דעת וה֯◦[

8]כ֯ול שכל מעולם הוא לוא ישנ֯ה֯[

9 ה]סגיר בעד ע֯ד מים ל֯בל[תי

10]ש֯מים ממעל לשמים ◦[

11]ל֯[

PAM 41.208, 41.389, 41.694, 43.390*

Notes on Readings

L. 6 ונש֯[מעה. An alternative restoration is ונש֯[כילה, which would mean 'we would consider'.

L. 9 After בעד the scribe wrote עד again in error.

Translation

1.] he prepared [
2.] a portion of their knowledge [
3.] he [
4.] [
5.] And how can a ma[n] understand who did not know and did not hear [
6. the]discernment, the inclination of our heart. With great intelligence He opened our ear, so that we would h[ear
7.] the inclination of understanding for all who pursue knowledge, and the [
8.] all intelligence is from eternity; it will not be changed[
9. He] shut (them) up before (the) waters so as no[t to
10.] heaven above heaven [
11.] [

Comments

In frg. 8 the notion that all knowledge and discernment comes from God is emphasized. All is at the same time predestined. At the end, the fragment appears to turn to the wonders of creation.

L. 6 יצר לב̊נ̊[ו]. Cf. Gen 6:5; 8:21.
L. 9 Cf. 1 Sam 1:6.

Frg. 9

1]ם̇ הא◦[
2]◦ שרים לי זרח א̊[ר]ץ̇ ל̊מ̇[
3 מ]לך נכב̇ד̇ והדר מלכותו מ̊לא̊[
4]א עם כול צב̊[א
5]א̊רך א[פים

PAM 41.694, 43.390*

NOTES ON READINGS
L. 1]ם̇. Also possible is]כי.
L. 4 צב̊[א. The reading and restoration are conjectural.

TRANSLATION
1.] [
2.] princes to Me, the shining of the la[n]d to [
3. the K]ing Who is honoured, and the majesty of His kingdom fills[
4.]with all the ho[st
5.]long su[ffering

COMMENTS
L. 3 מ]לך נכב̇ד̇. Cf. 2 Sam 6:20.
L. 3 והדר מלכותו. Cf. Ps 145:12.

Frg. 10

1]מ̊ל̊ך̇ [
2] וגב̊[ו]ר̊י̊ חיל יחזקו̇ מ[עמד
3 ר]ם̇ על כול גואים ישר̇א̊[ל
4]◦ וליצו̇ר ולחשוב̊[
5]ושופטים לכול לא̊[ומים

]◦ על כול מספרם ◦[

]ל֯[ ]◦ ו֯שופטים בין אביו֯[ן

]א֯תם לתכן כול עבודת֯[

]כול ממ[ש]לו֯ת֯ם ◦[

]◦◦ יוׄמםׄ[

]מׄוׄ ומחשׄ[בותם

PAM 41.321, 43.390*

TRANSLATION

1.]king [
2.]and mi[gh]ty warriors shall take (their) st[and
3. ex]alted over all the nations. Israe[l
4.] and to fashion and to think [
5.] and judges for all the na[tions
6.] according to all their numbers [
7.] and they judge between a poor ma[n
8.] for the measure of all work of [
9.] all of their do[mi]nion [
10.] by day[
11.] and their th[oughts

COMMENTS

Both frgs. 9 and 10 refer to the 'king', presumably God. God is described in frg. 10 as having set out the rulers for all the nations. Israel is apparently to be contrasted in some way.

L. 2 יחזקו֯ מ[עמד. Cf. 1QSa II 4–5; 1QM XIV 6; 1QH[a] IV 36; V 29–30; 1QS I 17. (On מעמד, see L. H. Schiffman, *The Eschatological Community of the Dead Sea Scrolls, A Study of the Rule of the Congregation.* SBLMS 38 [Atlanta: Scholars Press, 1989] 28–9.)

L. 4 Cf. Jer 18:11.

Frg. 11

]אה֯ ◦עׄ◦◦[

]◦◦ ◦◦[

]◦[

PAM 43.390

Frg. 12

]◦[1

]◦א כול מ֯ן֯[2

]◦◦◦ ולו◦[3

]ל֯[4

PAM 43.390

NOTES ON READINGS

L. 3 The final letter may be an *ʾalep* or *ʿayin*.

TRANSLATION

1.] [
2.] everything, from[
3.] and to (?)[
4.] [

Frg. 13

This fragment, as listed in Wacholder-Abegg, following Milik's entries in the *Preliminary Concordance*, is made up of two fragments which are identified here as frgs. 13a and 13b. Separate transcriptions are provided for each, followed by a reconstruction according to Milik's view.

Frg. 13a

]ח֯ול בין ה֯ט֯◦[1

י]שראל ואתכם[2

ה]לכו בה֯[3

PAM 43.390

NOTES ON READINGS

L. 3 ה]לכו. Also possible is מ]לכו, 'ruled over it'.

TRANSLATION

1.] between [
2. I]srael, and you[
3. wal]ked in it[

COMMENTS

L. 1 Perhaps restore: בין הקודש ל]חול בין הטמ[א לטהור, 'between the holy and the] profane, between the impu[re and the pure'. Cf. Lev 10:10.

L. 2 Or 'and with you'.

Frg. 13b

]המשיל אתכם[2

]ם ◦[3

PAM 43.390

TRANSLATION

2.]He made you rule[(or:]He likened you[)
3.] [

COMMENTS

L. 2 אתכם. A verb for this direct object pronoun must follow in the lacuna.

Frg. 13a-b

]חול בין הט֯◦[1

]המשיל אתכם[י]שׂראל ואתכם[2

]ם ◦[ה]לכו בה֯[3

COMMENTS

The fragment is joined according to Milik's reconstruction.

TRANSLATION

1.] between [
2.]he made you rule (or:]he likened you) [I]srael, and you [
3.] walked in it[

Frg. 14

]◦◦◦[1

]מל֯קוש ל֯◦[2

]◦ל֯י֯ה ובסוד֯ ◦[3

bottom margin

PAM 43.391

NOTES ON READINGS

L. 3 The last letter may be a *pe*. If so, perhaps read ובסוד[י] פ֯לא.

TRANSLATION

1.] [
2.]latter rain for [
3.] and in the counsel of [

Frg. 15

] ◦ [1

]ל֯ו֯א יגע[ח[ז֯ק֯]ות [ל֯כ֯ו֯]ל 2

vacat י֯חזק ◦◦ל֯◦[ ]י֯ת֯ם לשמ֯ע ◦◦ם[3

bottom margin

PAM 43.391

TRANSLATION

1.] [
2.] he shall not touch[st]ron[g] for al[l
3.]*vacat* He will strengthen [ ] to hear [

Frg. 16

]◦ עשה[1

]רוחכ֯ם[2

]◦◦◦[3

PAM 43.391

TRANSLATION

1.] he did (or made)[
2.]your spirit[
3.]   [

Frg. 17 i

]ע֯שׂה[1

מחוכמה[2

bottom margin

PAM 41.694, 43.391*

Although readable text is preserved only from col. i of this fragment, it appears that to the left of the margin there was writing on a second column. This margin, if it can be assumed that it was one, is considerably wider than those in frgs. 3a, 3c, and 6, raising the question of whether this indeed was a second column (rather than the end of a sheet) or whether perhaps this fragment does not belong to 4QMyst[a].

TRANSLATION

1.]he did (or made)[
2.]from (or because of) wisdom

Frg. 18

]יׄשלים פשעׄ[1

]בׄו וביוםׄ[2

]אׄהב[ ]מהטות[3

PAM 41.694, 43.391*

TRANSLATION

1.] he shall complete (or requite?) (the) transgression [
2.] in it, and on the day [
3.] I shall [ ] from inclining [

Frg. 19

]הׄמשל[1

]∘∘ [2

PAM 43.391

NOTES ON READINGS

L. 1]הׄמשל[. Perhaps read ומשל.

TRANSLATION

1.]the parable (or ruling) [
2.] [

Frg. 20

]חׄוׄקׄ תכׄוׄנׄם כיא אםׄ[1

]מׄשקל לתכון ∘∘∘[2

]יחׄד רוׄבם אם[3

PAM 43.391

NOTES ON READINGS

L. 3 רו̊בם. Perhaps read ריבם, 'their dispute'.

TRANSLATION

1.]the allotment of their measure, except[
2.]the weight, according to the measure of [
3.]together, most of them if[

Frg. 21

[◦◦ם] [נ̊ן ב̊] 1

[גליהם ביד ◦] 2

[◦ לוא כול כוח וכ̊] 3

[ו̊א̊וצר כול] 4

PAM 41.694, 43.391*

TRANSLATION

1.] [
2.] their heaps in the hand of [
3.] not every power and [
4.]and the one who stores up everything [

COMMENTS

L. 4 Cf. Hos 13:15.

Frg. 22

[מ̊פי] 1

[למחיו◦] 2

[◦י̇ מ◦] 3

PAM 43.391

Translation

1.]from the mouth of[
2.] [
3.] [

Frg. 23

]∘∘[1

] הוא א֯[2

]מ֯ו֯ד֯ה מנ֯[3

]∘ נפש[4

]∘ה אר֯כ֯ה֯[5

PAM 43.391

Translation

1.] [
2.] he [
3.]abundance [
4.] person [
5.] its length[

Frg. 24

]∘∘∘[1

]היאה מ֯[2

א]שר ה[3

]∘[4

PAM 43.391

TRANSLATION

1.] [
2.]it is [
3. wh]ich (?) the[
4.] [

Frg. 25

]○○[1

]ם̇ תפ֯[2

]א לוא[3

]○ׄי רש[4

PAM 43.391

TRANSLATION

1.] [
2.] [
3.] not[
4.] [

Frg. 26

מו]של ○[1

]ו̇נספרה֯[2

]○○ת לוא֯[3

]○ מ̇צ̇[4

PAM 43.391

NOTES ON READINGS

L. 1 מו]של. Perhaps restore מ]של.

TRANSLATION

1. ru]les [
2.]and let us recount[
3.] not[
4.] [

Frg. 27

]וׄא ◦[1

]ה על מ◦[2

]◦ מה מ[3

]אבן מ◦[4

]◦ ◦[5

PAM 43.391

TRANSLATION

1.] [
2.] on [
3.] what [
4.]stone [
5.] [

Frg. 28

]אׄ הילודים[1

]תׄמהו כן ילוׄדׄ[2

]לׄ[3

PAM 43.391

NOTES ON READINGS

L. 2]תׄמהו. Cf. Ps 48:6. Perhaps restore י]תמהו 'they will be astonished', or ו]תמהו 'and they were astonished'.

L. 2 ילוׄדׄ[. Perhaps restore ילוד]ים, 'those who are born'.

TRANSLATION

1.] those who are born[
2.]they were astonished, thus one who is born[
3.] [

COMMENTS

L. 2 The vocalization *ha-yilodim* occurs in Jer 16:3, and *ha-yeludim* occurs in 1 Chr 14:4.

Frg. 29

[◦מ◦◦] 1

[י֯ם ל◦ ◦◦◦] 2

[כ֯ל ח֯י ובמדה] 3

[י֯שׄבׄיע ◦◦] 4

PAM 43.391

TRANSLATION

1.] [
2.] [
3.]every living thing, and in a measure[
4.]he will swear [

COMMENTS

L. 4 This line may also be translated, 'He will satisfy'. Cf. the use of the *Hipʿil* of שבע in Ps 145:16, where כל חי appears, as it does here, in line 3.

Frg. 30

] [1

[א֯ בׄשׄלמו֯] 2

ח]ושך בח֯ו֯שך מ◦[3

[ד֯מוסר֯ לוא ◦] 4

[◦◦ הׄוסיף֯] 5

No photograph of this fragment could be found; it is reproduced based on the transcription of Milik compiled by Wacholder-Abegg.

TRANSLATION

1.] [
2.] when he completes[
3. da]rkness in darkness [
4.]the teaching (he) did not [
5.] he added[

COMMENTS

L. 3 Cf. Eccl 6:4.

L. 4 לוא ○]. Perhaps restore לוא ל[קח or לוא ל[קחו, 'he did not ac[cept' or 'they did not ac[cept'. The verb לקח followed by the object מוסר is regular in biblical usage, e.g. Jer 2:30, 5:3.

Frg. 31

[○ן י֯○] 1

[ב֯כול ○○] 2

[○ עוד ○○○] 3

[בידך] 4

PAM 43.391

TRANSLATION

1.] [
2.]in all [
3.] still [
4.]in your hand[

COMMENTS

L. 4 [בידך. This perhaps refers to God, 'in Your hand'. The fragment would then refer to God's control over the affairs of man and the world.

Frg. 32

]◦◦◦ [1

]◦שלו מה הוא המצוֹ[ה 2

מ]חזיק ותולדֹות המ[3

]אׄ◦[ ]מֹשקלֹ[4

PAM 43.391

Translation

1.] [
2.] what is the command[ment (?)
3. he h]olds fast, and the generations of the [
4.] weight[

Frg. 33

]◦◦ ◦[1

י]צֹרו ובמח◦[2

]◦◦שׁוי ואם ינשא[3

]מה גבורה בלוא[4

PAM 43.391

Translation

1.] [
2.]his [in]clination and [
3.] and if he will bear[
4.]what is might without[

Frg. 34

]∘∘מה יכון נ∘[1

]תו֯ ואם יהפכ֯[ו 2

]∘ מ֯ב֯י֯ן ∘[3

PAM 43.391

Translation

1.] he will establish [
2.] his [,] and if [they] will turn[
3.] one who understands [

Comments

L. 3 Or 'from between', which seems less likely.

Frg. 35

א]ל הדעות[1

]ב֯יד מלאכ[י 2

PAM 43.391

Notes on Readings

L. 2]ב֯יד מלאכ[י. Perhaps restore:]ביד מלאכ[י קודש.

Translation

1. G]od of knowledge[
2.]in the hand of the messenger[s of

Comments

L. 1 א]ל הדעות[. For this designation of God, see 1 Sam 2:3; 1QS III 15; 1QH[a] I 26, XII 10, and frg. 4 15. It occurs as well in the sapiential material from Qumran, e.g. 4Q**417** 2 i 8; 4Q**418** 43 6 and 55 5.

L. 2 'Through the agency of angels' or: 'through the agency of the prophets'. This is certainly the correct meaning as the fragment refers to God's making known His teachings through the biblical prophets. Cf. 2 Chr 36:15, where מלאך, literally 'messenger', may designate a prophet; cf. also 1QS III 21; IV 12.

Frg. 36

]לכל כ֯◦[

ה]ו֯א יהיה[

]◦◦ ◦[

PAM 43.391

TRANSLATION

1.]to all [
2. h]e will be[
3.] [

COMMENTS

L. 2 יהיה[. It is unlikely that the tetragrammaton should be read here, as it does not appear in this text.

Frg. 37

]◦[

]כ֯ול מע֯שה֯ ה[

]פ֯תח בפ◦◦[

PAM 43.391

NOTES ON READINGS

L. 3 בפ◦◦[. The attractive reading, בפנ]יהם, 'before them', is unlikely in light of the traces.

TRANSLATION

1.] [
2.]every deed of the[
3.]He opened [

COMMENTS

L. 2 מע֯שה֯. In Hebrew, מעשה may also refer to 'creature'.

L. 3 This line likely refers to God's having revealed His wisdom to man.

Frg. 38

]◦ לפני ◦◦[
]בה אוש◦[
]◦◦ם ◦[

PAM 43.391

Translation

1.] before [
2.] [
3.] [

Frg. 39

]בני יש[ראל
]לתכונם ◦[
]◦ד ◦◦[

PAM 43.391

Translation

1.]the children of Is[rael
2.]according to their measure [
3.] [

Frg. 40

] ומע[
]רם[

PAM 43.391

Frg. 41

]◦צו[1

]יאה[2

PAM 43.391

Frg. 42

]ב֯ה מ֯[1

]◦ד כי אם֯[2

]ל֯יהא לוא[3

]◦ החכמה[4

PAM 43.391

TRANSLATION

1.] [
2.] except[
3.] not[
4.] the wisdom[

Frg. 43

]◦ש֯ו֯ם֯[1

]ת֯ומכי ר[זי 2

]התב֯[וננו 3

]ם֯ תו[4

PAM 43.391

TRANSLATION
1.] [
2.]those who hold fast to the sec[rets of
3.] inve[stigate
4.] [

COMMENTS

L. 3 Or: 'they investigated'. The *Polal* of בון appears throughout the sapiential corpus from Qumran, with the meaning of to examine closely in order to discern the truth; cf. 4Q**413** 1 1.

Frg. 44

]לי֯ ומ֯○[1
]○ מעש[י 2
]ועתה[3

PAM 43.391

TRANSLATION
1.] [
2.] creature[s of
3.]And now[

COMMENTS

L. 2 מעש[י. Perhaps restore מעש[ה.

L. 3]ועתה[. This must have been the beginning of a section of a wisdom speech. This word serves to introduce such speeches throughout this literature. It often comes after a *vacat,* which indicates a new paragraph; cf. 4Q**413** 1 3, 4Q**418** 69 ii 5.

Frg. 45

]ה לב֯ם[1
]אמרו ○[2
ג]בורה [3

PAM 41.694, 43.392*

TRANSLATION

1.] their heart [
2.]they said [
3. m]ight [

Frg. 46

]○ ○[

]א֯ בוננ○[

]ה֯וא ○[

]○[

PAM 43.392

TRANSLATION

1.] [
2.]investigate [
3.]he [
4.] [

NOTES ON READINGS

L. 2]○בוננ. Probably read בוננו. Also possible are בוננת or בוננתם; see COMMENTS to frg. 43 3.

Frg. 47

]ש֯פ֯[

]ולברכ֯[

]ול֯ב[

PAM 43.392

COMMENTS

L. 2]ולברכ֯[. Perhaps read: ולברכ]ה.

Frg. 48

כו]ל̊ עו̇ב̊]רי 1
ו̇ב
]כול מ◦[2
[י̊ם̇] 3

PAM 43.392

TRANSLATION

1. al]l who pas[s
2.]and in every [
3.] [

COMMENTS

L. 1 עו̇ב̊]רי. Perhaps restore עוב]רי דרך, 'travellers', as in 1QH[a] VIII 8–9. But see 1QH[a] IV 26–27; 1QS V 7; also 4Q**299** 59 3.

L. 3 [י̊ם̇]. The preserved portion of this line, apparently the masc. pl. ending, would require that it be preceded by a noun or an adjective.

Frg. 49

[י̊מי א◦] 1

Frg. 50

[א̊] 1
[◦הד̊] 2

Frg. 51

[מלאכ̇י] 1

PAM 43.392

TRANSLATION

1.]messenger[s of

Comments

L. 1]מלאכׄ[יׄ. See comments to frg. 35 2.

Frg. 52

◦◦[1
◦◦◦◦[2
איש נו֯◦[3
בכורׄ[4

PAM 43.392

Translation

1. [
2. [
3. man [
4. in the furnace[

Comments

L. 4 בכורׄ[. The notion that man is refined through suffering is often expressed in terms of his having gone through a furnace; cf. CD VIII 26; 1QH^{a} V 16. This word may also be the noun בכור signifying the first-born. Cf. 1QH^{a} III 8, XIX 3.

Frg. 53

]תׄועׄבותׄ[1
]בׄקודשוׄ ◦◦[2
]ה בכם ◦◦◦[3
]◦ד ואין שם למוע[ד 4
]מׄשפט כיא צדיקׄ[5
ג[בׄורׄתו וחזקׄ[6
[לאל לנקום נקׄםׄ[7
[וריב על חזק ע[8

א]ל ובשמים מדור[ו 9

]◦ם̇ *vacat*[10

]יכם אשמיע̊[11

]ב̇ו עם מלך[12

bottom margin

PAM 40.612, 41.321, 41.695, 42.181, 43.392*

NOTES ON READINGS

L. 12]ב̇ו. Perhaps read]כי.

TRANSLATION

1.]abominations[
2.]in His holiness [
3.] among you [
4.] and there is no name for the peri[od
5.]judgement for [He is] righteous[
6.]His [m]ight and the power[of
7.] to God to exact vengeance[
8.] and a dispute against the strong [
9. G]od, and in the heavens is [His] dwelling[
10.] *vacat*[
11.]your [ ] I will announce[
12.]him (?) with the king[

COMMENTS

This fragment deals with the coming judgement in which God will avenge the violation of His law. From the heavens He will exact punishment in an age so awesome that it does not even have a name. After that, redemption will be announced.

L. 7 Cf. Num 31:2; Ezek 24:8; 25:12; CD XIX 24; 1QS V 12; 1QM IV 12.

Frg. 54

]◦◦ת̇ מ[1

]ם̇ עשוק וגזול ב◦◦◦[2

]◦ה̇ו כיא אהבת ח̇סד̇[3

]◦ בכו̇ל ◦◦◦ ל◦◦[4

]◦ ◦◦ ◦◦[5

PAM 40.612, 41.321, 43.392*

TRANSLATION

1.] [
2.] persecuted and robbed by [
3.] for loving-kindness[
4.] in all to[
5.] [

COMMENTS

L. 2 עשוק וגזול. See Deut 28:29; cf. Jer 22:3.

L. 3 אהבת חׄסׄדׄ[. Cf. Mic 6:8. The phrase is common in sectarian texts; cf. 1QS II 24; V 4, 25; VIII 2; X 26; CD XIII 18; 4Q**418** 169 3; 170 3.

Frg. 55

] קודש ◦◦◦◦[1

המשפ]טׄים הצדיקיׄםׄ[2

]◦הנו כיא המׄ[3

]אׄשר בחרׄוׄ בׄהׄ◦ אׄ[4

עבו]דׄת קודשו וׄלכפרׄ עׄל ◦◦[5

]עליהם לׄ[6

bottom margin

PAM 41.695, 42.181, 43.392*

NOTES ON READINGS

L. 4 בחרׄוׄ. Perhaps read ראו, 'they saw'.

TRANSLATION

1.] holiness [
2.]the righteous [judge]ments[
3.] for [
4.]which they chose [
5.]His holy [serv]ice, and to expiate for [
6.]upon them to[

COMMENTS

L. 2 Cf. Deut 4:8; cf. 4Q**412** 3 1; 4Q**418** 121 1; 214 2.

Frg. 56

]○[1

]שׁ֯ו֯פטם במשפטי֯[2

י]חזיקו ביד ○○○○[3

]○ל○○[ ]○[4

PAM 40.612, 41.321, 43.392*

TRANSLATION

1.] [
2.]their judge in the judgements of[
3. they shall] hold fast to the [
4.] [

COMMENTS

L. 3 Cf. Judg 7:20; 1QM VI 15; CD VI 21, XIV 14.

Frg. 57

]○[1

]נו בה[2

]א֯שר יעשה[3

]יע את אש[ר 4

]○○ ○○○[5

PAM 42.181, 43.392*

TRANSLATION

1.] [
2.] in it[
3.]which he will do[
4.] that whi[ch
5.] [

Frg. 58

]◦ע֯ ◦◦[

]◦ השיב ל◦[

bottom margin

PAM 41.321, 43.392*

TRANSLATION

1.] [
2.] he answered to [

Frg. 59

יק֯ד֯ש ◦[ ]◦[

ב֯משפט יריב א[ת

בכול עוברי פי֯ה֯[ו

עוזרי רשעה[

◦◦◦ עו֯ש֯[

vacat

◦◦◦ ונריבה ריב◦[

PAM 42.181, 43.392*

TRANSLATION

1. he will sanctify [
2. with justice he will contend wi[th
3. against all those who violate [His] command[
4. those who aid (in doing) evil[
5. those who do[
6. *vacat*
7. and let us contend in dispute[

Comments

One encounters again the motif of God's doing justice against those who violate His commandments.

L. 2 Cf. Mic 7:9; Ps 43:1.

L. 3 עוברי פיׄהׄ[ו. Literally, 'who violate [His] mouth'.

L. 7 ריב◦[. Perhaps read ריבו, 'His (God's) dispute'.

Frg. 60

]◦◦◦◦ ◦◦[1

]רצה ופקׄוד[2

] סגולה מכול [העמים 3

] וכול מלכי עׄמׄיׄ[ם 4

]◦ ◦[5

PAM 41.321, 43.392*

Translation

1.] [
2.]favour (?) and remember[
3.]treasured possession from among all [the nations
4.]and all kings of nation[s
5.] [

Comments

L. 3 סגולה מכול [העמים. Restored with Exod 19:5; Deut 7:6; 14:2.

L. 4 מלכי עׄמׄיׄ[ם. See Gen 17:16.

Frg. 61

]הׄ◦◦◦ הׄ◦◦◦שׄ◦[1

]בׄחוקים ◦[2

PAM 41.321, 43.392*

TRANSLATION

1.] [
2.]in the laws [

Frg. 62

]°° °[

]וא וריב רב֯[

] *vacat* ועתה מ°[

]שנאיכה לוא יוכל֯[ו

]ל֯חצרו[תי]ה֯מ֯ה֯ למ[

]°[

PAM 43.392

TRANSLATION

1.] [
2.] and dispute [
3.]*vacat* And now, [
4.]your enemies will not be abl[e
5.]to their courtyard[s
6.] [

COMMENTS

L. 3 ועתה. This is the customary beginning of a wisdom speech.

Frg. 63

]ש֯מע֯ו ו°°[

] °°ו֯בל °ל ד֯°[

]ו֯ישמילנו [

]כ֯ב֯ודו [

]א[

PAM 41.321

Fragment 63 appears in the *Preliminary Concordance* as frg. 60. It is not found on the most recent photograph (PAM 43.392) of this museum plate (mus. inv. 595) though it does appear on the earlier PAM 41.321.

TRANSLATION

1.]Listen and [
2.] [
3. and he will cause us to turn aside to the left (?) [
4.]His glory [
5.] [

COMMENTS

L. 1]ש̊מ̇ע̇ו. The common introduction to a hortatory speech, as noted above.

L. 3] ו̊ישמילנו[. The *Hipʿil* of שמאל means to turn from the true way (BDB, 970a).

L. 4]כ̊בודו. Taking the reference here as referring to the divine presence, designated by כבוד in Qumran sectarian texts.

Frg. 64

]ה̊שמים ל̊[1
]ג̊י̊ם קדו[ש 2
]◦◦ ◦הבל ◦[3
]◦◦[4
]א[5

PAM 43.392

PAM 43.392 includes a fragment, designated here as frg. 64, which is not found in the *Preliminary Concordance*.

TRANSLATION

1.]the heavens to[
2.] hol[y
3.] vanity [
4.] [
5.] [

Frg. 65

1]◦◦◦◦[ ]◦[
2]◦ינו שיד הואה[
3 מ]חסור ולמחיר֯[
4]◦◦◦ מ֯עׄלים עי֯[ן
5]◦לת לג֯ו֯יתו וא◦[
6]ת֯ ו◦[

PAM 41.321, 43.392*

NOTES ON READINGS

L. 3 מ]חסור. This word is very common in the sapiential texts, e.g. 4Q**416** 1 4, 6, and is the most likely restoration here.

TRANSLATION

1.] [
2.] he[
3. l]ack, and for the price of[
4.] they avert the ey[e
5.] to his body [
6.] [

COMMENTS

L. 4 Cf. Lev 20:4; Ezek 22:26; Prov 28:27 (preceded by מחסור; cf. line 3).

Frg. 66

1]◦◦ם ול֯שו֯נ֯ו[ת
2]ל֯ משפחות[
3]◦ל ישרא[ל
4]◦ יתנו[
5]ל֯[

PAM 40.614, 41.321, 43.393*

NOTES ON READINGS

L. 3]◦ל. Read either על or כול.

TRANSLATION

1.]   and tongue[s
2.] families[
3.] Israe[l
4.] they will give[
5.]   [

COMMENTS

L. 1]◦◦ם ולשׁ֯ו֯נ֯ו֯[ת. Perhaps read עמי]ם ולשונו[ת.

L. 2 משפחות֯[. Restore משפחות[האדמה, משפחות[הארץ, or משפחות[הארצות.

Ll. 1–2 Both these terms most probably designate the peoples of the earth. In some way the text contrasts them with Israel (line 3).

Frg. 67

1]ה◦ [
2]◦ כול משפחות֯[
   ע◦]
3] עׄמו מכוהן ◦[
4]ל֯ים֯ כל ר[
5]◦◦◦[

PAM 40.614

NOTES ON READINGS

L. 3 The supralinear correction cannot be interpreted since it is only partly preserved.

TRANSLATION

1.]   [
2.] all the families of[
3.] with him, from a priest [
4.]   all [
5.]   [

COMMENTS

L. 3 עׄמו, here translated 'with him', can also be 'his people'.

Frg. 68

יש]ראל ועמׄ[1

]◦ לׄבני ישרׄ]אל 2

ע]בודתו לׄ[3

]ם ידע[4

PAM 40.614, 41.321, 43.393*

TRANSLATION

1. Is]rael and the nation[
2.] to the children of Isra[el
3.]His [s]ervice to[
4.] he (or they) knew[

Frg. 69

א]חת בשנהׄ[1

אור]ים ותומים[2

]◦ כול האדם[3

bottom margin

PAM 43.393

TRANSLATION

1. O]nce in the year[
2. Ur]im and Thummim[
3.] every human being[

COMMENTS

It is possible that this fragment is out of place here, since it deals with the Day of Atonement or some similar ritual. The same is the case with frg. 79. 1Q**27** 3 and 6, however, deal with priestly and sacrificial matters, as do 4Q**419** 1 1–8 and 4Q**421** 13 1–6.

L. 1 א]חת בשנהׄ[. Cf. Lev 16:34 regarding the annual character of the Day of Atonement rituals.

Frg. 70

1]◦תם חוק֯[
2]ל֯וא ידעתם ◦[
3]ל֯חול ואת[ם
4]ל עם אשמה֯[

PAM 43.393

TRANSLATION

1.] the law[
2.]you did not know [
3.]to that which is profane, but yo[u
4.] with guilt[

COMMENTS

L. 2]ל֯וא ידעתם. Cf. Deut 11:28; 13:3, 14; Jer 33:3; Ezek 32:9.
L. 3]ל֯חול. Or: 'to the sand'.

Frg. 71

1 שבי פשׄ[ע
2 צ֯רׄב לכם ומ֯[
3 נאצתה ו֯[
4 ו֯י֯שפ֯ר ל֯[

PAM 41.695, 43.393*

TRANSLATION

1. those who have repented from transgres[sion
2. it burnt you and [
3. you reviled and[
4. and it was pleasing for[

COMMENTS

L. 1 שבי פשׄ[ע. Cf. Isa 59:20; 1QH[a] II 9; 4Q**400** 1 16; 4Q**512** 70–71 2; CD II 5.

Frg. 72

הו]אׄ קדוש הׄוׄאׄ] 1

ג]בׄורי צדק] 2

י]דעו כיאׄ] 3

[◦ על פׄ] 4

PAM 41.321, 43.393*

Translation

1. H]e is holy, He[
2. h]eroes of righteousness[
3.]they [k]new that[
4.] upon [

Comments

L. 1 קדוש הׄוׄאׄ]. Cf. 2 Kgs 4:9, referring to a man; Ps 99:3, 5, referring to God.

L. 3 י]דעו. Or: 'will know'.

Frg. 73

[◦ ◦] 1

[◦יׄ ואין] 2

[אׄל הדעׄ]ות 3

[◦ל] 4

PAM 43.393

Translation

1.] [
2.] and there is no[
3.]God of know[ledge
4.] [

Frg. 74

]°נ֯ו֯[1
]מׄשה פנים אבני[2
]לׄזׄכׄר קדושׄיׄםׄ על [3
]ל° וגב[4
]°°דׄ°[5

PAM 41.321, 43.393*

TRANSLATION

1.] [
2.]Moses, a face, stones of[
3.]for a remembrance of the holy ones, upon [
4.] [
5.] [

COMMENTS

L. 3]לׄזׄכׄר קדושׄיׄםׄ[. Cf. Ps 30:5; 97:12. קדושים most probably refers to the angels. Cf. COMMENTS to frg. 72.

Frg. 75

]°°ל תכלת[1
] כבוד לפתוחׄ[2

PAM 41.695, 43.393*

TRANSLATION

1.] blue[
2.] honour, to open[

Frg. 76

[ ]○ ומ֯○[1

[ ]מ֯פיהו לפת[וח 2

כול אבות העדה[3

ובºººº בין איש[4

[ ]ה[ ] 5

PAM 41.695, 43.393*

TRANSLATION

1. [ ] [
2. [ ]from his mouth, to op[en
3. all the fathers of the congregation[
4. and in [ ] between each (or a man) [
5. [ ] [

COMMENTS

L. 2]מ֯פיהו לפת[וח. Cf. Prov 24:7.

L. 3 אבות העדה[. Cf. Num 31:26; 1QSa I 16, 24; II 16; 1QM II 1, 7; III 4; and Schiffman, *Eschatological Community*, 21, 53, where אבות is taken as 'clans, households'.

L. 4 ובºººº בין איש[. Perhaps restore ובריב בין איש[לרעהו, 'and in a dispute between a man and his fellow'.

Frg. 77

]○○ איש֯[1

]כ֯ו֯ל בידכם[2

]○ ו֯ה֯ו֯א[3

PAM 43.393

TRANSLATION

1.] a man[
2.]all in your hands[
3.] and he[

COMMENTS

L. 2]כ֯ו֯ל בידכם[. Cf. Gen 9:2; Josh 9:11.

Frg. 78

]ח֯וקתיה[1

]ג֯בולותיה[2

]◦◦◦◦◦י֯ם֯[3

PAM 43.393

Translation

1.]its laws[
2.]its boundaries[
3.] [

Frg. 79

]◦ ם[1

]י֯שרים [2

]ד֯רך חיים [3

]◦ו֯ רצונו הל[4

]ארץ צביו וה֯וא ◦[5

]באהליהם ואהרון מ[6

ריח נ]י֯חוח לזכרון נב◦[7

] כול העמים ◦◦[8

]ליו להי]ות [ל[9

bottom margin

PAM 41.321, 43.393*

Translation

1.] [
2.]the upright [
3.]way of life [

4.] his will [
5.]the land of his delight, and he [
6.]in their tents, and Aaron [
7. a fragrant of]fering as a remembrance of [
8.] all the nations [
9.] to b[e] for[

COMMENTS

It is questionable whether this fragment is part of 4QMysteries, since it appears to be describing Aaron and the offering of sacrifices. Cf. the COMMENTS to frg. 69.

L. 3 דרך חיים. Cf. Jer 21:8; Prov 6:23.

L. 5]ארץ צביו. Cf. Dan 11:16, 41; Jer 3:19; Ezek 20:6, 15; 25:9.

Frg. 80

]◦◦ קרא אׄ[1

] ועתה פׄ[2

מ]שׄפׄטׄי צדק[3

]◦◦[4

PAM 43.393

TRANSLATION

1.] he called [
2.] And now, [
3. l]aws of righteousness[
4.] [

COMMENTS

L. 2 ועתה. This is a familiar wisdom introduction.

L. 3 מ]שׄפׄטׄי צדק[. Cf. Ps 119:7, 106, 164; 1QS III 1; IV 4.

Frg. 81

]הׄארץ למ◦[1

]◦ ישפוׄטׄ שׄ[2

PAM 43.393

Translation

1.]the land to [
2.] he will judge [

Frg. 82

]◦ז̇ו̇ת [1

]· ישים[2

]◦י̇ת̇י̇ ישראל[3

]◦י̇ו̇ם י̇י̇מס[4

]◦לים וק◦[5

PAM 43.393

Translation

1.] [
2.] he will put[
3.] Israel[
4.]day (?) [
5.] [

Frg. 83

]◦◦[1

]בקדם ◦[2

]◦ית ב◦[3

]ברית ה◦[4

עבו]ד̇ת קוד[ש 5

PAM 43.393

TRANSLATION

1.] [
2.]before (?)[
3.] [
4.]the covenant of the [
5.]the [ser]vice (?) of holi[ness

COMMENTS

L. 2 Perhaps, 'in the east'.

L. 5 קוד]ש. Perhaps restore קודשו, 'His holiness', or קודשך, 'Your holiness'.

Frg. 84

]מש֯◦[1

]מ◦◦[2

]ש◦◦[3

] ◦◦◦[4

PAM 43.393

Frg. 85

] ◦◦[1

]◦◦◦◦◦[2

]י֯צ֯◦◦◦[3

]ם לך◦◦[4

PAM 43.393

TRANSLATION

1.] [
2.] [
3.] [
4.] to you [

Frg. 86

1]∘∘∘∘[
2]שית מ∘[
3]הוא ∘[

PAM 43.393

TRANSLATION

1.]   [
2.]   [
3.]he [

Frg. 87

1]∘∘[
2]דׄת בלחמׄי[
3]∘ןׄ ∘∘∘[

PAM 43.393

TRANSLATION

1.]   [
2.] in the bread of[
3.]   [

Frg. 88

1 ע]בודׄתׄ [
2]קדשו ∘[
3]∘ מׄ[

PAM 43.393

TRANSLATION

1. se]rvice of the [
2.]His holiness [
3.] [

Frg. 89

]ם֯ [1

]י֯מ֯ים י֯[2

]∘∘א[3

PAM 43.393

TRANSLATION

1.] [
2.]days (?) [
3.] [

Frg. 90

]עוי֯ ∘[1

]∘ים ל[2

PAM 43.393

Frg. 91

]ים [1

]א֯∘∘ ל֯[2

PAM 43.393

Frg. 92

[∘∘∘]

[∘∘∘]

[ע̇מ∘∘]

[∘ל∘]

PAM 43.393

Frg. 93

[∘∘]

[∘מ̇]

PAM 43.393

Frg. 94

[∘ ∘]

[יד]

PAM 43.393

Frg. 95

[◦ וכ֯] 1

[ו֯ע◦] 2

PAM 43.393

Frg. 96

[ו֯כש֯] 1

[◦◦◦] 2

PAM 43.393

Frg. 97

[יושביׄ] 1

[◦◦◦] 2

PAM 43.393

TRANSLATION

1.] those who dwell in[
2.] [

Frg. 98

]מׄתׄןׄ[

]○○ לׄ○[

PAM 43.393

Frg. 99

] לכול ל○○[

] עשהׄ[

]○[

PAM 43.393

TRANSLATION

1.] to all [
2.] he did[
3.] [

Frg. 100

]רש[

] קר[

PAM 43.393

Frg. 101

[◦◦יׄב ◦] 1
[לוא באׄ] 2
[◦◦נ ◦] 3

PAM 43.393

Translation

1.] [
2.]not in [
3.] [

Frg. 102

ל[וא ◦] 1
[קר◦] 2

PAM 43.393

Translation

1. n]ot [
2.] [

Frg. 103

[◦◦] 1
[ם וד◦] 2
[◦ ◦] 3

PAM 43.393

Frg. 104

]מׄ ◦◦[1

] ◦◦[2

PAM 43.393

Frg. 105

]◦◦[1

]אׄ◦◦ג◦[2

]וׄיׄ◦[3

PAM 43.393

Frg. 106

]◦◦ ◦[1

]אבר[הם 2

]◦◦[3

PAM 43.393

Translation

1.] [
2.]Abra[ham (?)
3.] [

300. 4QMysteries^{b}

(PLATE VIII)

Preliminary publication: L. Schiffman, '4Q Mysteries^{b}, A Preliminary Edition', *RevQ* 16 (1993) 203–23. B. Z. Wacholder and M. G. Abegg, *A Preliminary Edition of the Unpublished Dead Sea Scrolls, The Hebrew and Aramaic Texts from Cave Four*, Fascicle Two (Washington, D.C.: Biblical Archaeology Society, 1992) 1–37.

Physical Description

THE manuscript is, for the most part, brown in colour, turning to darker brown where stained, and with a grey hue in some places. The skin is thin, wrinkled, and cracked. The width of the intercolumnar space (extant in frgs. 1a and 2) measures 1.4 cm. The top margin, preserved in frgs. 1a and 1b, measures 1.3 cm and is most probably complete. The single, preserved, bottom margin (extant in frg. 5) measures 1.1 cm and may be incomplete, though in 2QRuth^{a}, 4QDan^{b}, 4QQoh, the bottom margin is likewise smaller than the top margin. The average line height is 4 mm, but varies between 3 and 5 mm on some fragments (see, especially, frg. 8, which approaches 3 mm). The average letter height is 1 mm.

Vertical dry lines are visible and were followed by the scribe. Horizontal dry lines are also visible but were not always followed. The lines are ruled at a distance of 6 mm. The desire of the scribe to fit more onto his manuscript than was provided for by the original ruling probably led him to ignore the lines; hence the variation in line height.

Palaeography and Orthography

The script has been identified by F. M. Cross as a late Herodian formal bookhand.

The text as preserved does not exhibit features of Qumran orthography (except in the case of כסלכמה frg. 1b 2). However, certain lexical usages are familiar from the sectarian corpus.

Reconstruction

The reconstruction of 4Q**300** (4QMysteries^{b}) is aided by parallels in 1Q**27** and 4Q**299**. The present edition preserves the numeration of Milik followed in the *Preliminary Concordance* and, therefore, in Wacholder-Abegg. It remains, however, impossible to determine the order in which the material stood in the original composition.

Mus. Inv. 591
PAM 41.694, 43.388*

Frg. 1a i

top margin

]◦ראות
[*vacat*
]ם מׄעשי ארץ
מע]שׂה אׄף ועבודת

PAM 41.694, 43.388*

TRANSLATION

1.] see (?)
2.] *vacat*
3.] the deeds of the land
4. ac]tion (provoking) anger and the service of

COMMENTS

Frg. 1a contains parts of two columns and a well-preserved, intercolumnar space. This fragment deals with the sins of the people of Israel. It probably alludes to transgressions of the type committed by the inhabitants of Canaan, which led them to be dispossessed of the land.

Ll. 3–4 Cf. Lev 18:3 which shows that מעשי should not be taken as 'creatures'. Perhaps restore כנען at the beginning of line 4. In any case, line 4 as preserved is an appropriate continuation to a reference to the sinful actions of the Canaanites.

Frg. 1a ii

Parallel: 4Q**299** 3c 2 (underline)

[ ]תׄ◦[
ותעׄודות השׄמׄ]ים
אׄ]ז [תאמרו ל[
תסתׄ]ם מכם
נכחדת[
[ח]זׄוׄןׄ ◦[

PAM 41.694, 43.388*

TRANSLATION

1. [ ]
2. and the signs of the heav[ens
3. The[n]you will say [
4. it will be kept secr[et from you
5. hidden[
6. the [vis]ion [of

COMMENTS

Milik understood this column to be joined to a group of subfragments (frg. 1b) which he saw as the left side of frg. 1a ii. Although there is no material join between these fragments, the ends of lines of the proposed left side of the column seem to flow smoothly into the beginning of the lines of the right side. There is one point at which the proposed join produces the phrase חכמה נכחדת, 'hidden wisdom', known from elsewhere in the text (frg. 5 5). Note that frg. 1a ii preserves six lines of text whereas frg. 1b preserves only five. The fragments are here presented both as separate fragments and as a joined fragment, per Milik's reconstuction.

Frg. 1b

top margin

1 החר]טמים מלמדי פשע אמרו הׄמשל והגידו הׄחידה בטרם נדבר ואז תדעו אם הבטתם֯

2]כׄסלכמה כי חתום מכם[ח]תׄם החזון וברזׄי עד לא הבטתם ובבינה לא השכלתם

3]◦ה והמׄי֯[ ]כי לא הבטתם בשורש חוכמה ואם תפתחו החזון

4]כׄל חוכמת[כ]ם כי לכם המ◦[ ] שמו כׄי֯[מ]הׄ היא חכמה

5 עו]דׄ לא תהיהׄ[[

PAM 41.694, 43.388*

TRANSLATION

1. the mag]icians who are skilled in transgression, utter the parable and relate the riddle before it is discussed, and then you will know whether you have considered
2.]your foolishness, for the [s]eal of the vision is sealed from you, and you have not considered the eternal mysteries, and you have not come to understand wisdom.
3. [ ]for you have not considered the root of wisdom, and if you open the vision
4.]all [yo]ur wisdom, for yours is the [ ] his name, for [wh]at is wisdom (which is)
5. sti]ll there will not be [ ]

COMMENTS

The magicians are challenged to explain the hidden meaning of the parable or riddle to see whether they have properly understood the signs. The text makes clear that they cannot, since the true vision, perhaps that of prophecy, is hidden from them, and they do not understand the mysteries of God. They are apparently expected by the text to admit their lack of understanding. Further, even if they were to uncover the vision, they would not understand it. Their wisdom is for nought. So they are summoned to listen to a description of what the true hidden wisdom is.

L. 1 החר]טמים. Following Wacholder-Abegg. Milik restored מש]טמים, but the fem. sing. משטמה and pl. משטמות are the usual forms. The 'magicians' of Dan 1:20 and 2:2 are more like soothsayers who foretell the future, a meaning appropriate to this text's castigation of the purveyors of false wisdom.

L. 1 מלמדי פשע. Cf. Song 3:8 and 1 Chr 25:7 for the *Puʿal* participle (followed by a noun) meaning 'trained in' or 'skilled in' something.

L. 1 אמרו ה֯משל. A variant of the biblical phrase found in Num 23:7, 18; 24:3, 15, 20, 21, 23.

L. 1 והגידו ה֯חידה. Cf. Judg 14:14. For the occurrence together of משל and חידה, cf. Ezek 17:2.

L. 1 נדבר. The form is *Nipʿal*. It can also be the more usual *Piʿel* in the 1st person pl. 'we will speak'.

L. 1 הבטתם֯. This is from the root נבט, 'look', here meaning to 'look carefully, consider'. The root is a regular feature of the sapiential and mysteries texts from Qumran.

L. 2 חתום מכם[ח]ת֯ם החזון. This is based on Dan 9:24, ולחתם חזון, 'to seal the vision'. This passage, the seventy-weeks prophecy, is formative for the language and conception of 4QMyst[b]. For חזון, cf. 4Q**410** 1 9; 1QH[a] IV 18.

L. 2 ובבינה לא השכלתם. This is based on Dan 9:22, where בינה refers to the understanding of a hidden prophetic vision of the dawn of the messianic era (cf. verse 25). Cf. also 1 Chr 22:12; 2 Chr 2:11.

L. 3 בשורש חוכמה. For שורשי בינה, see 4Q**301** 2b 1.

L. 3 תפתחו. If you attempt to discover and reveal the hidden meaning of the vision; it is the opposite of חתם, to 'seal' or 'hide' the vision.

L. 4 מ]ה֯ היא. This begins a rhetorical wisdom question, which is the predominant literary device in the Mysteries texts. Such a usage of מה is also found in 4QMyst[c] (4Q**301**).

Frg. 1a ii-b

Parallels: 4Q**299** 3c 2 (underline)

top margin

1 [ ]ת֯◦[החר]טמים מלמדי פשע אמרו ה֯משל והגידו ה֯חידה בטרם נדבר ואז תדעו אם הבטתם֯

2 ותע֯ודות הש֯מ֯[ים]כסלכמה כי חתום מכם[ח]ת֯ם החזון וברז֯י עד לא הבטתם ובבינה לא השכלתם

3 א֯[ז]ת֯אמרו ל[ ]◦ה וה֯מ֯י֯[ ]כי לא הבטתם בשורש חוכמה ואם תפתחו החזון

4 תסת֯]ם מכם]כ֯ל חוכמת[כ]ם כי לכם המ◦[ ]
שמו֯ כי֯[מ]ה֯ היא חכמה

5 נכחדת[עו]ד֯ לא תהיה֯[ ]

6 [ח]ז֯ו֯ן֯ ◦[ ]

PAM 41.694, 43.388*

TRANSLATION

1. [ ] [the mag]icians who are skilled in transgression utter the parable and relate the riddle before it is discussed, and then you will know whether you have considered,
2. and the signs of the heav[ens]your foolishness, for the [s]eal of the vision is sealed from you, and you have not considered the eternal mysteries, and you have not come to understand wisdom.
3. The[n]you will say [ ] for you have not considered the root of wisdom, and if you open the vision
4. it will be kept secr[et from you]all [yo]ur wisdom, for yours is the [ ] his name, for [wh]at is wisdom (which is)
5. hidden[sti]ll there will not be [ ]
6. the [vis]ion [of]

Frg. 2 i

1 [

2 [

3 ם[

4 י֯לתו[

5 לענה[

PAM 41.694, 43.388*

TRANSLATION

1.]
2.]
3.]
4.]his[
5.]poison

COMMENTS

Frg. 2 contains parts two columns with a well-preserved, intercolumnar space.

L. 4 A feminine noun stood here, perhaps תפ]ילתו or תה]ילתו.

L. 5 Although לענה is actually the name of a specific plant, 'wormwood', it serves in this text as a word for 'poison'; see frgs. 6 5; 7 2; and 1QH[a] IV 14.

Frg. 2 ii

[ ]ימׄים [1

שקר מה פחד[לאדם 2

יעזוב קנאת מדנים[3

מעלו אשר מעל[4

רׄעׄ זולתו אׄהוב[5

PAM 41.694, 43.388*

TRANSLATION

1. [ ]days [
2. falsehood. What fear [for a person
3. he shall abandon the jealous strife[
4. his transgression which he committed[
5. evil, except for him, the beloved[

COMMENTS

Col. i mentions the poison, no doubt arguing that some behaviour is worse than poison for man. Col. ii, which is more substantial, refers to the transgressions of mankind, particularly jealousy which leads to strife and some form of trespass. If one judges from the scriptural use of the root מעל, the passage may refer to a cultic offence.

L. 3 קנאת מדנים[. Cf. מ]שלח מדנים in 4Q**412** 2 4.

L. 4 מעלו. See Ezek 18:24; 1 Chr 10:13 (both in sing.). Cf. Lev 26:40; Ezek 39:26; and Dan 9:7.

Frg. 3

Parallels: **1Q27** 1 i 1–7 (underline)

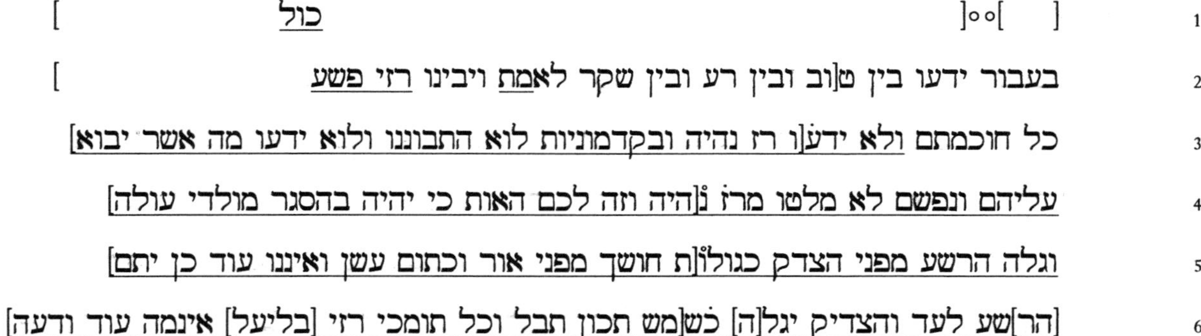

1 [ ]°°[כול]

2 בעבור ידעו בין ט[וב ובין רע ובין שקר לאמת ויבינו רזי פשע]

3 כל חוכמתם ולא ידע̇[ו רז נהיה ובקדמוניות לוא התבוננו ולוא ידעו מה אשר יבוא]

4 עליהם ונפשם לא מלטו מרז נ̇[היה וזה לכם האות כי יהיה בהסגר מולדי עולה]

5 וגלה הרשע מפני הצדק כגול̇ו̇[ת חושך מפני אור וכתום עשן ואיננו עוד כן יתם]

6 [הר]שע לעד והצדיק יגל[ה] כש[מש תכון תבל וכל תומכי רזי [בליעל] אינמה עוד ודעה]

PAM 41.694, 43.388*

TRANSLATION

1. [ ] [everything]
2. in order that they would know (the difference) between g[ood and evil, and between falsehood and truth, and that they might understand the mysteries of transgression]
3. all their wisdom. But [they] did not know [the mystery of that which was coming into being, and the former things they did not consider. And they did not know what shall befall]
4. them. And they did not save their lives from the mystery of that which was com[ing into being. And this shall be the sign to you that it is taking place: When the begotten of unrighteousness are delivered up,]
5. and wickedness is removed from before righteousness, as [darkness] is remove[d from before light. (Then,) just as smoke wholly ceases and is no more, so shall wick]edness [cease]
6. forever, and righteousness shall be reveal[ed] as the s[un (throughout) the full measure of the world. And all the adherents of the mysteries of [Belial] are to be no more. But knowledge]

COMMENTS

Frg. 3 is paralleled in **1Q27** and part of the continuation of the text following line 6 is preserved in both **1Q27** and **4Q299** 1. Accordingly, the transcription is here restored with text from **1Q27** 1. A poetic rendering combining elements of all three fragments to indicate the full extent of the text appears in the COMMENTS to **4Q299** 1, as does a summary of the poem as preserved in all three manuscripts.

L. 2 ידעו בין ט[וב ובין רע. Cf. Gen 3:5; Deut 1:39; 1QSa I 9–11.[1] See also 4Q**416** 1 15; 4Q**417** 2 i 8; 4Q**418** 2 7 and 43 5–6.

L. 3 רז נהיה. This refers to the secret of that which is in the process of coming into being. This usage of the *Nipʿal* is common in Qumran Hebrew. Cf. also Sir 42:19 and 48:25, where נהיות is parallel to נסתרות, 'secrets'.

[1] See L. H. Schiffman, *Sectarian Law in the Dead Sea Scrolls, Courts, Testimony and the Penal Code,* Brown Judaic Studies 33 (Chico, CA: Scholars Press, 1983) 62–5. The same passage is discussed from another perspective in L. H. Schiffman, *The Eschatological Community of the Dead Sea Scrolls: A Study of the Rule of the Congregation,* SBLMS 38 (Atlanta: Scholars Press, 1989) 16–20.

L. 3 ובקדמוניות לוא התבוננו. This refers to the investigation of the past which would provide the key to understanding the events of the future. Cf. בינה לקדמוניות in 4Q**418** 148 ii 6.

L. 4 ונפשם לא מלטו. Cf. 1 Kings 1:12; Jer 48:6; 51:6; Ezek 33:5; Amos 2:14-15; Ps 89:49; 116:4.

L. 4 מולדי. The participial form is not found in the Hebrew Bible. It is, however, found in manuscripts and mediaeval witnesses to *b. Ketub.* 72b.[2]

L. 5 כגולו֯]ת חושך מפני אור. Emend to כגלו]ת. Cf. Job 17:12 and the first evening benediction as quoted in *b. Ber.* 11b, גולל אור מפני חושך וחושך מפני אור, 'He (God) rolls away the light before the darkness and the darkness before the light'.

Ll. 5–6 יתם הר]שע]. Cf. Ps 104:35.

L. 6 רזי פלא. Emending to רזי בליעל in 1Q**27** as absolutely required by the context.

L. 6 אינמה עוד. Cf. Ps 104:35 which influenced lines 5–6.

Frg. 4

[○○ש○] 1

[ת ישל֯ם] 2

[○ב והוא ○○] 3

[לשו֯ם לט֯]וב 4

PAM 43.388

TRANSLATION

1.] [
2.] he will pay [
3.] and he [
4.] to place, for g[ood

[2] M. Herschler, ed., מסכת כתובות, vol. 2 (Jerusalem: Institute for the Complete Israeli Talmud, 1977) 178, variants to line 13 and n. 24.

Frg. 5

Parallels: 4Q**299** 3a ii-b 1–5 (underline)

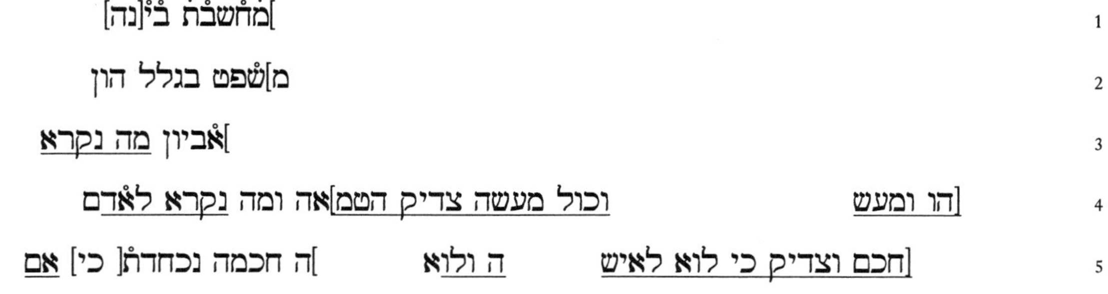

bottom margin

PAM 41.694, 43.388*

TRANSLATION

1.]thought of under[standing]
2. ju]dgement because of property
3.]poor man. What shall we call
4. [his and deed (?) and every action of the righteous has become imp]ure. And what shall we call a person
5. wise and righteous, for it is not for persons and not] hidden wisdom, [ex]cept

COMMENTS

Note that the overlap with 4Q**299** 3a ii-b 1–9 in extant, as opposed to restored, passages is only in four words which are themselves parts of stereotyped formulae that could be repeated throughout the text. The restoration from 4Q**299** is, therefore, extremely tentative. This fragment alludes to thoughts of understanding and probably to injustice relating to property. It presents a series of rhetorical questions dealing with the futility of man's attempt to be righteous and wise.

Ll. 3–4 מה נקרא . . . ומה נקרא. This is a series of rhetorical sapiential questions.

L. 4 מעשה צדיק. Cf. Eccl 8:14.

L. 5]חכם וצדיק. Cf. Eccl 9:1.

Frg. 6

Parallels: 4Q**299** 7 4–5 (underline)

1 י]דׄעו ההבׄ[דל

2]ת֯ גבר ומה מע[שה

3]עם יודע[י

4 <u>]ו֯הׄוא רחו[ק</u>

5 ואי]ן֯ לענה <u>לנגדו֯</u>[

6]מ֯הׄ עמוק לא[יש

7]ל֯[

PAM 41.694, 43.388*

TRANSLATION

1. they [will] know the diff[erence
2.]of a man and what is the de[ed of
3.]with [those] who know[of
4.] and it is dista[nt
5. and there is noth]ing more poisonous before him [
6.]how deep for a m[an
7.] [

COMMENTS

This fragment may overlap with 4Q**299** 7 4–5. It deals with the theme of man's lowly state. Something is the greatest poison to him. Probably, if we are to compare frg. 7, it is the bearing of a grudge.

L. 2 Immediately before the break, restore a feminine noun.

L. 2 ומה מע[שה. Cf. Gen 44:15, Judg 13:12. This begins another rhetorical question.

L. 3 Perhaps translate, 'the people who know' with Ps 89:16.

L. 5 לענה. See COMMENTS to frg. 2 i 5.

Frg. 7

Parallels: 4Q**299** 7 4–5 (underline)
4Q**300** 6 5 (overbar)

מה רע לאדם מ]רשע ומ֯ה ר֯ם לגבר מצדק֯[1

]ואין לענה לנגדו מנוקם לנטור בלו֯א֯[משפט 2

]ש משפט נפשו כי֯[א]צד֯יק בכל[דרכיו 3

מה]ר֯שע֯ משנו֯א֯[4

PAM 41.694, 43.388*

TRANSLATION

1. what is worse for a human being than]evil, and what is more exalted for a man than righteousness[
2.]and there is nothing more poisonous before him than one who takes vengeance by bearing a grudge un[justly[
3. Fo[r]He is righteous in all[His ways
4. what is]more evil than hating[

COMMENTS

Frg. 7 preserves part of a series of rhetorical questions. Evil is the worst thing for a person, and justice is the best. The worst poison for one's moral state is to bear a grudge. God is righteous and always seeks only justice. Nothing is worse than to hate one's fellow.

L. 1 ר֯ם לגבר מצדק֯[. Cf. Ps 89:17.

L. 2 לענה. See COMMENTS to frg. 2 ii 5.

L. 2 מנוקם לנטור. Cf. Lev 19:18; Nah 1:2; CD IX 2–8; VII 2–3; 1QS VII 8–9 (see Schiffman, *Sectarian Law*, 89–97).

L. 3 משפט נפשו. Cf. Ps 109:31.

L. 3]צד֯יק בכל[דרכיו. Restored with Ps 145:17.

Frg. 8

מ]ח֯זה ימינו֯[1

]מ֯ה קדם ומה אח[ור 2

]◦ים נפתח נ[3

]ונ֯ו֯ד֯י֯ע֯ה֯[4a

]◦◦עו להולכי פתי בכ֯ל֯ [4

]ל֯ה אתכם תומ֯כ֯י רזים א[5

ת]ד֯עו היש אתכם בינה ואמ֯[6

]ה ולא היה מה רז֯ א֯מ֯[7

] לאיש וה]וא 8

PAM 41.694, 43.388*

TRANSLATION

1. the vi]sion of our days[
2.]what is before and what is af[ter
3.] is open [

4a]and let us make known[

4.] to those who walk with simplicity in all[
5.] you who hold fast to the mysteries [
6. you]will know whether you have understanding and whether[
7.] and it was not. What mystery [
8.] to a man and h[e

COMMENTS

This fragment probably alludes to knowledge of what occurred before and what is to come after the world as we know it. Part of the hidden knowledge, as in the rabbinic esoteric tradition, concerned that which occurred before creation and that which would happen in the end of days. This text, and the related sapiential texts, encourage investigation of these secrets. The text goes on to describe those who observe God's law and understand his mysteries.

L. 2 Cf. Isa 9:11; Ps 139:5; Job 23:8; and especially *m.Ḥag.* 2.1 מה לפנים ומה לאחור, in regard to mystical speculation. See also *m. ʾAbot* 3.1.

L. 4a This line was written in the space between lines 3 and 4.

L. 4 Cf. 4Q**301** 1 3.

Frg. 9

]ס֯ודות לא השיגוהו ◦[1

]כ֯י֯א ב֯ו֯ יום הריב ◦[2

]מ֯ע֯ולם הוא וע֯]ד עולם 3

PAM 43.388

TRANSLATION

1.]secrets, they did not grasp it [
2.]for on it is the day of the dispute [
3.]it is from eternity and un[to eternity

COMMENTS

L. 1 Cf. [פן ישיגו בדברי] in 4Q**418** 188 7.

Frg. 10

[◦ לאיש ◦◦] 1

מ]שפט מה רע לא^{יש}◦◦ ואו◦[2

[◦ לא יקח] 3

[◦◦] 4

PAM 43.388

NOTES ON READINGS

L. 2 לא^{יש}◦◦. The scribe wrote לא and two illegible letters. He then corrected these by writing יש above the line.

TRANSLATION

1.] for a man [
2. ju]dgement. What is worse for a man than not [
3.] he will not take[
4.] [

Frg. 11

]צ̊ד̊ק̇ ◦◦◦[1

]ובידו משפט כלם וצד̊]ק 2

]ל[ ]◦◦ת̊◦[3

PAM 43.388

TRANSLATION

1.]righteousness [
2.]and in His hand is the judgement of all of them, and righteous[ness
3.] [

COMMENTS

The fate of everyone is in God's hands. This fragment represents the familiar notion of predestination known from the Qumran sectarian corpus.

Frg. 12

1 מ]תוק מה ◦[

PAM 43.388

TRANSLATION

1. sw]eet, what [

Frg. 13

1] היום [

PAM 43.388

TRANSLATION

1.] the day [

Frg. 14

1]ו̊◦[

301. 4QMysteries^{c}?

(PLATE IX)

Preliminary publication: B. Z. Wacholder and M. G. Abegg, *A Preliminary Edition of the Unpublished Dead Sea Scrolls, The Hebrew and Aramaic Texts from Cave Four*, Fascicle Two (Washington, D.C.: Biblical Archaeology Society, 1992) 35-7.

THIS text, 4Q**301** (4QMyst^{c}?), was classified as a copy of Mysteries by J. T. Milik, although no definite textual overlap exists with the other texts of Mysteries (1Q**27**, 4Q**299**, and 4Q**300**). The parallels between 4Q**301** and *hekhalot* literature, parallels not found in the other three manuscripts, would lead one to take a more cautious view of the relationship of 4Q**301** to the other Mysteries texts.

Physical Description

The skin is mostly tan in colour, with some light specks and some dark staining. Dry lines are not visible on these fragments, although the text is well aligned. The average line height is 7–8 mm. The letter height averages 2.5 mm. The letters are generally dark and well defined.

The manuscript preserves the top margins of at least two columns (cf. frgs. 1 and 2a–b) and the bottom margin of frg. 3. Since the original order of the fragments cannot be determined with any certitude, the numeration established by J. T. Milik in the *Preliminary Concordance* is retained. This order is followed also in the preliminary edition of B. Z. Wacholder and M. G. Abegg with some corrections. Frgs. 8–10 are not found in either the *Preliminary Concordance* or in Wacholder-Abegg.

Contents

1Q**27**, 4Q**299** and 4Q**300** were linked by the use of consistent terminology and by subject matter. Those compositions are of a genre and content similar to the so-called sapiential texts, especially 4Q**415–418**[1] Terms such as רז נהיה, הבט, התבונן and numerous others unite these texts. Yet these terms and the concern with mysteries are not found in 4Q**301**. In addition to this, the lack of any textual overlap makes it extremely unlikely that 4Q**301** (Myst^{c}?) and the other manuscripts constitute witnesses to the same composition. This is despite the fact that some linguistic parallels do exist between 4QMysteries^{c}? and the other mysteries texts.

---

[1] On this genre, see T. Elgvin, 'Admonition Texts from Cave 4', *Methods of Investigation of the Dead Sea Scrolls and the Khirbet Qumran Site, Present Realities and Future Prospects, Annals of the New York Academy of Sciences*, ed. M. O. Wise, *et al.* (New York: New York Academy of Sciences, 1994) 179–96.

The mysteries texts, like the Qumran sapiential literature in general, open up to us a new genre of wisdom literature. Hidden wisdom is available only to a select group of people endowed with an ability to interpret riddles and parables which transmit it. God is exalted in terms reminiscent of the later *hekhalot* poems, and His status is contrasted with the lowly state of mankind. What we have here is a marriage of wisdom and revealed knowledge; not only a new literary genre, but further testimony to the religious creativity of Second Temple Judaism.

Palaeography and Orthography

F. M. Cross has identified the script as a late Herodian, formal bookhand.

The orthography of 4Q**301**, like that of 4Q**299**, is prone towards characteristic Qumranic features: *scriptio plena*, special spelling of כיא, מיא, long forms of personal pronouns (e.g. frg. 3 5, 7). The long pronoun form הואה appears twice. As in 4Q**299**, the Masoretic-type forms are more numerous than the Qumranic ones, but the presence of some features of Qumran orthography points towards the copying of the text by a sectarian scribe.

Mus. Inv. 582
PAM 41.695, 43.394*

Frg. 1

top margin

1 א]ביעה רוחי ולמיניכם אחלקה דברי אליכם[

2 מ]של וחידה וחוקרי שורשי בינה עם תומכי ר[זי פלא

3]הולכי פותי ואנשי מחשבת לכול עבודת מעשיהם

4]עורף °° קודק[וד כ]ל [ה]מולת עמים עם °°°[

5]°[

PAM 43.394

Frg. 1 is a composite of sub-fragments. The text begins with what appears to be a hortatory, wisdom-type formula. Several common wisdom terms occur, as the text allude in various ways to those who possess wisdom and to those who do not.

Translation

1. I] will speak my mind and according to your kinds (?) I will apportion my words to you [
2. A par]able and a riddle, and those who search the roots of understanding with those who hold fast to [the wondrous] se[crets
3.]those who behave foolishly and the scheming people in all the work of their deeds
4.]neck ∘∘ cre[st of al]l [the] tumult of the peoples, with [
5.] [

Comments

L. 1 א]בׄיעה רוחי. Prov 1:23. Cf. 1QH[a] I 29, ומבע רוח . . . ומבעי רוחות.

L. 1 אׄחלקה דברי אליכׄם]. Cf. Prov 1:23 אודיעה דברי אתכם.

L. 2 מ]של וחידה. Cf. Ezek 17:2 and 4Q**300** 1 ii 1.

L. 2 שׄוׄרׄשי בינה. Also in 4Q**418** 55 9. Cf. שורשי חוכמה in 4Q**300** 1 ii 3.

L. 2 תומכי רׄ]זי פלא. Restored with 4Q**299** 40 2 and 4Q**300** 8 5, and the common phrase רזי פלא.

L. 3]הׄוׄלכי פותי. This expression also occurs in 4Q**300** 8 4.

L. 3 עׄבודת מעשיהם. עבודת מעשיהם occurs in 4Q**511** 63 iii 3 (*DJD* III, 48). Cf. also עבודת מעשו in 1QSa I 16. This illustrates the use of a construct of synonyms to express one idea.

Frg. 2a

top margin

משפטי כסיל ונחלת חכמׄ]ים 1

מה נכבדׄ לבב והוא ממשׄ]ל 2

מׄוׄשל ∘∘[ ]לׄ[ ]מׄ∘[3

] 4

] 5

] 6

] 7

PAM 43.394

Frg. 2 is made up of two fragments that were connected by Milik. In fact, there is no physical join between these fragments and no point at which the end of the line of one seems to run into the beginning of the line of the next. Accordingly, we will translate these separately, designating them as 2a and 2b. Frg. 2a was seen by Milik as preserving the beginnings of the line and frg. 2b as preserving all but one or two letters at the end of the line. In fact, neither contention can be considered definite from the photographs or from inspection of the original.

NOTES ON READINGS

L. 3 מׄושל. Alternatively מׄמשל, 'dominion' could be possible.

TRANSLATION

1. Judgements of a fool and the inheritance of sage[s
2. How honoured is the heart and it is from a parab[le
3. it rules [ ] [ ] [

COMMENTS

L. 2 מה נכבד. 2 Sam 6:20.

Frg. 2b

top margin

]ים ומה הׄחידה לכמה חׄו<ק>רי בׄשור{ש}שי בינה 1

]משל מה אדיר לכם והוא למשׁ]ל]◦[ ]מה שר [ ] [2

]בׄלוא חוזק וירד בו בשוט בלוא מחיר מיא יאמׄ[ר] 3

]ל◦◦[ ]ל[ ]◦ מׄיׄאׄ בׄכם דורש פני אור ומאׄ[ור] 4

]◦ תׄבנית זכר ללוא היהׄ[ ] 5

]במלאכי [ ] 6

מ]הללים[ ] 7

PAM 43.394

The text speaks about the honoured position of the riddle and parable to those who seek to understand wisdom. The passage makes use of rhetorical questions beginning with 'what'. Apparently, discernment is likened to light or to a luminary.

NOTES ON READINGS

L. 1 חׄו<ק>רי בׄשור{ש}שי בינה. Cf. above, frg. 1 2. Note that the *qop* was omitted accidentally by the scribe and the *šin* was written twice and then one was erased.

TRANSLATION

1.]s and what is the riddle for you, O you who sea<r>ch the roots of understanding
2.]parable. How majestic for you, and it is for a parab[le] [ ] [ ]
3.]without strength, and he will rule over him with a whip at no cost. Who will sa[y]
4.] [ ] [ ] Who among you seeks the presence of light and the lum[inary]
5.] the image of a male to whom there was not (?) [ ]
6.] with angels of [ ]
7. p]raising[ ]

COMMENTS

L. 2 מה אדיר. Ps 8:2, 10.

L. 3]בלוא חזק וירד. Cf. Ezek 34:4: ובחזקה רדיתם, 'and with force you have ruled them'.

L. 3 בשוט. Cf. 1QH^a VI 35.

L. 3 בלוא מחיר. Cf. אשר לוא במחיר in 1QS V 17 and 4Q**427** (4QHodayot^a) 7 ii 8 לאין מחיר.

L. 4 מיא בכם. Isa 42:23.

L. 4 דורש פני. Cf. Ps 24:6.

L. 4 פני . . . ומא[ור]. Cf. Ps 90:8.

L. 4 אור ומא[ור]. Cf. אורים ומאורי פלא in 4QBer^a 1 ii 3 and מאורים כמשפט האורים in 4QpIsa^d 1 5 (Allegro reads: מאירים).

L. 5 תבנית זכר. Deut 4:16 where it is connected with the prohibition of idolatrous images.

L. 7 מ]הללים[. Only in 1 Chr 23:5.

Frg. 3a–b

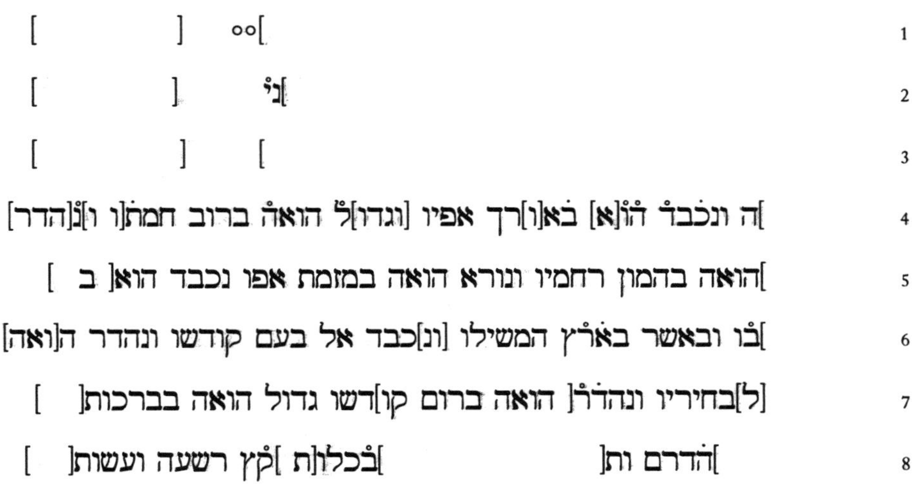

1]∘∘ [ ]

2]ני [ ]

3] [ ]

4]ה ונכבד הו[א] בא[ו]רך אפיו [וגדו]ל הואה ברוב חמת[ו ו]נ[הדר]

5]הואה בהמון רחמיו ונורא הואה במזמת אפו נכבד הוא[ב]

6]בו ובאשר בארץ המשילו [ונ]כבד אל בעם קודשו ונהדר ה[ואה]

7 [ל]בחיריו ונהדר[הואה ברום קו]דשו גדול הואה בברכות[ ]

8]הדרם ות[ ]בכל[ו]ת]קץ רשעה ועשות[ ]

bottom margin

PAM 43.394

This fragment consists of two pieces which are joined at one point in what is by no means a definitive manner. Only if one accepts the join, is it possible to assume, as does Milik, that the preserved width of the column would constitute practically the entire column. The narrowness of the column which results would argue against this join. We translate this column as joined by Milik, on the assumption that, if some text is missing, it would be to the left of the preserved portion of frg. 3a. Because of the uncertainty of the join, however, we place the portion deriving from frg. 3a in italics, while translating the portion deriving from frg. 3b in Roman type.

Together, frgs. 3a and 3b constitute part of a poetic text, reminiscent of some of the later *hekhalot* mystical hymns. Such poems are characterized by a sequence of adjectives describing the majesty and greatness of God,[2] as in this text. The lines of the poem would each begin with an adjectival description followed by הוא(ה). To illustrate this literary form, a poetic rendering is provided. An attempt to link this type of poetry to the Dead Sea scrolls was made by M. Smith before sufficient Qumran literature was known.[3] We were able to argue such links more extensively from a few of the fragments of the Sabbath Songs.[4] With the full publication of this text by C. Newsom,[5] these links are even clearer. There is no reason, therefore, to be surprised by the finding of further links between these corpora.[6]

Frg. 3b contains several unusual notations. To the right of these there appear to be *vacats*, with writing before that of line 2. (In the translation the signs are denoted by an X). This would mean that the lines above the preserved portion of text (i.e. lines 1–3) were shorter than the remainder of the fragment (lines 4 and below). E. Tov has suggested that these signs are probably letters from the Cryptic A script. However he notes: 'The context does not help us to understand the mystery of these signs . . . ' .[7]

The poetic text found in this fragment is a series of praises of God extolling His contrasting characteristics. God is praised for being long-suffering and extremely merciful, yet able to pour out His mighty wrath. Thereafter, we read of God's rule over the universe and of the honour he receives from His people. He is concurrently exalted among His chosen ones and in the holy habitation in heaven. His true greatness will be revealed when evil is entirely destroyed at the end of days.

TRANSLATION

1.] X[ ]
2.] X[ ]
3.] X[ ]
4.] *and honoured is H[e] in His l[o]ng suffering* [and grea]t is He in [His] great anger. [And] e[xalted]
5.]*is He in the multitude of His mercies and awesome* is He in the plan of His anger. Honoured is He [in
6.] *and who rules over the earth.* [And ho]noured is God by His holy people, and exalted is H[e]
7. [*for*] *His chosen ones. And exalted* [*is He* in the heights of] His [ho]liness. Great is He in the blessings[ ]
8.]*their glory and* [ ]when there comes to an en[d] the period of evil and the doing of[ ]

---

[2] Cf. G. Scholem, *Major Trends in Jewish Mysticism* (New York: Schocken, 1941) 57–63.

[3] M. Smith, 'Observations on Hekhalot Rabbati', *Biblical and Other Studies*, ed. A. Altmann (Cambridge: Harvard, 1963) 157.

[4] L. H. Schiffman, 'Merkavah Speculation at Qumran: The 4Q Serekh Shirot ʿOlat Ha-Shabbat', *Mystics, Philosophers, and Politicians, Essays in Jewish Intellectual History in Honor of Alexander Altmann*, ed. J. Reinharz, D. Swetschinski, with K. P. Bland (Durham: Duke University Press, 1982) 15–47.

[5] C. Newsom, *Songs of the Sabbath Sacrifice: A Critical Edition* (HSS 27; Atlanta: Scholars Press, 1985); final publication: *DJD* XI, forthcoming.

[6] See L. H. Schiffman, 'ספרות ההיכלות וכתבי קומראן', *Jerusalem Studies in Jewish Thought* 6 (Proceedings of the First International Conference on the History of Jewish Mysticism: Early Jewish Mysticism; Jerusalem: Hebrew University Press, 1987) 121–38.

[7] E. Tov, 'Letters of the Cryptic A Script and Paleo-Hebrew Letters Used as Scribal Marks in Some Qumran Scrolls', *DSD* 2 (1995) 330–39, esp. p. 334.

COMMENTS

L. 4 ונכבד̊ ה̊ו̊[א]. Cf. Gen 34:19.

L. 4 [וגדו]ל̊ הואה̊. Cf. Ps 99:3.

L. 5 בהמון רחמיו. Cf. Isa 63:15 המון מעיך ורחמיך, 'Your yearning and Your love' (NJPS); 1QH[a] IX 7–8. In later Hebrew, the usual meaning is 'multitude', as in the Additional Service for Festivals, שובה אלינו בהמון רחמיך, 'Return to us (O God) in Your abundant mercies'.[8]

L. 5 ונורא הואה. Cf. Ps 99:3.

L. 5 במזמת. Cf. 4Q**299** 3a-b 10.

L. 7 ל]בחיריו. Ps 105:6, 43; 1 Chr 16:13. The *Preliminary Concordance* has בחידיו with a question mark once but elsewhere בחיריו.

L. 8]ק̊ץ רשעה. Cf. CD VI 10, 14; XII 23; XIII 20; XV 7, 10; 1QpHab V 7–8. This usage certainly places the document as a 'sectarian' work, as it refers to the notion that the present age is evil, to be followed by the victory of the sectarians in the War of the Sons of Light against the Sons of Darkness. The context in which the root כלה is used in this passage is also typical of the sectarian compositions. Cf. לכל̇ת רשעה in 4Q**511** 35 1 (*DJD* VIII, 237).

POETIC RENDERING

] *and honoured is H*[*e*] *in His l*[*o*]*ng suffering*
[and grea]t is He in [His] great anger.
[And] e[xalted] *is He in the multitude of His mercies*
and awesome is He in the plan of His anger.
Honoured is He [in] *and in which the earth is His rule.*
[And ho]noured is God by His holy people,
and exalted is H[e *for*] *His chosen ones.*
And exalted [*is He* in the heights of] His [ho]liness.
Great is He in the blessings [ ] *their glory and* [ ]
when there comes to an en[d] the period of evil and the doing of[

Frg. 4

1]°°° בנ°°[
2]ת̊° כל רוח ב̊י̊נ̊ת̇ו לוא ידע̊[ו
3]עת בכול כבודו ומה אפר̊ [ועפר
4]זהר נהד̇ר הואה ב[
5]°°°°[ ]ל̊[

PAM 43.394

[8] D. Goldschmidt, ed., סדר רב עמרם גאון (Jerusalem: Mossad Harav Kook, 1971) 126.

This fragment also deals with the praise of God. His wisdom and glory are singled out and contrasted with the lowly state of man.

TRANSLATION

1.] [
2.] every spirit of His discernment [they] did not understand[
3.] in all His glory. And what is dust [and ashes
4.]splendour. Exalted is He in[
5.] [ ] [

COMMENTS

L. 2 כל רוח. Jer 49:32; Ezek 21:12.

L. 2 רוח ב֯י֯נ֯תו. Cf. רוח בינה in Shir[a], 4Q**510** 1 6 (*DJD* VII, 216), paralleled in 4Q**511** 10 6–7 (p. 225); and in 4Q**418** 58 2; as well as in the Songs for the Sabbath Sacrifice, 4Q**405** 17 3 (Newsom, 289) and in 4Q**444** 2 i 3.

L. 2 לוא ידע֯]ו. Or ‘will not know’.

L. 3 אפ֯ר] ועפר. Restored by Milik in the Preliminary Concordance. Cf. Gen 18:27; Job 30:19; 42:6. Gen 18:27 is apparently quoted in 4Q**267** (4QD[b] according to present numeration) 1 5. This fragment is part of the admonition at the beginning of the *Zadokite Fragments* which was not preserved in the medieval genizah manuscripts.

L. 4]זהר. Despite some hesitation, it seems reasonable to assume that this is the defective spelling of זוהר, which occurs with this meaning in 4QBer[a] 1 ii 3, 4 (2x), 4QBer[b] 2 5 and 4QS[h] 3 4.

Frg. 5

]ב֯נ֯[1

]היכל מלכות֯ו[2

מ]ה בשר כיא [3

א]ו֯ר גדול ונכב]ד הואה 4

]◦ אור ואורו [5

PAM 43.394

Here again mankind is contrasted with God whose royal sanctuary is mentioned. The stress is again placed on a great light, probably that of wisdom and discernment.

TRANSLATION

1.] [
2.]the Temple of His kingdom[
3. wh]at is flesh that [
4. a great [li]ght. And honou[red is He
5.] light, and his light

COMMENTS

L. 2 Or, 'His royal Temple'. Cf. בהיכלי מ[לכות in 4QBer[b] 2 11.

L. 3 בשר כיא. Num 11:18; Ps 136:25. Certainly, 'flesh' here refers to humanity.

L. 4 א[ו]ר גדול. Isa 9:1.

Frg. 6

1 כי]א אין לו מ[

2]ר̇ ה̊[ו]נו וצעד כבו[דו

3]ל̇∘∘ר̊ הואה למו הואה̊[

4]ה̊לוא ∘∘∘[ ]∘∘[

PAM 43.394

Frg. 6 may contrast the glory of God with the status of humans.

TRANSLATION

1. fo]r he does not have [
2.] his pr[op]erty and the step (?) of [His] glor[y
3.] he, to them, he[
4.]is it not [ ] [

Frg. 7

1]ר̇ש וג∘[

2]עד מלא̇[ת

3 רש]עת לבו ל∘[

4]לוא ∘∘[

PAM 43.394

Frg. 7 may refer to the evil of man's heart.

TRANSLATION

1.] [
2.]until the complet[ion of
3. the ini]quity of his heart [
4.]not [

COMMENTS

L. 2 עד מלא]ת[. For this expression, used frequently in the Rule of the Community, see 1QS VI 17, 18, 21; VIII 26; VII 20, 22; 1QSa I 10.[9]

L. 3 Perhaps restore רש]עת לבו, 'the [ev]il of his heart'.

Frg. 8

]○○○[1

]ונות ב○[2

]בֿחׄי [3

PAM 43.394

Frg. 9

]○[1

]רוׄח סי[2

נכב]דֿ הׄואה [ב 3

PAM 43.394

The poetic praise of God is apparently the subject of frg. 9.

TRANSLATION

1.] [
2.]the spirit of [
3. Honou]red is He [in

[9] See L. H. Schiffman, *Sectarian Law in the Dead Sea Scrolls, Courts, Testimony and the Penal Code* (BJS 33; Chico, CA: Scholars Press, 1983) 178 nn. 47–8; 182 n. 106.

COMMENTS

L. 3 As restored, the text would fit the poetic structure found in frgs. 3–5 and therefore, probably needs to be placed together with them.

Frg. 10

]◦[1

]ן בין א[2

]מ̊ח̊שב[ת 3

PAM 43.394

TRANSLATION

1.] [
2.] between [
3.]the pla[n of

302. 4QpapAdmonitory Parable

(PLATES X–XII)

4Q**302** (*olim* 4Q**302** and 4Q**302a**, two separate compositions) consists of twenty-three papyrus fragments, three of which contain major portions of text.[1] Frg. 1, the smallest of the three, contains parts of two columns: col. i consists of fourteen lines; col. ii consists of fifteen lines. Frgs. 2 and 3 preserve parts of three columns. Cols. i and iii are fragmentary and contain only a few words. However, col. ii contains several complete lines, thus indicating the entire column width. On this basis, the original column width can be estimated at 9–9.5 cm. The height of individual letters averages 2.5 mm, and the space between the dry lines is *c*.5–9 mm. A margin of *c*.1.5 cm separates the columns. There is no evidence of horizontal or vertical ruling. The papyrus sheet is very thin, and all the fragments are of a homogeneous light brown colour. The material state of the papyrus in plates 43.395 (Mus. Inv. 356) and 43.396 (Mus. Inv. 333) indicates that the fragments originated from the same scroll.

TABLE 1: *Measurements of Fragments (in cm)*

Frg.	Width	Height
1	8	11.2
1a	1.9	1.7
1b	4.3	6
2	16.7	8
3	16	9

Orthography

The orthography is, for the most part, defective, with occasional exceptions. The pronominal suffixes are defective: כדבריך (frg. 1 i 3); טֹוביך (frg. 1 i 5); לנגדך (frg. 3 ii 7); בריבך (frg. 3 ii 8); משבו (frg. 3 ii 9); מֹפניך (frg. 1a 2). The accusative marker for the 3rd person is written אתו (frg. 2 ii 6, twice). The noun אלהים is consistently written defectively (frgs. 1 i 4; 3 ii 2 אֹלהיכם, 6, 9). One finds the *plene* spelling of כוֹל (frg. 1 i 5); הלוא (frg. 2 ii 6); בֹלוא (frg. 2 iii 7). The *plene* spellings of לוא and בלוא are also attested in the Bible. But לא is written defectively in frgs. 3 ii 7, 3 iii 1. The verbs are spelled both

[1] Thanks are due to Prof. Jacob Milgrom for his helpful editorial advice and for the translation of the text into English.

in full and defectively; see להרבות (frg. 2 ii 7) and לרבת (frg. 2 ii 8); ישמר (frg. 2 ii 6) but ויכסמוהו (frg. 2 iii 6).

Palaeography

The fragments are written in a Hasmonaean semi-cursive script, *c.*125–100 BCE. Note the shapes of *he* and *ḥet*. The *samek* is not closed. *Waw* and *yod* are easily distinguishable. The *reš*, when written at the end of a word, has a long leg, e.g. לאחר (frg. 1 i 2); יחר (frg. 3 ii 1).

Genre

The composition, comprising two parts (a historical admonition and an accompanying parable), resembles a discourse or admonition of the *rib* (lawsuit) pattern, which is found in prophetic books and passages (Deuteronomy 32; 1 Sam 12:6-15; Isaiah 1; Jeremiah 2; Ezekiel 20; Amos 4; Mic 6:1-9 *et al.*), occasionally in psalmic passages (Psalms 50 and 82), and in post-biblical literature (e.g., *1 Enoch* 1–5; *Testament of Naphtali* 3–4). In Qumran literature one finds admonitions in the *rib* pattern in the non-canonical psalms 4Q**381** 69 and 76–77, and in the sectarian composition CD II–IV 12.[2]

Characteristics of the *rib* pattern appear in both parts of 4Q**302**; there is a direct address to the audience הׄבׄינׄוׄ נא בזאת החכמים (frg. 2 ii 2); בׄמעלכם, מידכם, לבבכם, אׄלהיכם, [מ]חשבתיכׄם (frg. 3 ii 2, 4, 6, 7). Singular direct address is also used, as noted in the COMMENTS. God is spoken of only in the 3rd person: אלהים צדיק; הוא יה (frg. 1 i 4, 8; and cf. also frg. 1 i 10; 1 ii 6); יקום אלוהים; אלהים בשמׄים משבו (frg. 3 ii 6, 9), in contrast to the use of second person address as in prayers.

Considering the whole text as a single composition, we find a declaration of God's justice in the introduction (frg. 1 i 4). A historical section, summarizing God's past actions both in the form of a survey (frg. 1 i 7–ii 15 + frg. 1b) and in the form of a parable (frg. 2 ii–iii), occupies the central part. An accusation and judgement (frg. 3 ii 4–7a), followed by a statement concerning a controversy (frg. 3 ii 7b–8), may be considered the conclusion of the historical section. In the last section of the preserved text a turn towards conciliation of God with Israel is suggested, possibly involving revenge upon His adversaries, the nations (frg. 3 ii 9–3 iii 3).

The sapiential parable within this text does not distinguish it from other examples of the *rib* pattern. Short parables or metaphorical statements are involved in many of the *rib* compositions, e.g., Deut 32:11; Isa 1:25, 30; Jer 2:13. The parable of the vineyard in Isa 5:1-7 is possibly an introduction to the following הוי admonitions and their

---

[2] For a survey of the research of this genre in the Bible, see K. Nielsen, 'History of Criticism', *Yahweh as Prosecutor and Judge* (JSOTSup 9; Sheffield, 1978) 1–26. L. Hartman discussed the *rib* pattern as it appears in *1 Enoch* (*Asking for a Meaning: A Study of Enoch 1–5* [CBNTS 12; Lund: CWK, 1979]); P. R. Davies discusses it in the context of CD ('The Damascus Covenant', *JSOT* 25 [1983] 56–104); and E. Schuller briefly compares the *rib* pattern in 4Q**381** 69, 76–77 with other compositions containing the pattern (*Non-Canonical Psalms from Qumran: A Pseudepigraphic Collection.* [HSS 28; Atlanta, GA: Scholars Press, 1986] 209–10; 224–6).

conclusion. Thus, the author of 4Q**302** follows the principles of the biblical *rib* pattern compositions. There are no specific Qumran sectarian ideas in 4Q**302**.

The sapiential element הבינו נא בזאת החכמים, and even the parable attached to it, do not impart a distinct sapiential nature to the composition, but do direct the reader towards a sapiential lesson in the admonition, as is customary in many biblical and Qumran compositions,[3] among them admonitions including historical surveys.[4] However, the admonitory nature of the composition may suggest that its post-biblical author intended the reader, by means of the parable, to apply the lesson learned from the historical setting to a specific situation in his own generation.

General Background

The vocabulary of 4Q**302** is biblical but not especially that of the *rib* pattern texts. Words of various biblical origins occur in the text; deuteronomic, prophetic, psalmic, and others, as noted in the COMMENTS. The orthography also follows the biblical pattern. Much of the subject matter of this poorly preserved composition is discernible because of its biblical origin. There is no apocalyptic or sectarian influence in 4Q**302**.

These features also characterize the non-canonical psalms from Qumran, and E. Schuller has concluded that the non-canonical psalms were composed earlier than the sectarian writings, possibly during the Persian or Hellenistic periods. This conclusion may also be relevant for 4Q**302**. Palaeographical analysis points to the early Hasmonaean period, but the text was probably composed earlier.

We have, on the one hand, a non-canonical composition that indicates a tendency to continue traditional literary ideas and practice. But on the other hand, the reuse of the *rib* pattern may be directed against specific persons involved in an actual event in the author's generation, which therefore requires a historical investigation. A separate reading of each of the non-canonical *rib* pattern compositions, 4Q**302**, 4Q**381** 69, and 4Q**381** 76–77—all of which are only partially preserved—renders it difficult to find references to a specific event. In reading these texts as a group of compositions of the same genre, however, a common theme is evident. Each of these texts mentions the foreign people from whose customs Israel was commanded to remain separate. 4Q**381**

---

[3] Among biblical and post-biblical works, such calls for a sapiential lesson appear at the opening or towards the conclusion of the work. These are written, not just in distinctly sapiential books such as Proverbs and Ben-Sira, or in the sapiential works from Qumran, as in 4Q**525** 14 ii 18 [ועתה מבין שמעה לי ושים לבכה ל], and others (see D. J. Harrington, 'Wisdom at Qumran', *The Community of the Renewed Covenant*, eds. E. Ulrich and J. VanderKam [CJAS 10; Notre Dame, IN: UNP, 1993] 137–52), but also in the non-canonical psalms of 4Q**381** and the admonitions of the ***Damascus Covenant***, and in other Qumran texts (ibid., esp. 138f.). The psalms of 4Q**381** are characterized by such calls within variegated contents (see Schuller, *Non-Canonical Psalms*, 23–4, and note their contexts).

[4] Noteworthy are such exhortative calls written in the context of historical surveys, in both biblical and post-biblical admonitions: Deut 32:7 בינו שנות דר ודר; CD I 1 שמעו כל יודעי צדק ובינו במעשי אל (cf. CD II 14); and in 4Q**381** 76–77 8 [שמעו] דברי ותשכילו לחכמה מפי תצא ותבינ[ו]. Another call, היש בינה תלמדו (4Q**381** 76–77 13) is written in the context of a dispute between God and Israel; בינו נא זאת שכחי אלוה (Ps 50:22) is written within another such dispute (cf. Ps 94:8). In 4Q**381** 69 4–5, the sending of prophets to teach Israel the lesson of their past transgressions is mentioned. However, none of these calls is followed by a parable. Some of the biblical parables have a header or an opening call, but of another type (cf. Judg 9:7; Isa 5:1; Ezek 19:1).

69 mentions the defilement of the land by its foreign inhabitants (lines 1–2) and the warning to Israel to turn from their deeds (line 5a); 4Q**381** 76–77 states that Israel is God's treasured people, who were chosen from many great peoples and nations (lines 5, 14–16); and 4Q**302** mentions the offspring of Abraham (frg. 1 i 7), God's '[ho]ly (people) Israe[l]' (frg. 1 i 10), who settled among the inhabitants of the land (frg. 1 i 12), but who were commanded not to follow their customs (frg. 1 ii 1–3?, 11–13). Although all of these statements refer to the past, one cannot ignore the analogous situation of the Jews in Judaea in the post-exilic period. There are insufficient details in 4Q**302** to enable the identification of the foreign peoples. Nevertheless, the mention of the inhabitants of the land among whom Israel had settled is noteworthy (frg. 1 i 12). If they symbolize actual people of the post-exilic period, one may tentatively identify them as the Samaritans, or the 'Samarians' (i.e., other persons in Samaria, distinguished from the Gerizim community).[5] There were relationships between Jews and Samaritans not just in the Persian period (Ezra 9–10), but also in the Hellenistic period, after the building of the Samaritan temple on Mt. Gerizim. According to Josephus, Jewish men who were excluded from Jerusalem at that time found shelter among the Samaritans (*Ant.* 11.346–347). These people perhaps participated in the worship at the Samaritan temple. In this context one may consider the central place that the building of the Temple in Jerusalem takes in the historical survey of frg. 1 ii 6–7. If its author intended to symbolize a polemic with the Jews who participate in the worship at the Samaritan temple, one may tentatively suggest that the text of 4Q**302** was composed at that time (around the third century BCE).[6] Clearer hints identifying the Samaritan danger at that time appear in another text from Qumran, 4Q**372**.[7] That text complains of the tendency of the Samaritans to prevail over the tribes of Jacob, while this text admonishes those Jews who transgress intentionally, possibly by following foreign customs. Nevertheless, the Samaritan danger in the land of Israel during that period may be assumed to be one of the historical situations dealt with in 4Q**302**. Another period when adherence to foreign customs was an issue in Judaea was during the Hellenistic period (1 Macc 1:41-53; 2 Macc 4:7-17). However, at that time, Jewish men followed the customs of the foreign rulers, not those of the inhabitants of the land.

On the basis of our general conclusion concerning the presectarian date of 4Q**302**, its literary characteristics can now be summarized. 4Q**302** may be joined to the collection of pre-Qumran, non-canonical compositions which adapt biblical motifs and patterns to new compositions, and which sometimes refer to actual historical situations. In the early Second Temple Period, the tendency to follow biblical patterns, motifs, vocabulary, and even content, still existed, as can be seen from the apocryphal writings of that period. However, in later sectarian compositions found at Qumran, this type of composition was superseded by new genres; one of these, that of the *pesharim*,

---

[5] See R. Egger, 'Josephus Flavius and the Samaritans', *Proceedings of the First International Congress of the Société d'études Samaritaines*, eds. A. Tal and M. Florentin (Tel-Aviv: Chaim Rosenberg School for Jewish Studies, Tel Aviv University, 1991) 109–14.

[6] According to Josephus at that time (*c.*300 BCE) the Samaritans enjoyed prosperity (*Ant.* 12.257). See Sir 50:26, and M. Z. Segal, ספר בן סירא השלם (Jerusalem: Bialik Institute, 1972) 349.

[7] See E. Schuller, '4Q372 1: A Text about Joseph', *RevQ* 14 (1989–90) 349–76; see especially 4Q**372** 1, 20–21, 27.

interpreted contemporary historical situations from a distinctly sectarian viewpoint.

Mus. Inv. 333, 356
PAM 41.975, 41.978, 43.395*, 43.396*

Frg. 1 i

1 [ ]אׄלׄ◦[ ]◦ וׄהוא
2 [ ]◦מכה לאחׄר
3 [מכה]◦◦◦ כדבריך באפים
4 [ ]הׄ *vac* אלהים צדיק
5 [ ]םׄ טׄוביך על כוׄל
6 [ ]◦םׄ *vacat*
7 [ ]רׄ זרע אברהם
8 [ ]כׄיׄ הוא יה
9 [ ]◦ ואׄ◦[ ]◦◦◦◦
10 [ק]דשו יׄשׄרא[ל]
11 [ ]◦◦◦[ ]ת בשמים
12 [ ]◦◦ וׄבקׄרׄבׄ עממים
13 [ ]◦תׄ יצר כל
14 [ ]◦

Mus. Inv. 333
PAM 41.975, 43.396*

NOTES ON READINGS

L. 2 ◦מכה[. The sign before the *mem* is unclear. It does not resemble *waw*, *šin*, or *yod*. Possibly it is not a remnant of a letter.

L. 2 לאחׄר. The *reš* has a long leg. See PALAEOGRAPHY.

L. 5 כוׄל. Although the second letter is damaged by a wrinkle in the papyrus, *waw* is more likely than a final *nun* (*PC* על כן). Traces of a *lamed* are also visible.

L. 7]רׄ. Based upon the long-legged *reš* (see PALAEOGRAPHY), the verb [בח]רׄ may have been written here.

TRANSLATION

1. [ ] [ ] and He
2. [ ] one affliction after
3. [*another*]◦◦◦ for your words. In anger (or: while you spoke angrily)
4. [ ] *vacat* God is righteous
5. [ ] Your bounty is over all (or: your good men [ ] for all)
6. [ ] *vacat*
7. [ ] the seed of Abraham
8. [ ] for He is the Lord
9. [ ] [ ]
10. [ ]His [ho]ly one, Israe[l]
11. [ ] [ ] in heaven
12. [ ] and in the midst of nations
13. [ ] He formed all
14. [ ]

COMMENTS

The top margin of frg. 1 i and the beginning of all its lines are damaged. The content is an admonition, but the opening—which may have been written on a no-longer extant, preceding column—is unknown. Two sections are apparent in this column: (1) a justification of God's judgement of Israel (lines 1–6) and (2) the choice of Israel to be the people of God (lines 7–13, and possibly frg. 1a, which may perhaps be placed at lines 14–15, see COMMENTS). A *vacat* at the end of line 6 separates these two sections. Both sections deal with the relationship between God and Israel in history. The first section may belong to a general introduction to the composition. In the second section a survey of the history of Israel is begun, which continues in frg. 1 ii, and possibly in some of the small fragments (e.g. frg. 1b). However, both sections may be considered to belong to the first part of an admonition directed to Israel, who stands before God's judgement, and the praise of God is to be understood in this context. The second part of **4Q302** (frgs. 2 ii–3 ii) is a parable concerning the same subject. The unity of the composition is apparent in the style, as well as the content. Israel is addressed in the second person singular and plural, and God is spoken of in the third person singular.

L. 1]אׄל◦[ ]◦ וׄהוא. The pronoun הוא refers to God rather than Israel (see below, lines 8, 10, 13).

L. 2]◦מכה לאחר. There are no lengthened suffixes in this text. Therefore, reconstructions such as [ש]מכה or [ישי]מכה are not plausible. Neither is a phrase such as [ש]מכה לאחר 'Your name to another' (see Isa 42:8; 48:11). The restored phrase may be מכה לאחר [מכה] 'one affliction after another'. Note the phrase מכה על מכה in 4Q**481c** 1 7 (PAM 43.550; PAM 41.468; 42.819), in the context of a prayer for God's mercy. See also the idea of smiting Israel sevenfold for its hostile acts against God in Lev 26:21, 24; Deut 28:59; Isa 1:6; Jer 6:7; *Jub*. 23:13; 4Q**504** 1–2 iii 6–13. The form לאחר (adverb with *lamed*) is used in Mishnaic Hebrew (see *m. Ber*. 6.6; 8.8; *m. Pe'a* 8.1, etc.).

L. 3 כדבריך. If the reading of line 2 is correct, it may be suggested that the afflictions mentioned there are associated with דברים of Deut 30:1, referring to the curses predicted by God. However, based on the prevailing style of the admonition, כדבריך is rather addressed to Israel, referring to its evil words that anger God (cf. Deut 4:21; Jer 33:24; Mal 2:17; 3:13 and see below frg. 3 ii 7–8). In this case כדבריך may be considered as either a nominal form with a prefix and a pronoun, or as the infinitive form כדברך 'while you spoke', of which the syllable before the pronoun ך- is spelled with *yod* and accented (see E. Qimron, 'Studies in the Hebrew of the Dead Sea Scrolls', *Hebrew Linguistics* 33–5 [1992] 79–92 [Heb]).

L. 3 באפים. This word may be a prepositional phrase used adverbially continuing the former clause, or it may begin a new sentence, describing God's wrathful smiting of Israel for its sins (lines 2–3; cf. Deut 29:27; 2 Kgs 17:18; Ezek 5:15).

L. 4 אלהים צדיק. This phrase is used here to declare the justification of God's punishment of Israel (cf. Dan 9:14; Ezra 9:15; Neh 9:33; 1QS I 26 [Licht's reconstruction][8]). In Ps 145:17 a similar phrase is used for praising God's justice in general.

L. 5 טׄוביך על כׄוׄל. This phrase may either refer to God or to Israel, depending on the meaning of טוביך. The definition is either 'your bounty' (טובך), with the syllable before the pronoun ך- being spelled with *yod* and accented (Qimron, HDSS, 33–5), or 'your good men'. For the first meaning cf. Ps 31:20; Neh 9:25, 35, where the Lord's bounty to Israel is specified. In this case, its connection with על כול may reflect a play on טוב ה' לכל ורחמיו על-כל-מעשיו 'The Lord is good to all, and His mercy is over all His works' (Ps 145:9). The author vocalizes the adjective טוב 'good' as the noun טוב 'bounty', rendering the first stiche as 'the bounty of the Lord is of all' and then combines it with על-כל from the second stiche, yielding 'Your bounty is over all'. However, the appeal to God should be explained in the light of lines 8, 10, and 14. As for the meaning 'good men', טובים appears in Biblical Hebrew (Ps 125:4; Prov 14:19; 15:3, etc.), referring to those men considered faithful to God. Yet, טובים with a pronoun is possibly reflected in the LXX version of Zech 6:10, 14 (χρησίμων [-μοις] αὐτῆς, i.e. טוֹבֶיהָ, BDB [Oxford 1907], 376), and see the Talmudic term טובי העיר (*b. Meg.* 26a). Its meaning here could be 'your best men' referring to the men of Israel, see lines 7–10 below, and the metaphor עץ טוב in frg. 2 ii 3. Its connection with על כול is understood if the author is referring both to Ps 145:9-10, modifying חסידיך of v. 10 into the synonym טוביך, and continuing with על כול from v. 9. In this case the whole phrase may have been [מודי]ם טוביך על כול] . . . 'Your good men [give thank]s for all [. . . ', directed to Israel.

L. 7 זרע אברהם. Cf. Isa 41:8; Jer 33:26; Ps 105:6; and 2 Chr 20:7 where this term defines Israel as the chosen people. See NOTES ON READINGS on line 7.

L. 8]כׄיׄ הוא יה. For the idea cf. Ps 105:7. The shortened tetragrammaton יה appears in Exod 17:16 and Ps 135:4.

L. 10 ק]דשו יׄשרא[ל]. These words may refer to Jer 2:3 קדש ישראל ליהוה, or possibly to עם הקדש (Isa 62:12), זרע קדש (Isa 6:13). Perhaps the author had in mind the verse היתה יהודה לקדשו ישראל ממשלותיו (Ps 114:2).

L. 11]ת בשמים. Possibly a remnant of a phrase such as ארובות בשמים (cf. 2 Kgs 7:2, 19), or rather אוצרות בשמים, referring to the heavenly storehouses containing the wind and water that God sends to the earth (cf. Deut 28:12; Jer 10:13 [= 51:16]; Ps 135:5-7; Job 38:22; $1QH^a$ I 12–13; 1QM X 12). These are defined in Jer 33:25; Job 38:33 as חקות שמים וארץ 'the laws of heaven and earth'. In frg. 2 ii 5 of this text יורה ומלקוש are mentioned. For the context here, see below, line 13.

L. 12 ובקׄרׄב עממים. This phrase may refer to the territory that God allotted to Israel among the peoples of Canaan and Transjordan. See the remembrances of these actions of God in Ps 135:10-12; Neh 9:22-24; 2 Chr 20:7.

L. 13 יצר כל. Note Jer 10:16 (= 51:19) יוצר הכל הוא (cf. Ps 135:6).

Frg. 1 ii

1 בׄהׄםׄ]

2 בׄם]

3 באלה תׄ◦]

[8] J. Licht, *The Rule Scroll* (Jerusalem: The Bialik Institute, 1965) 68 [Hebrew].

בח̊[ ] לוא̊[4

ו̊ל̊[ ]ת̊ם̊[5

מ̊קדשו̊ [6

ל̊עשות ל̊[7

ה̊א̊[8

◦◦[9

ו̊◦◦◦[10

ושמ̊אל [11

ואל ת̊[12

ואל ת̊[13

דבריו [14

לב̊ער א̊[15

Mus. Inv. 333
PAM 41.975, 43.396*

NOTES ON READINGS

L. 2] ב̊ם. *Bet* is assumed based on the upper right corner. There is a hole where the lower horizontal line would be placed.

L. 6] מ̊קדשו̊. A small space separates the *mem* from the *qop*. However, note the remains of the long diagonal line of the *mem*, which possibly necessitated leaving a small space before writing the *qop*.

TRANSLATION

1. in them [
2. in them [
3. in these [
4. [ ] not [
5. [ ] [
6. His sanctuary [
7. to make for [
8. [
9. [
10. and [
11. and left [
12. and do not [
13. and do not [
14. His words/commandments [
15. to eliminate [

COMMENTS

Only the first words of fifteen lines are preserved in this column, thereby making reconstruction of the phrases difficult. Some comments may be suggested based on the context of this column within the composition, and by following the biblical origins of the preserved words that fit the context. Indeed, some major motifs of the biblical history of Israel may be discerned in this way. It may be suggested tentatively, based on the preserved words, that the content deals with the distinction of Israel from other nations, mentioned in col. i, intending to say that all the nations worship idols, for 'there is no breath in them' (lines 1–2), but Israel has been chosen to adhere to God, by keeping his commandments, and worshipping him in his Temple, which was built to glorify his name (lines 3–8). Israel is warned not to turn from the way of God towards heathen ways, since they are useless. Thus sinners are punished and abandoned to destruction (lines 11–15). A hint of the punishment of Israel is preserved in frg. 1b 6. This fragment may be placed at the upper part of the following column.

L. 1 בׄהׄםׄ. This may refer to Ps 135:18 concerning the nations who trust in idols (cf. Jer 10:15 [= 51:18]).

L. 2 בׄם. This may refer to Jer 10:14 (= 51:17), concerning idols, for 'there is no breath in them'.

L. 3 באלה תׄ°[. This perhaps paraphrases Jer 10:16 (= 51:19) לא כאלה חלק יעקב 'not like these is the portion of Jacob', as לא באלה תב[חר 'not in these you will choose' (cf. Josh 24:14, 15, 23). One may also propose another phrase such as באלה תמ[אס 'in these you will reject' (cf. Isa 31:7).

L. 4 בח[ ]לוא[. If the first word is the verb בחר, this line may refer to Deut 7:6-8, which states that God chose Israel to be his treasured people, not because they were the most numerous of the peoples, but because he favoured them and kept the oath He made to their forefathers.

L. 6 מׄקדשוׄ. This word may refer to Ps 78:69 concerning the building of the Temple on Mt. Zion.

L. 7 לעשות ל[. If this phrase is concerned with the Temple it may refer either to the offerings 'producing an odour pleasing to the Lord' (Num 15:3); or to the idea of making a glorious name to God (Isa 63:14; 64:10; 1 Chr 22:5; 29:13, etc.). The latter may be completed in line 8 (see below). The idea of making Israel the people of God for the sake of his great name (1 Sam 12:22; 2 Sam 7:23; Isa 63:12; 1 Chr 17:8, 21) is less plausible at this stage of the survey.

L. 8 האׄ[. Possibly read הארצות; cf. 1 Chr 22:5 והבית לבנות ליהוה . . . לשם ולתפארת לכל הארצות 'house to be built to the Lord . . . to win fame and glory throughout all the lands'.

L. 11 ושמׄאל. This may refer to the warning of Deut 5:2, etc., not to turn from God's commandments to the right or to the left (cf. 11QT^{a} LVI 7–8; 1QS I 15; III 10).

L. 12 ואל תׄ[. This is possibly another phrase referring to the aforementioned warning, such as אל תט (Prov 4:27); אל תפן אל און (Job 36:21); אל תטמאו (Lev 18:24); אל תאמר בלבבך (Deut 9:4); אל תמרדו (Josh 22:19); אל תשת ידך עם רשע (Exod 23:1), and the like.

L. 13 ואל ת[. See above, line 12.

L. 14 דבריו. Perhaps this refers to the commandments of God (cf. e.g. Deut 4:36; Ps 147:19).

L. 15 לבׄער א[. A phrase such as לבער את (cf. 2 Sam 4:11) or לבער אחרי (cf. 1 Kgs 14:10; 21:21) may refer to God's determination to destroy the sinners of Israel from the earth.

Frg. 1a

]◦ ◦[1

]◦◦ מ֯פניך[2

Mus. Inv. 333
PAM 43.396*

TRANSLATION

1.] [
2.] from your presence [

COMMENTS

L. 2 מ֯פניך[. If this word refers to driving great nations from the path of Israel and possessing their land (cf. Deut 4:38 etc.), it may be positioned in line 14 or 15 of frg. 1 i on the basis of its context.

Frg. 1b

]◦◦[1

]◦**א**[2

]◦◦[ ]◦[3

]◦◦◦ *vacat* ם֯[4

]◦◦[ ] ן֯[ ] ◦◦◦◦וש ם[5

]להביא ושלישיו ◦[6

]◦◦[7

Mus. Inv. 333
PAM 43.396*

TRANSLATION

1.] [
2.] [
3.] [ ] [
4.] *vacat* [
5.] and [ ] [ ] [
6.] and his officers to bring [
7.] [

COMMENTS

L. 6 ושלישיו להביא[. These words may refer to Ezek 23:23 concerning the officers of the nations whom God intended to bring to Jerusalem in chariots in order to punish its inhabitants for their sins. שליש in this context may be the third man in the chariot (cf. Exod 14:7, and see BDB 1026). If this suggestion is correct, this fragment may follow frg. 1 ii, possibly at the beginning of the next column. Alternatively, להביא may start a new sentence.

Frg. 2 i

1]
2]
3]
4]◦
5]◦◦יף

Mus. Inv. 356
PAM 41.978, 43.395*

NOTES ON READINGS

L. 5]◦◦יף. There is a similarity between the two latter letters and those seen in frg. 12 1.

Frg. 2 ii

1 [ ]◦
2 הׄבינׄוׄ נא בזאת החכמים אׄם יהיה
3 לאיש עץ טוב וׄיׄגׄבה עד לשמים[ ]לׄ[ ]
4 לאׄ◦◦יׄ ארצות וׄעׄשהׄ פרי שמן ◦◦◦ ◦◦
5 יורה ומלקוש יׄ◦◦[ ] בׄחׄרׄוׄ◦ ובצמה
6 הלוא אתו יאׄ[הב]◦◦◦◦רׄ ואתו ישמר
7 [ ]ים להרבות עפי
8 [ ]ל מׄנצרו לרבת
9 [ ]רו ודלתיו

]לׄ[ ] 10

○[ ] 11

Mus. Inv. 356
PAM 41.975, 41.978, 43.395*

NOTES ON READINGS

L. 5 בׄחׄרׄוׄ○. Read either בחרוף for בחורף 'in winter' (see COMMENTS, below), or בחרוב for בחורב 'in scorching heat'. The former is preferred on the basis of the remains of the last letter that appears to be a final *pe* (see the final *pe* of ויף in frg. 12 1, pl XII).

L. 6 ואתו. *PC* suggests אינו, but *taw* seems to be the correct reading, even though its upper line is not complete.

L. 6 ○○○ךׄ. Or ○○○ד.

TRANSLATION

1. [ ]
2. Discern this, O wise men: If a man will possess
3. a good tree that towers unto the sky [ ] [ ]
4. lands, and it produces the best fruit
5. early and late rains [ ] in winter (or: in scorching heat and in thirst)
6. Is it not that he lo[ves] it [ ] and that he guards it
7. [ ] to increase branches
8. [ ] from its root to rear
9. [ ] and its branches
10. [ ] [
11. [ ]

COMMENTS

The admonition to Israel in frg. 2 ii–iii is written in the form of a sapiential parable. The opening formula הׄבׄינׄוׄ נא בזאת החכמים and the first lines of the parable are quite well preserved. Such formulae are used in the admonitions of 4Q**381** 76–77 8; CD I 1, II 2, 14, but also in sapiential works (cf. 4Q**413** 1 1). However, in the distinctly sapiential compositions from Qumran (4Q**416**–4Q**418**) different formulae are used which refer to a single listener and include phrases such as הבט [ ] ברז נהיה, רז נהיה דרוש and the like (see 4Q**416** 2 iii 14–15; 4Q**417** 2 i 6–8, 18–19 and parallels; 4Q**418** 77 1–3). The content and wording of the parable of 4Q**302** are based on parables of trees similar to those found in Isa 5:1-6; Jer 2:21, Ezek 19:10-14; Ps 80:9-17; and Dan 4:7-14, 17-18. Some words and phrases referring to the moral ending of the fable may be identified in frg. 3, while its beginning may be found in the historical survey of frg. 1. As in many of the biblical parables of trees, the tree here may symbolize Israel, whom God raised up and treated as His chosen nation but whom He intended to abandon and destroy, were Israel to sin. If the parable delivers an additional message it may be clarified in frg. 3 ii, or more likely in frg. 3 iii.

L. 2 הׄבׄינׄוׄ נא בזאת החכמים. An opening call (cf. Prov 8:5; 4Q**381** 1 2; 49 2; 76–77 8), addressed to the wise men; cf. Job 34:2; 1QH[a] I 35. 4Q**418** [4QInstruction A[a]] 81 20; cf. also CD I 1; II 2, 14). For בזאת ('in this') cf. 4Q**521** 2 ii + 4 4 הלוא בזאת תמצאו אדני כל המיחלים בלבם and also 4Q**418** 81 4 (בזה כבדהו

בהתקדשכה), referring to the words immediately following or mentioned generally in that context. Cf. also many biblical verses (e.g. Gen 34:15, 22; 42:15; Exod 7:17; Ps 50:22, etc.).

Ll. 2–3 אם יהיה לאיש. The opening clause אם יהיה is not an introduction to a conditional sentence (Gen 28:20; Judg 6:37 etc.), or to an oath (1 Kgs 17:2; Jer 22:24, etc.), but rather an introduction to a judicial case (possibly אם + verb is like כי + verb. [cf. Deut 21:15, 18; 22:23; and likewise Lev 25:26; etc.; e.g. 11QT[a] XLV 7; LXIV 6–7, 9]).

L. 3 עץ טוב ו̇ג̇בה עד לשמים]. Cf. the parables of a tree in Ezek 19:11; Dan 4:7-8, 17-18. The phrase עץ טוב appears in 2 Kgs 3:19, 25.

L. 4 ל̇א̇°° ארצות. This is either a statement concerning the height of the tree (cf. Dan 4:8 וחזותה לסוף כל ארעא), or concerning its roots which grew down deeply and filled the land (cf. Ps 80:10).

L. 4 ו̇ע̇שה̇ פרי שמן. Cf. Dan 4:9. שמן ('fat') symbolizes the best (cf. Gen 27:39).

L. 5 [ ]°°̇י יורה ומלקוש. The granting of the early rain and the late rain in their seasons symbolizes the steadfast love of God for his people (Deut 11:14; Jer 5:24; Ezek 34:26-27; 4Q**285** 1 5 [= 11Q**14** (11QBer) 1–2 7–8] and possibly 4Q**262** 3 6). A verb such as יתן ('grant', Deut 11:14), ישקה ('water', cf. e.g. Psalm 104:13), יוריד ('rain', 'fall', 'drop', cf. Ps 72:6) or ירוה ('soak', cf. Isa 55:10) was possibly written either at the end of line 4 or as the third word of line 5.

L. 5 ב̇ח̇ר̇ו̇° ובצמה. For בחרוף ובצמה (= בחורף ובצמה) cf. Zech 14:8 בקיץ ובחרף ('in summer and winter'). For בחרוב ובצמה (= בחורב ובצמא), cf. Hag 1:11. The form of both חרוף and חרוב instead of חורף and חורב may be considered as the *Qtul* form, which appears in Qumran writings in words such as תכון (e.g. 1QS V 3) instead of the biblical תכן (Exod 5:18; Ezek 45:11). Cf. for example the parallel forms of 1QM and 4QM[a] (4Q**491**) אמוץ, חזוק (1QM XIV 6, 7) = אומץ, חוזק (4QM[a] 8–10 4). See E. Qimron, *The Hebrew of the Dead Sea Scrolls*, HSS 29 (Atlanta: Scholars Press, 1986) 37 (§ 200.24); 65–6 (§ 330.1); E. Y. Kutscher, *The Language and Linguistic Background of the Isaiah Scroll (1QIsa[a])* (STDJ VI; Leiden: E. J. Brill, 1974) 201, 203. Although a reconstructed phrase [ברעב] ובצמה is plausible (cf. Deut 28:48; 2 Chr 32:11), the traces of the preserved letters do not favour this reconstruction. The spelling צמה may reflect the noun צִמְאָה (cf. Jer 2:25), or the orthographical replacement of radical *ʾalep* by *he* in final position (see Qimron, *HDSS* 23 § 100.7).

L. 6 הלוא אתו י̇א̇[הב. This is a metaphorical phrase expressing the idea of God's love for Israel (cf. e.g. Deut 23:6c; Isa 63:9; Jer 31:3; Ps 47:5).

L. 6 ואתו ישמר. This is a metaphorical phrase reflecting the idea of God's protection of Israel from all harm (cf. Jer 31:9; Ps 121:4-8). See also הגפן הנטעת אשמ[ר in 6Q**11** ('Allegory of the Vine'), line 6.

L. 7 להרבות עפי. Cf. Ezek 31:5; Dan 4:9a, 18a; cf. also עפאים (עפים Q^{MSS} Ps 104:12, see BHK), and the descriptions of Ezek 19:10; Ps 80:11. However, the Aramaic word עפי appears in biblical writings only in Dan 4:9, 11, 18. The form עפאים in Ps 104:12 is a loan word (BDB 779; GK § 93z). In Qumran writings see עפיו of 4Q**433a** 2 8 (4QpapHodayot-like Text, PAM 43.255; = recto of 4Q**255** [4QpapS[a]]). The word ויף in frg. 12 1 may be associated with this description (cf. Ezek 31:7 וייף בגדלו 'it was beautiful in its greatness'). However, its correct position in the scroll is unknown. The verb להרבות ('to multiply') may refer metaphorically to the idea of Deut 7:13; 28:63a; 1 Chr 27:23; see line 8.

L. 8 מ̇נצרו לרבת. The word מנצרו 'from its shoot' refers to Isa 11:1 and Dan 11:7, where it occurs in the context of a shoot of a kingdom, while in Isa 60:21 it occurs in the context of the shoot of Israel. The verb לרבת may be understood either as meaning 'to rear' (cf. Ezek 19:2), or 'to multiply' (cf., e.g. Gen 1:22; Deut 30:16). The idea of rearing may be appropriate here, but referring to Israel, not to a king. The latter meaning may refer to the multiplicity of Israel (cf. 1 Kgs 4:20; Isa 60:22).

L. 9]רו ודלתיו. דלתיו (= דליותיו) is the plural of דלת (= דלית, stem דלה), branch plus a 3rd masc. suffix. See GK § 84[a]; BDB 194, 1QH[a] VII 9, and 4Q**262** 3 2. For the defective spelling of this word see דלותו (= דליותיו) in 4Q**262** 3 1 (PAM 42.380, 43.267), and Qimron, *HDSS* 19 (§ 100.32).]רו may refer to a verb such as נשברו, in which case the statement would refer to the destruction of the tree (cf. Jer 11:16; Ezek 31:12). This idea appears clearly in frg. 2 iii (see lines 6–7).

Frg. 2 iii

]○○ ○○○ 1

קצי ○[2

] 3

] 4

] 5

ויכסמוהו חז̊]ירים 6

ויכ̇רת ב̇לוא ○[7

לכ̇[8

Mus. Inv. 356
PAM 43.395*

NOTES ON READINGS

L. 6 חז̊]ירים. The trace of the second letter is probably the *zayin* of חזיר/ים (cf. Ps 80:14). A *yod* suggesting חיות is less likely, despite the parallel idea in Isa 18:5-6; Jer 12:9; Ezek 31:13; 32:4, etc.

TRANSLATION

1. [
2. epochs [
3. [
4. [
5. [
6. bo[ars] ravaged [
7. and it was cut down without [
8. [

COMMENTS

The preserved words of lines 6–7 continue the parable of the tree, referring to the motif of its destruction, based on Ps 80:14 and other biblical verses. However, while the main wording of the composition is in Biblical Hebrew, the word קצי of line 2 represents a later term. According to the context, קצי may concern epochs of wrath or desolation.

L. 2 קצי ○[. A construct state of קצים. The pl. form is not attested in classical Hebrew, but in post-biblical and Mishnaic Hebrew, meaning 'periods' (Qimron, *HDSS* 68, 95, 103). See E. Y. Kutscher, 'The Hebrew and Aramaic Tongue of the Dead Sea Scrolls', *The Language and Linguistic Background of the Isaiah Scroll* (Jerusalem, 1959) 50–53, esp. 52 [Heb.]. Perhaps קצי חרון 'epochs of wrath' (cf. 1QH[a] III 28; frg. 1 5; CD I 5 [= 4QD[b] 2 i 10]; 4QD[b] 18 v 19; 4QD[a] 1 5 [= 4QD[b] 2 i 3]; 4QD[e] 11 ii 13; 4QpHos[a] I 12), or קצי חרבן 'epochs of desolation' (cf. CD V 20 [= 4QD[b] 3 ii 15]). If either of these reconstructions is correct, it may refer not to the future (1QH[a] III 28), but to the past or to the present.

L. 6 ויכסמוהו חׄז[ירים. Cf. Ps 80:14 יכרסמנה חזיר 'the boar . . . ravages it'. The author used a form of כסם ('shear', 'clip', BDB 493) in the plural, instead of the quadriliteral form כרסם, used in Ps 80:14 in the singular. The verb כסם appears in Ezek 44:20, quoted in *b. Sanh.* 22b; *b. Ned.* 51a; *Yal.* II.v.383; Maimonides, 'Laws of the Temple's Utensils', 5:6. E. Qimron (private communication) assumes that כרסם in Ps 80:14 represents the secondary form of כסם. For such cases of resolution of gemination with *reš*, see Aramaic כָּרְסֵא = Hebrew כִּסֵּא = Akkadian *kussū*; Aramaic דַּרְמֶשֶׂק = Hebrew דַּמֶּשֶׂק. According to the plural form, the noun was probably חזירים, 'boars'. As for the content and idea of this metaphor, the author may also have had in mind Isa 18:5-6 and Jer 22:7.

L. 7 ויכׄרת בׄלוא ◦[. The cutting of trees symbolizes the destruction of the land in Isa 18:5; Jer 22:7; 46:23; etc. בלוא may refer to the phrase בלוא הון and the like (cf. Ps 44:13; 4Q**504** 1–2 ii 15), meaning to despise something.

Frg. 3 i

1-6 [ ]
7]להי◦

Mus. Inv. 356
PAM 41.978, 43.395*

Frg. 3 ii

1 [ ]יד יתר
2 [ ]אׄלהיכם
3 [ ]◦◦
4 [ ]◦ לבבכם אׄ[ ]◦
5 [ ]בׄנׄפׄש חׄפצה *vacat*
6 [ ]יקום אלהים מידכם בׄמעלכם
7 [פרי מ]חשבתיכם ולא עמד לנגדך להוכח
8 עׄמך ולהשיב דבר בריבך *vacat*
9 [ ]◦ אלהים בשמׄים משבו וממ[שלתו]
10 בארצות בימים ◦[ ]◦◦◦ בהם וראׄ[
11 עׄמׄ ◦◦◦◦תׄ[ ]לׄ[

Mus. Inv. 356
PAM 41.975, 43.395*

NOTES ON READINGS

L. 1 יתר. The *reš* has a long leg. See PALAEOGRAPHY.

TRANSLATION

1. [ ]
2. [ ] your God
3. [ ]
4. [ ] your heart [ ]
5. [ ]with deep desire. *vacat*
6. [ ]God will take vengeance on you for your betrayal
7. [the fruit of] your [sch]emes, and he did not confront you to argue
8. with you and reply to your contention *vacat*
9. [ ] God's seat is in the heavens, and [His] he[gemony]
10. is over lands (and) seas [ ] in them and
11. [ ] [

COMMENTS

The text of this column consists of three sections, separated from each other by a *vacat* (lines 5, 8). The first section consists of a description of the guilt of Israel (lines 1–5, or 3–5). The second section comprises the decree of the punishment (lines 6–8) and the third section describes the inspection of God, the sovereign and judge of the universe (lines 9–10). These subjects may form the conclusion of the parable and its message. In the preserved lines of the parable there is no explicit reason for the abandonment of the tree, and indeed, none may been given, considering the possibility that it may have been alluded to in the historical survey of the preceding part (frg. 1 ii). In any event, from the text preserved in the first section of frg. 3 ii, it may be understood that Israel, being aware of breaking God's commandments (see above frg. 1 ii 11) is explicitly blamed for willful transgression, even taking delight in its transgressions (lines 4–5). Therefore, as stated in the second section, its punishment was predictable (lines 6–7a). Nevertheless, this section refers to a controversy between Israel and God (lines 7–8), possibly reacting against Israel's claims. According to biblical and post-biblical books, these may be either polemical claims against God's punishment of Israel (cf. Ezek 18:2; 20:32), or against the justice of God (cf. Hab 1:12-13 and later writings such as the book of Job, Mal 2:17; 3:14; 4Q**381** 76–77 10–11). Possibly the author of this composition may be referring to such claims against God's justice in his generation. However, from the statement in lines 7–8, it may be understood that God's decree is final, and Israel's claims will not even be considered. Moreover, the third section (lines 9–10) demonstrates the author's awareness of the justice of God, the supreme ruler of the whole universe. Therefore, this section ends with a conclusion that is not controversial, but refers to the wide spectrum of God's sovereignty and judgement. The words preserved in lines 10–11 may refer to the omnipresence of God, who views all the earth, watching all nations, even those who oppress Israel while it is being punished. If this assumption is correct, it may be suggested that a turning to God's mercy towards Israel and his wrath against Israel's enemies comes here.

L. 1 יד יתר[. The meaning of יתר is obscure. It could perhaps be a noun meaning 'remnant', or an adjective or adverb meaning 'exceeding'. Another suggestion is a verb in the 3rd person sing. of the *Piʿel* future, derived from יתר or from נתר, or possibly a defective spelling of the *Qal* יתור derived from תור. The latter suggestion may fit the context. Such a phrase as [תמ]יד יתר [לבבכם אחר גלוליכם], or the like, may fit the idea of line 5 (see below). Cf. Deut 29:16-17; Ezek 14:3-7; 1QS II 11; CD XX 9–10. For the collocation of תור and לב see Num 15:39; תרתי בלבי (Eccl 2:3); מתור לבו (1QS III 3).

L. 4 ◦[ ]לבבכם אֹ. This word may refer to verses such as Num 15:39, Deut 11:16 or the like. See below line 5.

L. 5 בְֹנֹפֹש חֹפצה[. This idiom, meaning 'deep desire' may be used positively, as in ועבדהו בלב שלם ובנפש הפצה (1 Chr 28:19, cf. Josh 23:5, 14 etc.), which might have been appropriate to lines 4–5. However, according to the context (see lines 6–7), a negative meaning such as that found in Isa 66:3 ובשקוציהם נפשם חפצה, 'in their abominations their soul takes delight', is more likely here.

L. 6 יקום אלהים מידכם בֹּמעלכם[. Cf. Lev 26:25; Ezek 39:23; CD I 3–4, 17–18. This idea is also reflected in 4QInstruction A[a] (4Q**418** 126 ii 6). For the idiom נקם מיד, cf. 2 Kgs 9:7.

L. 7 מ]חשבתיכם. A phrase such as [פרי מ]חשבתיכם may have been written here, harmonizing Jer 6:19 and 21:14. Other possibilities are [ורוע מ]חשבתיכֹם (cf. Prov 15:26), or [ואון מ]חשבתיכֹם (cf. Isa 59:7; Jer 4:14; Prov 6:18).

Ll. 7–8 ולא עמד לנגדך להוכח עֹמך ולהשיב דבר בריבך. See the idea of 4Q**381** 76–77 10 מי בכם ישיב דבר ויעמד בהתוכח עמו. E. Schuller has translated this, 'who among you will reply, and (who) will stand in controversy with Him', taking this statement as a continuation of the phrase of Mic 6:2 כי ריב ליהוה עם עמו ועם ישראל יתוכח (*Non-Canonical Psalms from Qumran*, HSS 28 [Atlanta: Scholars Press, 1986] 218, 222). A similar idea appears in Prov 21:30, including the statement אין . . . לנגד יהוה, 'no . . . can prevail against the Lord' (cf. Job 31:14; 2 Bar 14:9).

However, another facet of this idea may be indicated here. If the 2nd person in this statement refers to Israel, as is the case in 4Q**302** in general, this statement is possibly addressed to Israel, emphasizing that any attempt to dispute with God is useless because God's sovereignty and judgement are final (see below, lines 9–10), and he will not even attend to Israel's claims. For this idea, cf. Job 9:3. (According to Isa 1:15; Jer 7:16; 11:14; 15:1; Ps 5:6, Israel's invocations will not be listened to while it still transgresses God's laws.)

L. 9 אלהים בשמֹים משבו. See Ps 103:19, and cf. Isa 6:1; 66:1; Ezek 1:26; 4QBer[a] (= 4Q**286**) 1 ii 1; 4Q**405** 20 ii–22 9–10. In the context of 4Q**302** 3 ii this statement expresses God's sovereignty and judgement above all.

Ll. 9–10 וממ]שלתו בארצות בימים. See Ps 135:5-6 and Jer 10:11. Cf. Ps 47:3; 89:10-12; 103:22; 1 Chr 29:12; 2 Chr 20:6.

L. 10 וראֹ[. A verb וראה (perfect of *Qal* with *waw* consecutive) meaning 'will look, observe', concerning God who observes all the inhabitants of the earth from his heavenly dwelling, may be suggested here on the basis of Ps 138:6; Job 28:24 (see below). This word presupposes the introduction of a new subject, possibly the judgement of God against all nations, especially those who oppress Israel (see Deut 32:27-43). Cf. especially יראה in Deut 32:36.

Frg. 3 iii

ולא כן [1

יבערו [2

ואיךְ לֹ◦רנ◦[3

Mus. Inv. 356
PAM 41.975, 43.395*

TRANSLATION

1. but not so [
2. they shall behave foolishly [
3. and how [

COMMENTS

Only the first words of three lines are preserved in the upper part of frg. 3 iii. Nevertheless, presuming the biblical origins of the preserved words, one may tentatively postulate that these words refer to the foolish pride of the nations, Israel's adversaries (cf. Isa 16:6; Jer 10:8-10). Thus, the putative continuation of this subject may speak of a conciliation with Israel, possibly in the spirit of Deut 32:36 (להתנחם 'have compassion' [RSV] which is preserved in frg. 3c, or 'take revenge' [NJPS]; they may refer both to Deut 32:36 and Isa 1:24).

L. 1] ולא כן. If our suggestion concerning the context of frg. 3 ii 10–11 is correct, the negative clause ולא כן may refer to the negation of the pride of the nations over Israel (cf. Isa 16:6).

L. 2] יבערו. In Jer 10:8 one finds the verb יבערו concerning the ignorance and foolishness of nations that worship idols, but who are helpless against the wrath of God. This idea is appropriate here rather than the suggestion that this word refers to the punishment of the nations by fire (Isa 30:33; 34:9; Nah 2:14; Mal 3:19; Ps 83:15).

L. 3]°ואיך֯ ל֯°רנ. If the aforementioned reconstructed context is correct, one may detect here the idea found also in Isa 16:10 concerning the lament of the nations following their desolation. Here the verb may be reconstructed as להרנין (cf. Deut 32:43; Ps 81:2).

Fragments 3a, 3b, 3c

Fragments 3a and 3b (PAM 43.395, Mus. Inv. 356), containing a left margin, preserve the left edge of a column. Frg. 3b has in its last line the two beginning letters of a line from the next column. Based on their physical position, they may be placed to the right of frg. 3 ii. It is possible that the space at the upper edge of frg. 3a is a top margin. However, the poor preservation of the text in these fragments renders it impossible to ascertain their placement. Frg. 3c may also belong to the same column, or to column 3 ii, based not on its position, but on its contents (see COMMENTS).

Frg. 3a

]ימי 1
]° 2

Mus. Inv. 356
PAM 41.978; 43.395

Frg. 3b i

1 ◦◦◦◦[
2 ם◦◦[
3 *vacat* [
4 *vacat* [
5]ם ◦פל
6]◦זרע כ◦
7 [

Mus. Inv. 356
PAM 41.978; 43.395

TRANSLATION

6.] seed [

Frg. 3b ii

1–6 [ ]
7 [ ]◦ו

Mus. Inv. 356
PAM 43.395

COMMENTS

L. 7 The visible letters may be part of the opening word of frg. 3 ii 7, if frg. 3b ii pertains to the same sheet.

Frg. 3c

1]◦ להתנ̊חם̊

Mus. Inv. 356
PAM 41.978; 43.395

Translation

1.] to have compassion

Comments

L. 1 להתנחם. This may be a reference to Deut 32:36; Ps 135:14, seeking the compassion of God for His people on the last day.

Frg. 4

]◦ב[

] *vacat*

]◦◦◦[ ]◦[

Mus. Inv. 333
PAM 41.978; 43.396

Frg. 5

]לוא[

]ותיכם [

]פאים ◦[

]◦כמה *vacat*

]◦◦

Mus. Inv. 333
PAM 41.975; 43.396

Notes on Readings

L. 2]ותיכם. The first trace of a letter may be of *waw* or *yod*. The second vestige may be of medial *nun*, or of *taw*. *Taw* is suggested based on the trace of an upper horizontal line seen under a stain. A crack renders it impossible to detect a right leg on the papyrus.

L. 3]פאים. The first trace may be of medial *pe* or of *yod*. *Pe* is suggested based on the vestige of a horizontal lower line. For the form of the curled upper line cf. אפים in frg. 1 i 3 and frg. 10 2.

Frg. 6

1]
2 ל◦◦]
3 ב֯]
4 ל֯ח֯]

Mus. Inv. 333
PAM 41.975; 43.396

NOTES ON READINGS

This fragment consists of traces of letters from the right edge of the lines, and is to be placed at the right edge of a column.

Frg. 7

1]◦תצו ו◦[

Mus. Inv. 333
PAM 43.396

NOTES ON READINGS

L. 1]◦תצו. The first trace is of the lower horizontal line of a letter, perhaps a medial *nun*.

Frg. 8

1]◦◦ ◦◦ ◦[
2]◦ה מ֯י י֯מ֯◦◦
3]ש֯ה֯יו֯ *vacat*

bottom margin

Mus. Inv. 333
PAM 43.396. M123

NOTES ON READINGS

L. 3]שׄהׄיׄוׄ. *Waw* is suggested based on a small lower vestige that may belong to the leg of the letter.

TRANSLATION

3.] which were *vacat*

Frg. 9

]◦ם בׄמׄ◦[1

]רׄעו חיׄ◦[2

]א ל◦◦[3

Mus. Inv. 333
PAM 43.396

COMMENTS

L. 2]רׄעו. If the word reflects a form of רעה (pasture, graze), this fragment may have pertained to the parable of the tree.

Frg. 10

]◦מׄר ◦[ ]ו והנׄהׄ [1

]עׄפׄי שיח ◦◦◦◦[2

]לׄ[3

Mus. Inv. 333
PAM 41.978; 43.396

NOTES ON READINGS

L. 1]◦מׄר. The *reš* has a long leg (see PALAEOGRAPHY).

TRANSLATION

1.] [ ] and indeed [
2.] branches of the bush [
3.] [

COMMENTS

L. 2]עׄפׄי שיח. This phrase suggests that the fragment may pertain to the parable of the tree. The

Aramaic noun עפיה appears in Dan 4:9, 11, 18, concerning the branches of a tree.

Frg. 11

1]עׄרה ויזו[

2]לׄ[

Mus. Inv. 333
PAM 41.978; 43.396

COMMENTS

L. 1]עׄרה ויזו[. One may putatively suggest here a phrase such as [ה]ערה ויזו[בו מים] (cf. Gen 24:20; Isa 48:21; Ps 78:20; 105: 41), pertaining to the first part of the parable. However, a phrase concerning destruction such as ערה ויזו[עו] may belong to the latter part of the parable (cf. Zeph 2:14; Ps 137:7; Eccl 12:3; Hab 2:7; 1QS viii 8).

Frg. 12

1]ויף [

2]◦[

Mus. Inv. 333
PAM 43.396

COMMENTS

L. 1]ויף[. If the preserved letters are a complete word, meaning ‘it was beautiful’, it may pertain to the parable of the tree (cf. Ezek 31:7).

Frg. 13

1]◦מ[

2]◦ר◦◦[

Mus. Inv. 333
PAM 41.978; 43.396

Frg. 14

]◦◦ה̊ [

]לטה א[

Inv. 333
PAM 43.396

NOTES ON READINGS

L. 2 א[. *ʾAlep* is suggested based on vestiges of two upper arms and a lower trace at the right side.

Frg. 15

] וכ̊ב̊[

]◦[

Mus. Inv. 333
PAM 41.978; 43.396

Frg. 16

]ו אם ◦◦ר̇[

Mus. Inv. 333
PAM 41.978; 43.396

Frg. 17

]יו[ ]◦[

]ר יהיה [

Mus. Inv. 333
PAM 41.978; 43.396

NOTES ON READINGS

L. 2 ר[. The *reš* has a long leg (see PALAEOGRAPHY).

TRANSLATION

2.] will be [

Frg. 18

1 ◦[ ]◦[

2]◦ אׄת[

Mus. Inv. 333
PAM 41.978; 43.396

303. 4QMeditation on Creation A

(PLATE XIII)

Physical Description

THIS text (*olim* 4QMeditation on Creation A^{a}) consists of several fragments of dark brown skin. A clear upper margin is visible, but no left, right or bottom margin is preserved. Fourteen lines are extant.[1]

Contents

The title originally given to this text, 'Meditation on Creation A', is retained here, since it appropriately describes what appears to be a reflection on God's creation. Based on the narratives of the opening chapters of Genesis, 4Q**303** recounts the works of God in nature as well as in man: God has set up the eternal light and lustrous heaven and replaced the primordial emptiness and void; in man He has instilled the understanding of good and evil and given to him a woman/wife as helper. The context of this reflection on creation is not clear, but if the first two lines are rendered at all correctly, then it seems that lessons are being drawn from the created order to illustrate the wondrous work of God, an admonition that has at its heart moral and ethical implications.

Palaeography

The text is written in a late Hasmonaean or early Herodian formal hand, dating to *c.*50–1 BCE (see nos. 3 and 4, F. Cross, 'Development of the Jewish Scripts', *The Bible and the Ancient Near East: Essays in Honor of William Foxwell Albright*, ed. G. Ernest Wright [Garden City, N.Y.: Doubleday, 1961] 138).

Mus. Inv. 350
PAM 41.516, 43.397*

---

[1] Many thanks are expressed to E. Tov and P. Hayman for their comments on the preliminary draft of 4Q**303** and to E. Qimron for his notes and suggestions to 4Q**303–305**.

top margin

1]מבינים שמעו ו◦[

2]מ̇ים וישביתו מעל נ̇[

3]א{ס̇◦ר̇◦◦} נפלאות אל אש]ר

4]ל̊אור עולם ושמי טוה]ר

5 או]ר במקום תהווב[הו

6]כולמעשיהם עד ק◦[

7]ר בם מלך לכולם[

8]ר ושכל טוב ורע ל̇[

אדם

9]לוקח ממנה כי א̊[

10 ו]עשה לו עזר כ[נגדו

11]לו לאשה כיא ממנו[לקחה זאת

12]חה *vacat* [

13]ל לפי[

14]ל̇[

Notes on Readings

L. 1 Traces of a letter appear after the *waw*. B. Z. Wacholder and M. G. Abegg, *A Preliminary Edition of the Unpublished Dead Sea Scrolls. The Hebrew and Aramaic Texts from Cave Four. Fascicle Two* (Washington: Biblical Archaeology Society, 1992) 232, transcribe the final two letters as וי.

L. 2 Only tiny traces of the initial *mem* of מים can be seen. The final letter may be a *nun* or *kap*.

L. 3 There may be five or more letters at the beginning of this line.

L. 4 The top of a *lamed* can be seen at the beginning of the line.

L. 5 The transcription חוש]ך במקומי of Wacholder and Abegg, *Preliminary Edition*, 232, is unlikely. For the spacing of תהווב[הו cf. line 6 below.

L. 6 The *lamed* is written immediately before the *mem* of מעשיהם. It is unlikely, however, that this is a preposition, since there appear to be the tops of two further letters before it. It is better to consider the proximity of the *lamed* as a case of mistaken spacing. The reconstruction of כו for the first two letters and the word as כול is in keeping with the *plene* spelling of the word (cf. line 7, לכולם). Qimron suggests reading קץ, 'until the time of'.

L. 7 Wacholder and Abegg, *Preliminary Edition*, 232, restore the first word to אש]ר.

L. 8 The preserved portion of the first letter suggests that it is a *reš*. The angular stroke of the final letter of the line probably belongs to a *lamed*. Qimron suggests the restoration ל[הבין.

L. 9 Although traces of the last letter are too tiny for a secure identification, the conjunction has been restored to כיא in accordance with the Qumran spelling of the word (cf. line 11). אדם is a scribal correction written interlinearly above כיא.

L. 11 Gen 2:23. לו[is likely to be the preposition plus 3rd masc. sing. pronominal suffix.

L. 12 Gen 2:23. The *vacat* may indicate the end of a paragraph.

L. 13 Probably the beginning of a new section.

Translation

1.]having understood, they listened and[
2.]*mym* and they caused treachery to cease *n*[
3.] . . . . . wonderful acts of God whi[ch
4.]for eternal light and cle[ar] heaven[
5. ligh]t in place of emptiness and vo[id
6.]all their deeds until *q*◦[
7.]*r* among them, a king for all of them[
8.]*r* and insight of good and evil, to[
9.]a man takes from it because [
10. and]He made for him a helper fit[for him
11. He gave her] to him for a wife, because from him[she was taken
12.]*ḥh vacat*[
13.]*l* according to[
14.]*l*[

Comments

L. 1 שמעו. Alternatively 'listen' or 'hear'. Qimron suggests that the plural participle may refer to 'sages', namely those of understanding, and translates as 'sages listened and'. In a similar vein he restores the first word of line 2 to חכ]מים.

L. 3 נפלאות אל is found in Job 37:14. The notion that creation is the splendid work of God occurs in 1QH[a] 1 33–34 and 11 28. Perhaps the sense here is 'the wonderful acts of God which He has performed mightily' (or 'confirmed'; הגביר cf. 1QH[a] 2 24; 4 8, 23).

L. 4 Qimron suggests 'heaven of brightness'.

L. 5 תהוו]בהו. Gen 1:2 and Jer 4:23. The *reš* may have been the final letter of אור, 'light' (so Qimron).

L. 8 Cf. 1QH[a] 11 28.

L. 9 Or לוקח ממנה כי[א] אדם, 'one taking from it, because a man'. The antecedent of 'it' may be 'the ground'.

L. 10 Cf. אעשה לו עזר כנגדו ('I shall make for him a suitable helper') Gen 2:18.

L. 11 Perhaps read ונתנה (so Qimron). Cf. Gen 2:23.

304. 4QMeditation on Creation B

(PLATE XIII)

Physical Description and Palaeography

AT 2.8 cm (height) and 2.9 cm (width), this tiny fragment (*olim* 4QMeditation on Creation A^{b}) preserves a right and possibly also a top margin. It is written in a scribal hand of the Hasmonaean period and is different from the script of 4Q**305**.

Mus. Inv. 295
PAM 41.662, 42.934, 43.397*

top margin (?)

ואת הארץ וכו[ל צבאם

החשך על כן נ◦]

עשה ◦◦◦]

TRANSLATION

1. and the earth and al[l their host
2. the darkness, therefore *n* . [
3. He made . . . [

COMMENTS

L. 1 Gen 2:1. Cf. 4Q**422** 1 6 וכול[צבאם עשה דבר]ו.

305. 4QMeditation on Creation C

(PLATE XIII)

Physical Description and Palaeography

THE legible portion of 4Q**305** (*olim* 4QMeditation on Creation B) consists of some four lines with a clear top and right margin. To the right of this are tiny pieces belonging to the same skin that have been reinforced with paper tissue.[1] In *DJD* XIII (Oxford: Clarendon Press, 1994) 423, T. Elgvin and E. Tov suggested that this legible portion is in fact 'column ii' of the same text. It seems unlikely that the badly mutilated right side belongs to the same text as 'column i', since the upper margin is not aligned to that of the left side. So far as I am aware, there is no example of a Qumran text that has different top margins for adjacent columns of the same text. The handwriting, so far as can be determined, is the same for both the left and right sides; however, a scribe can copy more than one text on the same skin or papyrus. It seems more probable, then, that what is preserved here are two different texts, the left side of which is 'Meditation on Creation C', while the right has preserved single and partial letters of a different composition (perhaps 4Q**305a**).

Only the legible left side is translated below.

Mus. Inv. 295
PAM 41.797, 42.559, 42.610, 43.397*

Col. i

]○[1

]רי[ ]○[

○[ ]○מ○[2

]○○[ ]מ ל[3

]○י[4

[1] Thanks are expressed to T. Elgvin for checking this at the Rockefeller Museum.

Col. ii

top margin

ויברא בו חיות[ ]◦[1

נתן לאדם דע[ת 2

ורֹעֹ[ ]לדֹעֹתֹ[3

ל[4

NOTES ON READINGS

L. 1 Elgvin and Tov, *DJD* XIII, 423, can apparently read [הא]ר[ץ].

TRANSLATION

col. ii

1. and He created in it animals[
2. He gave to man knowled[ge
3. and evil(?)[ ]to know(?)[
4. *l*[

411. 4QSapiential Hymn

(PLATE XIV)

Physical Description

ONLY one fragment of this manuscript has survived.[1] The skin, of medium thickness, is buff in colour, turning to dark brown where stained. The back is extremely coarse and grey-yellow in colour. The surface is somewhat shiny; mottled, but well preserved. The ink is poorly fixed and has eroded in places. There are no traces of either horizontal or vertical dry lines, but guide dots for the ruling of lines are visible in col. ii (cf. e.g. 4Q**418** and 4Q**365**). The space between the lines is approximately 0.55 cm, with some irregularity (e.g. 0.7 cm between lines 8 and 9). The average letter height is approximately 0.2 cm. Remains of two columns are extant, separated by a sewn seam. Only the last two letters of the first line are preserved in col. i; the beginnings of the first seventeen lines remain in col. ii. The original number of lines per column is unknown. The right margin of the second sheet is approximately 1 cm wide, and the left margin of the preceding sheet may have been of a similar dimension. The top margin of the scroll measured at least 1 cm.

Palaeography

The hand is a formal Hasmonaean, dating from the first century BCE close to the beginning of the Herodian period. However, no *keraiai* are evident, and *bet*, for example, is still written with one stroke.

Orthography

In terms of orthography, the use of *ʾalep* instead of *he* for -*ê* is significant in the case of הנא instead of הנה in frg. 1 ii 4 (cf. also והנא twice in 4QD[a]).

Contents

The use of the tetragrammaton suggests a pre-Qumran origin of the work. The preserved section is perhaps hymnic in character; the topic of creation, especially, might indicate its sapiential nature.

---

[1] The editor wishes to extend cordial thanks to Prof. J. Strugnell for his advice and for making available to her his transcriptions and preliminary notes on 4Q**411**. Special thanks are due to Prof. E. Puech for re-examining the manuscript.

Mus. Inv. 292
PAM 41.286, 41.347, 42.836, 42.916*, 43.499

Frg. 1 i

1]לׄו

NOTES ON READINGS
Only remains of the end of the first line have been preserved.

Frg. 1 ii

1 [ו]תשמח בחכ֯[מה/ת
2 יהׄוה פן יס֯ח[ר
3 טוב יום אח֯ד[
4 הנא החלתי ל֯[
5 לאדם והוא ב֯[
6 ידעתי את [
7 מי חכם וׄ◦[
8 וגאל ב֯צה ◦[
9 ותבונתו מי [
10 ב֯אהל לש]בת
11 ב֯שר֯ יהו]ה ברא
12 יהוה ברא הׄ[
13 יהוה ברא ש֯[מים
14 הופיעו לא֯[
15 להרׄאות֯[
16 לשעש֯[וע(ים)

[י]הו̊ה̊[17

NOTES ON READINGS

L. 2 יס̊ח[ר. *Samek* is preferable to *qop*. Strugnell (*PC*) suggested יקח.

L. 7 ו̊○[. Remains of a letter after *waw* (read as certain in Strugnell's notes) have now eroded.

L. 8 ב̊צה ○[. The first letter is *bet* or *kap*; *pe* seems to be excluded (cf. lines 2 and 14). The last letter is perhaps *lamed*.

L. 10 ב̊אהל. *Bet* is preferable to *kap*; cf. חכם line 7.

L. 11 ב̊שר̊. The last letter is *reš* or *dalet*.

L. 13 ש̊[. *Šin* is preferable to *ʾalep*.

L. 16 לשעש̊[וע(ים). The second *šin* is probable.

L. 17 [י]הו̊ה̊[. *Ḥet* and *dalet* are also possible in place of the second *he*.

TRANSLATION

1. [and] you take pleasure in wis[dom
2. YHWH, lest he go ab[out
3. good is one day[
4. behold, I began to[
5. concerning man, and he [
6. I knew the [
7. who is wise and [
8. and redeemed a swamp [
9. and his understanding, who [
10. in a tent to d[well
11. flesh. YHW[H created
12. YHWH created [
13. YHWH created h[eaven
14. they shine out [
15. to appear[
16. for deli[ght
17. [Y]HWH[

COMMENTS

L. 3 Cf. Ps 84:11 ('better is') and Qoh 7:1.

L. 4 החלתי. 1st person sing. *Hipʿil* perfect; either God, a human being, or perhaps wisdom, could be the subject; cf. Deut 2:31 and 1 Sam 22:15.

L. 5 לאדם. 'Mankind' is indicated rather than 'Adam'.

L. 7 Cf. Hos 14:10.

L. 8 וגאל ב̊צה ○[. The meaning of this line is rather uncertain. גאל might be either from I גאל or from II גאל (*Piʿel*), 'pollute'. On בצה, cf. Job 8:11, 40:21. If I גאל, 'redeem', is correct (much more common than II גאל), and בצה is the object of the sentence, the closest parallels would be Lev 25:26, 33 and Ruth 4:4, 6. It might perhaps be an allusion to the redemption of mankind. כצה instead of בצה is contextually inappropriate.

Ll. 9–10 In the case that the palaeographically less probable כ̊ (instead of ב̊) should be correct, cf. Isa 40:22 (heavens).

L. 11 To fit the context of lines 12 and 13, יהו[ה ברא might perhaps be completed.

Ll. 12–13 On the sequence: designation for God + ברא, cf. 1QS III 17, 25. Read perhaps יהוה ברא ש]מים, cf. e.g. 1 Chr 16:26 (rather than e.g. יהוה ברא א]דם). The style of 4Q**411** might not have been highly elegant; see the repetition in lines 12 and 13.

L. 14 הופיעו לא̊[. 'Shine out' or 'cause to shine out'. The pl. הופיעו is uncommon. It might refer either to angels or to the sun, moon, and/or the stars. If the reading of *ʾalep* in the second word is correct, a form of אור might perhaps be completed at the end.

L. 15 *Nipʿal* or *Hipʿil*, 'cause to see'.

L. 16 The Torah might be the object of delight; cf. especially Psalm 119.

L. 17 Or, e.g. ו]הוד[or, less probably, י]הוד[ה.

412. 4QSapiential-Didactic Work A

(PLATE XIV)

Physical Description

FOUR fragments appear to belong to this manuscript, though it is uncertain whether frg. 4 is indeed part of 4Q**412**, as the handwriting is not identical.[1] The skin of 4Q**412** is stiff and of medium thickness. Its surface is mottled and is peeling in places. Its colour is dark brown turning to red. On the largest fragment, frg. 1, remains of the right margin are preserved (*c*.0.8 cm). The distance between lines is 0.5–0.7 cm, and the letter height is *c*.0.2–0.3 cm.

Palaeography and Orthography

The hand of 4Q**412** dates to the first century BCE. It is written in a late Hasmonaean or early Herodian formal script. The orthography shows a tendency to *plene* writing, see e.g. בכול (frg. 1 7), and מעוון (frg. 1 3), but note הדות (frg. 1 8), probably for הודות and ידעים for יודעים (frg. 4 4). Only long pronominal suffixes are used, see e.g. וללשונכה (frg. 1 5) and פיכה (frg. 1 7). Note the use of medial *mem* in final position יוממ ולילה] (frg. 1 10) and the writing in one word of דבתדבוב (frg. 1 3); in both cases the scribe might have intended to express graphically the close relationship of two words within a single expression.

Contents

4Q**412** seems to be a didactic collection, giving instructions for the life and behaviour of a person, as well as liturgical commands. If frg. 4 belongs to the manuscript, it also includes hymnic/prayer material. There is no evidence for a Qumran origin of the sapiential composition represented by 4Q**412**. It might have been part of the broader stream of pre-Essenic wisdom literature, such as Ben Sira.

Mus. Inv. 292
PAM 40.963, 41.138, 41.139, 41.401, 41.402, 41.893, 42.472, 42.861, 42.916*, 43.499

---

[1] The editor wishes to extend cordial thanks to Prof. J. Strugnell for his advice and for making available to her his transcriptions and preliminary notes on 4Q**412**. Special thanks are due to Prof. E. Puech for re-examining the manuscript.

Frg. 1

1 [ואת]הׄ אל תפעׄ[ל]

2 [קה(?)]לר֯בים אל תפעׄ[ל]◦ האר֯◦[ ]הוציא[ ]

3 [עלי]כׄה דבתדבוב *vac* וׄגׄם מעוון לדׄעׄתׄיׄ[ ]

4 [ו]תׄבׄוׄך באמרי יׄוׄ[ ]◦[ ]בׄיׄנׄה הוציא מליׄםׄ[ ]

5 [ש]יׄם מוסר על שׄפׄתׄיׄכׄהׄ[*vac?*] וללשונכה דלתי מ[גן *vac* ועתה בני שמע[ ]

6 ליׄ צדק הגה בהמהׄ[צ]דׄיׄקׄ(?) למבקשי[ ] בינה[ ]

7 בכול פיכה הלל ◦[ ]רׄעשכה[ ]

8 תן הדות לשמוׄ[ ]

9 בקהל רביׄם מׄ[ ]

10 יומם וליל[ה]

NOTES ON READINGS

L. 1 תפעׄ[ל. *ʿAyin* is uncertain (note its closeness to the preceding *pe*).

L. 2]לר֯בים. There is no space between *lamed* and the following letter. Read either רבים or דבים.

L. 2 PAM 41.402 shows remains of אר֯.

L. 3 [עלי]כׄה. *Kap* or *bet* are possible.

L. 3 וׄגׄם. It is not absolutely certain whether the scribe intended to write ואם (PC) or וגם. Faint traces of the vertical stroke of *waw* exist. If one reads וגם, also the head of *waw* is preserved. If one reads ואם, the right arm of *ʾalep* must have eroded, or *waw* was erased. וגם seems to be preferable.

L. 3 לדׄעׄתׄיׄ[or לדׄעׄתׄוׄ[is a preferable reading to לוׄאׄ תׄבׄ[(PC); *ʾalep*, especially, would be difficult, and there are traces of a letter at the bottom right part of *taw* which fit best with *ʿayin*; *dalet* is possible, but only traces of the right part of the head are preserved; the vertical stroke at the end is also possibly a *waw*.

L. 4 [ו]תׄבׄוׄך. *Taw* is almost certain; *bet* might be preferable to *mem*.

L. 4 יׄוׄ[. Or וׄיׄ. It is very difficult to distinguish between *waw* and *yod* in 4Q**412**.

L. 5 שׄפׄתׄיׄכׄהׄ is very probable but not certain. *Šin* is nearly certain (see the first three remains of ink); faint traces of the lower part of the vertical stroke and base of *pe* seem to exist. It touches a letter with a vertical stroke, which may well be *taw* (the surface of the skin has eroded where the left descender and foot of *taw* might be expected to appear).

L. 6 ליׄ. לו is also possible; a reading of *nun* before *yod* or *waw* is excluded because the stroke is too high and too close in relation to *yod/waw*, cf. frg. 2 4. Read בהמה rather than בהמון. After the lacuna, ק/יק is certain; it is preceded by two dots of ink which best fit *dalet*.

L. 7 רׄעשכה seems to be the most plausible reading. The traces of the first letter may be the hook and top of a *reš* or *dalet*, rather than the split head of a *he*.

Translation

1. [And yo]u, do not d[o(?)
2. [an assemb]ly of many(?). Do not d[o spreads]
3. [against] you evil defamation(?). *vacat* And also from iniquity to my knowledge(?)[
4. [and] you are confused(?) by the words of [ ] understanding, he spreads words [
5. [P]lace a bond on your lips(?) [*vacat*?] and for your tongue (place) doors of p[rotection *vac* And now, my son, listen]
6. to me, justice ponder in them [j]ust(?) concerning those who seek [understanding
7. with all your mouth praise [ ] your trembling[
8. give thanks to his name [
9. in an assembly of many [
10. day and nigh[t

Comments

L. 1 [ואת]ה אַל and not [ואת]ה אֵל; see especially the 2nd person sing. in line 5. The verb פעל, cf. line 2, is uncertain.

L. 2 It is uncertain whether *lamed* belongs to רבים or to the preceding word (there is enough space to read [קה]ל at the beginning of the line); see the small gap between אל and תפע]ל. If קהלרבים was intended, cf. the writing of דבתדבוב line 3; and cf. e.g. the writing of קהל־עם (with *maqqef*) in Ps 107:32. Nevertheless, קהל רבים is written in two words in line 9. Alternatively one might translate 'concerning the many/the slanderers', or 'the/an assembly of slanderers'; on the possibility of 'slanderers', cf. line 3.

L. 2 האׄרׄ°. Read, perhaps, a form of ארב, 'to lie in wait', or of ארח, 'path'.

L. 3 The unusual construction דבתדבוב, from the roots דִּבָּה ('whispering, defamation, evil report') and דָּבַב ('to glide over' [one's lips]), is written as one word. A similar phenomenon also occurs in other Qumran texts, see e.g. 1QS III 9; 4QS[a] 2 5, and 4Q**397** 18 12 (4QMMT C 12). An alternative translation to 'evil defamation' might be 'slander of the slanderer' (taking דבוב as a designation for an evil being). Cf. Num 14:36; Prov 10:18 and Sir 46:7 on the suggested reconstruction הוציא עליכה דבתדבוב.

L. 3 וגׄם. On ואם or וגם in sapiential texts, cf. e.g. 4Q**417** 1 i 3 or 1 i 19 (there also in similar 2nd person sing. formulations); both ואם or וגם indicate a collection of prescriptions.

L. 3 After לדעתי, a form of שוב might be expected; cf. Prov 22:17.

L. 4 [ו]תׄבׄוך. Read probably a *Nipʿal* of בוך, but a *Qal* imperfect form of תמך ('grasp, hold') cannot be excluded.

L. 4 יׄוׄ[. Read perhaps יׄוׄ]דעי . . . .

L. 4 מליׄםׄ[. Cf. frg. 3 2.

L. 5 מוסר. Cf. Ps 34:14. מוֹסֵר seems preferable to מוּסָר, 'reprimand'.

L. 5 דלתי מ[גן. Cf. 1QH[a] XIV 30 (Sukenik VI 27).

L. 6 On the suggested reconstruction ועתה בני שמע לי, cf. 4Q**525** 3 4, 14 ii 18, and [31 1], and—with a different word order—4QD[c] (4Q**268**) 1 9 and 4QD[e] (4Q**270**) 2 ii 19. On הגה + the accusative, see e.g. Ps 38:13; צדק + הגה is found in Ps 35:28 and 71:24. According to this restoration, the width of the column might have been *c*.11 cm (assuming a small *vacat* before ועתה), but this is very hypothetical. לו is less plausible, but cf. Gen 15:6 (ויחשבה לו צדקה). הגה should be understood as an imperative; cf. תן in line 8.

L. 7 הלל seems to be an imperative, as does תן in line 8.

L. 8 הדות should probably be read הודות. This defective form in not attested elsewhere; it might have been a scribal error.

L. 9 בקהל רביׄםׄ. Cf. on line 2.

L. 10 יומם ולילה] might be understood in the context of worship (cf. 1QM XIV 13 עם מ[בו]א יומם ולילה and see lines 7–8) rather than that of study, in which case an expression like דרש בתורה יומם ולילה (cf. 1QS VI 6) or יומם ולילה הגה ברז נהיה ודורש תמיד (cf. 4Q**418** 43 4 = 4Q**417** 2 i 6) would be expected. On יומם ולילה cf. also 1QH[a] XVI 30 (Sukenik VIII 29); 4Q**417** 1 i 22 (= 4Q**418** 7 7); 4Q**508** 41 2; and the Bible *passim*.

Frg. 2

]רתי̊ °°[1

]°ו̊ר̊תי̊ אל ת[2

]°°ן̊ שלוש̊[3

מ]שלח̊ מ̊דנים °[4

]ל[ ]לך רא̊[5

]°ד̊[6

Notes on Readings

L. 1]רתי̊. The final letter is *yod* or *waw*.

L. 2]°ו̊ר̊תי̊. The second letter is *waw* or *yod*. The third letter is either *reš* with a destroyed head, *dalet*, or a large *yod*. The final letter is *yod* or *waw*.

L. 3 The second *šin* is almost certain.

L. 5 Remains of *ʾalep* or *dalet* follow after *reš*.

L. 6 The last letter might be *dalet* or final *kap*.

Translation

2.] do not [
3.] three[
4. who] let loose strife [

Comments

Frg. 2 might deal with the same subject as frg. 1 1–5.

L. 2 Cf. perhaps frg. 1 1, 2.

L. 4 Cf. Prov 6:19 (also 6:14 and 16:28), and frg. 1 1–5.

Frg. 3

מ]שפטי צד̊[ק 1

] על מלי כ̊[2

Notes on Readings

L. 2 *Kap* seems preferable to *pe*; the remains of the head are almost horizontal.

Translation

1.] right[eous ju]dgements[
2.] according to the words of [

Comments

L. 1 This does not connect to frg. 1 6.

L. 2 Cf. frg. 1 4.

Frg. 4

]עֹ֯שרי֯ ינחי֯ל[1

כ]ר֯צונו ברא [2

]ם אקרא ו֯ק֯[ולי 3

מ]ל֯י֯ ו֯ידעים א֯[4

]◦ת֯ אנ֯וש [5

Notes on Readings

L. 1 עֹשרי֯ fits better than עֹשרו֯; note the large head of *yod*.

L. 3 ו֯ק֯[. *Lamed* is possible instead of *qop*.

L. 4 מ]ל֯י֯. *Yod* (cf. e.g. the second *yod* in וידעים) or *dalet* (Strugnell, *PC*).

Translation

1.]my wealth he will give as a possession[
2. according to] His will He created [
3.] I cry and [my] voi[ce
4.]my [wor]ds and those who know [
5.] man [

Comments

L. 3 'I cry' or 'I call', cf. perhaps Prov 8:4 אליכם אישים אקרא וקולי אל בני אדם.

L. 4 מ]ל֯י֯. If correct, cf. perhaps Job 34:4.

413. 4QComposition concerning Divine Providence

(PLATE XIV)

Preliminary publication: E. Qimron, 'A Work Concerning Divine Providence: 4Q*413*', in *Solving Riddles and Untying Knots: Biblical, Epigraphic, and Semitic Studies in Honor of Jonas C. Greenfield*, eds. Z. Zevit, S. Gitin, M. Sokoloff (Winona Lake, IN, 1995) 191–202.

Physical Description

ONLY two fragments of this manuscript, each containing four lines, have survived. Both fragments have upper margins; the larger one also has a left margin and the smaller one a right margin. Even though the two fragments do not join, they evidently belong to the top of the same column. The script is Herodian.

Contents

It is difficult to determine the nature of this work on the basis of such a short text. The four preserved lines contain an appeal (in the 1st person) exhorting the reader to consider carefully the historical events of the past, which demonstrate that whoever follows God has been rewarded, while whoever did not has failed to survive. This concept of divine providence is commonly found in other Qumran literary works, such as the *Damascus Document* (in the 'Admonition'). Cf. also 1QS III 13–25, the epilogue of 4QMTT, and 1Q**27**.

Mus. Inv. 127
PAM 40.618, 41.411, 41.903, 43.499*

Frgs. 1–2

top margin

1 מׄזׄמׄתׄ ד[עת מצאו] וחוכמה אלמדכמה והתבוננו בדרכי אנוש ובפועלות
2 בני אדׄ[ם כי באהבת]𐤀𐤋 את איש הרבה לו נחלה בׄדעת אמתו וכפי גועלו
3 כל רעׄ[ההולך אחר מ]שמע אוזניו ומראה עינו בׄלׄ יחיה *vacat* ועתה
4 חסד [ ]רׄאישונים ובינו בׄשׄני ד[ור ו]דׄור כאשר גלה 𐤀𐤋
5 *vacat* [ ]ל [ ] [ ]]לׄ[ ]

TRANSLATION

1. a plan of kn[owledge find] and let me teach you wisdom, and (thus) contemplate the conduct of man and the actions of
2. human beings. [For whenever] God [favoured] a person He increased his share in the knowledge of His truth; and as He despised
3. every wicked individual [who would follow what] his ears hear and what his eyes see (that wicked individual) would not survive (*vacat*). And now
4. (sons of) grace [(the events of)]the former years and contemplate the events of past [gene]rations as God has revealed.

COMMENTS

L. 1 מׄזׄמׄה. Both מזמה and the following related חוכמה are used in the sectarian Dead Sea scrolls in reference to divine providence. For the restoration, see Prov 8:12.

L. 1 וחוכמה. The *plene* orthography of this word occurs thirteen times in the nonbiblical Dead Sea scrolls. It represents an early *quṭla* pattern, as does its Tiberian and Babylonian vocalization. The alternative spelling of this word (חכמה) is, however more frequent in the Dead Sea scrolls (twenty eight times), and perhaps attests to another early pattern, for example *ḥikma* as in Syriac, Arabic, Samaritan Aramaic[1] and perhaps Qumran Aramaic.[2] Several cases of *ḥakma* are found in Hebrew.[3] It is less likely that all the cases of חכמה (without *waw*) are the defective spellings, since some of them occur in manuscripts that consistently mark any *u/o* vowel with a *waw*.

L. 1 אלמדכמה. Cf. Ps 34:12 יראת ה' אלמדכם. The long pronominal suffix is typical of the Hebrew of the Dead Sea scrolls.[4]

L. 1 והתבוננו. *Hitpolel* forms of בין occur in Biblical Hebrew, in the Hebrew and Aramaic of the Dead Sea scrolls, in the book of Ben Sira, and (rarely) in Mishnaic Hebrew.[5]

Ll. 1–2 בדרכי אנוש ובפועלות בני אד[ם]. דרך here means 'conduct'. It occurs here parallel to פְּעֻלָּה. Though this exact parallelism remains elsewhere unattested, the pairing of פְּעֻלּוֹת with ארחות is found in Ps 17:4 (cf. also 1QS IV 15; 1QpHab VIII 12–13). אנוש occurs in Biblical Hebrew exclusively in poetry. In the Dead Sea scrolls it is found in prose as well. For the spelling פועלות for פעולות, see Appendix 2 in Qimron, 'Work Concerning Divine Providence'.

L. 2 𐤀𐤋[באהבת]. For the restoration באהבת cf. CD VIII 16–18 באהבת אל את הראשנים . . . ובשונאו את בוני החיץ. אל here and in line 4 is written in palaeo-Hebrew script, as is the case in other scrolls.

L. 2 את איש. 'A person'. The use of את before the indefinite object is peculiar. Cf. the somewhat similar construction (with *lamed* rather than את) ואהבת חסד לאיש (1QS V 25; 4QS[d] reads ואהבת חסד without the object marker.[6]

L. 2 הרבה לו נחלה. Similar expressions occur in the Bible and in the Dead Sea scrolls: לרב תרבה נחלתו (Num 26:54; cf. 33:54); לפי נחלת איש בין רוב למועט (1QH[a] X 28–29); . . . באי]ש הרביתה נ̇ח̇ל̇ת̇ו̇ בדעת אמתכה (1QS IV 16) וכפי נחלת איש באמת יצדק (1QS IV 24). Note that the suffix in נחלתו in the biblical sources and in 1QH[a] is equivalent to לו in this text. Compare עינים להם ולא יראו (Ps 115:5) to ידיהם ולא ימישון (Ps 115:7).

---

[1] E. Y. Kutscher, *Hebrew and Aramaic Studies* (Jerusalem, 1977) 276 [Hebrew section].

[2] The form חכמה is attested fourteen times, and חוכמה only once.

[3] E. Qimron, 'A Grammar of the Hebrew Language of the Dead Sea Scrolls' (Ph.D. diss., Hebrew University, 1976) 43 n. 27 [Hebrew].

[4] See E. Qimron, *The Hebrew of the Dead Sea Scrolls* (HSS 29; Atlanta, 1986) §322.17 [henceforth *HDSS*].

[5] See M. Moreshet, 'Polel/Hitpolel in Mishnaic Hebrew and in Aramaic', *Bar-Ilan* 18–9 (1981) 248–69 [Hebrew].

[6] Cf. M. Kister, 'Biblical Phrases and Hidden Biblical Interpretations and *Pesharim*' in *The Dead Sea Scrolls: Forty Years of Research*, ed. D. Dimant and U. Rappaport (Jerusalem and Leiden, 1992) 30.

L. 2 בְדעת אמתו. The combination דעת + אמת occurs in 1QH[a] X 28–29 cited above and in 1QS IX 17. Similar combinations occur elsewhere. The juxtaposition of אמת + נחלה also occurs in 1QS IV 24.

L. 2 וכפי גועלו. כפי is equivalent to לפי or to the prepositions כ and ב. It is relatively more frequent in the Dead Sea scrolls than in the Hebrew Bible, especially before an infinitive. גועלו should be parsed as an inflected infinitive, rather than a *quṭl* noun (בגֹעַל נפשך, Ezek 16:5). The verb געל is an antonym of אהב.

L. 3 ההולך אחר מ[שמע אוזניו ומראה עינו]. This expression is taken from Isa 11:3 ולא למראה עיניו ישפוט ולא למשמע אזניו יוכיח. The form מִשְׁמַע is unique in the Hebrew Bible, while מַרְאֶה is common, occurring frequently in the combinations מראה עיניך, מראה עיניה, and the like. The passage in Isaiah 11 deals with the Messianic King, stating that he will judge through God's inspiration. The expression under discussion is generally taken as a metaphor for human frailty. At first glance the usage of this expression in this text seems different from its usage in Isaiah. Yet this is not necessarily the case. Fortunately we have a *pesher* on this biblical text that informs us about the ways in which the expressions under discussion were interpreted by the Qumran sectarians. It appears that the *pesher* interpreted this expression as a metaphor for a person acting according to his own will (in contrast to God's will). This is apparently the meaning of the expression here. It is an attribute of an evil person, who acts independently rather than following God's commands. Compare Isa 33:15 אטם אזנו משמע דמים ועצם עיניו מראות ברע (referring to a righteous person), and 1QH[a] VII 2–4, שעו עיני מראות רע אוזני משמוע דמים השם לבבי ממחשבת רוע. For a discussion of the relationship of this expression to the understanding of 4Q**161** 8–10 21–23 [4QpIsa[a]] and 11QT[a] LVIII 15–21, see Appendix 1 in Qimron, 'A Work Concerning Divine Providence'.

L. 3 בל יחיה. The negative בל occurs twenty seven times in the Dead Sea scrolls, always before an imperfect tense. In the Hebrew Bible it occurs sixty times, before various verbal forms. In Mishnaic Hebrew, it is not used freely but rather always in the combination בל תעשה (or יעשה) in the sense of a prohibitive law.

L. 4 ובינו. The conjunctive *waw* in ובינו suggests that another imperative form with a similar meaning (such as זכורו) preceded it (cf. Deut 32:7 זכר ימות עולם בינו שנות דור ודור). This would also be consistent with the occurrence of ועתה (after the *vacat* in line 3); ועתה indicates that the action expressed by the verb that follows is actual. This verb is frequently used in the imperative (or, the jussive), as in CD I 1 ועתה שמעו כל יודעי צדק ובינו במעשי אל. It thus appears that the beginning of the line contained a sentence parallel to ובינו בשני דור ודור. (Parallelism is characteristic of this text). The word חסד, which is materially quite certain, seems however, to be inconsistent with this suggestion. A possible solution is to read חסד as an abbreviation of בני חסד (one of the epithets of the Dead Sea sect; 1QH[a] VII 20) and to restore ועתה חסד [זכורו ימים] ראשונים 'And now members of the covenant, contemplate (the events of) the days gone by . . .'. Compare with Sir 41:11 הבל אדם בגויתו אך שם חסד לא יכרת.

For the imperative *Qal* בינו see CD I 1. The introduction of the object of בין in the *Hipʿil* and *Qal* by ב is typical of the Dead Sea scrolls and of late Biblical Hebrew.[7] The masc. pl. of שנה is used here instead of the archaic fem. pl. form used especially in biblical poetry, as in, for example, the parallel, biblical source, Deut 32:7.

L. 4 כאשר גלה אל. The *vacat* at the beginning of line 5 shows that אל is the last word of the sentence. The verb thus has no object. Compare 1QS VIII 16 כאשר גלו הנביאים ברוח קודשו.

---

[7] See A. Hurvitz, *The Transition Period in Biblical Hebrew* (Jerusalem, 1972) 136–7 [Hebrew]; Qimron, *HDSS*, 88.

420. 4QWays of Righteousness[a]

(PLATE XV)

Previous discussion: T. Elgvin, 'Admonition Texts from Qumran Cave 4', *Methods of Investigation of the Dead Sea Scrolls and the Khirbet Qumran Site: Present Realities and Future Prospects*, eds. M. Wise, N. Golb, J. Collins, D. Pardee (New York: The New York Academy of Sciences, 1994) 179–94.

4QWAYS of Righteousness is a sapiential composition preserved in two copies.[1] Both copies display a Herodian script, and 4Q**420** is somewhat earlier than 4Q**421**. Where the two copies overlap, approximately one line of text of 4Q**420** 1a ii-b is missing in 4Q**421** 1a ii-b. This is probably due to a scribal error, not to any difference in versions. 4Q**421** was rolled in the less usual way with its beginning on the inside, a fact which probably indicates that this scroll was in active use in the Qumran library in the final period of the settlement's history.[2]

4Q**421** 12 and 13, which probably belonged to the latter part of the composition, deal with matters connected with the Temple service. This section covered more than one column of text. 4Q**421** 1a i deals with the organization of the *yaḥad* and abounds with sectarian terminology, which proves the sectarian origin. 4QWays of Righteousness thus demonstrates that sapiential works, including those containing wisdom sayings, were written (or at least edited) within the *yaḥad*, while others were imported to the Qumran community.

4QWays of Righteousness seems to be a composite work. The first preserved section (which must be close to the beginning of the composition) deals with sectarian organization. The second part, wisdom sayings about the righteous man, is introduced by an admonition to submit to the yoke of wisdom. The third is a section dealing with matters connected with the Temple. Different sources have probably been compiled together by a sectarian editor. Some of the sources may be pre-sectarian: the parts of the work containing wisdom sayings do not usually reflect a specific sectarian theology, although some sayings easily can be interpreted in a sectarian way. The section on the Temple probably has its origin in a pre-sectarian priestly milieu. The wisdom sayings do not display any priestly characteristics. This composition is thus another indication that the *yaḥad* reflects a merger between priestly and lay circles in the mid-second century BCE.[3]

The similarities with sections in 1QS and CD dealing with the organization of the *yaḥad* could point to a date of origin in the late second century BCE for the composition as a whole.

---

[1] I am indebted to L. H. Schiffman, M. Weinfeld and J. A. Fitzmyer for valuable comments and proposals for this edition of 4Q**420** and 4Q**421**.

[2] Cf. T. Elgvin, 'The Reconstruction of Sapiential Work A', *RevQ* 16 (1993–95) 559–80, esp. 564 n. 13.

[3] See T. Elgvin, 'Wisdom, Revelation, and Eschatology in an Early Essene Writing', *SBLSP* 34 (1995) 440–63.

Physical Description

The skin is very thin. Frg. 2 has shrunk and darkened due to deterioration. The colour varies from light to dark brown on both sides of the fragments. Frg. 1a is dark brown, though lighter where the surface is gone. The smaller fragments 3, 4, and 5 are dark brown.

Col. ii of frg. 1a-b is quite narrow. Three of the lines can be reconstructed with the overlapping text from 4Q**421**. Line 2 has 45–47 letter-spaces, line 4 probably 46. The length of the writing block of this column can be calculated to *c*.7.5 cm.

Palaeography

The script is a Herodian formal script which is difficult to date precisely; it is possibly from the turn of the era. The letters are thin-lined. *ʾAlep* is characterized by an elegant inverted 'v'-style of penning the oblique axis and left leg. The baseline of the *bet* is drawn from left to right, and often extends beyond the vertical right downstroke. *Gimel* is early Herodian in style, it is not thickened at the top. The head of *yod* is shaded; *yod* is shorter than *waw* and can easily be distinguished from the latter. The head of the *ṭet* is extensively curled. The hook of the *lamed* is slightly enlarged, but less than in 4Q**421**.

Orthography and Morphology

Although the evidence is scarce, 4Q**420** seems to reflect the so-called Qumran practice of orthography and morphology. לוא and כול are written *plene* (with one probable exception, frg. 1a ii 7 כ̊ל[). The pronominal suffix of the third person plural is -*māh* (frg. 2 9).

Mus. Inv. 509
PAM 41.349, 41.706, 41.855, 41.966, 42.633, 42.818, 43.534*

Frg. 1a i

]]ק[ ]◦חוב 3
] ה[ו̊ן̊ רשעים 4
]]◦ות אל 5

PAM 42.633, 43.534*

NOTES ON READINGS

Frg. 1 is composed of a join between two fragments: frg. 1a and frg. 1b. Frg. 1a contains parts of cols. i and ii; frg. 1b contains part of col. ii.

L. 4 ה]ון. Or:]ן.

TRANSLATION

3.] [ ]

4. pro]perty(?) of the wicked

5.] God/to(?)

COMMENTS

Col. i can be located close to the beginning of the composition (see below on 4Q**421**). These lines, which correspond to the lower (missing) part of 4Q**421** 1a i, most likely belong to the first part of the book which dealt with sectarian organization. The theme seems to be the need to separate the property of the sectarians from those outside the community, cf. 1QS I 12–13; V 2, 16–20; VII 25; IX 8; CD XIII 11–16.

L. 4 ה]ון רשעים. This phrase belongs to sectarian vocabulary, cf. CD VI 15, VIII 5 הון רשעה; 1QS X 19; 1QpHab VIII 11 הון (אנשי) חמס; 1QS IX 8 הון אנשי הרמיה.

Frg. 1a ii-b

Parallels: 4Q**421** 1a ii-b (underline)

top margin

1]בדרכי אל לעשות צדקה [בזות לוא ישיב בטרם ישמ]ע[

2 ו]לוא ידב[ר ב]טרם יבין [בארוך אפים ישיב פתגם וש[ ]

3 יוציא דבר[ידר]ש אמת משפט ובמחקר צדק

4 ימצא תוצ]אותיה איש[עניו ונכי שכלו ל]ו[א ישוב א]חור[

5 עד י[מ איש]נאמן לוא יסור מדרכי צדק[ויש]מ[

6]לבו ל ול עצ]מותיו וכפיו בצדק נגא]ל[

7 בבינה כל[ ]ל[ ]שדותיו גבולו [ ]

8 [ ]ל]עשות צ[דקה[ ]

PAM 41.706, 41.855, 41.966, 42.633, 43.534*

NOTES ON READINGS

L. 1 בּ֯ז֯ו֯ת. The first preserved letter is *bet*, *kap*, *pe*, or *ṭet* (the lower horizontal stroke is preserved), of the next two letters the lower part of two vertical strokes are preserved, here tentetivly read as *zayin* and *waw*.

L. 2 ו֯]לוא. A trace of the first letter can be seen with a microscope on frg. 1a.

L. 2 בארוך אפים. 4Q**421** 1a ii 14 has בארך א֯]פים.

L. 2 וש֯[. The last preserved letter is *šin*, *ʿayin*, or *ṣade*.

Ll. 2–3 The parallel text of 4Q**421** 1a ii-b 14 has a lacuna with space for only three or four of the ten words between **אפים** and צדק; this means that approximately six words were omitted by the scribe of 4Q**421**, probably by error.

L. 4 ימצא תוצ]אותיה א֯יש] עניו. The reconstruction assumes that there is only one word between תוצ]אותיה and עניו. **איש** is the obvious option, yielding a line of 46 letter-spaces.

Ll. 5–6 וישם לבו ל ול עצ]מ֯ותיו וכפיו [. For the reconstruction, cf. 4Q**525** 14 ii 18 ושים לבכה ל∘[. The reconstructed text has a parallelism; the first part talks about man's heart, the second about his bones and hands.

L. 6 נג֯א]ל[. There is space for one more word on the line, but the line could also have ended with this word. The latter option seems most probable when one compares the length of the line in the parallel text 4Q**421** 1a ii-b 17. For the first option could be reconstructed something like בצדק נגא]ל משכיל] בבינה כ֯ל֯[or בצדק נגא]ל נפשו] בבינה כ֯ל֯[.

TRANSLATION

1. [in the ways of God, to do righteousness] as follows: he will not answer before he hea[rs,]
2. and [not spea]k be[fore he understands.]With great patience will he give answer and [ ]
3. he will utter a word[he will see]k true judgement, and by studying righteousness
4. he will understand [its conseq]uences. [A man] who is humble and meek in mind will n[o]t turn a[way]
5. until [A man]who is trustworthy will not turn from ways of righteousness.[He will set]
6. [his heart on and on]his [bo]nes and his hands. By righteousness is he redee[med],
7. through understanding all[ ]his fields, its borders[ ]
8. [ ]to[do ri]ghteousness[ ]

COMMENTS

This text is preceded by 4Q**421** 1a ii-b 5–12. 4Q**421** 1a ii-b 9–10 admonishes man to submit to the yoke of wisdom. Then follows a section of wisdom sayings about the righteous man, similar to biblical proverbs, of which this text is a part.

Each unit of the text is introduced with the word **איש** followed by one or two adjectives: אי]ש֯ משכיל ונבון (4Q**421** 1b 10); י]ו֯כח תוכחת משכיל איש ∘[(4Q**421** 1a ii-b 11–12); [א֯יש עניו ונכי שכלו (4Q**420** 1a ii-b 4); איש [נ֯אמן (line 5). A key word is צדק, which occurs thrice, lines 3, 5, 6. The verb is always in imperfect, in *yiqtōl/lô yiqtōl*-style. A key word in the wisdom sayings is צדק/צדקה (lines 3, 5, 6, 8; cf. 4Q**421** 11 4 מלאכת צ֯]דק; 4Q**424** 3 2 להצדיק צדיק; 3 9 צדקה לאביוני]ם[; 3 10 בני צד֯ק).

A similar section containing wisdom sayings is found in the sapiential composition 4Q**424**, where frg. 1 7–13 and frg. 3 1–7 describe the attitude to the foolish man in *ʾal tiqtōl*-style (vetitive), while frg. 3 7–10 describe the righteous in indicative *yiqtōl*-style. Another sapiential scroll, 4Q**525** (4QBeatitudes), employs various syntactical means: *ʾašrê qōtēl . . . wĕlōʾ yiqtōl, ʾal tiqtōl,* as well as the imperative. 4Q**425** is characterized by longer wisdom speeches and wisdom instructions, not the shorter sentences of 4Q**424** and 4Q**420/421**. In contrast to 4Q**420/421**, 4Q**424** and 4Q**525** do not exhibit specific sectarian phrases. Lines 1–7 can be seen as a list of virtues, a common literary pattern in the Hellenistic world and New Testament epistles; cf. also 1QS V 3–4. The priestly torah about the righteous and the ungodly in Ezekiel 18, is one of the sources of inspiration for the wisdom sayings of this text.

Lines 1–4 deal with expressing one's opinion in a dispute or matter of discussion. Close parallels to this passage are found in Sir 5:9-15 and 4Q**525** (4QBeatitudes) 14 ii 18–27, the admonition to be careful with one's words is well known from Proverbs (10:19; 13:3; 15:23; 16:23; 17:27; 21:23; 25:11). The knowledgeable man should know a matter thoroughly and hear all sides before he gives his opinion. These lines could be considered guidelines for discussions during the meetings of the *yaḥad*. Lines 4–5 deal with humility and honesty. Lines 5–8 talk about the trustworthy man who walks in the ways of righteousness. Line 7 mentions the borders of his fields, possibly meaning that his fields will be safe because of his understanding and honesty.

Ll. 1–4 The knowledgeable man shall be careful in his judgement and not express his opinion before he knows the matter in question. A close parallel is Sir 11:7-8 בטרם תחקר אל תסלף בקר לפנים ואחר תזיף. בני אל תשיב דבר בטרם תשמע ובתוך שיחה אל תדבר, 'Before investigating, find not fault; examine first, then criticize. My son, before hearing, answer not, and interrupt no one in the middle of his speech'. 4Q**420** 1a ii-b 1–2 and Sir 11:7-8 seem to be two versions of the same saying. Cf. also Sir 5:9-15, especially vv 11-12 היה ממהר להאזין ובארך רוח השב פתגם אם יש אתך ענה רעך ואם אין ידך על פיך 'Be quick to listen, and considerate when you give your opinion. Only if you know, answer your neighbour. If not, put your hand over your mouth'. A contrasting description which uses many of the same words is found in the sapiential composition 4Q**424** 3 1–2 אל תמשילהו ברודפי דעת כי לא יבין משפטם להצדיק צדיק ולהרשיע [רשע] איש שופט בטרם ידרוש ומאמין בטרם [יבחן] 'A man who judges before he has investigated and forms his opinion before he has [checked the matter], you shall not set him up in charge of those who pursue knowledge, for he will not understand how to judge them, to declare innocent the righteous and deem guilty [the wicked]'. Cf. also the (early Ptolemaic) Demotic *Instruction of Anksheshonqy* 7.23: 'Do not hasten when you speak, lest you give offense', and the rules for speaking in the common meeting of the *yaḥad*, 1QS VI 9–13, where the members are asked to express their opinions on matters of importance for the community. The advice of this passage about careful judgement could have been considered relevant for such meetings of the *yaḥad*.

L. 1 לוא ישיב בטרם ישמׄ[ע]. Cf. 4Q**525** 14 ii 22–24 ולפי שומעכה ענה . . . אל] תשפוך שיח טרם תשמע את מליהם . . . לפנים שמע אמרם ואחר תשוב בׄ[דבריכה] 'According to what you have heard you shall answer . . . Do not] speak before you have listened to their words . . . First listen to their argument and only afterwards shall you give [your opinion]'.

L. 2]בארוך אפים ישיב פתגם. For פתגם, cf. Esth 1:10; Qoh 8:11; Sir 5:11; 8:9, where this word has the meaning 'decree, word'. Cf. 4Q**525** 14 ii 24–25 [בארך] אפים הוציאם וענה נכון 'with great] patience you shall utter them and give a right answer'.

L. 3 ובמחקר צדׄק. Cf. 4Q**525** 14 ii 20 בענות צדק הוצא אמרי[כה א]ל תתן['Give [your] opinion with justice and humility. Do[n]ot give['.

L. 4 תוצ]אותיה. In Biblical Hebrew, תוצאות has the meanings 'source/origin' (Prov 4:23), 'deliverance', and, more frequently, 'endpoint of a bordering line' (for the latter option here cf. line 7]שׄדותיו גבולו). In Qumran literature the word occurs only in the sapiential material: twice in the Book of Mysteries (1QMyst 1 i 12 = 4QMyst[a] 1 4; 4QMyst[a] 1 7 [where Schiffman translates תו]צאותם '[that which re]sults from them'; see above]); 4Q**426** 7 1; twice in 4QWays of Righteousness (here and in 4Q**421** 3 1); and once in 4QInstruction[c], 4Q**417** 2 i 11–14. The latter passage runs as follows: ובכושר מבינות נודׄ[ע נס]תׄרי מחשבתו עם התהלכו [ת]מׄיׄ[ם בכול מ]עׄשיו אלה שחר תמיד והתבונן [בכו]ל תוצאותמה ואז תדע בׄכבוד עׄ[ולם ע]ם רזי פלאו וגבורות מעשיו ואתהׄ מבין רוש פעלתכה בזכרון הׄעׄ[ת '. . . and with proper understanding [the hid]den things of His thoughts are kno[wn] when one walks [b]lameless[ly in all]one's d[ee]ds. These things seek always, and meditate [on al]l that results from them. Then you will have knowledge of [eterna]l glory [wi]th His wondrous mysteries and mighty deeds. And you will understand the origin of your deed when you remember the ti[me'. In this occurrence, the only case where the context for the word is preserved,

תוצאותמה refers to the hidden secrets of God which have been revealed to the elect. The addressee is admonished to meditate on these mysteries and reflect on 'their outcome'. The word probably carries the same meaning—'outcome/results of the matter/ consequences'—in the other sapiential works, besides this text.

L. 4 א̊יש] עניו. עניו, עני, and ענוה רוח are common designations for the covenanters and their spirit in sectarian literature; cf. e.g. 1QS II 24; III 8; IV 3; V 25; 1QM XIV 7. Consequently, even if this material is pre-sectarian in its origin, in the sectarian setting this text portrays the ideal for a member of the *yaḥad*.

L. 4 ל[ו]א ישוב א[חור]. In the Bible the expression שוב אחור means 'turn back', cf. Ps 9:4 בשוב אויבי אחור, Ps 56:10 אז ישובו אויבי אחור or 'turn away', Lam 1:8 ותשב אחור. In 1QH[a] XIII 18, 19 and 1Q**27** (1QMyst) 1 i 8 לוא ישוב אחור has the meaning that a word or prophecy 'will not be cancelled', possibly also in 1QH[a] 1 9–10 ואדעה כיא אמת [יצא מפיכה . . . ולוא ישוב] אחור, for which cf. Ps 132:11 נשבע יהוה לדוד אמת לא ישוב ממנה 'God has sworn to David, it is true and He will not cancel it', Isa 45:23 בי נשבעתי יצא מפי צדקה דבר ולא ישוב.[4] The phrase is found in 4QMMT C 22 ולוא ישובו א̊ח̊ו[ר, where Qimron chooses the second option and interprets it as the blessings and curses (of line 20) which will 'not be cancelled'.[5] In this text the phrase has the meaning 'turn away' or 'backslide', cf. the parallel phrase לוא יסור מדרכי צדק in the next line.

L. 5 איש [נאמן. In the sectarian setting the root אמן is often connected with trusting in the Teacher and the covenant of God with the community, cf. 1QpHab II 3–4 כי[א ל]ו[א האמינו בברית אל, VIII 2–3 בעבור עמלם ואמנתם במורה הצדק. Yerushalmi uses the word נאמן about a trustworthy member (i.e. a full member) of a Pharisaic *ḥaburah*, אבל ברבים אינו נאמן עד שיקבל עליו ברבים. ר' אמי בשם ר' ינאי אפילו אני איני נאמן עד שנקבל עליי ברבים 'but as regards the *rabbim* he is not to be trusted until he assumes his obligations in the presence of the *rabbim*. R. Ami in the name of R. Yannai said: "Even I would not be trusted [by the *Rabbim*] until I assumed my obligations in the presence of the *rabbim*"'.[6] This parallel could indicate that איש נאמן means 'a member of the community'. Cf. also Num 12:7 on Moses, בכל־ביתי נאמן הוא.

L. 5 לוא יסור מדרכי צדק]. A close parallel is found in CD I 15–16, referring to unbelieving Israel ולסור מנתיבות צדק. CD I 13; II 6, uses סרי/סררי דרך for the antagonists of the *yaḥad*. Cf. also 1QS I 15 ולוא לסור מחוקי אמתו ללכת ימין ושמאול; III 10 ולוא לסור ימין ושמאול; 4Q**525** 3 ii 12 וא[ל תסו̊ר]ו מאמרי פי. The phrase דרכי צדק is not found in the Bible (on the parallel phrase דרכי אל, see 4Q**421** 1a ii-b 12), but occurs in 1QS IV 2; *Jub.* 1:20, 23:26 ('path of righteousness'); *1 Enoch* 91:18-19; 92:3; 94:1; 99:10; 4Q**213** (4QLevi[a] ar) 5 ii 9 א]רחת קשטא תשבק[ו]ן 'the w]ays of righteousness you will aba[n]don'; cf. Tob 1:3 ὁδοῖς ἀληθείας . . . καὶ δικαιοσύνης. Strugnell and Dimant reconstruct in 4Q**385** (4Qps Ezek[a]) 2 2–3 וילכו

---

[4] In Akkadian, the equivalent to לוא ישוב אחור, a-na ku-tal-li-šú ú-ul i-ta-a-ar, has the meaning 'cancel the treaty' (Treaty between Mattiuaza of Mitanni and Subbiluliumi of Hatti, line 26, cf. Esarhaddon's vassal treaty line 377). See M. Weinfeld, 'The Vassal Treaties of Esarhaddon—An Annotated Translation', *Shnaton* 1 (1975) 89–127 (Hebrew) 105 n. 66; E. F. Weidner, *Politische Dokumente aus Kleinasien. Die Staatsverträge in akkadischer Sprache aus dem Archiv von Boghazköi* (Hildesheim/New York: Georg Olms Verlag, 1970) 42–3; D. J. Wiseman, 'The Vassal-Treaties of Esarhaddon', *Iraq* XX (1958) 1–99, pp. 57–8. D. Flusser notes that the original wording of the blessing after the Haftarah was ודברך אחור לא ישוב, '"The Book of Mysteries" and a Synagogal Prayer', *Knesset Ezra. Literature and Life in the Synagogue. Studies Presented to Ezra Fleischer,* eds. S. Elizur, M. D. Herr, G. Shaked, A. Shinan (Jerusalem: Ben-Zvi Institute, 1994) 3–20, p. 5 n. 14 (Hebrew).

[5] *DJD* X, 60–61. Since this text testifies to the meaning 'turn away, backslide' of the phrase in a sectarian text, the proposal of M. Wise (R. H. Eisenman, M. Wise, *The Dead Sea Scrolls Uncovered. The First Complete Translation and Interpretation of 50 Key Documents Withheld for Over 35 Years* [Shaftesbury: Element, 1992] 199–200] to reconstruct 4QMMT C 21–22 שישובו בישר[אל] לת[ורת אל בכול לבם] ולוא ישובו א̊ח̊ו[ר and translate 'when (those) in Isra[e]l are to return to the La[w of God with all their heart,] never to turn bac[k] (again)' seems preferable. In MMT the subject of this sentence is contrasted with the wicked who act wickedly, and it seems better to read the phrase about the righteous remnant in Israel of the last days, which will not any more turn away from God. For the phrase שישובו לת[ורת אל, cf. 1QS V 8 where לשוב אל תורת מושה clearly means 'return to the Law'.

[6] *Y. Dem.* 2.2, 22d; cf. S. Lieberman, 'The Discipline in the So-called Dead Sea Manual of Discipline', *JBL* LXXI (1952) 199–206.

בׄדרכי] צדק. The parallel expression נתיבות צדק/צדקה is used in CD I 16; 1QH[a] VII 14. In the sectarian context, the sentence איש נ]אמן לוא יסור מדרכי צדק would be interpreted 'a trustworthy member will not turn from the way of the *yaḥad*'. The absolute form (ה)דרך is found in *Jub.* 23:20 'in order to return them to "the Way"'; 1QS IX 18, 19, 21; CD I 13; II 6. For the *yaḥad* the term (ה)דרך 'the Way' was connected to the eschatological fulfilment of Isa 40:3 במדבר פנו דרך יהוה through the Community, cf. 1QS IX 19. There is no allusion to Isa 40:3 in this text.

Ll. 5–6 וישם לבו ל ול עצ]מׄותיו וכפיו]. The reconstruction yields a parallelism which expresses that the righteous one mobilizes his heart as well as his bones and hands. The missing words could be אמת and צדק: 'He will set [his heart on truth,] and his [bo]nes and his hands [on righteousness']. As a man has brought all his resources into the *yaḥad* (previous column; cf. 4Q**421** 1a i 2–3), so shall he dedicate his body to righteousness; cf. Rom 6:13, 12:1.

L. 6 בצדק נגאׄ]ל[. The verb is a perfect or participle.

L. 7 גבולו. The suffix -ו is probably appended to a plural form (cf. *HDSS*, 59).

L. 8]לׄ[עשות צ]דׄקה[. Cf. 1QS V 3–4 לעשות אמת יחד וענוה צדקה ומשפט ואהבת חסד.

Frg. 2 (olim frg. 3)

1 ארך] אפים [

2]תׄנלוים עדׄ[

3 להו]סׄיף(?) מדתם [

4] על נגועי משפ[ט

]יׄם
5]וׄזרעם על תנחומׄ[ים

6]◦ות אשר דברׄ[

7]לכול גורריוׄ ◦[ ]◦ ◦[

8]ובׄתׄלמיה יחרוׄש ותמיד[

9 צ]דׄיקים[ ]מה בלבב מׄ[שכילים(?)

10]לׄגערתו וׄ◦[

PAM 41.349, 41.966, 42.633, 43.534*

Notes on Readings

In the *Preliminary Concordance*, this fragment was identified as frg. 3.

L. 2]תׄנלוים. The first letter after the lacuna can be a *taw* or *nun*. There is no space between this letter and the following word.

L. 5]יׄם. This is written above the line.

L. 5 תנחומׄ[ים. Only a trace is preserved of the last letter before the lacuna.

TRANSLATION

1. long] patience [
2.]they are joining until[
3. to ad]d their tributes/measures(?) [
4.] on those stricken by judgeme[nt
5.]and their seed, for the sake of consolatio[n
6.] which he spoke[
7.]to all who pull it/him [
8.]and in its furrows he will plough and (he will) always [
9. ri]ghteous ones, thei[r] in the heart of the k[nowledgeable ones (?)
10.]his rebuke [

COMMENTS

The fragmentary character of this text makes it difficult to understand. The theme of lines 3–4 may be consolation for those who are stricken. The subject in the third person (lines 6, 8, 10) can either be God or the righteous. In line 8 (and possibly line 7) we meet the image of ploughing and furrows, probably used symbolically, as is also done in Job 4:8; 31:38; Ps 129:3. Another option would be to see in lines 7–8 (or 5–8, cf.]וזרעם, line 5) sayings about the way of the farmer, for which cf. Isa 28:24-29; Sir 38:25-26.

L. 2]תנלוים עד[. We read נלוים as a separate word, *Nip'al* participle of לוה 'join'. The *Nip'al* of לוה in BH is followed by the prepositions אל, על or עם with the meaning 'join oneself to'. However, the last letter before the lacuna is *dalet*.

L. 3 מדתם. The word מדה can mean either 'measurement' or 'tax, tribute' (on the fields), as מנדה/מדה in Ezra 4:13, 20; 6:8; 7:24 (Aramaic); Neh 5:4 (Hebrew). The latter meaning could fit the theme of ploughing in line 8. Qimron notes that מדה 'measurement' in Qumran literature can have the spiritual meaning 'nature, way' as in Mishnaic Hebrew.[7]

L. 5]וזרעם. The word can mean either 'their seed/offspring' or 'their arm/strength'.

L. 7]לכול גורריו. Since the subject of the next line is ploughing, the object for גרר could be a plough.

L. 8]ובתלמיה יחרוש. The object could be שדה.

Frg. 3

מ]שפט] 1

]∘∘ היה משק]ל צדק 2

bottom margin

PAM 41.966, 43.534*

TRANSLATION

1. ju]dgement [

---

[7] *HDSS*, 101; cf. 1QS VIII 4 במדת האמת.

2.] was a [just] balan[ce

COMMENTS

This small fragment seems to deal with just balances, a well-known biblical theme from prophetic and sapiential literature.

L. 2 משק]ל צדק. Cf. Ezek 45:10 מאזני צדק; Prov 16:1; Job 31:6 מאזני משפט; 1QH[a] VI 26 ומשקלת א]מת. 4QInstruction connects the words משקל and מוזני צדק to God's creation of man and woman and His judging them; see 4Q**415** 9 12; 4Q**418** 127 6; and further about testing a prospective bride, see 4Q**418** 167 2 (= 4Q**415** 11 02); 4Q**415** 11 8.

Frg. 4

]ו֯תדׄ]בר 1

א]מתׄ נ∘∘[2

PAM 42.818, 43.534*

TRANSLATION

1.]and you will s[peak
2. tr]uth [

Frg. 5

מו[1

דׄ[2

PAM 43.534*

Frg. 6

ע]ל כול דׄב֯[ר 1

]פק[ ]לדרו[תם(?) 2

]∘[ ]∘ אׄמת ד֯[3

PAM 41.855, 43.534*

NOTES ON READINGS

L. 2]פק[. Possibly reconstruct from the root פקד: פק]ודה[or פק]ודת אל[. A tempting reconstruction is פק]ד אותם [לדרו]תם 'He comman[ded them]for [their] generation[s to . . .'.

TRANSLATION

1. up]on every wor[d
2.]for [their] generation[s (?)
3.] truth [

COMMENTS

This fragment is not located on Mus. Inv. 509.

Frg. 7

1]ם̊[

2]חר̊ג̊[

PAM 43.534*

COMMENTS

This fragment is not located on Mus. Inv. 509.

421. 4QWays of Righteousness[b]

(PLATE XVI)

4QWAYS of Righteousness is a sapiential composition preserved in two copies: 4Q**420** and 4Q**421** (see INTRODUCTORY COMMENTS to 4Q**420** for general remarks on the two manuscripts).

The skin of 4Q**421** is relatively thick. The colour is medium to dark brown; frgs. 2 and 12 are very dark brown. Frg. 1b, the lower part of frg. 1a, and frg. 12 have shrunk substantially. Frgs. 4, 11, 12, and 13 are difficult to read due to the darkening of the skin. On frg. 1b one can see the vertical ruling line which indicated the left margin of the column. On frg. 1b 12, 15 one can see parts of the horizontal ruling lines. The margin between cols. i and ii in frg 1a is *c*.12 mm; the left margin of frg. 1b is larger (16 mm from the vertical ruling line to the edge of the fragment), which could indicate the end of a sheet. This remains only a possibility. If so, this would be the end of the first sheet of the scroll (see below).

The text of frg. 1a ii-b 13–17 runs parallel to 4Q**420** 1a ii-b 1–7. Approximately one line of text from 4Q**420** 1a ii-b 2–3 is missing in 4Q**421** and was probably omitted by scribal error. A comparison between the two fragments which preserve the same text shows that the length of the lines 4Q**421** 1a ii-b seems to be approximately the same as in 4Q**420** 1a ii-b, which is reconstructed with 45–47 letter-spaces per line. 4Q**421** 1a ii-b 13 has at least 48 letter-spaces per line; line 14 is therefore reconstructed with 40 letter-spaces; line 15 with 44; line 17 with *c*.48. The length of the writing block was *c*.9–9.5 cm.

Placement of Fragments

When a transparent photocopy of frg. 1b is placed on top of frg. 1a, the wear pattern is obvious (the pattern of deterioration below the word משכיל of frg. 1b ii 10 corresponds to that of frg. 1a alongside the word ידלם of line 11). If the column was 9.5 cm wide, the length of the turn of the scroll at this point would be 7.5 cm. An examination of both sides of the fragments reveals that frg. 1a was located on top of frg. 1b: the verso of frg. 1a is darker exactly on the section where it was not covered from below by frg. 1b (these two fragments were possibly lying with their verso sides upwards after the fragmentation of the scroll). This observation shows that frg. 1a was located one turn further inwards than frg. 1b, and that the scroll was rolled in an unusual way with its beginning on the inside.

Scrolls that were rolled with the beginning on the inside were loosely wrapped; the circumference of such a scroll in its innermost turn can be quite large (1QS: 5 cm, 1QH[a]: 7 cm; 1QM: 9 cm). Such loosely rolled scrolls have no constant increase in circumference per turn as one proceeds outwards (an examination of 1QS shows great variation in the increase in circumference per turn, from 1 to 5 mm).[1] It is therefore difficult to calculate the distance from the beginning of the scroll to frg. 1a, but frg. 1a i must be close to its beginning. It could be the first column of the scroll, or, at the most, two columns could have preceded it. It is thus less probable that frg. 1b preserves the end of a sheet.

Frgs. 11, 12, and 13 demonstrate many similarities in their physical shape and must have been together in one wad, with frg. 11 on top, frg. 12 in the middle, and frg. 13 at the bottom.[2] These three fragments represent three consecutive columns. Since the scroll was rolled with its beginning on the inside, the sequence in the original scroll was frgs. 11, 12, 13. While frg. 11 probably belongs to the section containing wisdom sayings, frgs. 12 and 13 deal with matters connected with Temple service, which are not mentioned in any other fragments. The fact that these two fragments derive from a wad that included frg. 11 excludes the option that frgs. 12 and 13 might belong to a different scroll. An examination of the script and the skin confirms that frgs. 11–13 belong to the same scroll as frgs. 1–10. More than one column of text dealt with Temple matters, as frgs. 12 and 13 represent the same lines in two consecutive columns. Since frgs. 11, 12, and 13 represent three consecutive columns, they cannot represent the first part of the scroll which preceded frg. 1, but rather derive from a more external part. Frg. 11 probably represents the last column containing wisdom sayings, which was followed by the section on Temple matters.

The sequence of the fragments and main sections of the scroll was thus:

Frg. 1a i + frg. 2: Sectarian organization.

Frg. 1a ii-b, possibly frg. 3: Beginning of the wisdom sayings.

Frgs. 4, 5, 6, 9, and 10: These fragments belong to the section containing wisdom sayings. Their internal sequence cannot be determined.

Frg. 11: Probably the last column containing wisdom sayings.

Frgs. 12–13: Two columns on Temple matters.

The distance between frg. 1a and frg. 11 in the original scroll (and thus the length of the section containing wisdom sayings) cannot be ascertained. The location of the text of 4Q**420** 2 within the book is difficult to ascertain.

---

[1] H. Stegemann, 'Methods for the Reconstruction of Scrolls from Scattered Fragments', *Archaeology and History in the Ded Sea Scrolls—The New York University Conference in Memory of Yigael Yadin*, ed. L. H. Schiffman (Sheffield: Sheffield University Press, 1990) 196; T. Elgvin, 'The Reconstruction of Sapiential Work A', *RevQ* 16 (1993–95) 559–80, esp. 564–5 nn. 13, 17.

[2] The top and left edges of frgs. 12 and 13 cover each other well; frg. 11 has the same shape of the top edge, but sticks further out to the left. When one checks the verso of the fragments, frg. 13, which was at the bottom of this wad, is darkest. The lower part of the front side of frg. 13, which was not covered by frg. 12, is darker than the rest of the fragment.

Palaeography

The script is a developed Herodian formal script, from the first half of the first century CE.[3] The baseline of the *bet* is drawn from left to right, and in one case it extends beyond the vertical right downstroke (frg. 1a ii 14). Other occurrences of *bet* do not demonstrate this trait, which is typical for a developed Herodian script. *Waw* and *yod* are sometimes difficult to distinguish from one another. The hook of the *lamed* extends to the baseline. A peculiar final form of *dalet* is found in עד (frg. 1b 15), which is similar to a final *kap*. The *dalet* is clear on the parallel text in 4Q**420** 1 5. Elsewhere in 4Q**421** an ordinary form of *dalet* is used. In frg. 1b 15 we have a final, more ornamental, form of *dalet* due to the fact that it is the last letter on the line. For a similar phenomenon, see the *reš* in כבכור in 4Q**423** 8 4, which also is the last letter on the line. A similar final form of *dalet* is found in 4Q**212** (4QEnoch^{g}).[4]

Orthography and Morphology

4Q**421** reflects the so-called Qumran practice of orthography and morphology. לוא, כול, and כיא are written plene (with one exception: כל in frg. 9 3). For the pronominal suffix of the 3rd person pl. we find both *-hem* (frg. 1a ii 7), *-māh* (after a singular noun, frg. 1a ii 8) and *-hemmāh* (frg. 13 1). Final *mem* is used regularly, but medial *mem* occurs twice in final position (frg. 1b 16; frg. 13 1). Note also the form הרישון (frg. 1a i 4).

Mus. Inv. 512
PAM 41.706, 41.780, 41.860, 41.997, 42.633, 42.970, 42.974, 43.537*

Frg. 1a i

1 [ ]ם̊ באיבת ע̊[ולם
2 [ ]יב̇יא את כול ח]כ̊מתו ודעתו ובינ̊תו וט̊וב̊ו̊ [ביחד]
3 [אל]◦ל לסרך הכול איש לפני רע[הו]
4 [ ]יצ[א̊ הגו̊ר̊ל הרישון וכן יצ̊א̊ו

[3] Cf. F. M. Cross, 'The Development of the Jewish Scripts', *The Bible and the Ancient Near East: Essays in Honor of William Foxwell Albright*, ed. G. E. Wright (Garden City, N. Y.: Doubleday, 1961) 139, line 6.

[4] See the palaeographical chart in E. Eshel, H. Eshel, A. Yardeni, 'A Qumran Composition Containing Part of Ps. 154 and a Prayer for the Welfare of King Jonathan and his Kingdom', *IEJ* 42 (1992) 221.

5] י]תֿישרו אמרינו

6] א]וֿתֿו ליסרו

7] [ ]לֿ[[

8–13] [

14]]בֿל

15]]עֿשר

16]]שֿ

PAM 41.706, 42.633, 43.537*

NOTES ON READINGS

L. 1]םֿ באיבֿת עֿ]ולם. Only a trace is preserved of the last letter after the lacuna, here read as *mem*. The *Preliminary Edition*[5] reads]◦ באימֿתֿ. The fourth letter of the first complete word is clearly a *bet*, not a *mem*. The lower horizontal stroke is stretched into the *taw* to the left; this would not be the case for a *mem*.

Ll. 2–3 יביא את כול ח]כֿמתו ודעתו וביֿנתו וטֿובֿו [ביחד אל. For the reconstruction, cf. 1QS I 11–12 וכול הנדבים לאמתו יביאו כול דעתם וכוחם והונם ביחד אל.

TRANSLATION

1. [ ] with e[ternal] enmity [
2. [he shall bring all] his [wi]sdom and knowledge and understanding and good things [into the Community]
3. [of God] to muster everyone, each before [his] neighbo[ur]
4. [ ]the first lot [will fa]ll, and then they will go out
5. [ ]our words [will be ma]de straight
6. [h]im, to discipline him
7. [ ] [ ]

8–13. [ ]

14. [ ]shall not
15. [ ]ten/wealth/tithe (?)
16. [ ]

COMMENTS

This section deals with sectarian organization. The text refers either to the yearly mustering of the *yaḥad*, cf. 1QS I–II, or more probably to the joining of new members, cf. CD XIII 11–12. Line 1 describes the enmity between the *yaḥad* and the sons of the pit, lines 2–3 talk about bringing one's resources into the *yaḥad*, lines 3–4 about the mustering of the community, lines 5–6 about improving the ways of the

[5] B. Z. Wacholder, M. G. Abegg, *A Preliminary Edition of the Unpublished Dead Sea Scrolls. The Hebrew and Aramaic Texts from Cave Four. Fascicle Two* (Washington: Biblical Archaeological Society, 1992) 161.

members. Parallels to these lines are found especially in 1QS, but also in CD and 1QM.

L. 1 באיבת ע]ולם. This phrase is found in Ezek 25:15, 35:5, and in 1QS IV 17, where it describes the eternal enmity between the spirits of truth and evil; cf. also 4Q**415** (4QInstruction[d]) 2 ii 5 ואויבת לנפשך. In this text the phrase probably describes the enmity between the Community/the covenanters and outsiders, for which cf. also 1QS I 4, 10–11.

Ll. 2–3 יביא את כול ח]כמתו ודעתו ובינתו וטובו [ביחד אל. This phrase has a close parallel in 1QS I 11–12 (see above under NOTES ON READINGS); III 2 ודעתו וכוחו והונו לוא יביאו בעצת יחד and CD XIII 11 וכל הנוסף לעדתו יפקדהו למעשיו ושיכלו וכוחו וגבורתו והונו. A member of the Community shall bring all his resources into the Community and submit to its rules.[6] This sentence either speaks about new members entering the Covenant or about the continuous obligation of the covenanters to steward their property according to the rules of the *yaḥad*.

L. 3 לסרך הכול איש לפני רע]הו[. In the sectarian writings the verb סרך has the specific meaning 'to muster, to inscribe in (their) order';[7] cf. 1QM II 1, 6; 1QS V 23 וכתבם בסרך איש לפני רעהו 'They shall inscribe them in order, each man before his neighbour'; CD XIII 12 וכתבוהו במקומו כפי היותו בגורל הא]ור. This text carries the same meaning: the members shall be inscribed in the Community in a specific order, according to the maturity of each one.

L. 4 יצ]א הגורל הרישון וכן יצאו. Cf. CD XIII 4 about the order for living in the camps in the time before that of the coming of the anointed ones: ויצא הג]ו[רל לצאת ולבוא על פיהו כל באי המחנה. 1QM I 13–14 and XVII 16 mention the seven lots of the eschatological war. The theme of this text is not marching out to war, but the order of the Community, as in CD XIII and 1QS II; cf. 1QS II 21–23: וכול העם יעבורו בשלישית בסרך זה אחר זה . . . לדעת כול איש ישראל איש בית מעמדו ביחד אל . . . ולוא ישפול איש מבית מעמדו ולוא ירום ממקום גורלו. Schiffman proposes that הגורל הרישון could mean 'the first decision' (i.e. the decision about his membership). We note that all three main elements of lines 2–4 (the bringing of resources into the Community, the inscription of members in their order, the lot of each member) are found in the same sequence in CD XIII 11–12, which deals with new members entering the Community.

L. 5 י]תישרו אמרינו. That the way of the members shall be made straight is a theme known from sectarian writings; cf. 1QS IV 2; 1QH[a] VII 14. See also 4Q**219** (4QJub[d]) 1 ii 12 (*Jub.* 21:15) למען תי]שר בכול מעשיכה 'so that you may behave pr]operly in all your actions'. The reconstruction presupposes the *Hitpa'el* form of ישר, which is not used in the Bible or elsewhere in sectarian writings. Another, less probable option would be to read a *Pi'el* 2nd person sing. with suffix, תישרו[, and let the next word start a new sentence: 'you will make him straight. Our words . . .'.

L. 6 ליסרו. According to the sectarian writings the members must walk according to the discipline and ethics of the Community; cf. CD IV 8; VII 5, 7–8; 1QS IX 10. In this text the *Pi'el* form indicates that a superior member disciplines another member.

L. 15 עשר[. Or מ]עשר 'tithe'. See frg. 5 2.

---

[6] Cf. M. Weinfeld, 'All who freely devote themselves to His truth shall bring all their knowledge, powers and possessions into the Community of God (1QS I 12)', *Bible Studies. Y. M. Grintz in Memoriam*, ed. B. Uffenheimer (Tel Aviv: Tel Aviv University, 1982) 37–41 (Hebrew). For a recent interpretation of the fellowship of property among the Essenes, see H. Stegemann, *Die Essener, Qumran, Johannes der Täufer und Jesus* (Freiburg: Herder, 4th ed. 1994) 245–63.

[7] On the root סרך in Qumran literature, cf. L. H. Schiffman, *The Halakhah at Qumran* (Leiden: E. J. Brill, 1975) 60–68.

Frg. 1a ii-b

Parallels: 4Q**420** 1a ii-b (underline)

]   [
]   [
]   [
]   [
וׄיׄדׄ◦]   [
מושל בׄ]   [
פעמיהם עׄלׄ]   [
הרפאמה עלׄ]   ]אׄשר
אשר דבר]   ]◦נטׄ]]לׄשׂאׄתׄ
עול חכמׄ]ה   אי]שׄ משכיל ונבון
ידלם וישחׄ]   איש   י]וׄכח תוכחת
משכיל איש ◦]   ]ללכת בדרכי אל
לעשות צדקהׄ] בׄזׄוׄת לוא ישיב בטרם יש]מׄע ולוא ידבר בטרם
יבין בארך אׄ]פים ישיב פתגם ובמחקר צ]דק ימצא
תוצאותיה אׄ]יש עניו ונכי שכלו לוא ישו]ב אחור עד
]יׄ]מׄ]   איש נאמן לוא יסור מדרכי צדק]וישמ
]לבו ל   ול   עצמׄוׄתיו וכפיו בצדק נגׄאל בבינ]הׄ כול
]   שׄדותיו גבולו   [
]   לׄעשות צדׄקה   [

PAM 41.706, 42.633, 43.537*

NOTES ON READINGS

Ll. 8–9]אׄשר אשר. The repetition of אשר is due to dittography.

L. 14 The parallel text in 4Q**420** has approximately one line more of text. The scribe of 4Q**421** seems to have omitted one full line from his *Vorlage*, probably by error. The reconstructed line is based on a guess of which words were omitted by the scribe. The lacuna could possibly have space for one more word than what is reconstructed here.

L. 14 בארך אׄ]פים. 4Q**420** 1a ii-b 2 has בארוך אפים.

L. 15 א֯]יש. Only a trace of the first letter is preserved before the lacuna. Syntactically it is a natural solution to close one sentence with תוצאותיה and open the next one with איש, without any additional word between the two.

L. 16]מ֯[. Either *mem* or *bet*. This letter is the fourth on the line.

TRANSLATION

1–4. [ ]
5. [ ]
6. ruling in[ ]
7. their times because[ ]
8. their healing because[ ] which/who
9. (which/who) spoke[ ] [ ] to carry
10. the yoke of wisd[om . A ma]n who is knowledgeable and has understanding
11. will draw them up and [. A man of will recei]ve the admonition of the
12. knowledgeable. A man of [ ]to walk in the ways of God,
13. to do righteousness[as follows: he will not answer before he h]ears and not speak before
14. he understands. With great pa[tience will he give answer, and by studying ri]ghteousness will he understand
15. its consequences. A m[an who is humble and meek in mind will not tur]n away until
16. [ ] [A man who is trustworthy will not turn from ways of righteousness.]He will set
17. [his heart on and on his bones and his hands. By righteousness is he redeemed, through understan]ding all
18. [his fields, its borders]
19. [to do righteousness]

COMMENTS

The theme(s) of lines 5–8 cannot be ascertained from the fragmentary character of the text (the word הרפאמה in line 8 possibly derives from a warning which describes the ungodly). The theme of lines 9–10 is to submit to the yoke of wisdom, a theme known from Ben Sira. Lines 12–19 consist of wisdom sayings about the righteous man, with four units introduced by the word איש followed by one or two adjectives (lines 10, 12, 15, 16). For lines 13–19, see COMMENTS on **4Q420** 1a ii-b.

The admonition to submit to the yoke of wisdom serves as a prolegomenon to the wisdom sayings, which give concrete guidelines for the life of the member of the Community, as the discourses on wisdom in Proverbs 1–9 relate to the sayings in chapters 10–31. The knowledgeable man submits to the yoke of wisdom (lines 9–10), he is prepared to receive admonition (lines 11–12), and he walks according to the ways of God (lines 12–13). These ways are then described in the wisdom sayings.

L. 8 הרפאמה. Construct infinitive, *Nipʿal* of רפא 'heal' with suffix.

Ll. 9–10]לש֯א֯ת֯ עול חכמ֯]ה. Although עול can mean both 'evil' and 'yoke', 'yoke' is clearly the meaning in this context, and the continuation should be reconstructed חכמ֯]ה or חכמ֯]ת אל. (For the expression נשא עול 'carry a yoke'; cf. Lam 3:27). On the yoke of the wisdom of God, cf. the discourses on wisdom in Sir 6:22-31; 51:13-30; and esp. 6:24, 30, and 51:26 וצואריכם בעלה הביאו ומשאה תשא נפשכם 'Bend your neck to her yoke, and your soul will receive teaching'. The tradition of the yoke of wisdom is taken up both in the New Testament (Matt 11:29 ἄρατε τὸν ζυγόν μου ἐφ' ὑμᾶς καὶ μάθετε ἀπ' ἐμοῦ, 'Take my yoke upon you and learn from me') and in rabbinic literature (*m. Ber.* 2.2 כדי שיקבל עליו עול מלכות שמים תחלה ואחר כך יקבל עליו עול מצות 'so that one may first take upon oneself the yoke of the Kingdom of Heaven and then the yoke of the commandments'; *m. ʾAbot* 3.5 'He who takes upon himself the yoke of Torah [כל המקבל עליו על תורה] is thereby released from the burdens of the state and of worldly affairs'; *b. ʿAbod.*

Zar. 5b, 'Man should always set himself towards words of Torah as an ox to a yoke and as an ass to its burden' [translation mine]). This text shows that the intertestamental tradition of the yoke of Wisdom also was known in the Qumran community.[8]

The expression 'the yoke of Wisdom' refers to the Wisdom of God as a hypostatic concept. The tradition of hypostatic wisdom is found in a number of compositions from the Qumran caves.[9] 4Q**184** (4QWiles of the Wicked Woman) and 4Q**185** (4Qsapiential work) portray Lady Folly and Lady Wisdom, and elaborate these motifs from Proverbs 1–9 and Job 28. The addressees are exhorted to keep away from Lady Folly and hearken to Lady Wisdom and follow her ways. We enounter hypostatic wisdom also in 4Q**525** (4QBeatitudes) 2 ii 2–9; 4 6–13; 11QPs^{a} 154:5-15; 11QPs^{a} Sirach; as well as *1 Enoch* 42. In contrast to 4QWays of Righteousness, none of these compositions reveals signs of sectarian authorship.

Similar to Sirach 24 and Baruch 3:9–4:4, 4QBeatitudes and 11QPs^{a} 154 explicitly connect wisdom and Torah: 4Q**525** 2 3–4 אשרי אדם השיג חוכמה ויתהלך בתורת עליון, 'Blessed is the man who attains wisdom and walks in the Torah of the Most High'; 11QPs^{a} 154:14 שיחתם בתורת עליון 'their meditation is on the Torah of the Most High'.

'Lady Wisdom' does not figure clearly in the writings of the *yaḥad* or the presectarian 4QInstruction (olim Sap. Work A): God's wisdom and power are intrinsically connected to God himself and not related to any derived hypostatic figure (see e.g. 1QH^{a} IX 16–17 וכגב[ורת]כה אין בכוח ולכבודכה אין [חקר ו]לחכמתכה אין מדה 'there is no power to compare with Your mig[ht]. There is no [bound] to Your glory, and to Your wisdom, no measure'). To a large extent 'Lady Wisdom' seems to have been replaced by the apocalyptic concept *raz* or *raz nihyeh*, the unfolding mystery of God. The *yaḥad* knew the tradition of Lady Wisdom through books they had inherited and copied. In their own writings, however, they reinterpreted this concept. The text under discussion here is the only significant exception. This observation supports our assertion that the wisdom sayings contained in 4QWays of Righteousness represent earlier tradition adopted by the *yaḥad*.

Ll. 10, 12 משכיל. In sectarian literature this word can mean 'the knowledgeable' (CD XII 21; 1Q IX 12, 21; 1QH^{a} XII 11; 4Q**417** [4QInstruction^{c}] 2 i 25) or the 'authoritative teacher' (1QS III 13; 1QSb III 22; V 28; possibly CD XIII 22). In line 10, אי[שׁ משכיל ונבון clearly means a 'knowledgeable man'. משכיל probably carries the same meaning in line 12, although י[וֹכח תוכחת משכיל (lines 11–12) can be interpreted as 'recei]ve the admonition of the teacher'.

L. 11 ידלם. A verb with a 3rd person pl. suffix, possibly from the root דלה 'draw'.

Ll. 11–12 י[וֹכח תוכחת משכיל. י[וֹכח is either *Hipʿil* or *Hopʿal* of יכח. The latter option is easier in the context. In the *yaḥad* the root יכח refers to a formalized procedure of reproof with the aim of correcting a member who has erred; cf. Lev 19:17-18; CD IX 2–8; 1QS V 24–VI 1; VII 8–9; IX 16–18.[10]

L. 12 ללכת בדרכי אל. Perhaps reconstruct יצניע [ללכת בדרכי אל, for which cf. 4Q**438** 5 2. For דרכי אל, cf. 2 Sam 22:22; Ps 18:22; 138:5 דרכי יהוה; 4Q**438** (4QBarki Nafshi^{e}) 4 ii 2 [ללכת] בדרכי אל; 5 2–3 ולהצניע

---

[8] M. Kister ('Biblical Phrases and Hidden Biblical Interpretations and *Pesharim*', *The Dead Sea Scrolls: Forty Years of Research*, eds. D. Dimant, U. Rappaport [STDJ 10; Leiden/Jerusalem: Brill, Magnes, 1992] 27–39) finds a similar motif in CD I 13–19: in his opinion this passage portrays unbelieving Israel, the stubborn heifer of Hos 10:11, who receives God's yoke as burden and punishment in contrast to the faithful who chose to accept the Divine yoke and God's upright commandments. This text, however, does not mention any yoke in such a positive sense.

M. Weinfeld ('The Loyalty Oath in the Ancient Near East', *Ugarit-Forschungen* 8 [1976] 406–7; *idem*, *Social Justice in Ancient Israel and in the Ancient Near East* [Jerusalem: Magnes; Minneapolis: Fortress, 1995] 206, n. 66) has noted that in Hellenistic use 'to take upon oneself a yoke' designates entry into a religious community and acceptance of its authority (see Apuleius, *Metamorph.* XI, 15), and proposes that 'yoke' in such a context signifies freedom, not burden (cf. *m. ᵓAbot* 6:2 '. . . graven upon the tables. Read not *graven* [חָרוּת] but *freedom* [חֵרוּת], for no man is free but he who occupies himself with the Law', and the phrase חירות עולם 'freedom of their yoke' in the Evening Prayer).

[9] See M. Küchler, *Frühjüdische Weisheitstraditionen. Zum Fortgang weisheitlichen Denkens in Bereich des frühjüdischen Jahweglaubens* (Göttingen: Vandenhoeck and Ruprecht, 1979) 95, 102–3.

[10] Cf. L. H. Schiffman, *Sectarian Law in the Dead Sea Scrolls. Courts, Testimony and the Penal Code* (Chico: Scholars Press, 1983) 89–109.

ללכת [בדרכי אל; 4Q**215** (4QTNaph) 2 ii 5–6 להשכיל [כול אנש] בדרכי אל. 1QS uses both דרכי אל (III 10) and דרכי צדק (IV 2). Our text also uses both phrases: דרכי צדק is used in the continuation, line 16. In 4Q**423** (4QInstruction[e]) 9 3 we find the phrase דרכי קודש with the same meaning, פן ישוגו ב]דרכי קודש (see below, n. 24). 4Q**473** (4QThe Two Ways) presents the two ways in a context of blessings and curses; 2 1–2 בה שׁ[תי]דרכים אחת טוב[ה ואחת רעה אם תלך בדרך הטובה הואה ישמורכה(?)] ויברככה ואם תלך 3–4 2 ;הדרך אשר תלך(?)] בדרך ה[רעה 't[wo]ways, one goo[d and one evil. If you walk on the good way He will guard you(?)] and bless you. But, if you walk on the [evil] way'.

L. 13 לעשות צדקה. This is a biblical term which also occurs in 1QS VIII 2; 4Q**200** (4QTobit[e]) 2 9 (with the meaning 'give alms'); 4Q**258** (4QS[d]) 1 i 3.

Frg. 2 (olim frg. 5)

1]ש בפיה[ו

2] דבר לברך ◦[

3 כו]ל[א]יש לפני[רעהו

PAM 42.633, 43.537*

TRANSLATION

1.] in [his] mouth[
2.] a word to bless [
3. ever]y[m]an before[his neighbour

COMMENTS

Frg. 2 belongs to the same section on sectarian organization as frg. 1a i. It could refer to the communal meal, cf. 1QS VI 2–13.

L. 3 כו]ל[א]יש לפני[רעהו. Cf. frg. 1a i 3 לסרך הכול איש לפני רע[הו] and the references *ad locum*.

Frg. 3 (olim frg. 4)

1]ד על תוצ[אות

2]◦ איש ושומר[

3 ע]ל אמתו יוצי[א דברו

PAM 41.706, 42.633, 43.537*

NOTES ON READINGS

L. 2 ושומר[. Or read: ישימו[.

TRANSLATION

1.] regarding resu[lts

2.] a man, and one guarding[
3. be]cause of his truthfulness he will bring for[th his opinion

COMMENTS

Frg. 3 belongs to the section containing wisdom sayings. Since line 3 is similar in topic to frg. 1a ii-b 13–14, this fragment could possibly be inserted into the lacuna in frg. 1a ii-b 10–12, yielding a possibly reconstructed text of line 12: משכיל איש ח]סיד(?) ע[ל אמתו יוצ֯י֯]א דברו ילמד(?) [ללכת בדרכי אל, 'knowledgeable. A [piou]s(?) man, [be]cause of his truthfulness, will bring for[th his opinion; he will learn(?)]to walk in the ways of God'.

L. 3 ע]ל אמתו יוצ֯י֯]א דברו. The topic is similar to frg. 1a ii-b 13–14.

Frg. 4 (olim frg. 2)

]◦ י֯שמור

]ובלבו

PAM 41.780, 42.633, 43.537*

TRANSLATION

1.] he will guard
2.]and in his heart

COMMENTS

Frg. 4 belongs to the section containing wisdom sayings which describes the righteous man.

Frg. 5 (olim frg. 3)

א]ם ישיׄב[

]ע֯ש֯ר לדעת ו◦[

PAM 42.970, 43.537*

TRANSLATION

1. i]f he answers[
2.]wealth(?), to know [

Comments

This fragment is only recorded on the latest photograph of this composition, which places it in lines 14 and 15 of frg. 1a ii-b, between frgs. 1a and 1b. The text of the first line can easily be fitted together with the text of frg. 1a ii-b 14 (as reconstructed from the parallel in **4Q420** 1a ii-b 2): יבין בארץ א̊[פי]ם̊ ישיב̊] פתגם. The text of the second line, however, does not fit with 4Q**421** 1a ii-b 15, so that this option should be discarded. The fragment belongs to the section containing wisdom sayings.

L. 2 ע̊שר֗]. Or מ[ע̊שר֗ 'tithe'. The same word occurs in 1a i 15.

Frg. 6

1 [ת̊ ◦]

2 [◦ר֗ו מש◦◦]

3 [א̊שר איננו ◦]

4 [ר̊ א֗יש כ֗◦]

PAM 41.997, 42.633, 43.537*

Translation

1.] [
2.] [
3.]who is not [
4.] a man [

Comments

Frg. 6 belongs to the section containing wisdom sayings.

Frg. 7

1 [י̊כ̊ה̊ ◦]

2 [◦מים עמ]

PAM 41.997, 42.633, 43.537*

Frg. 8

]◦ שׁורר̊ ב[1

מג]ל̊ת ספר לקרוא̊[2

PAM 42.633, 42.970, 43.537*

TRANSLATION

1.] is ruling over[
2. the sc]roll of a book to read[

COMMENTS

L. 1 שׁורר̊ ב[. The meaning of שׂרר ב- is 'rule over'. Other options are שׁורר̊ ב]אל(?) 'rising against[God, or, שׁורר̊ ב]ו(?) 'rising against[him(?) (from שׁרר 'rise up against', cf. Ps 5:9; 27:11).[11]

L. 2 מג]ל̊ת ספר. The phrase מגלת ספר is found in Jer 36:2, 4; Ezek 2:9; Ps 40:8; but not elsewhere in Qumran literature.

Frg. 9

]◦ יאמץ לנ◦[1

ח]ב̊ריו לחזק לבב̊ נ̊ג̊]ועים(?) 2

]ל̊[כ]לות כל עבדי ר̊[שע(?) 3

]ל̊[ ]◦◦[4

PAM 42.633, 43.537*

NOTES ON READINGS

L. 2 ח]ב̊ריו לחזק לבב̊ נ̊ג̊]ועים. The reconstruction is tentative. The first word could be reconstructed ד[ב̊ריו 'his [w]ords'.

TRANSLATION

1.] he will have courage to[
2.]his [fr]iends, to strengthen the heart of the st[ricken(?)
3.]to [exter]minate all the servants of e[vil(?)
4.] [ ] [

[11] Cf. BDB 1004, *HALAT* 1349.

COMMENTS

Frg. 9 belongs to the section containing wisdom sayings. Line 2 deals with exhortation within the *yaḥad*.

L. 2 (?)לחזק לבב̇ נ̇ג̇[ועים. In the Bible לחזק לב means ‘harden somebody’s heart’. In Qumran literature, however, it means ‘strengthen/encourage somebody’s heart’: 4Q**504** (4QDibHam[a]) 1–2 v 8–9 כי אתה חזקתה את לבבנו ‘you strengthened our heart’; 1QM XVI 13–14 ותחזק את לבכם; 4Q**436** (4QBarki Nafshi[c]) 1 i 1 בינה לחזק לב נדכה; ‘. . . understanding, to encourage the heart of the downcast’; 1 i 4 ותחזק על לב]י ‘you strengthened [my] heart’.

L. 3]ל̊[כ]לות כל עבדי ר̊[שע. If the reconstruction ל̊[כ]לות is correct, we have a reference to God’s judgement of the wicked. This theme is not mentioned in any of the other preserved fragments of this composition, but it is prominent in other sapiential writings such as the Book of Mysteries and 4QInstruction. The continuation could be reconstructed as here or כל עבדי ב̊[ליעל ‘all the servants of B[elial’, for which cf. 1QS II 4–5 כול אנשי גורל בליעל; 4Q**286** (4QBer[a]) 7 ii 6 כול בני בלי]על. Cf. 1Q**27** (1QMyst) 1 i 7 וכל תומכי רזי פש̊ע̊ אינמה עוד.

Frg. 10

1 אי]ש נאמן בכו̊[ל דרכו(?)
2]ל̊ו עד ל[

PAM 42.633, 43.537*

TRANSLATION
1. a] faithful [ma]n in al[l his ways(?)
2.] until [

COMMENTS

Frg. 10 belongs to the section containing wisdom sayings.

L. 1 אי]ש נאמן בכו̊[ל דרכו. Or: אי]ש נאמן בכו̊[ל ביתו. This sentence may allude to the description of Moses in Num 12:7 בכל ביתי נאמן הוא. For the word נאמן, cf. COMMENTS to 4Q**420** 1a ii-b 5.

Frg. 11 (olim frg. 12)

1]◦ ◦◦ תצא̊◦[ ]ושא[
2 ב]טוח לאכול ולשתות ממנו כ̊ו̊ל ◦[
3]ס̊פ̊ר והיה חינ̇ם אל ישאב ממנו ◦[
4]כ̊יא מלאכת צ̊[דק]היאה אל י̊חל[
5]ו̊איש בחד̊[ ]ל[
6 כ]ו̊ל ◦[

PAM 41.860, 41.997, 42.633*, 43.537

NOTES ON READINGS

L. 3 חינׄם. Wacholder and Abegg read חוׄנה, which does not make sense. The unusual plene spelling חינׄם is to be preferred, although the same word is written defectively in frg. 12 4.

L. 4 כׄיא מלאכת צׄ]דק[היאה[. Only a trace is preserved of a *ṣade*, *ʿayin*, or *šin* before the lacuna. Wacholder and Abegg reconstruct מלאכת עׄ]בד [which yields the translation 'for it is the work of a s[lave'. A dot (visible on the photograph only) below the *nun* of the word חינם in line 3 might be the head of a *lamed*. If so, both proposals should be discarded for a word beginning with *ṣade*, *ʿayin*, or *šin*, and with *lamed* as its second letter.

L. 5 בחרׄ[. The last letter before the lacuna could be *reš*, which could yield the reconstruction ואׄיש בחרׄ]פתו.

TRANSLATION

1.]
2. r]eliable(?), to eat and drink from it all [
3.]counted(?), and it will be in vain. Let him not draw from it [
4.]for a rig[hteous] deed it is. Let him not wait[
5.] man in [
6. a]ll[

COMMENTS

The precise theme of frg. 11 is not easy to comprehend. It seems to deal with human sustenance. Line 2 deals with a positive source for food and drink and could allude to the condition of man in the Garden of Eden.[12] Line 3 mentions a disappointing source from which one should not draw water.

Frg. 11 was located one column before frg. 12, which followed the section containing wisdom sayings. Frg. 11 could belong to the first part of the section on Temple and priestly matters, but more probably derives from the last part of the section containing wisdom sayings. While the wisdom sayings of frgs. 1a ii-b, 3, 9 and 10 are formulated in the indicative, the sayings or rules in frgs. 11–13 are formulated in the vetitive (*ʾal yiqtol*) or prohibitive (*lōʾ yiqtol*). This form could indicate that these rules were considered halakhically binding for the *yaḥad*. Frg. 11 3–4 could preserve remnants of two wisdom admonitions with motive clauses:[13] 'Let him not draw from it [ ]for a righteous deed it is. Let him not wait['.

L. 2 ב[טוח. Some form of the root בטח 'trust' can be reconstructed here, possibly as the passive participle 'be reliable' or 'feel secure'. Alternatively one could reconstruct להב[טיח, a *Hipʿil* with the meaning 'to make a promise' as in Sir 13:6; 20:23. Another option is the passive participle ש[טוח 'spread out'.

---

[12] Cf. 4Q**423** (4QInstruction A^e) 1–2, which use the Eden-theme to describe man's conditions and tasks on earth as well as his spiritual-eschatological share.

[13] In the biblical material the wisdom sentence (*mašal*) can be divided into the separate forms of *wisdom admonition* (*Mahnwort*) and *wisdom saying* (*Aussage*) on form-critical grounds. While wisdom sayings are formulated in the indicative mood, wisdom admonitions are formulated in the imperative (or relevant mood) and are characterised by a subordinate motive clause. See P. J. Nel, *The Structure and Ethos of the Wisdom Admonitions in Proverbs* (Berlin, New York: de Gruyter, 1982) 4–5, 18–74; H.-J. Hermisson, *Studien zur israelitischen Spruchweisheit* (Neukirchen: Neukirchener, 1968) 160–62.

L. 2 לאכול ולשתות ממנו. 1QH[a] VIII 12–13 uses similar terminology to express the idea that ordinary people have no access to the spring of life: בל י]בוא ב[מעין חיים ועם עצי עולם לא ישתה מי קודש '[will] not [reach] the spring of life, nor with the everlasting trees will it drink the waters of holiness'.

L. 2 כׄולׄ °[. Possibly reconstruct something like כול י]מי חיו 'all the d[ays of his life'.

L. 3]סׄפׄר. The exact meaning of this word from the root ספר cannot be ascertained.

L. 3 והיה חינׄם אל ישאב ממנו. For a similar theme, cf. Jer 2:13 אתי עזבו מקור מים חיים לחצב להם בארות בארת נשברים אשר לא יכלו המים, rephrased in *1 Enoch* 96:6 'Woe to you who drink water from every fountain. For suddenly you shall be consumed and wither away, because you have forsaken the fountain of life'.

L. 4 מלאכת צׄ]דק. If one follows Wacholder and Abegg's reconstruction [מלאכת עׄ]בד, the slave is mentioned both here and one column later in the scroll, in frg. 12 2. The meaning of lines 3–4 could then be 'let him not draw water from the well, that is the work of a slave'.

Frg. 12 (olim frg. 11)

]° °כׄה ימׄאׄ[

]° וכול עבד ואמה לוא יוכל במׄ[קדש אל(?)

]אׄ ואל יבא בשער חצרו ובשעׄ[ר

אל יבי]אׄ ממקומו חנׄם ואם בא כׄ[ו]ל[

]מׄה או בׄ[ ]לׄ[

PAM 41.997, 42.633, 43.537*

NOTES ON READINGS

L. 2 במׄ]קדש. The last letter before the lacuna is *mem* or *nun*.

L. 4 חנׄם. Wacholder and Abegg read חנׄו, which does not make sense.

TRANSLATION

1.] your [
2.] and no slave or maidservant shall eat in the t[emple of God(?)
3.] and he shall not enter by/bring into the gate of its court or by/into the gat[e of
4. he shall not brin]g from its/His place in vain. And if a[n]y [ ] enters [
5.]their [ ] or [

COMMENTS

Frgs. 12 and 13 deal with matters having to do with the Temple, a topic not mentioned in any other fragment of this composition. Frg. 12 possibly contains four prohibitions related to the Temple in the prohibitive (לוא יוכל) and the vetitive (אל יבא): line 2 prohibits gentile slaves from partaking of sacrificial meals in the Temple, line 3 prohibits a certain group from entering the Temple courts; the first part of line 4 is possibly a prohibition to bring something from the altar; the second part could mention another group which is excluded from entering the Temple or a part of it.

Exclusion from the Temple and the assembly of Israel is a topic mentioned in a number of biblical and post-biblical texts. Deut 23:1-8 prohibits Ammonites, Moabites, those born in forbidden marriages, and castrated persons from joining the community of God. 2 Sam 5:8 records the saying from the First Temple period: 'The blind and the lame shall not come into the house'.[14] *Tg. Pseudo-Jonathan* 2 Sam 5:8 translates 'sinners and wicked ones' על כין יימרון חטאיא וחייביא לא ייעלון לביתא. According to *m. ᶜEd.* 5.6 and *b. Moᶜed Qaṭ.* 15b, banned persons were excluded from the Temple court and thus from offering sacrifices.[15] *M. Roš Haš.* 1.8 puts gamblers, usurers, pigeon-trainers, and dealers in produce of the sabbatical year on the same footing as slaves (i.e. gentile slaves) with regard to testimony.[16] *Jub.* 16:25 uses the example of Abraham to assert that one should not celebrate a festival together with an alien or uncircumcised man (cf. also Exod 12:43, 48). According to *Pss. Sol.* 17:22, 28, aliens and foreigners (probably reflecting גר ונוכרי) will not reside in Jerusalem or partake in the messianic kingdom.

The sectarian writings[17] combine Deut 23:1-2 with Lev 21:16-24, regarding the restrictions on priests with blemishes, and further with 2 Sam 5:6-8, Exod 4:11, and Ezek 44:6-9 in their exegesis of who can enter the *yaḥad*. 4QMMT B 39–49 repeats the prohibition of Deut 23:1-8 regarding Ammonites, Moabites, those born in forbidden marriages, and castrated persons; they should neither enter the Temple nor intermarry with Israelites. 4QMMT B 49–54 specifies that the blind and deaf, although they are physically unable to obey the law fully, do have access to the sacred food. 1QSa II 3–8 excludes from the *yaḥad* anyone who is lame, blind, deaf, dumb, or smitten with a visible blemish. 4Q**267** (4QD^b) 17 i 6–9 fills the lacuna at the end of CD XV: 'Fools, madmen, simpletons and imbeciles, the blind, the maimed, the lame, the deaf, and minors, none of these may enter the midst of the Community'. 11QT^a XLV 12–14 forbids the blind to enter the Temple. 4QFlor I 3–4 extends the restriction of Deuteronomy 23: the Ammonite, the Moabite, the half-breed, the proselyte, and the stranger are forbidden from entering the eschatological Temple.[18] 1QM VII 4–6 forbids the lame, blind, crippled, or those afflicted with a lasting bodily blemish from marching out to war. 11QT^a XXXIX 7 and XL 6 indicate that women were permitted only to enter the outer court, not the middle one, of the Temple. According to the

---

[14] According to M. Weinfeld, this saying reflects a Davidic adaptation of Hittite custom to exclude the crippled from the temple: 'Traces of Hittite Cult in Shiloh, Bethel and in Jerusalem', *Religionsgeschichtliche Beziehungen zwischen Kleinasien, Nordsyrien und dem Alten Testament, OBO* 129 (1993) 458–9.

[15] Cf. G. Alon, 'On the Halakhot of the Early Sages', *Jews, Judaism and the Classical World* (Jerusalem: Magnes, 1977) 138–45.

[16] J. Jeremias, *Jerusalem in the Time of Jesus* (London: SCM, 1969) 303–16.

[17] Cf. J. M. Baumgarten, *Studies in Qumran Law* (Leiden: E. J. Brill, 1977) 75–87; L. H. Schiffman, *The Eschatological Community of the Dead Sea Scrolls. A Study of the Rule of the Congregation* (Atlanta: Scholars Press, 1989) 37–52; E. Qimron and J. Strugnell, *DJD* X, 142–7, 158–61.

[18] The lacuna at the beginning of line 4 has space for two or three initial categories of those to be excluded. A. Steudel proposes [ערל לב וערל ב]שׂרֹ[עד]עֹולם '[der am Herzen Unbeschnittene noch der am Fl]eisch [Unbeschnittene für]immer' (*Der Midrasch zur Eschatologie aus der Qumrangemeinde (4QMidrEschat$^{a.b}$)* [Leiden: E. J. Brill, 1994] 25, 31). Yadin proposed [איש אשר בב]שׂרֹ[ו מום]עֹולם ('A Midrash on 2 Sam. vii and Ps. i–ii (4Q *Florilegium*)', *IEJ* IX [1959] 95–8), while Vermes translates 'unclean and uncircumcised', *DSSE*, 3rd. ed., 1990, 293.

Temple Scroll, menstrually impure women would be excluded from עיר המקדש.[19] 4Q**267** (4QD^b) 6 ii 4–7 prescribes that a priest who has been a captive among the gentiles can no longer enter the priestly court, participate in the Temple sacrifices, or eat of the sacrificial meat: ואל יוכל את קודש ה֯[. The latter paragraph from 4QD^b seems to provide the clearest parallel to this text.

L. 2 וכול עבד ואמה לוא יוכל במ֯]קדש אל. This prohibition must refer to gentile slaves who are prohibited from partaking of sacrificial meals in the Temple, in contrast to physically handicapped Israelites, for which cf. 4QMMT B 49–54. It is hardly comprehensible that the sectarians would exclude Israelite slaves from entering the Temple or from partaking of sacrificial meals. CD XII 10–11 prescribes that a master should not sell his slaves (of gentile origin) to gentiles, 'because they have entered with him the Covenant of Abraham' (i.e. circumcision) ואת עבדו ואת אמתו אל ימכור להם אשר באו עמו בברית אברהם.[20] We note that this text from CD mentions the pair עבד and אמה. The same is the case in Lev 25:44 which also deals with gentile slaves ועבדך ואמתך אשר יהיו לך מאת הגוים. This text preserves a restrictive attitude to gentiles in relation to the Temple, as does 4QMMT B 3–9 which opposes the sacrifices of the gentiles and the use of grain grown by gentiles in the Temple.

For the matter of eating in the sanctuary, cf. 4Q**513** (4QOrd^b) 10 ii 6–7 which mentions טהרה 'pure food' in connection with המקדש; the subject is probably a prohibition of mixing priestly and lay sacrificial meat.[21] If במ֯]קדש is correctly reconstructed, the prohibition deals with the Temple area and not the communal meals. The passage might preserve early Temple halakha which provided the basis for similar sectarian teaching connected to the communal meal and its purity.

L. 2 לוא יוכל. A common theme in the sectarian writings is the criteria for partaking of the sacred food. Similar terminology to כול . . . לוא יוכל is found in the Rule of Discipline and 4QS fragments, cf. 4QS^d 1 i 9] ואל יואכל איש מאנשי הקדש (= 4QS^b 5 10–11); 4QS^d 1 7–8 (= 4QS^b 5 8–9) לוא יגעו לטהרת אנשי [הקוד]ש ואל יוכל אתו ב[יחד; 1QS V 16 ואשר לוא יוכל מהונם כול ולוא ישתה. Cf. also 4Q**514** (4QOrd^c) where אל יאכל appears four times in connection with states of impurity (frg. 1a ii-b 2, 3–4, 7, 8);[22] 4Q**513** (4QOrd^c) 11 1 אם יא֯[וכל]ו מהמ֯[ה; 24 3 ולוא יוכאלו[.[23] For the subject matter, cf. 4QMMT B 23 (on one who has carried a carcass) לוא י[גש לטהרת ה֯[קודש 'he shall not have access to the sacred food'.

L. 3 ואל יבא בשער חצרו ובשע֯[ר. A prohibition for a certain group to enter the Temple courts or a prohibition to bring something into the Temple. This line also could refer to gentile slaves; they 'should not eat in the t[emple of God . . .] and not <even> enter the gate of its courts . . .' At the end of the line, reconstruct either ובשע֯[ר בית אלהים (cf. Jer 36:10; Ezek 8:14 שער בית יהוה—the tetragrammaton would

---

[19] According to Yadin (*The Temple Scroll*, vol. I, 289, 306), the *Temple Scroll* excludes women from living in the entire city of Jerusalem. Schiffman disagrees; menstrually impure women would be excluded from the 'Temple City' (which in his view is the expanded Temple area), but ritually pure women were allowed into the outer court; see 'Exclusion from the Sanctuary and the City of the Sanctuary in the Temple Scroll', *HAR* 9 (1985) 301–20. Qimron and Strugnell assert that MMT supports Yadin's view: for the sectarians all Jerusalem, not only the Temple area, is a sacred area (*DJD* X, 142–5).

[20] Cf. L. Ginsberg, *An Unknown Jewish Sect* (New York: The Jewish Theological Seminary of America, 1976) 78. On gentile slaves, see Billerbeck IV, 716–44; J. Jeremias, *Jerusalem in the Time of Jesus* (London: SCM, 1969), 345–51. According to the rabbis, a slave did not belong to the community of Israel although he had gone through proselyte baptism and circumcision. He had lost the status of a heathen but not yet attained that of a Jew (*b. Sanh.* 58b; *b. B. Qam.* 88a).

[21] J. M. Baumgarten, 'Halakhic Polemics in New Fragments from Qumran Cave 4', *Biblical Archaeology Today: Proceedings of the International Congress on Biblical Archaeology, Jerusalem, April 1984*, ed. J. Amitai (Jerusalem: Israel Exploration Societey, 1985) 392.

[22] According to 4Q**514**, the impure can only partake of the pure food after ablution; cf. J. Milgrom, *The Dead Sea Scrolls. Hebrew, Aramaic, and Greek Texts with English Translations, vol. 1. The Rule of the Community and Related Documents,* ed. J. H. Charlesworth (Tübingen: Mohr; Louisville: Westminster John Knox, 1994) 177.

[23] According to Schiffman (Charlesworth, *The Dead Sea Scrolls*, vol 1, 171), 4Q**513** 24 probably deals with parturients; this line contains a prohibition against eating pure food by new mothers before their purification.

usually be avoided in a sectarian text); ובשע֯[ר המזבח (cf. Ezek 8:5); or ובשע֯[ר מזבחו. The phrase שער החצר is frequent in Exodus 35–40. 4QShirShab frequently mentions the gates of the heavenly Temple through which the angels pass during their praises, but this text certainly deals with the earthly Temple. The mention of the gate and the courtyard makes it clear that this text deals with the Temple, and not with the Essene house of prayer (בית השתחות CD XI 22).[24] אל יבא is a halakhic term which in sectarian literature carries the meaning 'he shall not bring' (1QS VI 1; CD XI 9), or 'he shall not come' [1QS V 13; 1QSa I 20; II 4; 4Q**271** (4QD^{f}) 3 i 15]. In this text it should probably be read as *Qal* 'he shall not come', not as *Hipʿil* 'he shall not bring'. A *Hipʿil* would hardly be written defectively by this scribe [cf. frg. 3 3 י֯וצ֯י[א, see, however, the spelling אל יבא for 'he shall not bring': 4Q**258** (4QS^{d}) 1 ii 5; 4Q**263** (4QS^{i}) 1 1; CD XI 9; 4Q**269** (4QD^{d}) 10 5; 4Q**270** (4QD^{e}) 5 17; 7 21; 10 v 14; 4Q**271** (4QD^{f}) 1 i 10; 1 ii 8; 3 i 5]. 4Q**389a** (4QapocrJer E) 6 3 uses ויביאם בשער for bringing something into the temple.

L. 4 אל יבי[א ממקומו חנם. This is possibly a prohibition to bring something from the altar. The word חנם 'in vain' is found (written plene) in frg. 10 3; cf. also CD VI 11–14 which quotes Mal 1:10 on kindling fire in vain on the altar: לבלתי בוא אל המקדש להאיר מזבחו חנם.

L. 4 ואם בא כ֯[ו]ל[. The beginning of a prohibition or a conditional clause.

Frg. 13

[כ֯יא אם אלפ֯[ני]ה֯מ֯ה֯] יפלו(?)

כ]ו֯ל העולות והזבחים א֯[

[ם אל יחשב֯] לו   ]◦◦[

[דברי קו֯דש כחוק]

] אל יער איש א֯[

[ש֯ ב֯כ֯[ו]ל֯ ה֯ק֯ר֯[בנות

PAM 41.860, 42.633, 42.974, 43.537*

NOTES ON READINGS

L. 1 אלפ֯[ני]ה֯מ֯ה֯[. The reading is tentative. There is no space between the *lamed* and the *pe*.

TRANSLATION

1.]but on their f[aces they should prostrate
2. a]ll the holocausts and the sacrifices [
3.] let it not be credited[to him
4.]the holy things according to the law [
5.] let a man not uncover himself [
6.] and in a[l]l the sac[rifices

[24] Cf. A. Steudel, 'The Houses of Prostration *CD* XI, 21–XII, 1—Duplicates of the Temple', *RevQ* 16 (1993–95) 49–68.

COMMENTS

Frg. 13 seems to preserve priestly halakha on the Temple service. Mentioned are sacrifices and their validity, the holy matters, and how to approach the altar. This passage might raise anew the question of the relation of the Qumran community to the Temple as well as the question of sacrifices in Qumran.[25] On the Essenes' relation to the Temple, cf. *Ant.* XVIII 19; CD VI 11–14; XI 17–21; XVI 13; 1QS IX 4 (on the spiritual sacrifices); 1QM II 4–5 (on the priestly service in the renewed Temple of the last days); 4QMMT B 3–13. Priestly material is also found in three other sapiential writings: 4Q**299** (4QMyst[a]) 52 (e.g. line 5]◦◦ ע֯ל ו֯לכפ֯ר קודשו [עבו]ד֯ת), 65, and 75; 4Q**419** (4QSap. Work B) 1, which deals with the priestly duties (e.g. line 6 ולגיש ניחוח); 4Q**423** (4QInstruction[e]) 3, which probably contains a liturgical formula for the redemption of the first born. These Qumran sapiential compositions demonstrate the same phenomenon as 4QWays of Righteousness: priestly matters are mentioned in only a small minority of the preserved fragments.

L. 1 כ֯יא אם אלפ֯[ני]ה֯מ֯ה֯] יפלו(?). אל is probably a scribal error for על. נפל על פנים is a technical term for prostrating/falling face down, frequent in the priestly stratum of the Pentateuch. The term fits well in this Temple context. Alternatively, the line could preserve a suffixal form of אֱלְפָּן 'custom', 'training', instruction', known from rabbinic literature.

L. 2 כ]ו֯ל העולות והזבחים. עולות וזבחים are often mentioned as a pair in the Bible; cf. Exod 10:25; 1 Sam 15:22; 2 Kgs 10:24; 1 Chr 29:21; 2 Chr 7:1. In Qumran literature we find the phrase in 1QM II 5; cf. 1QS IX 4 on the spiritual sacrifices מבשר עולות ומחלבי זבח.

L. 3 אל יחשב֯] לו. The terminology of this prohibition in the vetitive is drawn from Lev 7:18 which deals with an invalid sacrifice that will not be credited to the offering person לא ירצה המקריב אתו לא יחשב לו פגול יהיה. The same terminology is found in 4Q**225** (4QpsJub[a]) 2 i 8 יתחשב לו צדקה.

L. 4 דברי קודש כחוק. The phrase דברי קודש is not found in the Bible (בגדי קודש and כלי הקודש are common, however), but does occur in Qumran literature: 4Q**403** (4QShirShabb[d]) 1 i 24 בשב֯[עה]ד֯ברי קודש פל֯א֯[ו, about angelic words of blessing; 4Q**436** (4QBarki Nafshi) 1 i 7 ולשוני פתחתה לדברי קודש, about words of prayer; and 4Q**418** 188 (4QInstruction[a]) 7 פ֯ן֯ ישוגו בדברי֯] קודש, 'lest they err regarding the holy matters'.[26] In this text, דברי קודש probably refers to matters related to the Temple or priestly ministry. 4Q**414** (4QBaptLit) 3 1 talks about 'the laws of holiness' ו֯תט֯ה֯]ר [ב֯ו לחוקי קו֯ד֯ש, while 4Q**419** (4QSap. Work B) 1 1 uses the word משפטים about priestly precepts: אשר תעשו על פי כול המשפ֯[טים.

L. 5 אל יער. A prohibition in the vetitive of ערר *Qal* 'uncover oneself', cf. Isa 32:11. For the subject matter, cf. Exod 20:26 ולא תעלה במעלת על מזבחי אשר לא תגלה ערותך עליו. It is likely that this text carries the same meaning: the priest should not uncover his pudenda when approaching the altar.

[25] Cf. the suggestion of J.-B. Humbert that sacrifices were offered in the first period of the Essene settlement at Qumran, 'L'espace sacré à Qumran. Propositions pour l'archéologie', *RB* 101 (1994) 161–211. For recent discusions on the subject, see E. Qimron, 'Celibacy in the Dead Sea Scrolls and the Two Kinds of Sectarians', *The Madrid Qumran Congress: Proceedings of the International Congress on the Dead Sea Scrolls, Madrid 18-21 March 1991*, eds. J. Trebolle Barrera and L. Vegas Montaner (Madrid: Editorial Complutense; Leiden: Brill, 1992) 287–94; A. Steudel, 'The Houses of Prostration', 49–68; A. I. Baumgarten, 'Josephus on Essene Sacrifice', *JJS* XLV (1994) 169–83.

[26] When one compares 4Q**418** (4QInstruction[a]) 188 7 with the parallel text in 4Q**423** (4QInstruction[e]) 9 3, it is clear that 4Q**418** had בדברי֯] קודש where 4Q**423** has ב]ד֯רכי קודש. Both readings are meaningful.

Concluding Comments

Three Qumran compositions (4Q**424** sapiential work, 4Q**420/421** Ways of Righteousness, and 4Q**415–418**, **423** Instruction) contain parenetic material in the form of short sentences (descriptive wisdom sayings, wisdom admonitions with motive clauses, commands and prohibitions). 4QInstruction contains wisdom admonitions, commands and prohibitions, but not wisdom sayings. 4Q**420/421** and 4Q**424** contain both wisdom sayings and wisdom admonitions (and 4Q**420/421** prohibitions as well), but not commands. The sentences in these three compositions do not reflect the structure or theology of the *yaḥad* and seem to derive from presectarian sapiential milieus. Two of these compositions reveal another literary stratum: the first part of 4QWays of Righteousness which deals with the organisation of the *yaḥad* and inclusion of new members into the community, shows that this composition has undergone sectarian editing. 4QInstruction contains, in addition to wisdom admonitions, a number of lengthy discourses which deal with the revelation of God's mysteries to a community and has much in common with the thinking of the *yaḥad*. These discourses display a variety of genres we do not encounter in the shorter sentences (wisdom instruction, rhetorical dialogue, trial speech, admonition speech, announcement of judgement and salvation, theophany report, exhortation to praise). Both 4QWays of Righteousness and 4QInstruction thus demonstrate that earlier parenetic material could be adopted and edited in the *yaḥad* or circles close to it.[27] The close relation of 4Q**420** 1a ii-b 1–2 to Sir 11:7-8 points to a date in the early second century BCE for the wisdom sentences of 4Q**420/421**. The sectarian joining of three different kinds of material into one scroll should probably be dated to the late second century BCE (see introduction to 4Q**420**).

---

[27] J. H. Ulrichsen draws similar conclusions as to the literary growth of the *Testament of the Twelve Patriarchs*. Ulrichsen concludes that the *Urschrift* from *c*.200 BCE was purely parenetic, while apocalyptic and prophetic passages represent later strata, added from *c*.150 BCE onwards: *Die Grundschrift der Testamente der Zwölf Patriarchen. Eine Untersuchung zu Umfang, Inhalt und Eigenart der ursprünglichen Schrift* (Uppsala: Almquist and Wiksell, 1991) 255–345.

425. 4QSapiential-Didactic Work B

(PLATE XVII)

Physical Description

SIX fragments belong to this manuscript.[1] The skin is of medium thickness and is light buff-grey in colour. The ink has eroded in many places although the surface of the skin is still intact. In some cases it is difficult to decide between the presence of a *vacat* or writing that has eroded (see esp. frgs. 1 7 and 4 ii 2, 5). The largest fragment, frg. 1, has eleven partially preserved lines. Neither the number of lines per column nor the column width is known. A margin measuring 0.7 cm in width is evident between columns i and ii on frg. 4. Frg. 1 preserves a *vacat* in line 9. If the suggested reconstruction is correct, the *vacat* did not occupy the entire line; rather, the line was inscribed at its beginning. No vertical or horizontal dry lines are visible except on frg. 1 where the imprint of a horizontal line appears between lines 2 and 3, and probably within line 1. If this was the original ruling, the scribe did not keep to the lines. The distance between the inscribed lines is 0.5–0.6 cm, and the letter height is approximately 0.3 cm. The distances between the letters and the words are quite irregular. Frgs. 5 and 6—if they have been correctly identified—were written with a much thinner pen. Supralinear corrections/additions exist on frg. 2 1a and frg. 4 ii 1a.

A material join exists between frgs. 2 and 4.[2] It is likely that frgs. 1 and 3 also belong together, though there is no direct material join. The pattern of deterioration of joined frgs. 1+3 corresponds to that of joined frgs. 2+4, suggesting that they originate from the same horizontal level, and in close proximity to one another—perhaps coming from the same skin sheet. It is not clear which combination came first in the scroll. Frgs. 5 and 6 also seem to correspond each other, but their sequence and their relationship to frgs. 1+3 and 2+4 are uncertain.

Palaeography

4Q**425** belongs to the formal tradition, but it includes also semi-cursive elements (see e.g. the looped *taw*, frg. 4 ii 4, and *reš*, frg. 4 ii 5). It stems from the first century BCE, near the transition from the Hasmonaean to the Herodian period (*keraiai* are not yet found but letters like *ṭet* and *mem* have already developed a straight base).

---

[1] The editor wishes to extend cordial thanks to Prof. J. Strugnell for his advice. Unfortunately, Strugnell's preliminary notes and transcription of 4Q**425** are lost. The latter is reflected in the *Preliminary Concordance* (*PC*). Special thanks are due to Prof. E. Puech for re-examining the manuscript.

[2] This join can be seen on the plate in the Rockefeller Museum. According to L. Libman, conservator, the join of frgs. 2 and 4 had been fixed with cellophane tape. None of the photos show this join, but it looks perfect.

Orthography

4Q**425** shows a clear tendency towards *plene* writing, e.g. לוא (frgs. 1+3 3) and חוק (frg. 5 5). The long form of the 3rd sing. personal pronoun הואה is probably used in frg. 5 2.

Contents

Frg. 1 partly overlaps with 4Q**424** 3, but the two fragments do not give the same text. אל is used as the designation for God instead of the Tetragrammaton. There are no indications that this sapiential-didactic collection was a Qumranic composition. It bears similarities to the Book of Proverbs.

Mus. Inv. 501
PAM 41.209, 41.504, 42.499, 43.219, 43.541*

Frgs. 1 + 3

]ל֯ מוסׄרׄ תועׄבה֯ דב[ר]מב[1
]◦ ב֯עׄד לבו לבלתי ה֯[2
]◦תנובׄה לוא ימׄר◦[3
]שקׄרׄ קטן כ◦[4
]◦[ ]◦[ ]ולשון ולוא [ ]◦[5
]ת א֯יׄש֯[ ]◦[ ] דכרׄכיו ובמׄ[ש]קׄל֯ ל֯ו֯אׄ י[עשה פעלתו 6
]◦◦◦ איש ב֯ל֯י֯[על] איש שוע ע֯י֯נ֯י֯ם[ ](◦)[7
]◦שים כ֯[ ]אוילי לב ו֯[ש]ג֯ע֯ו֯נ֯ו֯[ ]◦◦◦[8
]ל◦(◦)[ ] *vacat* [9
]בים לו לפ֯ל֯[ס 10
]ל דרכיו֯[11

NOTES ON READINGS

Frg. 3 probably precedes frg. 1 in lines 5–9. There is no material join between the fragments.

L. 1 ל֯[. Remains of the head of *lamed* curving into the hook seem to exist. On the fragment, it is almost certain.

L. 1 תוע֯בה֯. *ʿAyin* is faint but clear. The last letter very probably is *he* and not *taw*; the surface has deteriorated on the left side of the head, but the right side speaks against *taw*. Also *he* sometimes has a small foot on its left leg, cf. e.g. frg. 4 ii 2.

L. 2 ב֯ע֯ד. *Bet* and *ʿayin* are almost certain.

L. 3 ◦תנוב֯ה[. *Bet* seems to be certain; *kap* would be narrower.

L. 3]◦ימ֯ר. Strugnell (*PC*) read *mem* as certain.

L. 5 ולשון[. The first *waw* probably belongs to לשון and not to the preceding word.

L. 6]◦[ ]איש֯. The *šin* is relatively far from the *yod,* but this manuscript exhibits irregular spacing. Traces of a base stroke exist on the left border of frg. 3.

L. 6 דכר֯כיו. A reading of דכרניו, as suggested by J. Maier (*Die Qumran-Essener: Die Texte vom Toten Meer*, vol. II [Munich/Basel, 1995] 504 n. 522), is palaeographically impossible; note the head of the letter.

L. 6 ובמ֯[ש]קל לו֯א֯. Remains of the lower part of *qop* exist as well as remains of both *lamed*s and *ʾalep*.

L. 7 After עינים, the ink seems to have eroded for a space of approximately 0.7 cm, possibly followed by the faint trace of a letter. However, a *vacat* cannot be totally excluded.

L. 8 At the left border of frg. 3, the top right corner of a probable *kap* or *taw* is preserved. The traces after לב might best be understood as ו֯[ש]ג֯ע֯ו֯נ֯ו֯; *ʿayin* touches *gimel*. The last preserved remains of this line consist of the lower parts of letters.

L. 10 לו לפ֯ל]ס. There is almost no space between לו and the following word. *Pe* is nearly certain.

L. 11 Strugnell (*PC*) read]ל[ ] דרכיו ל[, but the remains he identified as part of the last *lamed* belong in fact to the bottom of the *pe* in the preceding line.

TRANSLATION

1.] correction, abomination, a thin[g of
2.] for his heart without [
3.] produce, not shall [
4.] a small deception [
5.] and (the) tongue, and not [
6.] a man [ ] his ways (?) and in respect to weight, not shall [do his work
7.] a worthless man, a man of smeared over eyes [you shall not send
8.] those with foolish hearts and his (?) [m]adness[
9.] *vacat* [
10.] him to make leve[l
11.] his ways [

COMMENTS

L. 1 מוסר֯. 'Correction, discipline', rather than 'bond'. The syntax is not clear, e.g. 'correction of abomination' would also be possible.

L. 3 ◦תנוב֯ה[. 'Produce' or 'fruit'.

L. 4 שקר֯ קטן[. Or 'small lie'. But it is questionable whether both words belong together, or whether one should understand 'deception/lie, small'.

L. 6 דכר֯כיו might be a mistake for דכדכיו, or perhaps even more probably for דרכיו (see line 11).

L. 6 On במשקל in the Bible cf., e.g. Lev 26:26; 1Chr 28:14, 18 (by weight); and Lev 19:35 (in respect to weight). The end of line 6 overlaps with 4Q**424** 3 1 which has ובמשקל לא יעשה פעלתו איש שופט בטרם ידרוש ומאמין בטרם [יבחן].

L. 7 4Q**424** 3 2 continues differently, but איש שוע עינים is found in 4Q**424** 3 3 with a preceding *vacat*. If our combination of 4Q**425** frgs. 1+3 is right, the text would differ from that of 4Q**424**: instead of the *vacat* we would have איש בליעל. It is impossible to know whether a new syntactical unit begins with איש שוע עינים, or whether it is in apposition (an enumeration is less probable). On שוע עינים, 'smeared over eyes' (= blind) see Isa 6:10; on איש בליעל in a sapiential context in the Bible, see Prov 16:27. It is possible, but not certain that the line continued like 4Q**424** 3 3 with איש שוע עינים אל תשלח לחזות לישרים.

L. 8 אויל is frequently used in the Book of Proverbs, cf. e.g. Prov 10:21; 11:29, but the expression אוילי לב is only found in 4Q**418** 58 1 (singular). On שגעון cf. Deut 28:28; 2 Kgs 9:20; Zech 12:4 and 4QDibHam[a] 1 ii 4; 4Q**387** 3 ii 4; on the combination of אויל and משוגע see CD XV, 15.

L. 10 לפ̊ל̊[ס]. 'To make level' or 'as a balance'. On פלס as verb cf. 4Q**424** 1 7; 3 4. On פלס as noun see esp. Prov 16:11 and Sir 42:4.

Frgs. 2 + 4 i

1]○[

2a]ש[

2]○○[ ]○○○○○[ ]○[ ]ה̊

3]ם̊ לשון למכ̊ו̊ן̊[ ]○[

4]ע̊ים סולה ○[ ]ת̊ו̊

5]ל לוקחי [ר]ש̊ף̊

6]ת[ ]נ̊ו○[ ]○עת̊

7]א̊מ̊ת̊[ ]ו○[

8]○[ ]○○○

9]לו

NOTES ON READINGS

Frg. 2 directly precedes frg. 4 i 2–6.

L. 2]ה̊. *He* is almost certain.

L. 3]ם̊. Final *mem* is almost certain. Read probably למכון rather than למכש]ל (*šin* is almost impossible, see a vertical trace of ink under the first oblique stroke which can be clearly seen on the original and which does not seem to be accidental).

L. 4]ע̊ים *ʿAyin* is certain—part of the left stroke going down to the right is preserved below the point where the right arm touches this stroke; read]ע̊ים or]ע̊ום. It is possible that the remains of an exceptionally long *lamed* from line 5 (perhaps due to the space between the words) appear after סולה. If not, the remains belong to a letter in line 4.

L. 4]ת֯ו֯. Probably תו/י rather than ○נו/י.

L. 5 A *lamed* perhaps appears at the left border of frg. 2; see note on line 4.

L. 5]רשׂ֯ף֯. *Šin* is almost certain. Read either *pe* or *kap* in final position.

L. 7]א֯מ֯ת֯[ ]ו○[. *ʾAlep* is rather uncertain; *mem*, and especially *taw*, are almost certain. The *waw* may be a *yod*.

L. 9]לו֯. Or]לי.

TRANSLATION

3.] tongue to a place[

4.] weighed [

5.] those who take [f]lame(?)

6.

7.]truth [

COMMENTS

L. 3]למ֯כ֯ו֯ן֯. 'To' or 'as'; 'place' or 'foundation'. Cf. similarly perhaps 1QH[a] XIX 7–8 (Sukenik XI 4–5).

L. 6 One might expect a form of כנע or מנע after כול.

Frg. 4 ii

1a ת֯ן֯[

1 מ֯ה נ֯דד֯ת֯[

2 [ ]תרדמ֯ה מ[ ]○○[

3 [ב]כ֯ו֯ל מ֯חשׁ֯בת ק֯וד֯[ש(ו) להלל]

4 [ו]להודות לאל על כו֯[ל

5 [ ]מזהר ל֯○○○ט֯[

6 א[ו]מ֯ר֯[ ]○[

7 ל֯[

NOTES ON READINGS

The column width is unknown.

L. 1a]ת֯ן. The first preserved word of this fragment is certainly a supralinear addition, note the much smaller distance between the lines, also the letters are smaller. *Taw* is uncertain; *he* and *ḥet* are also possible.

L. 1 מ֯ה. Strugnell (*PC*) was able to read *mem* clearly.

L. 2 The ink seems to have eroded at the beginning of the line; a *vacat* is also possible. The first *mem* is almost certain.

L. 3 [ב]כ֯ול מ֯ח֯ש֯בת ק֯וד[ש(ו)]. קהל, as has been suggested by Strugnell (*PC*), seems unlikely; the remains do not belong to the lower part of a *qop* in line 3 but to the curving of the head of *lamed* in line 4. [ו]כול is possible, but [ב]כול is preferable as it fits the space well. מחשבת is possible if a relatively large *ḥet* and *šin* are assumed. *Qop* and *dalet* are quite certain.

L. 4 [ו]להודות fits the space; להודות is too short.

L. 5 A lacuna at the beginning of the line is preferable to a *vacat*, i.e. the ink seems to have eroded there. Traces of the head of the *lamed* seem to exist. *Ṭet* at the end is almost certain because of the characteristic curving of its right part.

L. 6 א[ו]מ֯ר֯ seems preferable to א[ו]ר֯ך֯. The last letter might be either *reš* or final *kap*. The remains of the preceding letter indicate *mem* rather than *reš*.

L. 7 ל֯[. Very probably the top of *lamed* exists which joins the bottom of *ʾalep* from line 6.

TRANSLATION

1a. give [
1. what do you flee [
2. [ ] deep sleep [
3. [in] the whole plan of [his?] holine[ss to offer praise]
4. [and] to offer thanksgiving to God because of al[l
5. [ ] . . . [
6. w[o]rd[

COMMENTS

L. 1a The supralinear addition must have been longer than only one word. If the reading תן is correct, one might complete, e.g. תן הדר (4Q**416** 2 III 10, 4Q**418** 9, 11) or תן הודות (4Q**412** 1 8).

L. 1 נ֯דד֯ת֯[. 'Flee' or 'stray'.

L. 2 Cf. Prov 19:15 עצלה תפיל תרדמה ('Idleness lulls a man to deep sleep . . .').

L. 3 On בכול מחשבת קודש cf. e.g. 1QS XI 19; 1QM XIII 2.

L. 4 On the restoration להלל ולהודות cf. 4QTest 21; on להודות לאל cf. 1QS XI 15.

L. 5 The meaning of מזהר is unclear. It might either come from I זהר, 'to be light, shining', or II זהר, 'to warn, instruct'.

L. 6 א[ו]מ֯ר֯[. The text probably refers to אמר 'word'. Alternatively, a verbal form of אמר might be read.

Frg. 5

1]◦[ ]◦[ ]ש֯ ק[ל]ו֯ן

2]◦נ֯ה֯ ה֯ו֯אה[

3]מ֯של ב֯רוחו֯[

4]ר֯ש֯ע ו֯◦[

5]חוקי ◦[

NOTES ON READINGS

L. 1 The letter before *qop* might be *šin*, but *bet* is also possible (cf. the head of *bet*, frg. 6 3). The letter before *nun* is either *yod* or *waw*; *lamed* between *qop* and *waw/yod* is quite possible.

L. 2 There are remains of two letters before נׄהׄ. Instead of *he*, *ḥet* might be possible.

L. 3]מׄשל בׄרוחׄו[. The first letter might be *mem*, but this is uncertain.

TRANSLATION

1.] dis[ho]nour [
2.] he [
3.] is master of himself [
4.] wickedness and [
5.] statutes of [

COMMENTS

L. 1 One might assume an expression like איש קלון, cf. frg. 1 + 3 6–7.

L. 3 If the reading משל is right, one might compare Prov 16:32 טוב ארך אפים מגבור ומשל ברוחו מלכד עיר ('Better an equable man than a hero, a man who is master of himself than one who takes a city').

L. 4 On רשע cf. frg. 6 5.

Frg. 6

]◦לׄ◦◦[1

] ואל ידב[ר 2

(אלׄ?)]יׄשפט ביום [3

]יעוה ובלשונו[4

] רשע ◦הׄ◦[5

NOTES ON READINGS

L. 1 The letter after *lamed* might be *kap* or *mem*.

L. 3]יׄשפט. A small trace appears before *šin* at a distance which suggests *yod* or *waw*.

L. 4]יעוה ובלשונו. ועוה and ובלשוני are also possible.

L. 5 *He* is certain; note the slightly curved stroke of its head.

TRANSLATION

1.] . . . [
2.] and let him not spea[k
3.]let him [not (?)] judge at the day [
4.]he commits iniquity and with his tongue[
5.] wickedness [

COMMENTS

L. 2 Cf., e.g. 1QS V 25; VI 10, 11; CD X 17 (concerning דבר נבל ורק on the Sabbath day).

L. 3]יׄשפט. *Qal* or *Nipʿal* ('he will be judged' or 'he will enter into controversy'). As in line 2, the sentence might well have been a negative one: 'let him [not] . . .'. It is tempting to restore [אל ישפט ביום השבת על] . . ., cf. CD X 18 (concerning הון and בצע), cf. line 2.

L. 4 עוה could be either *Qal*, *Nipʿal* ('be bent, bowed down, twisted') or *Piʿel* ('twist, distort'). A negative formulation ('let him not . . .') as in line 2 (and line 3?) cannot be excluded. The fact that עוה is usually used in the perfect and not in the imperfect might favour reading ועוה instead of יעוה, but this is speculative.

426. 4QSapiential-Hymnic Work A

(PLATE XVIII)

Physical Description

THIS manuscript consists of thirteen fragments.[1] It is written on fairly thin skin which was originally light buff-grey in colour. Most of the fragments have darkened over the course of time and have turned brown. Frg. 8, which is almost black, has broken into several pieces. Surface flaking has occurred on some of the fragments (e.g. frgs. 1 i and 7). Frgs. 1 and 2 come from the top of the scroll. The top margin is 1.1 cm. Bottom margins have not been preserved on any of the fragments. The inter-columnar margin on frg. 1 measures 1.1 cm. Horizontal dry lines and vertical margin lines are still visible on frg. 1. The line height is approximately 0.5–0.6 cm. Letter height is 0.2–0.3 cm. The original dimensions of the columns are uncertain: neither the lengths of the lines nor the number of lines per column is known. The maximum number of lines preserved is fourteen on frg. 1 i (maximum height of frg. 1 i is 9 cm). There are patches of uninscribed skin in frg. 1 i 3, 7 at the end of the lines, and frg. 1 ii 1 at the beginning of the line. In all three cases it is uncertain whether the entire lines were *vacat*s or whether only parts of the lines were left blank. A supralinear addition written in a second, tiny hand appears in frg. 4 3a. The same script is also found in frg. 8 2, where it immediately follows the first hand. It may possibly have been added later in a former *vacat* or written over an erasure. Single letters are cancelled by the placing of a dot above the letter (see frg. 1 i 12; ii 4; 11 2). Additions of single letters above the line, probably by the original scribe correcting orthographical mistakes, are found in frgs. 1 i 4; ii 4; 8 3. A special scribal mark, also known from 1QIsa[a], appears above the blank space at the beginning of frg. 1 ii 1.

A material reconstruction of the manuscript might be possible in parts. The horizontal proximity of some of the fragments is indicated by corresponding patterns of deterioration (e.g. frgs. 1 and 2; frgs. 1 and 5).

Contents

4Q**426** represents a sapiential work which—as far as can be concluded from its poor state of preservation—contained prayer, hymnic, and didactic elements. First and third person speech occurs. אל is the designation for God. The lack of the tetragrammaton *might* argue against an early dating of the composition, i.e. the third century BCE or earlier. There are no clear indications that the work was a Qumranic composition.

---

[1] The editor wishes to extend cordial thanks to Prof. J. Strugnell for his advice. Unfortunately, Strugnell's preliminary notes and transcription of 4Q**426** are lost. The latter is reflected in the *Preliminary Concordance* (*PC*). Special thanks are due to Prof. E. Puech for re-examining this manuscript.

Palaeography

Two different hands are distinguishable in 4Q**426**: that of the scribe of the main text, and the hand of the scribe responsible for the additions/corrections in frg. 4 3a and frg. 8 2. The main hand represents the formal Hasmonaean tradition, originating from the second half of the second century or the early first century BCE. *ʿAyin* is still small, while medial *nun* (see especially frg. 1 ii 3) and also medial *kap* are still large; the latter remains narrow. The right downstrokes of medial *pe* and *mem* already turn down at a right angle into a straight base. Medial *ṣade* on the other hand has not yet developed a typical Hasmonaean base stroke (but see frg. 1 i 2). Final *mem* is open at the bottom. Medial letters are used twice in a final position: medial *pe* in frg. 5 2 (no final *pe* exists in the manuscript), and medial *mem* in frg. 1 5 and frg. 10 4. There is still a difference in the writing of *waw* and *yod*. *Waw* usually has a small head and its base stroke is straight, while the head of *yod* is generally bigger and the downstroke is slightly more curved. Nonetheless, in many cases it is almost impossible to distinguish between these two letters; they are often virtually identical. 4Q**426** contains excellent examples of typical *he* in the formal tradition (cf. 4Q**364**): the crossbar is not shaded, as is often assumed, but is written in two strokes (from left to right and from right to left), which can best be seen in ובינה in frg. 1 i 4 and in ונחלה in frg. 1 ii 6. The hand responsible for the supralinear addition in frg. 4 3a and the addition/correction in frg. 8 2 belongs to the cursive tradition, see especially the writing of *he*, *yod,* and *šin*. A dating of this hand is almost impossible as only a few letters are preserved.

Orthography

The orthography of 4Q**426** tends clearly to *plene* writing (see for example כול, לוא, מצוותיו, and אורך), but see a perhaps defective spelling of the participle ידע in frg. 1 ii 5. Phonetic characteristics might be found in frgs. 1 i 9 and 1 ii 4 and 6.

Mus. Inv. 276
PAM 41.321, 41.518, 41.858, 42.836, 42.909, 43.541*

Frg. 1 i

top margin

כב]וֹד ומדת דעת ואורך ימים
שו]מֹרי כול מצוותיו וזרע רשעים
[*vacat*

]נתן אל בלבבי דעה ובינה 4

]ל֯[ ]למ ו֯לנ֯וצ֯ר֯[י אמ[ת֯ אמרי 5

]◦◦ו֯ה֯ ש֯◦[א/י]ח֯יהו֯ 6

[*vacat* 7

]לה֯ לוא יהיו 8

]כול תור בתבל 9

]ל֯ ו֯כול זר א֯ין 10

]ה֯ וא֯וכל טוב ענפיה 11

]ת בסתר֯ מלפניו֯ ה֯יו֯ם 12

]ה ◦ול למלכי ארץ רוד[ף֯] 13

]ים ונשי֯ם֯ 14

NOTES ON READINGS

L. 5 Read probably medial *mem* in final position (cf. frg. 10 4) after the second *lamed*. The reading ו֯לנ֯וצ֯ר֯[י is highly probable. Read either אמרי or אמרו.

L. 6 *Waw* or *yod* is possible. After this comes either *he* or *taw*. Read then either *šin* or *ṣade*, followed by a letter with an angle at its bottom (*mem*, *kap*, etc.). *Ḥet* is nearly certain.

L. 8 Only slight traces of the first three letters are visible; J. Strugnell (*PC*) was able to read]לה לוא.

L. 11 וא֯וכל. *ʾAlep* is possible but not certain.

L. 12 ה֯יו֯ם. *He* is followed by a letter with a vertical stroke; יו֯ fit the space well.

L. 13]ה ◦ול. Or]ה ◦יל.

L. 14 ונשי֯ם֯. *Yod* is quite certain; final *mem* is possible.

TRANSLATION

1. hon]our and a measured portion of knowledge and length of days
2. those who k]eep all His commandments, but the seed of (the) wicked ones
3.] *vacat*
4.]God has put into my heart knowledge and understanding
5.]and for (those) who observe [the tru]th(?), words of
6.]his [b]rother(?)/He] sustains him(?)
7.] *vacat*
8.] they shall not be
9.]all beauty in the world
10.] and every stranger is not
11.] and its branches are good food
12.] secretly from before {him} the day
13.] to the kings of the earth, pur[suing]
14.] and women(?)

Comments

L. 1 On the connection between דעה and כבוד, frequent in Qumran texts, see cf. e.g. 1QS III 15-16; on the connection of wisdom—which seems to be the topic discussed here—and length of days (= long life), cf. Job 12:12b and Prov 3:2.

L. 2 The sentence in line 2 and the beginning of line 3 might be completed 'God loves/never leaves those who k]eep all his commandments, but the seed of (the) wicked ones[will be cut off forever]'; cf. Ps 37:28.

Ll. 4–6(7) Note the rather short unit of text framed by *vacat*s in lines 3 and 7.

L. 5 An alternative reconstruction is ו̇לנ̊ו̊צ̊ר̊[י ברי]ת̇; cf. Deut 33:9, Ps 25:10.

L. 6 י]ח̊יה̊ו̊ may be a *Piʿel* 3rd sing. imperfect + suffix (cf. Ps 41:3), if not אחיהו or part of a longer word.

L. 9 תור is very probably phonetically תאר 'beauty', see 11QPs[a] XXVIII 9; cf. תוארכה in 4Q**525** 14 i 12. תור 'turtledove' (Cant 2:12) is less probable.

L. 10 Cf. perhaps Lev 22:10, 13 (וכל זר לא יאכל קדש/ בו). The context of this line may be the same as the beginning of line 11, but this is highly hypothetical.

L. 11 The significance of 'good food'—if the reading and grammatical understanding are correct—is uncertain. It might perhaps mean the opposite of a poor, ascetic meal, or perhaps—although not attested—a type of אוכל קדש, cf. note on line 10. A verbal form of יכל seems to be excluded. A verbal form of אכל could also be possible; one might translate alternatively e.g. 'eating the good of its branches'.

L. 13 God might be the subject; cf. Ps 76:13; cf. also Ps 89:28, there referring to the 'firstborn' (cf. frg. 1 ii 2); both psalms have למלכי ארץ.

L. 13 One might alternatively restore רוד]ד 'beating down'. On רודף, cf. e.g. Judg 4:22; on רודד, cf. Ps 144:2.

L. 14]ים ונשי̊ם̊. Perhaps אנש]ים ונשים may be restored (cf. Jer 40:7 and Ezra 10:1).

Frg. 1 ii

top margin

1] *vacat*

2 בכור ארים ש]

3 יתבונן ואגידה לכמה̊]

4 ואתבוננו בפ^ו^עלות אנ̊ו̊[ש

5 צעדו איש ידע י°]

6 ישר ונחלה ואל̊]

7 ואל יביאני עד]

8 תשוך בעדי̊]

9 איש °]

טוב̇[10

יפלס̇[11

א̊[12

NOTES ON READINGS

A scribal mark exists above line 1; it is slightly split by a break in the skin. The right part of the sign is placed in the margin; the left part is within the column. Although the placement of this sign is unique, the sign itself is comparable to an already well-developed scribal mark, also occurring in 1QIsa[a] XXVIII, XXXII, XXXVIII, XLIII, XLIX and perhaps in **4Q428** 14 1. In **4Q426** it seems to consist of a horizontal hook, which is a common paragraph mark in the Qumran manuscripts (e.g. in 1QS), with a *pe* above it (rather than a small hook; see the base stroke of *pe* reaching into the horizontal hook; *pe* is of average letter height); cf. also 1QIsa[a] XXII (part of a larger sign). It most likely marks a new text passage. This is confirmed by the fact that the preserved beginning of line 1 is a *vacat* (cf. the evidence in 1QIsa[a]). It might be surmised tentatively that *pe* stands for פרש/ פרשה. It is noteworthy that this sign is unique to manuscripts of the Hasmonaean period.

L. 3 לכמה̊[. Traces of the head make *he* plausible.

L. 5 A vertical stroke is all that remains of the last letter.

L. 6 ואל̊[. Traces of the head of *lamed* exist (under the final *yod* in line 5).

L. 7 יביאני. Or יביאנו.

L. 8 בעדי̊[. Or בעדו.

TRANSLATION

1. *vacat* [
2. a firstborn(?) I will raise [
3. he will understand, and I will tell you [
4. and I will consider him in the deeds of me[n
5. his step. A learned man, he [/ a man will know/knows his step [
6. uprightness and inheritance and do not[
7. [ ] and let him/Him not bring me to[
8. you (protectingly) fence me about[
9. man [
10. good[
11. he will weigh out[

COMMENTS

L. 2 The syntax is not clear: if the whole of line 1 was a *vacat*, בכור ארים is the beginning of a new passage. If the new passage started in line 1, which is more likely, ' . . . (as) a firstborn. I will raise . . . ' may be read. Alternatively, one might understand בכור as כור + ב (see e.g. 1QM V 11, 1QH[a] XI 13 [Sukenik III 12]).

L. 4 Since התבונן + ב means 'pay attention to', this line might be more easily understood by assuming אתבוננו = התבוננו (phonetically) 'and they will pay attention to the deeds of m[en' (Strugnell).

L. 5 צעדו. 'His step', i.e. the course of his life. A *Hipʿil* of כון may perhaps be completed at the end of line 4 (cf. Jer 10:23; Prov 16:9), assuming either the righteous man or preferably God to be the subject; in that case read יְדַע. Alternatively—and perhaps preferably—one might read 'a man will know/knows his step', cf. Job 31:37.

L. 6 ישר. 'Upright' or 'uprightness'; alternatively 'wealth', representing a phonetic spelling of עשר (Strugnell).

L. 6 ואל֯]. Or 'and God'; cf. line 7.

L. 7 A reading 'and let him not bring him/it . . . ' is not excluded. The altered sequence of subject and verb seems to speak against understanding 'and God will bring me even to'; cf. Ezekiel 40–47 (always יבאני אל).

L. 8 בעדי֯]. Or 'him'. Cf. Job 1:10.

L. 11 יפלס֯]. 'Weigh out' or 'make level'; cf. 4Q**424** 1 7 and 3 4, which might suggest a negative clause, in which case לוא /אל would have to be restored at the end of line 10. Both cases refer to a man who is unable to do something correctly.

Frg. 2

top margin

]איש הבהב ל[וא] ישר֯[1

]◦ ולו֯[א] יפ֯לג֯[2

]א֯ו֯ת֯ם֯[3

NOTES ON READINGS

Corresponding patterns of deterioration suggest a proximity between frg. 2 and frg. 1. Frg. 2 might have belonged at the top of the column before frg. 1 i, or at the top of the column after frg. 1 ii. It does not come from the right margin of a column (note the trace of ink before ולו֯[א] in line 2).

L. 1 The second *he* in הבה֯ב is certain. The head is broken, but the two strokes at the left side of the head are still visible. The last letter of the line might be *reš*.

L. 2 יפ֯לג֯]. *Pe* is almost certain. Its base has eroded due to an abrasion of the skin but part of the lower angle seems to be preserved.

L. 3 Read *taw* plus traces of one or two letters at either side. In the latter case *yod/waw* should be read before and after *taw*.

TRANSLATION

1.]a greedy man is n[ot] upright(?)[
2.] and he shall no[t] divide [
3.]them[

COMMENTS

L. 1 הבהב comes from יהב and means 'greedy', cf. Prov 30:15 הב הב, literally, 'give, give!'.

Frg. 3

1]○○ *vacat* [

2]בׄיׄ/וׄ[

Frg. 4

1]○[

2]אׄוהב ב[

3a]○ ושלושה [

3 לו]אׄ ישג יה○[

4 ב]חׄר בשרׄיׄםׄ תׄ[

5]םׄ טמא](ה)

6]צׄא○[ ]○○[

7]לׄ[

Notes on Readings

L. 1 The remains are from a letter with a horizontal base.

L. 3a The preserved uninscribed space after this word is relatively large; this might speak for the end of the addition.

L. 3 אׄ[. Strugnell (*PC*) read לא[. Perhaps he erroneously read the first traces of line 3a as the head of *lamed*. However, this would have been too far to the left (and it would contradict the usual *plene* writing of לוא in 4Q**426**).

L. 4 חׄר בשרׄיׄםׄ תׄ[. *Ḥet* is almost certain. In the second word, *yod* or *waw* is possible; final *mem* is possible but uncertain; the last letter is more possibly *taw* than *he* (see the top right angle which seems to be curved, while the position of the legs might as well fit *he*). The tiny piece of ink at the top left side might belong to the leg of *taw* (if *he*, it would belong to the crossbar).

L. 5 םׄ[. The traces of ink indicate the left upper part of final *mem* rather than *reš*. The surface of the skin has eroded where the left vertical stroke would be expected.

L. 6 Strugnell (*PC*) read צאצׄ]איו [○לו○[, which is possible, but *ṣade* is, in fact, uncertain, and remains of only two letters are still visible at the end. The first *ṣade* could also be *taw*.

Translation

2.] loving [

3a.] and three [

3.] he does [no]t(?) reach[
4. has cho]sen leaders [
5.] unclean [

COMMENTS

L. 2]אׄוהב ב. On אהב + ב, cf. Qoh 5:9 (אהב בהמון; the second *bet* is considered dittographical by BHS).

Ll. 3a+3] ◦שלושה.]אׄ ישג 'reach' or 'bring'. לו]א may perhaps be restored at the beginning of line 3. The beginning of the addition which has been lost is unclear, as is its exact relationship with line 3.

L. 4 Even if the reading is correct, the meaning of this line is uncertain. It is uncertain whether *bet* is part of the root, or whether it is a preposition. In the first case, בשר 'flesh', might be read in the rare plural form (Prov 14:30). In the second case, it might be understood as a plural of שר 'leader', with the preposition *bet*. A restoration of ב]חר preceding בשרים would fit both possibilities.

L. 5 טמא](ה). '(Become) unclean' or 'uncleanness'.

Frg. 5

]ח֯דרי שא[ול 1

]◦פ שקוצים[2

]ה א[ת] אשרׄ ◦[3

]לת ל◦[4

]אׄ מ֯י֯ משולח֯ ל֯ו֯אׄ[5

]ל֯ו֯א֯ ישו֯ב֯[6

NOTES ON READINGS

Frg. 5 might belong in the proximity of frg. 1. Similar patterns of deterioration and corresponding line-spacing indicate this. Frg. 5 1 is best placed on a level with frg. 1 i 7, probably either in the column preceding frg. 1 i, or in the column following frg. 1 ii.

L. 1 *Ḥet* is almost certain. Strugnell (*PC*) was able to read שא[. This piece of skin has broken away, and except for a small trace of ink (*šin*?), the letters are already missing on the photographs.

L. 2]◦פ. Medial *pe* is used in final position.

L. 5 The reading of מ֯י֯ is almost certain.

L. 6 ישו֯ב֯[. Or ישיב.

TRANSLATION

1.] the chambers of She[ol
2.] detested things [
3.] h[o]w(?) [
4.] . . . [
5.] one who is sent off [shall] not [
6.] shall not turn/bring back[

Comments

L. 1 Cf. 1QH[a] XVIII 36 (Sukenik X 34) and Prov 7:27. For שאול, see also frg. 8 3.

L. 3 א[ת] אשר. Cf. e.g. Deut 9:7; 2 Sam 11:20.

L. 6]לוא ישוב[. Cf. e.g. 1QS VII 2, 17, 24; VIII 23; IX 1; for לוא ישיב, cf. e.g. 1QS V 15.

Frg. 6

ו]עתה אלי[1

]ימל[2

Notes on Readings

L. 1 Traces of the right leg and top of the probable *he* are apparent. The *ʾalep* is possible.

L. 2 *Yod* or *waw*.

Translation

1. and] now, my God[

Comments

L. 1 Cf. e.g. 2 Sam 7:25; 2 Chr 1:9.

L. 2 Reconstruct perhaps]ימל[ך.

Frg. 7

]◦ ותוצאת[1

]שכל יחש[ב 2

]יפתח אוצ[ר(ו) (?) 3

Notes on Readings

L. 1 *Ṣade* is certain, and the second *taw* is nearly certain.

L. 2]שכל. Parts of the left stroke of *šin* seem to exist. Remains of the head make *lamed* certain.

L. 3 The first letter may be *yod* or *waw*. The reading of *waw* and *ṣade* at the end of the line, suggested by Strugnell, seems probable based on the traces (head of *waw* and right arm of *ṣade*).

Translation

1.] and the consequence of[
2.] prudence he shall thin[k
3.] he shall open [his] sto[re/trea[sury

COMMENTS

L. 1 The sing. **תוצאה** is attested only in later Hebrew, but see the pl. form, e.g. in 1Q**27** 1 i 12 and 4Q**421** 1 ii 15; it is perhaps a defective plural here.

L. 2]שׂ̊כל[appears to be a noun rather than a verb.

L. 3 Cf. 1QS X 2 concerning the times of day (light and darkness). But cf. also Deut 28:12 (God opens the heavens to let it rain), and Jer 50:25 (God opens the armory). See **אוצר** in frg. 10 1.

Frg. 8

1]◦◦◦[

2]◦תה {כי אל̊י̊}[

3]◦ שאולה[

4 א]יש לץ ◦[

NOTES ON READINGS

L. 1 Traces of some letters seem to exist at the right edge of the fragment.

L. 2]{כי אל̊י̊}. These words are written in the same small hand as frg. 4 3a, either in a *vacat* or in an erasure following ◦תה[. Several tiny dots are visible on frg. 8, especially at its top, and also perhaps under the addition in line 2, which might indicate that the addition itself was cancelled. But, inexplicably, the same type of dots also appear on the right side of frg. 8, where they do not make any sense. Therefore the marks on frg. 8 may be random ink spots. It is impossible to gain any clarification from the fragment as it has become completely black.

L. 3 Read a final letter, e.g. *pe*, followed by שאולה (E. Puech, oral communication), and not א̊]י[ש עילה[as read by Strugnell (*PC*) (the first trace of ink is too deep for *ʾalep*; *ʿayin* is impossible, see the ink remains at the lower right side and the ductus of the strokes; the only possibilities are *ʾalep* and *ḥet*).

L. 4 Read either *ʾalep*, *dalet*, or *he* at the end.

TRANSLATION

2.] {because my God } [
3.] to She<o>l [
4. a m]an who is a scorner [

COMMENTS

L. 3 Cf. frg. 5 1. שאולה (שאול + locative *he*) is very often used with a form of ירד in the Bible, see e.g. Gen 42:38; Ezek 31:17 (שאלה).

Frg. 9

]תו נמאר̊[1

]◦ו נחרצה̊[2

]ירחיב[3

NOTES ON READINGS

L. 1]נמאר̊.]נמאס̊ is excluded because intact, uninscribed skin is apparent at the left margin of the fragment where one would expect ink for *samek*.

L. 2 A rather thin oblique stroke remains from the left upper part of the first letter; *ʿayin* and *ṣade* are possible. The second letter is *yod* or *waw*. The final letter could also be *taw*.

L. 3 The first letter is *yod* or *waw*.

TRANSLATION

1.] malignant [
2.] strict decision [
3.] he shall enlarge[

COMMENTS

L. 1 On נמאר, cf. also 1QH[a] XIII 30 (Sukenik V 28). One is tempted to restore [צרע]תו נמאר[ת 'his [lepros]y is malign[ant]'; cf. Lev 13:51, 52; 14:44 (ממארת); and 4QD[a] 6 i 5 and 4QD[g] 1 i 13, but the genre is different.

L. 2]נחרצה̊. 'Strict decision' (a *Nipʿal* fem. participle). This word occurs in the Bible together with כלה as an expression for God's judgement (see Isa 10:23, 28:22; Dan 9:27; cf. Dan 9:26, 11:36); cf. also 4QBeat 22 2 and 4QPrayer of Enosh 1 i 6.

Frg. 10

]מ̊◦[ ]אוצר̊[1

]א̊יש̊ בינה ◦[2

ל/י]תעב כול עובד̊י̊[3

כו]ל[ ]מ̊ל̊כ̊ים א◦[4

NOTES ON READINGS

L. 1 Remains of *mem* are quite certain, joined by a vertical trace of ink.

L. 2]א̊יש̊. The remains at the beginning of the line fit איש well; note the traces of the left leg of *ʾalep* and remains of the right part of a quite oblique *yod* (cf. e.g. *yod* in frg. 11 3) almost touching the *ʾalep*. The only possible alternative to *šin* is *ḥet*. The space between]א̊יש̊ and בינה is quite large, but it does not seem to be a *vacat* (cf. the distance between בינה and the following word, which is also rather wide). At the end read a letter which turns into its base stroke with a curve, e.g. *kap*.

L. 3 ל/י]תעב. The space between *taw* and עב is slightly larger than usual, but a single word seems to be indicated.

L. 4]מׄלׄכׄיׄם. Medial *mem* is in final position. The first *mem* is now broken away, but it was still there when Strugnell read it. *Kap* and *yod* are quite certain.

TRANSLATION

1.] store/treasury[
2.]man(?) of understanding [
3. to] abhor all who serve[
4. al]l kings [

COMMENTS

L. 1 Cf. frg. 7 3.

L. 2 On איש בינה cf. 4Q**382** 45 5.

L. 3 A verbal form of תעב, probably in *Piʿel*, should be expected ('to abhor' or 'he abhors'). One might complete e.g. עובדי]עולה at the end. Cf. similarly 1QH^a VI 37 (Sukenik XIV 26) and VIII 28–29 (Sukenik XVI 10–11).

L. 4 Cf. frg. 1 i 13.

Frg. 11

]נׄחׄלתו *vac* (◦)[1

]הׄפכהׄנׄ ישכון לׄ[2

]לרׄוׄחו לוא יש[3

נ]פשׄוׄ אש[ר (?) 4

NOTES ON READINGS

L. 1 *Nun* and *ḥet* are quite certain. The length of the *vacat* is not certain; a tiny trace of ink appears at the left side of the fragment which might be a letter in line 1. Alternatively, the ink remains might belong to the head of *lamed* from the line below.

L. 2 The first *he* is certain (see the double-stroke head), and also the second, which might be written as a correction on a former letter (see the unusual thickness of the strokes). *Nun* is erased by a dot above. Faint traces of a letter exist at the end which could fit *lamed* (traces of which may exist in line 1).

L. 3 לרׄוׄחו. The surface of the skin has eroded under the head of the first *waw* (or *yod*) and also under the left side of *ḥet*.

L. 4 נ]פשׄוׄ. There is a dot above *šin* which, if not an erasure, might be a random ink spot. At the end of the word read *waw*, *yod* or final *nun*.

TRANSLATION

1.] his inheritance *vac* [
2.] turns, he will inhabit[

3.] concerning his spirit. Not [
4.] his [s]oul(?) whi[ch

Comments

L. 2 הׄפכה[. Different verbal forms of הפך, either in *Qal* or *Nipʿal*, are possible or, alternatively, a noun הפכה ('overthrow'; cf. Gen 19 29).

L. 3 On לרוחו, cf. e.g. 1QS VI 17.

Frg. 12

]◦יה לוא ה[1

]דרׄשו ומשפחותׄ[2

(בני שם) עילם וא]שׄור וארפכשד ול[וד וארם 3

]וׄכול שוכני[4

Notes on Readings

L. 1 ◦יה[. The second letter is *yod* or *waw*.

L. 4 וׄכול[. The first *waw* is almost certain.

Translation

1.] not [
2.] they search(ed) and clans[
3. (Shem's sons:) Elam, A]sshur, Arpachshad, L[ud, and Aram
4.] and all inhabitants of [

Comments

L. 3 See Gen 10:22; 1 Chr 1:17; cf. 1QM II 10–13; it is somewhat strange to find this in a wisdom context.

Frg. 12a

]אׄמׄ[1

Notes on Readings

This tiny fragment, obviously belonging to frg. 12 (see the photographs), has blackened and broken into three pieces. Its placement is unknown.

L. 1 *Mem* is certain and *ʾalep* is almost certain; see the remains of the left leg and the oblique stroke.

Frg. 13

]ש המ֯[

NOTES ON READINGS

L. 1]המ֯. The remains of the second letter appear to be *mem*; see the oblique base stroke (cf. e.g. למלכי frg. 1 13) and remains of the left portion.

CONCORDANCES

THESE concordances refer to all the Hebrew words occurring in the texts covered by this volume, together with their respective contexts. All independent words are covered, thus excluding the attached morphemes -ב, -ה, -כ, and -ל. From left to right, each entry contains the reference, lemma, and in-context phrase. The concordance has been prepared by S. Pfann. The volume's editors have reviewed the concordances, and the lemmatizations and readings reflect their preferences.

SIGLA

/	beginning of line
//	beginning of column
א̊	possible letter
א̇	probable letter
‸א	supralinear insertion
~~אב~~	word crossed out
{{א}}	scribal deletion
{א}	erasure
(א)	modern editor's deletion
<א>	modern editor's addition
[א]	reconstructed letter

4Q298 cryptA WORDS OF A MASKIL TO ALL SONS OF DAWN

298 3-4ii7	אהב	]ו֯אהבו חסד הוסיפו / ענוה
298 3-4i9	אוֹצָר	]° אוצר בינות / [
298 1-2i1	אזן	האזי]נו לי כ]ול אנשי לבב / [ורוד]פ֯י צדק
298 3-4ii4	אזן	ועתה / האזי֯נ֯]ו חכמים] וידעים שמעו
298 1-2i1	אִישׁ	האזי]נו לי כ]ול אנשי לבב / [ורוד]פ֯י צדק
298 1-2i3	אִישׁ	וְהָשיב֯]ו לאורח]ח֯יים א֯[נשי] / [רצו]נ֯ו
298 3-4ii4	אִישׁ	ואנשי/ בינה ה֯[וסיפו לק]ח֯
298 3-4ii6	אִישׁ	ואנשי / אמת רד֯פ֯[ו צדק]
298 3-4i4	אֵל	]נתן אל / [
298 1-2i3	אֱלֹהַ	וי]ד֯עים דר֯[ש]ו֯[א]ל֯ה֯
298 1-2i2	אֵמוּן	/ [ורוד]פ֯י צדק הבי[נ]ו֯ במלי
298 3-4ii6	אֹמֶץ	יו֯[דעי הדרך]ה֯וסיפו אומץ
298 3-4ii7	אֱמֶת	ואנשי / אמת רד֯פ֯[ו צדק]
298 1-2i1	אֲשֶׁר	דבר]י֯ משכיל אשר דבר לכול בני שחר
298 3-4i10	אֲשֶׁר	מ]לתי ואשר /
298 3-4ii8	אֲשֶׁר	אשר / פת֯ר֯[י]ה֯ם֯[אספ]ר֯
298 3-4ii3	אֵת	...]ו֯ת את ג֯בולה
298 1-2i2	בין	/ [ורוד]פ֯י צדק הבי[נ]ו֯ במלי
298 2ii3	בין	/ התב֯ו֯נן °[
298 3-4ii9	בין	ב֯ע֯בור תב֯ינו בקץ / עולמ֯ות
298 3-4i9	בִּינָה	]° אוצר בינות / [
298 3-4ii5	בִּינָה	ואנשי/ בינה ה֯[וסיפו לק]ח֯
298 3-4ii2	בִּלְתִּי	]ך֯ לבלתי רום / מת֯[כונה
298 1-2i1	בֵּן	דבר]י֯ משכיל אשר דבר לכול בני שחר
298 1-2i2	בקש	/ [ורוד]פ֯י צדק הבי[נ]ו֯ במלי
298 3-4ii1	גבוּלָה	]ומספר גבלותיה / [
298 3-4ii3	גבוּלָה	...]ו֯ת את ג֯בולה
298 5ii9	גבוּלָה	] / גבולותיו֯[
298 5ii10	גבוּלָה	] / שם גבולות֯[
298 1-2i1	דבר	דבר]י֯ משכיל אשר דבר לכול בני שחר
298 1-2i1	דָּבָר	דבר]י֯ משכיל אשר דבר לכול בני שחר
298 3-4ii8	דַּעַת	וה֯ו֯[סיפו ד]ע֯ת֯[י]מ֯י תעודה
298 5i9	דרך	]ת֯ לדרוך / [
298 1-2i3	דרש	וי]ד֯עים דר֯[ש]ו֯[א]ל֯ה֯
298 3-4ii5	דרש	ודורש[י] משפט הצניע / לכת
298 3-4i8	הלך	ת]כונם להתהלך / [
298 3-4ii6	הלך	ודורש[י] משפט הצניע / לכת
298 3-4i1	זְבוּל	]זבול /
298 1-2i3	חַיִּים	וְהָשיב֯]ו לאורח]ח֯יים א֯[נשי] / [רצו]נ֯ו
298 3-4ii7	חֶסֶד	]ו֯אהבו חסד הוסיפו / ענוה
298 1-2i4	חֵקֶר	ו֯[אור]עולמ֯י[ם לאין] חקר ב֯[
298 1-2i3	ידע	וי]ד֯עים דר֯[ש]ו֯[א]ל֯ה֯
298 3-4ii4	ידע	ועתה / האזי֯נ֯]ו חכמים] וידעים שמעו
298 3-4ii6	ידע	יו֯[דעי הדרך]ה֯וסיפו אומץ
298 3-4ii10	ידע	ובקד֯[מ]וניות תביטו לדעת //
298 3-4ii8	יוֹם	וה֯ו֯[סיפו ד]ע֯ת֯[י]מ֯י תעודה
298 3-4ii5	יסף	ואנשי/ בינה ה֯[וסיפו לק]ח֯
298 3-4ii6	יסף	יו֯[דעי הדרך]ה֯וסיפו אומץ
298 3-4ii7	יסף	]ו֯אהבו חסד הוסיפו / ענוה
298 3-4ii8	יסף	וה֯ו֯[סיפו ד]ע֯ת֯[י]מ֯י תעודה
298 2ii1	יצא	/ שורשיה יצ֯[או
298 1-2i1	כֹּל	דבר]י֯ משכיל אשר דבר לכול בני שחר
298 1-2i1	כֹּל	האזי]נו לי כ]ול אנשי לבב / [ורוד]פ֯י צדק
298 1-2i2	כֹּל	ש֯[מע]ו֯ ל֯מלי בכול / [מ]וצ֯א שפת֯[י
298 3-4i5	כֹּל	]ב֯כול תבל /[
298 1-2i1	לֵבָב	האזי]נו לי כ]ול אנשי לבב / [ורוד]פ֯י צדק
298 3-4ii5	לֶקַח	ואנשי/ בינה ה֯[וסיפו לק]ח֯
298 3-4i6	מדד	] מדד תכונם / [
298 3-4i2	מָה	]ל֯ ובמה /
298 1-2i3	מוֹצָא	ש֯[מע]ו֯ ל֯מלי בכול / [מ]וצ֯א שפת֯[י
298 1-2i2	מִלָּה	/ [ורוד]פ֯י צדק הבי[נ]ו֯ במלי
298 1-2i2	מִלָּה	ש֯[מע]ו֯ ל֯מלי בכול / [מ]וצ֯א שפת֯[י
298 3-4i10	מִלָּה	מ]לתי ואשר /
298 2ii2	מִן	/ בתהום מת֯[חת
298 3-4i7	מִן	מת]ח֯ת שם /[
298 3-4ii3	מִן	]ך֯ לבלתי רום / מת֯[כונה
298 3-4ii1	מִסְפָּר	]ומספר גבלותיה / [
298 3-4ii5	מִשְׁפָּט	ודורש[י] משפט הצניע / לכת
298 3-4ii10	נבט	ובקד֯[מ]וניות תביטו לדעת //
298 3-4i4	נתן	]נתן אל / [
298 3-4ii9	ספר	אשר / פת֯ר֯[י]ה֯ם֯[אספ]ר֯
298 3-4ii9	עָבוּר	ב֯ע֯בור תב֯ינו בקץ / עולמ֯ות
298 1-2i4	עוֹלָם	ו֯[אור]עולמ֯י[ם לאין] חקר ב֯[
298 3-4ii10	עוֹלָם	ב֯ע֯בור תב֯ינו בקץ / עולמ֯ות
298 3-4ii8	עָנָו	]ו֯אהבו חסד הוסיפו / ענוה
298 3-4i3	עָפָר	] עפר / [
298 3-4ii3	עַתָּה	ועתה / האזי֯נ֯]ו חכמים] וידעים שמעו
298 3-4ii9	פְּתַר	אשר / פת֯ר֯[י]ה֯ם֯[אספ]ר֯
298 1-2i2	צֶדֶק	האזי]נו לי כ]ול אנשי לבב / [ורוד]פ֯י צדק
298 3-4ii5	צנע	ודורש[י] משפט הצניע / לכת
298 3-4ii10	קַדְמֹנִי	ובקד֯[מ]וניות תביטו לדעת //
298 3-4ii9	קֵץ	ב֯ע֯בור תב֯ינו בקץ / עולמ֯ות
298 1-2i2	רדף	האזי]נו לי כ]ול אנשי לבב / [ורוד]פ֯י צדק
298 3-4ii7	רדף	ואנשי / אמת רד֯פ֯[ו צדק]
298 3-4ii2	רום	]ך֯ לבלתי רום / מת֯[כונה
298 1-2i4	רָצוֹן	וְהָשיב֯]ו לאורח]ח֯יים א֯[נשי] / [רצו]נ֯ו
298 1-2i3	שׁוּב	וְהָשיב֯]ו לאורח]ח֯יים א֯[נשי] / [רצו]נ֯ו
298 3-4i7	שִׂים	מת]ח֯ת שם / [

298 5ii10	שִׂים	] / שם גבולות̇[
298 1-2i1	שַׁחַר	דבר]ו̇ משכיל אשר דבר לכול בני שחר
298 5ii8	שַׁחַר	] / השחר וק̇[
298 1-2i1	שׂכל	דבר]ו̇ משכיל אשר דבר לכול בני שחר
298 1-2i2	שמע	ש̇[מעו]ן̇ למלי בכול / [מ]וצא̇ שפת̇[י
298 3-4ii4	שמע	ועתה / האזינ̇[ו חכמים] וידעים שמעו
298 1-2i3	שָׂפָה	ש̇[מעו]ן̇ למלי בכול / [מ]וצא̇ שפת̇[י
298 2ii1	שֹׁרֶשׁ	/ שורשיה יצ̇[או
298 3-4i5	תֵּבֵל	]ב̇כול תבל /[
298 2ii2	תְּהוֹם	/ בתהום מת̇[חת
298 2ii2	תַּחַת	/ בתהום מת̇[חת
298 3-4i7	תַּחַת	מת]ח̇ת שם / [
298 3-4i6	תִּכּוֹן	] מדד תכונם / [
298 3-4i8	תִּכּוֹן	ת]כונם להתהלך / [
298 3-4ii3	תִּכּוֹן	]ך̇ לבלתי דום / מת̇[כונה
298 5i8	תִּכְלֶת	] תכלית / [
298 3-4ii8	תְּעוּדָה	והו̇[סיפו ד]ע̇ת̇[י]מ̇י תעודה

4Q**299–301** MYSTERIES[a–b, c?]

299 6ii5	אָב	/ מה אב לבנים מאיש̇[
299 76,3	אָב	/ כול אבות העדה[
299 10,7	אֶבְיוֹן	]ל[ ]◦ ו̇שופטים בין אביו̇[ן
300 5,3	אֶבְיוֹן	]אביון מה נקרא /
299 27,4	אֶבֶן	]אבן מ◦[
299 74,2	אֶבֶן	]מ̇שה פנים אבני[
299 106,2	אַבְרָהָם	]אבר[הם
301 2b,2	אַדִּיר	]משל מה אד̇יר לכם
299 3a ii-b,3	אָדָם	ומה]נקרא לאד̇[ם] / חכם וצדיק
299 69,3	אָדָם	]◦ כול האדם[
300 5,4	אָדָם	ומה נקרא לא̇דם /
299 54,3	אהב	]◦ה̇ו כיא אהבת ח̇סד̇[
300 2ii5	אהב	/ ר̇ע̇ זולתו א̇ה̇וב[
299 79,6	אֹהֶל	]באהליהם ואהרון מ[
299 79,6	אַהֲרוֹן	]באהליהם ואהרון מ[
299 6ii15	אוֹ	/ מ̇ודה או תכלית י̇[
299 6ii3	אֱוִיל	/ אוילי כסה ◦[
299 21,4	אוֹצָר	]ו̇אוצר כול[
299 5,2	אוֹר	גב]ו̇רות רזי אור ודרכי חוש̇[ך
299 6ii10	אוֹר	/ חוש[ך] ו̇א[ור
301 2b,4	אוֹר	]◦ מ̇יא̇ ב̇כם דורש פני אור ומא̇[ור
301 5,4	אוֹר	א]ו̇ר גדול ונכב[ד הואה
301 5,5	אוֹר	]◦ אור ו̇אורו̇ [
301 5,5	אוֹר	]◦ אור ו̇אורו̇ [
299 69,2	אוּרִים	אור]י̇ם ותומים[
300 1a ii-b,1	אָז	ואז תדעו אם הבטתמ̇
300 1a ii-b,3	אָז	/ א̇[ז]ת̇אמרו ל[
299 8,6	אֹזֶן	ברוב שכל גלה אוזננו
299 6ii16	אֶחָד	/ תכון אחד ולוא יש̇[בע
299 69,1	אֶחָד	א]חת בשנה̇[
300 8,2	אָחוֹר	]מ̇ה קדם ומה אח[ור
299 4,5	אַיִן	]אינה לשלו̇ם̇[
299 6ii9	אַיִן	/ אשר אין ל◦◦[

299 53,4	אַיִן	]◦ד ואין שם למו̇ע[ד
299 73,2	אַיִן	]◦י̇ ואין[
300 6,5	אַיִן	ואי]ן̇ לענה לנגדו̇[
300 7,2	אַיִן	]ואין לענה לנגדו
301 6,1	אַיִן	כי]א אין ל̇ו̇ מ[
299 1,5	אִישׁ	]אנשי מחשבת לכול /
299 3a ii-b,4	אִישׁ	כי לוא לאיש̇[
299 6ii5	אִישׁ	/ מה אב לבנים מאי̇ש̇[
299 6ii13	אִישׁ	/ מאיש נואל הון הון ◦[
299 7,3	אִישׁ	/ [מה הוא רחו]ק̇ לאיש ממעש̇[ה
299 7,4	אִישׁ	/ מ̇ו̇ל̇ אי̇ש̇ והוא ר̇ח̇וק מ◦[
299 52,3	אִישׁ	/ איש נ̇ו̇◦[
299 76,4	אִישׁ	/ וב◦◦◦◦ בין איש[
299 77,1	אִישׁ	]◦◦ איש̇[
300 6,6	אִישׁ	]מ̇ה̇ עמוק לא[יש
300 8,8	אִישׁ	] לאיש ו̇ה̇[וא
300 10,1	אִישׁ	]◦ לאיש ◦◦[
300 10,2	אִישׁ	מה רע לא◦◦י̇ש̇ ואי◦[
301 1,3	אִישׁ	]ה̇ו̇לכי פותי ואנשי מחשבת
299 35,1	אֵל	א]ל הדעות[
299 53,7	אֵל	] לאל לנקום נקו̇ם̇[
299 53,9	אֵל	א]ל ובשמים מדור[ו
299 73,3	אֵל	]א̇ל הדע̇[ות
301 3a-b,6	אֵל	[ונ]כבד אל בעם קודשו
301 1,1	אֵל	ולמיניכם א̇חלקה דברי אליכם̇[
299 3a ii-b,5	אִם	כי] / אם חוכמת עורמת רוע ומ̇[חשבת בליעל
299 3a ii-b,6	אִם	כ̇יא אם [ ] / ד̇בר עושו
299 6ii6	אִם	/ כיא אם ארץ להדר ◦[
299 6ii7	אִם	/ ממנו כי אם רוח ◦ע̇[
299 6ii18	אִם	/ ואם דש̇ יוסיף ל[
299 20,1	אִם	]ח̇ו̇ק תכ̇ונם כיא אם̇[
299 20,3	אִם	]יח̇ד̇ רו̇בם אם[
299 33,3	אִם	]◦◦שוי ואם ינשא[

299 34,2	אִם	]תו ואם יהפכ[ו
299 42,2	אִם	]°ד כי אם[
300 1a ii-b,1	אִם	ואז תדעו אם הבטתם
300 1a ii-b,3	אִם	ואם תפתחו החזון / תסת[ם מכם
300 5,5	אִם	]ה חכמה נכחדת[כי] אם /
300 8,6	אִם	ת]דעו היש אתכם בינה ואם[
299 6i6	אמר	]יאמר להם ויתנו /
299 45,2	אמר	]אמרו °[
300 1a ii-b,1	אמר	אמרו המשל והגידו החידה
300 1a ii-b,3	אמר	/ א[ז]תאמרו ל[
301 2b,3	אמר	מיא יאמ[ר]
299 1,2	אֱמֶת	הלוא מפי כול לאומים שמע] האמת
299 9,5	אַף	]ארך א[פים
300 1a i,4	אַף	מע]שה אף
301 3a-b,4	אַף	]ה ונכבד הו[א] בא[ו]רך אפיו [
301 3a-b,5	אַף	ונורא הואה במזמת אפו נכבד הוא[ב]
301 4,3	אֵפֶר	]עת בכול כבודו ומה אפר [ועפר
299 6ii12	ארב	/ לב רעו ואורב מ°[
299 9,5	אֹרֶךְ	]ארך א[פים
299 23,5	אֹרֶךְ	]°ה ארכה[
301 3a-b,4	אֹרֶךְ	]ה ונכבד הו[א] בא[ו]רך אפיו [
299 4,3	אֶרֶץ	]ארץ וכמהו ל[
299 6ii6	אֶרֶץ	/ כיא אם ארץ להדר °[
299 9,2	אֶרֶץ	]° שרים לי זרח א[ר]ץ למ[
299 79,5	אֶרֶץ	]ארץ צביו והוא °[
299 81,1	אֶרֶץ	]הארץ למ°[
300 1a i,3	אֶרֶץ	]ם מעשי ארץ /
301 3a-b,6	אֶרֶץ	/]בו ובאשר בארץ המשילו
299 70,4	אַשְׁמָה	]ל עם אשמה[
299 1,3	אֲשֶׁר	]מי גוי אשר לוא גזל / [הון]
299 3a ii-b,6	אֲשֶׁר	/ מעשה אשר לוא יעשה עוד
299 3a ii-b,7	אֲשֶׁר	ומה (ו)הוא אשר יעשה ג[בר
299 6ii8	אֲשֶׁר	/ עמים מהיא אשר[
299 6ii9	אֲשֶׁר	/ אשר אין ל°°[
299 7,6	אֲשֶׁר	/ אש[ר מ]על ועשה[
299 24,3	אֲשֶׁר	א]שר ה[
299 55,4	אֲשֶׁר	]אשר בחרו בה° א[
299 57,3	אֲשֶׁר	]אשר יעשה[
299 57,4	אֲשֶׁר	]יע את אש[ר
300 2ii4	אֲשֶׁר	/ מעלו אשר מעל[
301 3a-b,6	אֲשֶׁר	/]בו ובאשר בארץ המשילו
299 3a ii-b,8	אֵת	/ המרה את דבר עושו
299 13a+b,2	אֵת	]המשיל אתכם[י]שראל ואתכם[
299 13a+b,2	אֵת	]המשיל אתכם[י]שראל ואתכם[
299 57,4	אֵת	]יע את אש[ר
299 59,2	אֵת	/ במשפט יריב א[ת
300 8,5	אֵת	]לה אתכם תומכי רזים א[
300 8,6	אֵת	ת]דעו היש אתכם בינה ואם[
299 10,8	אַתֶּם	]אתם לתכן כול עבודת[
299 70,3	אַתֶּם	]לחול ואת[ם
301 3a-b,7	בָּחִיר	ונהדר ה[ואה] / [ל]בחיריו
299 1,6	בחן	]°°ם נבחנה דברים /
299 3a ii-b,14	בחן	בחן וינחילנו[
299 55,4	בחר	]אשר בחרו בה° א[
299 10,7	בֵּין	]ל[ ]° ושופטים בין אביו[ן
299 13a+b,1	בֵּין	]חול בין הט°[
299 76,4	בֵּין	/ ובי°°° בין איש[
300 3,2	בֵּין	/ בעבור ידעו בין ט[וב ובין רע
301 10,2	בֵּין	]ן בין א[
299 8,5	בין	]°° ומה יתבונן גב[ר]
299 34,3	בין	]° מבין °[
299 43,3	בין	]התב[וננו
299 46,2	בין	]א בוננ°[
299 8,6	בִּינָה	ה]בינה יצר לבנ[ו]
299 8,7	בִּינָה	]יצר בינה
300 1a ii-b,2	בִּינָה	ובבינה לא השכלתם /
300 5,1	בִּינָה	]מחשבת בי[נה] /
300 8,6	בִּינָה	ת]דעו היש אתכם בינה ואם[
301 1,2	בִּינָה	וחוקרי שורשי בינה
301 2b,1	בִּינָה	לכמה חו‹ק›רי בשור(ש)שי בינה /
301 4,2	בִּינָה	]ת° כל רוח בינתו לוא ידע[ו
299 1,4	בַּיִת	]בית מולדים נשטרה °/
299 3a ii-b,13	בַּיִת	]ל [מ]חשבת בית מולדים
299 5,5	בַּיִת	]ובית מולדים[
299 52,4	בְּכוֹר	/ בכור[
299 4,1	בִּלְתִּי	לב]לתי המו[
299 8,9	בִּלְתִּי	ה]סגיר בעד עד מים לבל[תי
299 6ii5	בֵּן	/ מה אב לבנים מאיש[
299 39,1	בֵּן	]בני יש[ראל
299 68,2	בֵּן	]° לבני ישר[אל
299 8,9	בְּעַד	ה]סגיר בעד עד מים לבל[תי
299 3a ii-b,16	ברא	/ ומה]עמים כ[י] בראם ומעש[יהמה
299 6i7	ברא	] בגברתו ברא /
299 83,4	בְּרִית	]ברית ה°[
301 3a-b,7	בְּרָכָה	גדול הואה בברכות[ ]
301 5,3	בָּשָׂר	מ]ה בשר כיא [
299 78,2	גבולָה	]גבולותיה[
299 10,2	גִּבּוֹר	] וגב[ו]רי חיל יחזקו מ[עמד
299 72,2	גִּבּוֹר	ג]בורי צדק [
299 5,2	גְּבוּרָה	גב]ורות רזי אור ודרכי חוש[ך
299 6i7	גְּבוּרָה	] בגברתו ברא /
299 6i16	גְּבוּרָה	]°ת כול גבורה /

]מה גבורה בלוא[	גְּבוּרָה	**299** 33,4
ג]בורה [	גְּבוּרָה	**299** 45,3
ג]בֿוֿרתו וחזק[	גְּבוּרָה	**299** 53,6
ומה (ו)הוא אשר יעשה ג[בר	גֶּבֶר	**299** 3a ii-b,7
]◦ עבֿודת גבר /	גֶּבֶר	**299** 6i18
]◦◦ ומה יתבונן גבֿ[ר	גֶּבֶר	**299** 8,5
]תֿ גבר ומה מע[שה	גֶּבֶר	**300** 6,2
ומהֿ רם לגבר מצדקֿ[	גֶּבֶר	**300** 7,1
[וגדו]לֿ הואהֿ ברוב חמתֿ[ו	גָּדוֹל	**301** 3a-b,4
גדול הואה בברכות[ ]	גָּדוֹל	**301** 3a-b,7
א]וֿר גדול ונכב[ד הואה	גָּדוֹל	**301** 5,4
]מֿי גוי אשר לוא גזל / [הון]	גּוֹי	**299** 1,3
ר]ם על כול גואים ישראֿ[ל	גּוֹי	**299** 10,3
]◦לת לגֿויתו וא◦[	גְּוִיָּה	**299** 65,5
]מֿי גוי אשר לוא גזל / [הון]	גזל	**299** 1,3
]םֿ עשוק וגזול ב◦◦◦[	גזל	**299** 54,2
] גליהם ביד ◦[	גַּל	**299** 21,2
ו]יגל בלוא ה[ון	גלה	**299** 2,2
ברוב שכל גלה אוזננו	גלה	**299** 8,6
/ וגלה הרשע מפני הצדק	גלה	**300** 3,5
כגולוֿ[ת חושך מפני אור	גלה	**300** 3,5
והצדיק יגל[ה] כש[מש	גלה	**300** 3,6
מ]שֿפט בגלל הון /	גְּלַל	**300** 5,2
ברק]ים עשה לנצח גשמים /	גֶּשֶׁם	**299** 6i4
בטרם נדבר	דבר	**300** 1a ii-b,1
]◦◦םֿ נבחנה דברים /	דָּבָר	**299** 1,6
כיא אם [ ] / דבר עושו	דָּבָר	**299** 3a ii-b,7
/ המרה את דבר עושו	דָּבָר	**299** 3a ii-b,8
ולמיניכם אֿחלקה דברי אליכםֿ[	דָּבָר	**301** 1,1
/ ואם דש יוסיף ל[	דוש	**299** 6ii18
]בֿדין מועדי חום עם קֿצֿ[י	דִּין	**299** 5,3
לֿכֿוֿל רודפי דעת וה◦[	דַּעַת	**299** 8,7
א]ל הדעות[	דַּעַת	**299** 35,1
]אֿל הדע[ות	דַּעַת	**299** 73,3
גב]וֿרות רזי אור ודרכי חושֿ[ך	דֶּרֶךְ	**299** 5,2
]דרך חיים [	דֶּרֶךְ	**299** 79,3
]◦ מֿיֿאֿ בֿכם דורש פני אור ומא[ור	דרש	**301** 2b,4
י]דעו ההב[דל	הֶבְדֵּל	**300** 6,1
]◦◦ ◦הבל ◦[	הֶבֶל	**299** 64,3
/ כיא אם ארץ להדר ◦[	הָדָר	**299** 6ii6
מ]לך נכבד והדר מלכותו מֿלאֿ[	הָדָר	**299** 9,3
ו]נֿ[הדר /]הואה בהמון רחמיו	הָדָר	**301** 3a-b,4
ונהדר ה[ואה] / [ל]בחיריו	הָדָר	**301** 3a-b,6
ונהדרֿ[הואה ברום קו]דשו	הָדָר	**301** 3a-b,7
]הדרם ות[	הָדָר	**301** 3a-b,8
]זהר נהדר הואה ב[	הָדָר	**301** 4,4

]הוא /	הוא	**299** 3a i,4
ומה (ו)הוא אשר יעשה ג[בר	הוא	**299** 3a ii-b,7
/ הוֿ[אה מק]דם עולם	הוא	**299** 3a ii-b,12
הואה שמו ולעֿ[ולם	הוא	**299** 3a ii-b,12
/ הוא י◦[ ]ל[ ]מ[	הוא	**299** 6ii19
]הֿוא אֿ[	הוא	**299** 7,1
/ מֿוֿלֿ אֿישֿ והוא רֿחֿוק מ◦[	הוא	**299** 7,4
]הֿוא הכין ע[	הוא	**299** 8,1
]ןֿ הוא ◦[	הוא	**299** 8,3
הוא לוא ישנה[	הוא	**299** 8,8
] הוא אֿ[	הוא	**299** 23,2
]◦שלו מה הוא המצוֿ[ה	הוא	**299** 32,2
ה]וא יהיה[	הוא	**299** 36,2
]הֿוא ◦[	הוא	**299** 46,3
]◦ינו שיד הואה[	הוא	**299** 65,2
הו]א קדוש הוֿאֿ[	הוא	**299** 72,1
הו]א קדוש הוֿאֿ[	הוא	**299** 72,1
]◦ וֿהֿוֿא[	הוא	**299** 77,3
]ארץ צביו והוא ◦[	הוא	**299** 79,5
]הוא ◦[	הוא	**299** 86,3
]◦ב והוא ◦◦[	הוא	**300** 4,3
]וֿהוא רחו[ק	הוא	**300** 6,4
] לאיש וה[וא	הוא	**300** 8,8
]מֿעולם הוא ועֿ[ד עולם	הוא	**300** 9,3
והוא ממשֿ[ל	הוא	**301** 2a,2
והוא למש[ל]◦[	הוא	**301** 2b,2
]ה ונכבדֿ הוֿ[א] בא[ו]רך אפיו [	הוא	**301** 3a-b,4
[וגדו]לֿ הואהֿ ברוב חמתֿ[ו	הוא	**301** 3a-b,4
ו]נֿ[הדר /]הואה בהמון רחמיו	הוא	**301** 3a-b,5
ונורא הואה במזמת אפו נכבד הוא[ב]	הוא	**301** 3a-b,5
ונורא הואה במזמת אפו נכבד הוא[ב]	הוא	**301** 3a-b,5
ונהדר ה[ואה] / [ל]בחיריו	הוא	**301** 3a-b,6
גדול הואה בברכות[ ]	הוא	**301** 3a-b,7
]זהר נהדר הואה ב[	הוא	**301** 4,4
]ל◦◦רֿ הואה למו הואהֿ[	הוא	**301** 6,3
]ל◦◦רֿ הואה למו הואהֿ[	הוא	**301** 6,3
נכב]דֿ הֿואה [ב	הוא	**301** 9,3
/ עמים מֿהיא אשרֿ[	הִיא	**299** 6ii8
]היאה מֿ[	הִיא	**299** 24,2
כי[מ]ה היא חכמה / נכחדת[	הִיא	**300** 1a ii-b,4
ו]יגל בלוא ה[ון	הוֹן	**299** 2,2
/ מאיש נואל הון הון ◦[	הוֹן	**299** 6ii13
/ מאיש נואל הון הון ◦[	הוֹן	**299** 6ii13
מ]שֿפט בגלל הון /	הוֹן	**300** 5,2
]ד הֿ[ו]נו וצעד כבו[דו	הוֹן	**301** 6,2
/ כן יהיה כֿ[	היה	**299** 6ii11

299 36,2 היה ה]וׄא יהיה[
299 79,9 היה]ל֯יו להי֯[ות]ל[
300 1a ii-b,5 היה עו]ד֯ לא תהיהׄ[
300 3,4 היה ונפשם לא מלטו מרזׄ נׄ[היה
300 8,7 היה]ה ולא היה
301 2b,5 היה]◦ תׄבנית זכר ללוא היהׄ[ ]
301 5,2 הֵיכָל]היכל מלכותוׄ[
299 13a+b,3 הלך]ם ◦[ה]לכו בהׄ[
300 8,4 הלך להולכי פתי בכׄל֯ [
301 1,3 הלך]הׄולכי פותי ואנשי מחשבת
301 2b,7 הלל מ]הללים[ ]
301 3a-b,5 הָמוֹן ו]נׄ[הדר /]הואה בהמון רחמיו
301 1,4 הֲמוּלָּה קודקׄ[וד כ]ל [ה]מׄולת עמים
299 34,2 הפך]תוׄ ואם יהפכׄ[ו
299 6i8 הַר]אׄ[ ]◦ל [ה]ר֯יה כול /
299 6i12 הרה]ו להרות לכול /
301 4,4 זֹהַר]זהר נהדׄר הואה ב[
300 2ii5 זוּלַת / ר֯עׄ זולתו אׄהׄוב[
299 74,3 זֵכֶר]לזׄכׄר קדושיׄםׄ על [
301 2b,5 זָכָר]◦ תׄבנית זכר ללוא היהׄ[ ]
299 5,1 זִכָּרוֹן מאור]ות כוכבים ל֯זׄ[כר]וׄן שמׄ[ו
299 79,7 זִכָּרוֹן ריח נ]יׄחוח לזכרון נב◦[
299 9,2 זרח]◦ שרים לי זרח אׄ[ר]ץׄ ל֯מׄ[
299 3a ii-b,15 חֶבֶל]כׄוׄל רז וחבלי כול מעשה
299 6i14 חֶדֶר]◦כול מקויהם וחדר /
299 70,3 חוֹל]לׄחול וׄאת[ם
300 1a ii-b,2 חוֹתָם כי חתום מכם[ח]תׄם החזון
300 1a ii-b,2 חָזוֹן כי חתום מכם[ח]תׄם החזון
300 1a ii-b,3 חָזוֹן ואם תפתחו החזון / תסתׄ[ם מכם
300 1a ii-b,6 חָזוֹן / [ח]זׄוׄןׄ ◦[
299 6i3 חזק]◦םׄ עבודׄתם יחזקו /
299 6i15 חזק]נתׄן ממשל לחזק /
299 6i17 חזק] וׄמׄחזק כול /
299 10,2 חזק] וגבׄ[ו]רׄיׄ חיל יחזקוׄ מ[עמד
299 15,3 חזק *vacat* יחזק ◦◦ל֯◦[
299 32,3 חזק מ]חזיק ותולדׄות המ[
299 53,6 חזק ג]בׄורׄתו וחזקׄ[
299 56,3 חזק י]חזיקו ביד ◦◦◦◦[
301 2b,3 חזק]בׄלוא חוזק
299 15,2 חָזָק ח]זׄקׄ[ות]ל֯כׄוׄ[ל
299 53,8 חָזָק] וריב על חזק ע[
299 6ii2 חַי / ועליכם החי ◦[
299 29,3 חַיָּה]כׄל חׄיׄ ובמדה[
299 79,3 חַיִּים]דׄרך חיים [
300 1a ii-b,1 חִידָה אמרו הׄמשל והגידו הׄחידה
301 1,2 חִידָה מ]של וחידה

301 2b,1 חִידָה]ים ומה הׄחידה
299 10,2 חַיִל] וגבׄ[ו]רׄיׄ חיל יחזקוׄ מ[עמד
299 3a ii-b,4 חָכָם ומה]נקרא לאדׄ[ם] / חכם וצדיק
301 2a,1 חָכָם / משפטי כסיל ונחלת חכמ[ים
299 3a ii-b,5 חָכְמָה כי] / אם חוכמת עורמת רוע ומׄ[חשבת בליעל
299 17i2 חָכְמָה]מחוכמה /
299 42,4 חָכְמָה]◦ החכמה[
300 1a ii-b,3 חָכְמָה]כי לא הבטתם בשורש חוכמה
300 1a ii-b,4 חָכְמָה]כׄל חוכמת[כ]ם
300 1a ii-b,4 חָכְמָה כׄיׄ[מ]הׄ היא חכמה / נכחדת[
300 3,3 חָכְמָה / כל חוכמתם
300 5,5 חָכְמָה]ה חכמה נכחדתׄ[כי] אם /
301 1,1 חלק ולמיניכם אׄחלקה דברי אליכםׄ[
299 5,3 חֹם]בׄדין מועדי חׄום עׄם קׄצׄ[י
301 3a-b,4 חֵמָה [וגדו]ל֯ הואהׄ ברוב חמתׄ[ו
299 54,3 חֶסֶד]◦הׄו כיא אהבת חׄסדׄ[
299 62,5 חָצֵר]ל֯חצרוׄ[תי]הׄמׄהׄ לם [
299 20,1 חֹק]חׄוׄק תכׄונם כיא אםׄ[
299 61,2 חֹק]בׄחׄוקים ◦[
299 70,1 חֹק]◦תם חוקׄ[
299 78,1 חֹק]חׄוקתיה[
301 1,2 חקר וחוקרי שׄוׄרׄשי בינה
301 2b,1 חקר לכמה חׄו‹ק›רי בׄשור(ש)שי בינה /
300 1a ii-b,1 חַרְטֹם החר]טמים מלמדי פשע
299 10,4 חשב]◦ וליצוׄר ולחשובׄ[
299 5,2 חֹשֶׁךְ גב]וׄרות רזי אור ודרכי חושׄ[ך
299 6ii10 חֹשֶׁךְ / חוש[ך] וׄא[ור
299 30,3 חֹשֶׁךְ ח]ושך בחׄוׄשך מ◦[
299 30,3 חֹשֶׁךְ ח]ושך בחׄוׄשך מ◦[
300 1a ii-b,2 חתם כי חתום מכם[ח]תׄם החזון
299 6i10 טַבּוּר]מׄטׄברו פרש /
300 3,2 טוֹב / בעבור ידעו בין ט[וב ובין רע
300 4,4 טוב]לשוםׄ לטׄ[וב
299 3a ii-b,3 טָמֵא / וכול מעשה צׄדׄיׄקׄ הטמׄ[אה
300 5,4 טָמֵא וכול מעשה צדיק הטמ]אה
300 1a ii-b,1 טֶרֶם בטרם נדבר
299 6ii13 יאל / מאיש נואׄל הון הון ◦[
299 21,2 יָד] גליהם ביד ◦[
299 31,4 יָד]בידך [
299 35,2 יָד]ביׄד מלאכ[י
299 56,3 יָד י]חזיקו ביד ◦◦◦◦[
299 77,2 יָד]כׄוׄל בידכם[
300 11,2 יָד]ובידו משפט כלם וצדׄ[ק
299 23,3 ידה]מׄוׄדׄה מנׄ[
299 4,4 ידע י]דׄע ונספרוׄ רישׄ[ונות
299 8,5 ידע בלוא יׄדׄעׄ ולוא שמע [

]ם ידע[	ידע	**299** 68,4
]לוֹא ידעתם ∘[	ידע	**299** 70,2
י]דעו כיא[	ידע	**299** 72,3
ואז תדעו אם הבטתםׄ	ידע	**300** 1a ii-b,1
/ בעבור ידעו בין ט]וב ובין רע	ידע	**300** 3,2
ולא ידע]ו רז נהיה	ידע	**300** 3,3
י]דׄעו ההבׄ]דל	ידע	**300** 6,1
]עם יודע]י	ידע	**300** 6,3
]ונוֹדׄיׄעׄה[	ידע	**300** 8,4a
ת]דׄעו היש אתכם בינה ואםׄ[	ידע	**300** 8,6
]תׄם כל רוח בׄינׄתו לוא ידעׄ]ו	ידע	**301** 4,2
]בׄו וביוםׄ[	יוֹם	**299** 18,2
]∘יׄוׄם יׄומס[	יוֹם	**299** 82,4
]וׄמׄים יׄ[	יוֹם	**299** 89,2
]ימיםׄ [	יוֹם	**300** 2ii1
מ]חׄזה ימינוׄ[	יוֹם	**300** 8,1
]כׄיא בׄוׄ יום הריב ∘[	יוֹם	**300** 9,2
] היום [	יוֹם	**300** 13,1
]∘∘ יוׄמםׄ[	יוֹמָם	**299** 10,10
]יחׄד רׄובם אם[	יַחַד	**299** 20,3
]שנאיכה לוא יוכלׄ]ו	יכל	**299** 62,4
]אׄ הילודים[	יָלוּד	**299** 28,1
]תׄמהו כן ילודׄ[	יָלוּד	**299** 28,2
/ ואם דשׄ יוסיף לׄ[	יסף	**299** 6ii18
]∘∘ הׄוסיףׄ[	יסף	**299** 30,5
]∘ וליצוׄר ולחשובׄ[	יצר	**299** 10,4
ה]בׄינה יצר לבׄנׄ]ו	יֵצֶר	**299** 8,6
]יׄצׄר בינה	יֵצֶר	**299** 8,7
י]צׄרו ובמח∘[	יֵצֶר	**299** 33,2
ונורא הואה במזמת אפו נכבד הוא[ב]	ירא	**301** 3a-b,5
/ מׄשפט כן ירד המ[	ירד	**299** 6ii17
וירד בו בשוט בלוא מחיר	ירד	**301** 2b,3
היש שפה ולשן /]מחזקת בה	יֵשׁ	**299** 1,2
ת]דׄעו היש אתכם בינה ואםׄ[	יֵשׁ	**300** 8,6
] יושבׄיׄ[	ישב	**299** 97,1
]ישרים [	יָשָׁר	**299** 79,2
ר]םׄ על כול גואים יׄשׄרׄאׄ]ל	יִשְׂרָאֵל	**299** 10,3
]המשיל אתכם[י]שׄראל ואתכם[	יִשְׂרָאֵל	**299** 13a+b,2
]בׄנׄי ישׄ]ראל	יִשְׂרָאֵל	**299** 39,1
]∘ל ישראׄ]ל	יִשְׂרָאֵל	**299** 66,3
יש]רׄאל ועםׄ[	יִשְׂרָאֵל	**299** 68,1
]∘ לׄבני ישרׄ]אל	יִשְׂרָאֵל	**299** 68,2
]∘יׄתׄי ישראל[	יִשְׂרָאֵל	**299** 82,3
מ]לך נכבׄד והדר מלכותו מׄלׄאׄ[	כבד	**299** 9,3
/ מה נכבׄד לבב	כבד	**301** 2a,2
]ה ונכׄבׄד הׄוׄ]א[בׄא]ו[רך אפיו [	כבד	**301** 3a-b,4

ונורא הואה במזמת אפו נכבד הוא[ב]	כבד	**301** 3a-b,5
]ונ[כבד אל בעם קודשו	כבד	**301** 3a-b,6
א]וׄר גדול ונכב]ד הואה	כבד	**301** 5,4
נכב]דׄ הׄואה]ב	כבד	**301** 9,3
]כׄבׄודו [	כָּבוֹד	**299** 63,4
] כבוד לפתוחׄ[	כָּבוֹד	**299** 75,2
]עת בכול כבודו ומה אפׄרׄ]ועפר	כָּבוֹד	**301** 4,3
]דׄ הׄ]ו[נו וצעד כבו]דו	כָּבוֹד	**301** 6,2
]∘ׄעׄמו מכוהן ∘[	כֹּהֵן	**299** 67,3
מאור]ות כוכבים לׄזׄ]כר[וׄן שׄמׄ]ו	כּוֹכָב	**299** 5,1
/ תכון אחד ולוא ישׄ]בע	כון	**299** 6ii16
]הׄוא הכין ע[	כון	**299** 8,1
]∘∘מה יכון נ∘[	כון	**299** 34,1
]לתכונם ∘[	כון	**299** 39,2
]∘ לוא כול כוח וכׄ[	כֹּחַ	**299** 21,3
כׄיׄ[מ]הׄ היא חכמה / נכחדת[	כחד	**300** 1a ii-b,5
]ה חכמה נכחדתׄ[כי] אם /	כחד	**300** 5,5
כי לוא לאישׄ[	כִּי	**299** 3a ii-b,4
כׄיא אםׄ [ ] / דׄבר עושו	כִּי	**299** 3a ii-b,6
]∘שׄבׄו כי לבנו	כִּי	**299** 3a ii-b,14
/ ומה]עׄמים כׄ]י[בׄראם ומעשׄ]יהמה	כִּי	**299** 3a ii-b,16
כי מה /]היא חכמה נכחדת	כִּי	**299** 3c,3
]כׄי מעפר מבניתם /	כִּי	**299** 6i13
/ כיא אם ארץ להדר ∘[	כִּי	**299** 6ii6
/ ממנו כי אם רוח ∘עׄ[	כִּי	**299** 6ii7
]חׄוׄק תכׄוׄנם כיא אםׄ[	כִּי	**299** 20,1
]∘ד כי אםׄ[	כִּי	**299** 42,2
]מׄשפט כיא צדׄיׄקׄ[	כִּי	**299** 53,5
]∘הׄו כיא אהבת חׄסדׄ[	כִּי	**299** 54,3
]∘הנו כיא המ[	כִּי	**299** 55,3
י]דעו כיא[	כִּי	**299** 72,3
כי חתום מכם[ח]תׄם החזון	כִּי	**300** 1a ii-b,2
]כי לא הבטתם בשורש חוכמה	כִּי	**300** 1a ii-b,3
כי לכם המ∘[	כִּי	**300** 1a ii-b,4
נפשו כׄי]א [צדׄיק בכל[דרכיו	כִּי	**300** 7,3
]כׄיׄא בׄוׄ יום הריב ∘[	כִּי	**300** 9,2
מ]ה בשר כיא [	כִּי	**301** 5,3
כי]א אין לוׄ מ[	כִּי	**301** 6,1
]אנשי מחשבת לכול /	כֹּל	**299** 1,5
]ולכׄ]ול[/	כֹּל	**299** 1,8
/ וכול מעשה צׄדׄיׄקׄ הטמׄ]אה	כֹּל	**299** 3a ii-b,3
ימחה שמו מפי כולׄ[	כֹּל	**299** 3a ii-b,8
/ עולם ומזמות כול מעשה ומׄ]חׄ[שבות	כֹּל	**299** 3a ii-b,10
/ כול רז וׄמׄכׄין כול מחשבת	כֹּל	**299** 3a ii-b,11
/ כול רז וׄמׄכׄין כול מחשבת	כֹּל	**299** 3a ii-b,11
עושה כולׄ[הנהיות	כֹּל	**299** 3a ii-b,11

]כׄוׄל רז וחבלי כול מעשה	כֹּל	**299** 3a ii-b,15
]כׄוׄל רז וחבלי כול מעשה	כֹּל	**299** 3a ii-b,15
]אׄ[ ]◦ל [ה]ריה כול /	כֹּל	**299** 6i8
]◦◦ כׄל צאצאיׄהׄ /	כֹּל	**299** 6i9
]ו להרות לכול /	כֹּל	**299** 6i12
]◦כול מקויהם וחדר /	כֹּל	**299** 6i14
]◦ת כול גבורה /	כֹּל	**299** 6i16
] וׄמׄחׄזק כול /	כֹּל	**299** 6i17
/ נסתרה מכול תומכׄ[י	כֹּל	**299** 6ii4
לׄכׄוׄל רודפי דעת וׄהׄ◦[	כֹּל	**299** 8,7
]כׄוׄל שכל מעולם	כֹּל	**299** 8,8
]א עם כול צבׄ[א	כֹּל	**299** 9,4
ר]םׄ על כול גואים ישׄראׄ[ל	כֹּל	**299** 10,3
]ושופטים לכול לאׄ[ומים	כֹּל	**299** 10,5
]◦ על כול מספרם ◦[	כֹּל	**299** 10,6
]אׄתם לתכן כול עבודתׄ[	כֹּל	**299** 10,8
]כול ממ[ש]לוׄתׄם ◦[	כֹּל	**299** 10,9
]◦א כול מןׄ[	כֹּל	**299** 12,2
ח]זׄקׄ[ות]לׄכׄוׄ[ל	כֹּל	**299** 15,2
]◦ לוא כול כוח וכׄ[	כֹּל	**299** 21,3
]ואׄוׄצר כול[	כֹּל	**299** 21,4
]כׄל חׄיׄ ובמדה[	כֹּל	**299** 29,3
]בׄכול ◦◦[	כֹּל	**299** 31,2
]לכל כׄ◦[	כֹּל	**299** 36,1
]כׄול מעׄשׄה ה[	כֹּל	**299** 37,2
כו]לׄ עובׄ[רי	כֹּל	**299** 48,1
]ובׄכול מ◦[	כֹּל	**299** 48,2
]◦ בכול ◦◦◦ ל◦◦[	כֹּל	**299** 54,4
/ בכול עוברי פיהׄ[ו	כֹּל	**299** 59,3
] סגולה מכול [העמים	כֹּל	**299** 60,3
] וכול מלכי עׄמׄיׄ[ם	כֹּל	**299** 60,4
]◦ כול משפחותׄ[	כֹּל	**299** 67,2
]ליׄםׄ כל ר[	כֹּל	**299** 67,4
]◦ כול האדם[	כֹּל	**299** 69,3
/ כול אבות העדה[	כֹּל	**299** 76,3
]כׄוׄל בידכם[	כֹּל	**299** 77,2
] כול העמים ◦◦[	כֹּל	**299** 79,8
] לכול ל◦◦[	כֹּל	**299** 99,1
]כׄל חוכמת[כ]ם	כֹּל	**300** 1a ii-b,4
/ כל חוכמתם	כֹּל	**300** 3,3
נפשו כיׄ[א]צדׄיק בכל[דרכיו	כֹּל	**300** 7,3
להולכי פתי בכׄלׄ [	כֹּל	**300** 8,4
]ובידו משפט כלם וצדׄ[ק	כֹּל	**300** 11,2
לכול עׄבודת מעשיׄהם	כֹּל	**301** 1,3
קׄודקׄ[וד כ]ל [ה]מׄולת עמים	כֹּל	**301** 1,4
]תׄ◦ כל רוח בׄיׄנׄתו לוא ידעׄ[ו	כֹּל	**301** 4,2
]עת בכול כבודו ומה אפׄרׄ [ועפר	כֹּל	**301** 4,3
]בׄכלו[ת]קׄץ רשעה ועשות[	כלה	**301** 3a-b,8
/ כן יהיה כׄ[	כֵּן	**299** 6ii11
/ מׄשפט כן ירד המ[	כֵּן	**299** 6ii17
]תׄמהו כן ילוׄדׄ[	כֵּן	**299** 28,2
/ אוילי כסה ◦[	כסה	**299** 6ii3
/ משפטי כסיל ונחלת חכמ[ים	כְּסִיל	**301** 2a,1
]כׄסלכמה	כֶּסֶל	**300** 1a ii-b,2
עבו]דת קודשו ולׄכפרׄ עׄלׄ ◦◦[	כפר	**299** 55,5
]מׄיׄ גוי אשר לוא גזל / [הון]	לא	**299** 1,3
]לא יצׄלׄחׄ[	לא	**299** 2,1
ו]יגל בלוא ה[ון	לא	**299** 2,2
כי לוא לאישׄ[	לא	**299** 3a ii-b,4
]הׄ ולׄו[א ה חכמה נכחדת כי]	לא	**299** 3a ii-b,4
/ מעשה אשר לוא יעשה עׄוד	לא	**299** 3a ii-b,6
/ ל]וא ◦◦◦[	לא	**299** 6ii1
/ תכון אחד ולוא ישׄ[בע	לא	**299** 6ii16
מנׄוטׄרׄ [לנ]קׄ[ו]ם בלוא מׄשׄ[פט	לא	**299** 7,5
בלוא ידׄעׄ ולוא שמע [	לא	**299** 8,5
בלוא ידׄעׄ ולוא שמע [	לא	**299** 8,5
הוא לוא ישנׄהׄ[	לא	**299** 8,8
]לׄוׄאׄ יגע[	לא	**299** 15,2
]◦ לוא כול כוח וכׄ[	לא	**299** 21,3
]א לוא[	לא	**299** 25,3
]◦◦ת לואׄ[	לא	**299** 26,3
]הׄמוסרׄ לוא ◦[	לא	**299** 30,4
]מה גבורה בלוא[	לא	**299** 33,4
]ליהא לוא[	לא	**299** 42,3
]שנאיכה לוא יוכלׄ[ו	לא	**299** 62,4
]לׄוׄא ידעתם ◦[	לא	**299** 70,2
]לוא באׄ[	לא	**299** 101,2
ל]וא ◦[	לא	**299** 102,1
וברזׄי עד לא הבטתם	לא	**300** 1a ii-b,2
ובבינה לא השכלתם /	לא	**300** 1a ii-b,2
]כי לא הבטתם בשורש חוכמה	לא	**300** 1a ii-b,3
עו]דׄ לא תהיהׄ[	לא	**300** 1a ii-b,5
ולא ידעׄ[ו רז נהיה	לא	**300** 3,3
ונפשם לא מלטו מרזׄ נׄ[היה	לא	**300** 3,4
מנוקם לנטור בלׄוׄאׄ[	לא	**300** 7,2
]ה ולא היה	לא	**300** 8,7
]סׄודות לא השיגוהו ◦[	לא	**300** 9,1
]◦ לא יקח[	לא	**300** 10,3
]בׄלוא חוזק	לא	**301** 2b,3
וירד בו בשוט בלוא מחיר	לא	**301** 2b,3
]◦ תׄבנית זכר ללוא היהׄ[ ]	לא	**301** 2b,5
]תׄ◦ כל רוח בׄיׄנׄתו לוא ידעׄ[ו	לא	**301** 4,2

301 6,4	לא	]הלוא ◦◦◦[ ]◦◦[
301 7,4	לא	]לוא ◦◦[
299 10,5	לְאֹם	]ושופטים לכול לא[ומים
299 3a ii-b,14	לֵב	]◦שבו כי לבנו
299 6ii12	לֵב	/ לב רעו ואורב מ◦[
299 8,6	לֵב	ה]בינה יצר לבנ[ו]
299 45,1	לֵב	]ה לבם[
301 7,3	לֵב	רש]עת לבו ל◦[
301 2a,2	לֵבָב	/ מה נכבד לבב
299 87,2	לֶחֶם	]דת בלחמי[
299 5,4	לַיְלָה	מבוא יום]ומוצא לילה[
300 1a ii-b,1	למד	החר]טמים מלמדי פשע
300 2i5	לַעֲנָה	]לענה /
300 6,5	לַעֲנָה	ואי]ן לענה לנגדו[
300 7,2	לַעֲנָה	]ואין לענה לנגדו
299 3a ii-b,13	לִפְנֵי	פתח לפ[ניהם
299 38,1	לִפְנֵי	]◦ לפני ◦◦[
300 10,3	לקח	]◦ לא יקח[
299 1,2	לָשׁוֹן	היש שפה ולשן / [מחזקת בה
299 66,1	לָשׁוֹן	]◦◦ם ולשונו[ת
299 6ii15	מְאֹד	/ מודה או תכלית י[
299 5,1	מָאוֹר	מאור]ות כוכבים לז[כר]ון שמ[ו
301 2b,4	מָאוֹר	]◦ מיא בכם דורש פני אור ומא[ור]
299 6i13	מבנית	]כי מעפר מבניתם /
299 29,3	מִדָּה	]כל חי ובמדה[
299 53,9	מָדוֹר	א]ל ובשמים מדור[ו
300 2ii3	מְדָן	/ יעזוב קנאת מדנים[
299 2,3	מָה	מה[מ מחים כי אם כול
299 3a i,5	מָה	]מה /
299 3a ii-b,2	מָה	/ מה נקרא ה[
299 3a ii-b,7	מָה	ומה [ו]הוא אשר יעשה ג[בר
299 3a ii-b,15	מָה	ומה [
299 3c,3	מָה	כי מה / [היא חכמה נכחדת
299 6ii5	מָה	/ מה אב לבנים מאיש[
299 6ii8	מָה	/ עמים מהיא אשר[
299 6ii14	מָה	/ לפי תבאות ומה ב◦[
299 8,5	מָה	]◦◦ ומה יתבונן גב[ר]
299 27,3	מָה	]◦ מה מ[
299 32,2	מָה	]◦שלו מה הוא המצו[ה
299 33,4	מָה	]מה גבורה בלוא[
300 1a ii-b,4	מָה	כי[מ]ה היא חכמה / נכחדת[
300 2ii2	מָה	/ שקר מה פחד[לאדם
300 5,3	מָה	]אביון מה נקרא /
300 5,4	מָה	ומה נקרא לאדם /
300 6,2	מָה	]ת גבר ומה מע[שה
300 6,6	מָה	]מה עמוק לא[יש

300 7,1	מָה	ומה רם לגבר מצדק[
300 8,2	מָה	]מה קדם ומה אח[ור
300 8,2	מָה	]מה קדם ומה אח[ור
300 8,7	מָה	מה רז אם[
300 10,2	מָה	מה רע לא◦◦יש ואי◦[
300 12,1	מָה	מ]תוק מה ◦[
301 2a,2	מָה	/ מה נכבד לבב
301 2b,1	מָה	]ים ומה החידה
301 2b,2	מָה	]משל מה אדיר לכם
301 4,3	מָה	]עת בכול כבודו ומה אפר [ועפר
301 5,3	מָה	מ]ה בשר כיא [
299 7,4	מול	/ מול איש והוא רחוק מ◦[
299 1,4	מוֹלָד	]בית מולדים נשטרה ◦/
299 3a ii-b,13	מוֹלָד	]ל [מ]חשבת בית מולדים
299 5,5	מוֹלָד	]ובית מולדים[
299 30,4	מוּסָר	]המוסר לוא ◦[
299 5,3	מוֹעֵד	]בדין מועדי חום עם קצ[י
299 53,4	מוֹעֵד	]◦ד ואין שם למוע[ד
299 5,4	מוֹצָא	מבוא יום]ומוצא לילה[
299 3a ii-b,10	מְזִמָּה	/ עולם ומזמות כול מעשה ומח[שבות
301 3a-b,5	מְזִמָּה	ונורא הואה במזמת אפו נכבד הוא[ב]
299 3a ii-b,8	מחה	ימחה שמו מפי כול[
300 8,1	מַחֲזֶה	מ]חזה ימינו[
299 65,3	מְחִיר	מ]חסור ולמחיר[
301 2b,3	מְחִיר	וירד בו בשוט בלוא מחיר
299 65,3	מַחְסוֹר	מ]חסור ולמחיר[
299 1,5	מַחֲשָׁבָה	]אנשי מחשבת לכול /
299 3a ii-b,5	מַחֲשָׁבָה	/ אם חוכמת עורמת רוע ומ[חשבת בליעל
299 3a ii-b,10	מַחֲשָׁבָה	/ עולם ומזמות כול מעשה ומח[שבות
299 3a ii-b,11	מַחֲשָׁבָה	/ כול רז ומכין כול מחשבת
299 3a ii-b,13	מַחֲשָׁבָה	]ל [מ]חשבת בית מולדים
299 10,11	מַחֲשָׁבָה	]מו ומחש[בותם
300 5,1	מַחֲשָׁבָה	]מחשבת בי[נה] /
301 1,3	מַחֲשָׁבָה	]הולכי פותי ואנשי מחשבת
301 10,3	מַחֲשָׁבָה	]מחשב[ת
299 1,3	מִי	]מי גוי אשר לוא גזל / [הון]
301 2b,3	מִי	מיא יאמ[ר]
301 2b,4	מִי	]◦ מיא בכם דורש פני אור ומא[ור]
299 6i1	מַיִם	]מים /
299 6i5	מַיִם	מי]ם ובמשורה ישקו /
299 8,9	מַיִם	ה]סגיר בעד עד מים לבל[תי
301 1,1	מִין	ולמיניכם אחלקה דברי אליכם[
299 3a ii-b,11	מָכוֹן	/ כול רז ומכין כול מחשבת
299 9,3	מלא	מ]לך נכבד והדר מלכותו מלא[
301 7,2	מלא	]עד מלא[ת
299 35,2	מַלְאָךְ	]ביד מלאכ[י

Reference	Lemma	Context
299 51,1	מַלְאָךְ	]מלאכ֯י[
301 2b,6	מַלְאָךְ	]במלאכי [ ]
300 3,4	מלט	ונפשם לא מלטו מרז נ֯]היה
299 9,3	מֶלֶךְ	מ]לך נכב֯ד והדר מלכותו מ֯לא֯[
299 10,1	מֶלֶךְ	]מ֯ל֯ך [
299 53,12	מֶלֶךְ	]ב֯ו֯ עם מלך[
299 60,4	מֶלֶךְ	] וכול מלכי ע֯מ֯י֯]ם
299 9,3	מַלְכוּת	מ]לך נכב֯ד והדר מלכותו מ֯לא֯[
301 5,2	מַלְכוּת	]היכל מלכותו֯[
299 14,2	מַלְקוֹשׁ	]מלקוש ל֯◦[
299 6i15	מִמְשָׁל	]נת֯ן ממשל לחזק /
299 10,9	מֶמְשָׁלָה	]כול ממ]ש[לו֯תם ◦[
299 3a ii-b,8	מִן	ימחה שמו מפי כול[
299 3c,2	מִן	]תסתם מ֯כם /
299 6i10	מִן	]מ֯טברו פרש /
299 6i13	מִן	]כ֯י מעפר מבניתם /
299 6ii4	מִן	/ נסתרה מכול תומכ֯[י
299 6ii5	מִן	/ מה אב לבנים מאי֯ש֯[
299 6ii7	מִן	/ ממנו כי אם רוח ◦ע֯[
299 6ii13	מִן	/ מאיש נואל הון הון ◦[
299 7,3	מִן	/]מה הוא רחו[ק לאיש ממעש֯]ה
299 7,4	מִן	/ מ֯ו֯ל֯ אי֯ש֯ והוא ר֯ח֯וק מ◦[
299 7,5	מִן	מנו֯ט֯ר]לנ[ק֯]ו[ם בלוא מ֯ש֯]פט
299 8,8	מִן	]כ֯ו֯ל שכל מעולם
299 8,10	מִן	]ש֯מים ממעל לשמים ◦[
299 12,2	מִן	]◦א כול מ֯ן֯[
299 17i2	מִן	]מחוכמה /
299 18,3	מִן	]א֯הב[ ]מהטות[
299 22,1	מִן	]מ֯פי[
299 53,9	מִן	א]ל ובשמים מדור[ו
299 60,3	מִן	] סגולה מכול]העמים
299 67,3	מִן	]◦ע֯מ֯ו מכוהן ◦[
299 76,2	מִן	[ ]מ֯פיהו לפת]וח
300 1a ii-b,2	מִן	כי חתום מכם[ח]ת֯ם החזון
300 3,4	מִן	ונפשם לא מלטו מרז נ֯]היה
300 3,5	מִן	/ וגלה הרשע מפני הצדק
300 7,1	מִן	ומה֯ ר֯ם לגבר מצד֯ק֯[
300 7,2	מִן	מנוקם לנטור בל֯ו֯א֯[
300 7,4	מִן	מה]ר֯ש֯ע֯ משנוא֯[
300 9,3	מִן	]מ֯ע֯ו֯לם הוא ו֯ע֯]ד עולם
301 2a,2	מִן	והוא ממש֯]ל
299 10,6	מִסְפָּר	]◦ על כול מספרם ◦[
299 7,6	מעל	/ אש֯]ר מ[ע֯ל ועשה֯[
300 2ii4	מעל	/ מעלו אשר מעל[
299 8,10	מַעַל	]ש֯מים ממעל לשמים ◦[
300 2ii4	מַעַל	/ מעלו אשר מעל[

Reference	Lemma	Context
299 10,2	מַעֲמָד	] וגב]ו[ר֯י֯ חיל יחזקו מ]עמד
299 3a ii-b,2	מַעֲשֶׂה	]הו ומעש[יו
299 3a ii-b,3	מַעֲשֶׂה	/ וכול מעשה צ֯ד֯י֯ק֯ הטמ]אה
299 3a ii-b,6	מַעֲשֶׂה	/ מעשה אשר לוא יעשה עו֯ד
299 3a ii-b,10	מַעֲשֶׂה	/ עולם ומזמות כול מעשה ומ֯ח֯]שבות
299 3a ii-b,15	מַעֲשֶׂה	]כ֯ו֯ל רז וחבלי כול מעשה
299 3a ii-b,16	מַעֲשֶׂה	/ ומה]ע֯מים כ֯[י] ב֯ראם ומעש[יהמה
299 3c,6	מַעֲשֶׂה	]◦ מ֯עשו יהו[
299 7,3	מַעֲשֶׂה	/]מה הוא רחו[ק לאיש ממעש֯]ה
299 37,2	מַעֲשֶׂה	]כ֯ול מעש֯ה֯ ה[
299 44,2	מַעֲשֶׂה	]◦ מעש[י
300 1a i,3	מַעֲשֶׂה	]ם֯ מ֯עשי ארץ /
300 1a i,4	מַעֲשֶׂה	מע]שה אף
300 6,2	מַעֲשֶׂה	]ת֯ גבר ומה מע[שה
301 1,3	מַעֲשֶׂה	לכול ע֯בודת מעשיהם
299 32,2	מִצְוָה	]◦שלו מה הוא המצו֯]ה
299 6i14	מִקְוֶה	]◦כול מקויהם וחדר /
299 3a ii-b,8	מרה	/ ה֯מרה את דבר עושו
299 74,2	מֹשֶׁה	]מ֯שה פנים אבני[
299 6i5	מְשׂוֹרָה	מי]ם֯ ו֯במשורה ישקו /
299 13a+b,2	משל	]המשיל אתכם[י]שראל ואתכם
299 26,1	משל	מו]של ◦[
301 2a,3	משל	מ֯ו֯של ◦◦[
301 2b,2	משל	]משל מה אדיר לכם
301 2b,2	משל	והוא למש]ל [◦]
301 3a-b,6	משל	/]ב֯ו֯ ובאשר בא֯ר֯ץ המשילו
299 19,1	מָשָׁל	]ה֯משל [
300 1a ii-b,1	מָשָׁל	אמרו ה֯משל והגידו ה֯חידה
301 1,2	מָשָׁל	מ]של וחידה
301 2a,2	מָשָׁל	והוא ממש֯]ל
299 66,2	מִשְׁפָּחָה	]ל֯ משפחות[
299 67,2	מִשְׁפָּחָה	]◦ כול משפחות֯[
299 6ii17	מִשְׁפָּט	/ מ֯שפט כן ירד המ[
299 7,5	מִשְׁפָּט	מנו֯ט֯ר]לנ[ק֯]ו[ם בלוא מ֯ש֯]פט
299 53,5	מִשְׁפָּט	]משפט כיא צדיק֯[
299 55,2	מִשְׁפָּט	המשפ]טים הצדיקים֯[
299 56,2	מִשְׁפָּט	]ש֯ופטם במשפטי֯[
299 59,2	מִשְׁפָּט	/ ב֯משפט יריב א]ת
299 80,3	מִשְׁפָּט	מ]ש֯פ֯ט֯י֯ צדק[
300 5,2	מִשְׁפָּט	מ]שפט בגלל הון /
300 7,3	מִשְׁפָּט	]ש משפט
300 10,2	מִשְׁפָּט	מ]שפט
300 11,2	מִשְׁפָּט	]ובידו משפט כלם וצד֯]ק
301 2a,1	מִשְׁפָּט	/ משפטי כסיל ונחלת חכמ]ים
299 20,2	מִשְׁקָל	]משקל לתכון ◦◦◦[
299 32,4	מִשְׁקָל	]מ֯שקל[

ע]בודת [	עֲבוֹדָה	**299** 88,1
ועבודת /	עֲבוֹדָה	**300** 1a i,4
לכול עבודת מעשיהם	עֲבוֹדָה	**301** 1,3
/ בעבור ידעו בין ט]וב ובין רע	עָבוּר	**300** 3,2
כו]ל עוב]רי	עבר	**299** 48,1
/ בכול עוברי פיה]ו	עבר	**299** 59,3
]שו ◦◦רזי עד /	עַד	**299** 3c,5
וברזי עד לא הבטתם	עַד	**300** 1a ii-b,2
כן יתם] / [הר]שע לעד	עַד	**300** 3,6
ה]סגיר בעד עד מים לבל]תי	עַד	**299** 8,9
]עד מלא]ת	עַד	**301** 7,2
/ כול אבות העדה[	עֵדָה	**299** 76,3
/ מעשה אשר לוא יעשה עוד	עוֹד	**299** 3a ii-b,6
]◦ עוד ◦◦◦[	עוֹד	**299** 31,3
עו]ד לא תהיה[	עוֹד	**300** 1a ii-b,5
הלוא כול העמי]ם שנאו עול /	עָוֶל	**299** 1,1
/ עולם ומזמות כול מעשה ומח]שבות	עוֹלָם	**299** 3a ii-b,10
/ הו]אה מק]דם עולם	עוֹלָם	**299** 3a ii-b,12
הואה שמו ולע]ולם	עוֹלָם	**299** 3a ii-b,12
]כול שכל מעולם	עוֹלָם	**299** 8,8
]מעולם הוא ועו]ד עולם	עוֹלָם	**300** 9,3
/ יעזוב קנאת מדנים[	עזב	**300** 2ii3
/ עוזרי רשעה[	עזר	**299** 59,4
]◦◦◦ מעלים עי]ן	עַיִן	**299** 65,4
/ ועליכם החי ◦[	עַל	**299** 6ii2
ר]ם על כול גואים ישרא]ל	עַל	**299** 10,3
]◦ על כול מספרם ◦[	עַל	**299** 10,6
]ה על מ◦[	עַל	**299** 27,2
] וריב על חזק ע[	עַל	**299** 53,8
עבו]דת קודשו ולכפר על ◦◦[	עַל	**299** 55,5
]עליהם ל[	עַל	**299** 55,6
]◦ על פ[	עַל	**299** 72,4
]לזכר קדושים על [	עַל	**299** 74,3
ולוא ידעו מה אשר יבוא] / עליהם	עַל	**300** 3,4
]◦◦◦ מעלים עי]ן	עלם	**299** 65,4
/ ומה]עמים כ]י] בראם ומעש]יהמה	עַם	**299** 3a ii-b,16
/ עמים מהיא אשר[	עַם	**299** 6ii8
] וכול מלכי עמי]ם	עַם	**299** 60,4
יש]ראל ועם[	עַם	**299** 68,1
] כול העמים ◦◦[	עַם	**299** 79,8
קודק]וד כ]ל [ה]מולת עמים	עַם	**301** 1,4
[ונ]כבד אל בעם קודשו	עַם	**301** 3a-b,6
]בדין מועדי חום עם קצ[י	עִם	**299** 5,3
]א עם כול צב]א	עִם	**299** 9,4
]בו עם מלך[	עִם	**299** 53,12
]◦ עמו מכוהן ◦[	עִם	**299** 67,3

מ]תוק מה ◦[	מָתוֹק	**300** 12,1
/ נאצתה ו[	נאץ	**299** 71,3
ואז תדעו אם הבטתם	נבט	**300** 1a ii-b,1
וברזי עד לא הבטתם	נבט	**300** 1a ii-b,2
]כי לא הבטתם בשורש חוכמה	נבט	**300** 1a ii-b,3
א]ביעה רוחי	נבע	**301** 1,1
אמרו המשל והגידו החידה	נגד	**300** 1a ii-b,1
ואין לענה] / לנגדו	נֶגֶד	**299** 7,5
ואי]ן לענה לנגדו[	נֶגֶד	**300** 6,5
]ואין לענה לנגדו	נֶגֶד	**300** 7,2
]לוא יגע[	נגע	**299** 15,2
בחן וינחילנו[	נחל	**299** 3a ii-b,14
/ משפטי כסיל ונחלת חכמ[ים	נַחֲלָה	**301** 2a,1
]אהב[ ]מהטות[	נטה	**299** 18,3
מנוטר [לנ]ק[ו]ם בלוא מש]פט	נטר	**299** 7,5
מנוקם לנטור בלוא[	נטר	**300** 7,2
ריח נ]יחוח לזכרון נב◦[	נִיחוֹחַ	**299** 79,7
]◦ נפש[	נֶפֶשׁ	**299** 23,4
ונפשם לא מלטו מרז נ]היה	נֶפֶשׁ	**300** 3,4
נפשו כי]א]צדיק בכל[דרכיו	נֶפֶשׁ	**300** 7,3
ברק]ים עשה לנצח גשמים /	נֶצַח	**299** 6i4
מנוטר [לנ]ק[ו]ם בלוא מש]פט	נקם	**299** 7,5
] לאל לנקום נקם[	נקם	**299** 53,7
מנוקם לנטור בלוא[	נקם	**300** 7,2
] לאל לנקום נקם[	נְקָמָה	**299** 53,7
]◦◦שוי ואם ינשא[	נשא	**299** 33,3
]סודות לא השיגוהו ◦[	נשג	**300** 9,1
]יאמר להם ויתנו /	נתן	**299** 6i6
]נתן ממשל לחזק /	נתן	**299** 6i15
]◦ יתנו[	נתן	**299** 66,4
] סגולה מכול [העמים	סְגֻלָּה	**299** 60,3
ה]סגיר בעד עד מים לבל]תי	סגר	**299** 8,9
]◦ליה ובסוד ◦[	סוֹד	**299** 14,3
]סודות לא השיגוהו ◦[	סוֹד	**300** 9,1
י]דע ונספרו ריש]ונות	ספר	**299** 4,4
]ונספרה[	ספר	**299** 26,2
]תסתם מכם /	סתם	**299** 3c,2
ואם תפתחו החזון / תסת[ם מכם	סתם	**300** 1a ii-b,4
/ נסתרה מכול תומכ[י	סתר	**299** 6ii4
]◦ם עבודתם יחזקו /	עֲבוֹדָה	**299** 6i3
]◦ עבודת גבר /	עֲבוֹדָה	**299** 6i18
עב]ודתו /	עֲבוֹדָה	**299** 6i19
]אתם לתכן כול עבודת[	עֲבוֹדָה	**299** 10,8
עבו]דת קודשו ולכפר על ◦◦[	עֲבוֹדָה	**299** 55,5
ע]בודתו ל[	עֲבוֹדָה	**299** 68,3
עבו]דת קוד[ש	עֲבוֹדָה	**299** 83,5

Reference	Word	Context
299 70,4	עִם	]ל עם אשמה[
300 6,3	עִם	]עם יודע[י
301 1,2	עִם	עם תומכי ר[זי פלא
301 1,4	עִם	עם ◦◦◦[
300 6,6	עָמֹק	]מה עמוק לא[יש
299 6i13	עָפָר	]כי מעפר מבניתם /
299 3a ii-b,5	עָרְמָה	כי] / אם חוכמת עורמת רוע ומ[חשבת בליעל
301 1,4	עֹרֶף	]עורף ◦◦ קודק[וד
299 3a ii-b,6	עשׂה	/ מעשה אשר לוא יעשה עוד
299 3a ii-b,7	עשׂה	כיא אם [ ] / דבר עושו
299 3a ii-b,7	עשׂה	ומה (ו)הוא אשר יעשה ג[בר
299 3a ii-b,8	עשׂה	/ המרה את דבר עושו
299 3a ii-b,11	עשׂה	עושה כול] הנהיות
299 6i4	עשׂה	ברק[ים עשה לנצח גשמים /
299 7,6	עשׂה	/ אש[ר מ]על ועשה[
299 16,1	עשׂה	]עשה ◦[
299 17i1	עשׂה	]עשה[
299 57,3	עשׂה	]אשר יעשה[
299 59,5	עשׂה	/ ◦◦◦ עושי[
299 99,2	עשׂה	] עשה[
301 3a-b,8	עשׂה	]בכלו[ת]קץ רשעה ועשות[
299 54,2	עשׁק	]ם עשוק וגזול ב◦◦◦[
299 6i11	עֵת	]◦◦◦◦דם עת בעת /
299 6i11	עֵת	]◦◦◦◦דם עת בעת /
299 44,3	עַתָּה	]ועתה[
299 62,3	עַתָּה	] *vacat* ועתה מ◦[
299 80,2	עַתָּה	] ועתה פ[
299 3a ii-b,8	פֶּה	ימחה שמו מפי כול[
299 6ii14	פֶּה	/ לפי תבאות ומה ב◦[
299 22,1	פֶּה	]מפי[
299 59,3	פֶּה	/ בכול עוברי פיה[ו
299 76,2	פֶּה	[ ]מפיהו לפת[וח
300 2ii2	פחד	/ שקר מה פחד] לאדם
299 8,2	פלג	]◦ פלג שכלם[
299 74,2	פָּנֶה	]משה פנים אבני[
300 3,5	פָּנֶה	/ וגלה הרשע מפני הצדק
301 2b,4	פָּנֶה	]◦ מיא בכם דורש פני אור ומא[ור]
299 60,2	פקד	]רצה ופקוד[
299 6i10	פרשׁ	]מטברו פרש /
299 18,1	פֶּשַׁע	]ישלים פשע[
299 71,1	פֶּשַׁע	/ שבי פש[ע
300 1a ii-b,1	פֶּשַׁע	החר]טמים מלמדי פשע
299 3a ii-b,13	פתח	פתח לפ[ניהם
299 75,2	פתח	] כבוד לפתוח[
299 76,2	פתח	[ ]מפיהו לפת[וח
300 1a ii-b,3	פתח	ואם תפתחו החזון / תסת[ם מכם

Reference	Word	Context
300 8,3	פתח	]◦ים נפתח נ[
299 37,3	פֶּתַח	]פתח בפ◦◦[
300 8,4	פֶּתִי	להולכי פתי בכל [
301 1,3	פֶּתִי	]הולכי פותי ואנשי מחשבת
299 6i9	צֶאֱצָא	]◦◦ כל צאצאיה /
299 9,4	צָבָא	]א עם כול צב[א
299 79,5	צְבִי	]ארץ צביו והוא ◦[
299 3a ii-b,3	צַדִּיק	/ וכול מעשה צדיק הטמ[אה
299 3a ii-b,4	צַדִּיק	ומה]נקרא לאד[ם] / חכם וצדיק
299 53,5	צַדִּיק	]משפט כיא צדיק[
299 55,2	צַדִּיק	המשפ]טים הצדיקים[
300 7,3	צַדִּיק	נפשו כי[א]צדיק בכל] דרכיו
299 72,2	צֶדֶק	ג]בורי צדק [
299 80,3	צֶדֶק	מ]שפטי צדק[
300 3,5	צֶדֶק	/ וגלה הרשע מפני הצדק
300 3,6	צֶדֶק	והצדיק יגל[ה] כש[מש
300 7,1	צֶדֶק	ומה רם לגבר מצדק[
300 11,1	צֶדֶק	]צדק ◦◦◦[
300 11,2	צֶדֶק	]ובידו משפט כלם וצד[ק
299 2,1	צלח	]לא יצלח[
301 6,2	צַעַד	]ד ה[ו]נו וצעד כבו[דו
299 71,2	צרב	/ צרב לכם ומ[
299 64,2	קָדוֹשׁ	]גים קדו[ש
299 72,1	קָדוֹשׁ	הו]א קדוש הוא[
299 74,3	קָדוֹשׁ	]לזכר קדושים על [
299 3a ii-b,12	קֶדֶם	/ הו[אה מק]דם עולם
299 83,2	קֶדֶם	]בקדם ◦[
300 8,2	קֶדֶם	]מה קדם ומה אח[ור
301 1,4	קָדְקֹד	קודק[וד כ]ל [ה]מולת עמים
299 59,1	קדשׁ	/ יקדש ◦[ ]◦[
299 53,2	קֹדֶשׁ	]בקודשו ◦◦[
299 55,1	קֹדֶשׁ	] קודש ◦◦◦◦[
299 55,5	קֹדֶשׁ	עבו]דת קודשו ולכפר על ◦◦[
299 83,5	קֹדֶשׁ	עבו]דת קוד[ש
299 88,2	קֹדֶשׁ	]קדשו ◦[
301 3a-b,6	קֹדֶשׁ	[ונ]כבד אל בעם קודשו
301 3a-b,7	קֹדֶשׁ	ונהדר[הואה ברום קו]דשו
300 2ii3	קִנְאָה	/ יעזוב קנאת מדנים[
299 5,3	קֵץ	]בדין מועדי חום עם קצ[י
301 3a-b,8	קֵץ	]בכלו[ת]קץ רשעה ועשות[
299 3a ii-b,2	קרא	/ מה נקרא ה[
299 3a ii-b,3	קרא	ומה]נקרא לאד[ם] / חכם וצדיק
299 80,1	קרא	]◦◦ קרא א[
300 5,3	קרא	]אביון מה נקרא /
300 5,4	קרא	ומה נקרא לאדם /
299 7,2	קָרֹב	]קרוב [

]°ראות /	ראה	**300** 1a i,1
י]דע ונספרו רישונות	רֵאשִׁית	**299** 4,4
]יחד רובם אם[	רַב	**299** 20,3
ברוב שכל גלה אוזננו	רֹב	**299** 8,6
[וגדו]ל הואה ברוב חמתו	רֹב	**301** 3a-b,4
לכול רודפי דעת והי°[	רדף	**299** 8,7
/ ממנו כי אם רוח °ע[	רוּחַ	**299** 6ii7
]רוחכם[	רוּחַ	**299** 16,2
א]ביעה רוחי	רוּחַ	**301** 1,1
]ת° כל רוח בינתו לוא ידעו[	רוּחַ	**301** 4,2
]רוח סי[	רוּחַ	**301** 9,2
/ כול רז ומכין כול מחשבת	רָז	**299** 3a ii-b,11
]כול רז וחבלי כול מעשה	רָז	**299** 3a ii-b,15
]שו °°רזי עד /	רָז	**299** 3c,5
גב]ורות רזי אור ודרכי חוש[ך	רָז	**299** 5,2
]תומכי ר[זי	רָז	**299** 43,2
וברזי עד לא הבטתם	רָז	**300** 1a ii-b,2
ונפשם לא מלטו מרז נ[היה	רָז	**300** 3,4
]לה אתכם תומכי רזים א[	רָז	**300** 8,5
מה רז אם[	רָז	**300** 8,7
עם תומכי ר[זי פלא	רָז	**301** 1,2
/ [מה הוא רחו]ק לאיש ממעש[ה	רָחוֹק	**299** 7,3
/ מול איש והוא רחוק מ°[	רָחוֹק	**299** 7,4
]והוא רחו[ק	רָחוֹק	**300** 6,4
ו]נ[הדר /]הואה בהמון רחמיו	רַחַם	**301** 3a-b,5
/ במשפט יריב א[ת	ריב	**299** 59,2
/ °°° ונריבה ריב°[	ריב	**299** 59,7
]וא וריב רב[	ריב	**299** 62,2
] וריב על חזק ע[	רִיב	**299** 53,8
/ °°° ונריבה ריב°[	רִיב	**299** 59,7
]כיא בו יום הריב °[	רִיב	**300** 9,2
ר]ם על כול גואים ישרא[ל	רָם	**299** 10,3
ומה רם לגבר מצדק[	רָם	**300** 7,1
/ רע זולתו אהוב[	רַע	**300** 2ii5
מה רע לא°°יש ואי°[	רַע	**300** 10,2
/ לב רעו ואורב מ°[	רֵעַ	**299** 6ii12
כי] / אם חוכמת עורמת רוע ומ[חשבת בליעל	רֹעַ	**299** 3a ii-b,5
]רצה ופקוד[	רצה	**299** 60,2
]°ו רצונו הל[	רָצוֹן	**299** 79,4
/ וגלה הרשע מפני הצדק	רֶשַׁע	**300** 3,5
כן יתם] / [הר]שע לעד	רֶשַׁע	**300** 3,6
מה רע לאדם מ]רשע	רֶשַׁע	**300** 7,1
מה]רשע משנוא[	רֶשַׁע	**300** 7,4
/ עוזרי רשעה[	רִשְׁעָה	**299** 59,4
]בכלו[ת]קץ רשעה ועשות[	רִשְׁעָה	**301** 3a-b,8
רש]עת לבו ל°[	רִשְׁעָה	**301** 7,3

/ תכון אחד ולוא יש[בע	שׂבע	**299** 6ii16
]ושביע °°[	שׂבע	**299** 29,4
]° השיב ל°[	שׁוב	**299** 58,2
/ שבי פש[ע	שׁוב	**299** 71,1
יש]וה בה	שׁוה	**299** 2,3
וירד בו בשוט בלוא מחיר	שׁוט	**301** 2b,3
] ישים[	שׂים	**299** 82,2
]לשום לט[וב	שׂים	**300** 4,4
]בית מולדים נשטרה °/	שׁטר	**299** 1,4
]°ינו שיד הואה[	שִׂיד	**299** 65,2
ובבינה לא השכלתם /	שׂכל	**300** 1a ii-b,2
]° פלג שכלם[	שֵׂכֶל	**299** 8,2
ברוב שכל גלה אוזננו	שֵׂכֶל	**299** 8,6
]כול שכל מעולם	שֵׂכֶל	**299** 8,8
]אינה לשלם[	שׁלם	**299** 4,5
]ושלים פשע[	שׁלם	**299** 18,1
]א בשלמו[	שׁלם	**299** 30,2
]ת ישלם[	שׁלם	**300** 4,2
]°°א שמה /	שָׁם	**299** 3c,4
]°ד ואין שם למוע[ד	שָׁם	**299** 53,4
ימחה שמו מפי כול[	שֵׁם	**299** 3a ii-b,8
הואה שמו ולע[ולם	שֵׁם	**299** 3a ii-b,12
מאור]ות כוכבים לז[כר]ון שמ[ו	שֵׁם	**299** 5,1
שמו		
]וישמילנו [	שׁמאל	**299** 63,3
]שמים ממעל לשמים °[	שָׁמַיִם	**299** 8,10
]שמים ממעל לשמים °[	שָׁמַיִם	**299** 8,10
א]ל ובשמים מדור[ו	שָׁמַיִם	**299** 53,9
]השמים ל[	שָׁמַיִם	**299** 64,1
/ ותעודות השמ[ים	שָׁמַיִם	**300** 1a ii-b,2
/ { } שמעו תומכי °[	שׁמע	**299** 3a ii-b,9
שמעו	שׁמע	**299** 3c,3
בלוא ידע ולוא שמע [	שׁמע	**299** 8,5
]יתם לשמע °°ם[	שׁמע	**299** 15,3
]יכם אשמיע[	שׁמע	**299** 53,11
]שמעו ו°°[	שׁמע	**299** 63,1
והצדיק יגל[ה] כש[מש	שֶׁמֶשׁ	**300** 3,6
הלוא כול העמי]ם שנאו עול /	שׂנא	**299** 1,1
]שנאיכה לוא יוכל[ו	שׂנא	**299** 62,4
מה]רשע משנוא[	שׂנא	**300** 7,4
הוא לוא ישנה[	שׁנה	**299** 8,8
א]חת בשנה[	שָׁנָה	**299** 69,1
היש שפה ולשן / [מחזקת בה	שָׂפָה	**299** 1,2
]ושופטים לכול לא[ומים	שׁפט	**299** 10,5
]ל[ ]° ושופטים בין אביו[ן	שׁפט	**299** 10,7
]שופטם במשפטי[	שׁפט	**299** 56,2

]° ישפוט שׁ[	שפט	**299** 81,2
/ ויׄשפׄר לׄ[	שפר	**299** 71,4
מי]ם ובׄמשורה ישקו /	שקה	**299** 6i5
/ שקר מה פחד[לאדם	שֶׁקֶר	**300** 2ii2
]° שרים לי זרח אׄ[ר]ץׄ לׄמׄ[	שַׁר	**299** 9,2
]כי לא הבטתם בשורש חוכמה	שֹׁרֶשׁ	**300** 1a ii-b,3
וחוקרי שׁׄוׄרׄשי בינה	שֹׁרֶשׁ	**301** 1,2
לכמה חׄו<ק>רי בׄשור{ש}שי בינה /	שֹׁרֶשׁ	**301** 2b,1
/ לפי תׄבאות ומה בׄ°[	תְבוּאָה	**299** 6ii14
]° תׄבנית זכר ללוא היהׄ[ ]	תַבְנִית	**301** 2b,5
מ]חזיק ותולדׄות המ[	תוֹלָדָה	**299** 32,3
]תׄוׄעׄבׄותׄ[	תוֹעֵבָה	**299** 53,1
]לׄ[תו]צׄאותם /	תוֹצָאָה	**299** 1,7

]חׄוׄקׄ תכׄונם כיא אׄםׄ[	תְכוּן	**299** 20,1
]מׄשקל לתכון °°°[	תְכוּן	**299** 20,2
/ מׄודה או תכלית יׄ[	תְכֵלֶת	**299** 6ii15
]°°ל תכלת[	תְכֵלֶת	**299** 75,1
]אׄתם לתכן כול עבודתׄ[	תֹכֶן	**299** 10,8
]תׄמהו כן ילוׄדׄ[	תמה	**299** 28,2
אור]ים ותומים[	תֻמִּים	**299** 69,2
/ { } שמעו תומכי °[	תמך	**299** 3a ii-b,9
/ נסתרה מכול תומכׄ[י	תמך	**299** 6ii4
]תׄומכי ר[זי	תמך	**299** 43,2
]לׄה אתכם תומׄכׄי רזים א[	תמך	**300** 8,5
עם תומכי רׄ[זי פלא	תמך	**301** 1,2
/ ותעׄודות השׁמׄ[ים	תְעוּדָה	**300** 1a ii-b,2

4Q**302** papADMONITORY PARABLE

]רׄ זרע אברהם /	אַבְרָהָם	**302** 1i7
/ הלוא אתו יׄאׄ[הב	אהב	**302** 2ii6
]°מכה לאחׄר / [מכה	אַחַר	**302** 1i2
/ ואיךׄ לׄ°רנ°[	אֵיךְ	**302** 3iii3
אׄם יהיה / לאיש	אִישׁ	**302** 2ii3
/ ואל תׄ[	אַל	**302** 1ii12
/ ואל ת[	אַל	**302** 1ii13
/ בׄאלה תׄ°[	אֵלֶּה	**302** 1ii3
]הׄ *vacat* אלהים צדיק /	אֱלֹהַ	**302** 1i4
]אׄלהיכם /	אֱלֹהַ	**302** 3ii2
]יקום אלהים מידכם בׄמעלכם /	אֱלֹהַ	**302** 3ii6
]° אלהים בשמׄים משבו	אֱלֹהַ	**302** 3ii9
אׄם יהיה / לאיש	אִם	**302** 2ii2
]°°° כדבריך באפים /	אַף	**302** 1i3
ארצות	אֶרֶץ	**302** 2ii4
וממ[שלתו] / בארצות בימים °[	אֶרֶץ	**302** 3ii10
/ הלוא אתו יׄאׄ[הב	אֵת	**302** 2ii6
]°°°רׄ ואתו ישמר	אֵת	**302** 2ii6
]° ושלישיו להביא[	בוא	**302** 1b,6
/ הׄבׄיׄנׄוׄ נא בזאת החכמים	בין	**302** 2ii2
/ לבׄער א[	בער	**302** 1ii15
/ יבערו [	בער	**302** 3iii2
עץ טוב ויׄגׄבה עד לשמים[	גבה	**302** 2ii3
]°°° כדבריך באפים /	דָּבָר	**302** 1i3
/ דבריו [	דָּבָר	**302** 1ii14
ולהשיב דבר בריבך *vacat* /	דָּבָר	**302** 3ii8
]רו ודלתיו	דָּלִיָּה	**302** 2ii9
]° וׄהׄוא /	הוא	**302** 1i1
]כׄיׄ הוא יה /	הוא	**302** 1i8

אׄם יהיה / לאיש	היה	**302** 2ii2
]שׄהׄיוׄ *vacat*	היה	**302** 8,3
]ר יהיה [	היה	**302** 17,2
]ו והנׄהׄ [	הִנֵּה	**302** 10,1
/ הׄבׄיׄנׄוׄ נא בזאת החכמים	זֶה	**302** 2ii2
]רׄ זרע אברהם /	זֶרַע	**302** 1i7
]°זרע כ° /	זֶרַע	**302** 3bi6
/ ויכסמוהו חזׄ[ירים	חֲזִיר	**302** 2iii6
/ הׄבׄיׄנׄוׄ נא בזאת החכמים	חָכָם	**302** 2ii2
]בׄנׄפׄש חׄפצה *vacat* /	חָפֵץ	**302** 3ii5
] בׄחׄרׄוׄ° ובצמה	חֹרֶב	**302** 2ii5
] בׄחׄרׄוׄ° ובצמה	חֹרֶף	**302** 2ii5
]םׄ טׄוביך על כוׄלׄ /	טוֹב	**302** 1i5
עץ טוב ויׄגׄבה עד לשמים[	טוֹב	**302** 2ii3
]םׄ טׄוביך על כוׄלׄ /	טוּב	**302** 1i5
]יקום אלהים מידכם בׄמעלכם /	יָד	**302** 3ii6
]כׄיׄ הוא יה /	יה	**302** 1i8
/ יורה ומלקוש יׄ°°[	יוֹרֶה	**302** 2ii5
ולא עמד לנגדך להוכח / עׄמך	יכח	**302** 3ii7
וממ[שלתו] / בארצות בימים °[	יָם	**302** 3ii10
]°תׄ יצר כל /	יצר	**302** 1i13
ק]דשו יׄשרא[ל] /	יִשְׂרָאֵל	**302** 1i10
]כׄיׄ הוא יה /	כִּי	**302** 1i8
]םׄ טׄוביך על כוׄלׄ /	כֹּל	**302** 1i5
]°תׄ יצר כל /	כֹּל	**302** 1i13
/ ולא כן [	כֵּן	**302** 3iii1
/ ויכסמוהו חזׄ[ירים	כסם	**302** 2iii6
/ ויכׄרת בׄלוא °[	כרת	**302** 2iii7
/ בח[ ] לוא[	לא	**302** 1ii4

302 2ii6	לא	/ הלוא אתו יׄאׄ[הב
302 2ii7	לא	/ ויכׄרת בׄלוא ◦[
302 3ii7	לא	ולא עמד לנגדך להוכח / עׄמך
302 3iii1	לא	/ ולא כן [
302 3ii4	לֵבָב	]◦ לבבכם אׄ[ ]◦ /
302 3ii9	מוֹשָׁב	]◦ אלהים בשמׄים משבו
302 3ii7	מַחֲשָׁבָה	[פרי מ]חשבתיכׄם /
302 1i2	מַכָּה	]◦מכה לאחׄר / [מכה
302 2ii5	מַלְקוֹשׁ	/ יורה ומלקוש יׄ◦◦[
302 3ii9	מֶמְשָׁלָה	וממ[שלתו] / בארצות בימים ◦[
302 1a,2	מִן	]מׄפניך ◦◦[
302 2ii8	מִן	]ל מׄנצרו לרבת
302 3ii6	מִן	]יקום אלהים מידכם בׄמעלכם /
302 3ii6	מַעַל	]יקום אלהים מידכם בׄמעלכם /
302 1ii6	מִקְדָּשׁ	/ מׄקדשׁוׄ [
302 2ii2	נָא	/ הׄבׄינׄוׄ נא בזאת החכמים
302 3ii7	נֶגֶד	ולא עמד לנגדך להוכח / עׄמך
302 3c1	נחם	]◦ להתנחׄםׄ
302 3ii5	נֶפֶשׁ	]בׄנׄפׄש חׄפצה *vacat* /
302 2ii8	נֵצֶר	]ל מׄנצרו לרבת
302 3ii6	נקם	]יקום אלהים מידכם בׄמעלכם /
302 2ii3	עַד	עץ טוב ויׄגׄבה עד לשמים[
302 1i5	עַל	]םׄ טׄוביך על כוׄלׄ /
302 1i12	עַם	]◦◦ וׄבקׄרׄבׄ עממים /
302 3ii8	עִם	ולא עמד לנגדך להוכח / עׄמך

302 3ii7	עמד	ולא עמד לנגדך להוכח / עׄמך
302 2ii7	עֳפִי	]ים להרבות עפי
302 10,2	עֳפִי	]עׄפׄי שיח ◦◦◦◦[
302 2ii3	עֵץ	עץ טוב ויׄגׄבה עד לשמים[
302 1ii7	עשׂה	/ לׄעשות ל[
302 2ii4	עשׂה	וׄעׄשׂהׄ פרי שמן ◦◦◦
302 1a,2	פָּנִים	]מׄפניך ◦◦[
302 2ii4	פְּרִי	וׄעׄשׂהׄ פרי שמן ◦◦◦
302 1i4	צַדִּיק	]הׄ *vacat* אלהים צדיק /
302 2ii5	צִמְאָה	] בׄחׄרׄוׄ◦ ובצמה
302 1i10	קֹדֶשׁ	ק]דשו יׄשׂרא[ל] /
302 2iii2	קֵץ	/ קצי ◦[
302 1i12	קֶרֶב	]◦◦ וׄבקׄרׄבׄ עממים /
302 2ii8	רַב	]ל מׄנצרו לרבת
302 2ii7	רבה	]ים להרבות עפי
302 3ii8	רִיב	ולהשיב דבר בריבך *vacat* /
302 3ii8	שׁוב	ולהשיב דבר בריבך *vacat* /
302 10,2	שִׂיחַ	]עׄפׄי שיח ◦◦◦◦[
302 1b,6	שָׁלִישׁ	]◦ ושלישיו להביא[
302 1ii11	שְׂמֹאל	/ ושמׄאל [
302 1i11	שָׁמַיִם	]ת בשמׄים /
302 2ii3	שָׁמַיִם	עץ טוב ויׄגׄבה עד לשמים[
302 3ii9	שָׁמַיִם	]◦ אלהים בשמׄים משבו
302 2ii4	שֶׁמֶן	וׄעׄשׂהׄ פרי שמן ◦◦◦
302 2ii6	שׁמר	]◦◦◦רׄ ואתו ישמר

4Q**303** MEDITATION ON CREATION A

303 1,9	אָדָם	]לוקח ממנה אדם כיאׄ[
303 1,4	אוֹר	]לׄאור עולם ושמי טוה[ר
303 1,5	אוֹר	או]ר במקום תהווב[הו
303 1,3	אֵל	] נפלאות אל אש[ר
303 1,11	אִשָּׁה	]לו לאשה כיא ממנו[לקחה זאת
303 1,3	אֲשֶׁר	] נפלאות אל אש[ר
303 1,5	בֹּהוּ	או]ר במקום תהווב[הו
303 1,1	בין	]מבינים שמעו ו◦[
303 1,4	טֹהַר	]לׄאור עולם ושמי טוה[ר
303 1,8	טוֹב	]ר ושכל טוב ורע ל[
303 1,9	כִּי	]לוקח ממנה אדם כיאׄ[
303 1,11	כִּי	]לו לאשה כיא ממנו[לקחה זאת
303 1,6	כֹּל	]כולמעשיהם עד ק◦[
303 1,7	כֹּל	]ר בם מלך לכולם[
303 1,9	לקח	]לוקח ממנה אדם כיאׄ[
303 1,7	מֶלֶךְ	]ר בם מלך לכולם[
303 1,9	מִן	]לוקח ממנה אדם כיאׄ[

303 1,11	מִן	]לו לאשה כיא ממנו[לקחה זאת
303 1,2	מַעַל	]מׄים וישביתו מעל נׄ[
303 1,6	מַעֲשֶׂה	]כולמעשיהם עד ק◦[
303 1,5	מָקוֹם	או]ר במקום תהווב[הו
303 1,6	עַד	]כולמעשיהם עד ק◦[
303 1,4	עוֹלָם	]לׄאור עולם ושמי טוה[ר
303 1,10	עֵזֶר	ו]עשה לו עזר כ[נגדו
303 1,10	עשׂה	ו]עשה לו עזר כ[נגדו
303 1,13	פֶּה	]ל לפי[
303 1,3	פלא	] נפלאות אל אש[ר
303 1,8	רַע	]ר ושכל טוב ורע ל[
303 1,2	שׁבת	]מׄים וישביתו מעל נׄ[
303 1,8	שֶׂכֶל	]ר ושכל טוב ורע ל[
303 1,4	שָׁמַיִם	]לׄאור עולם ושמי טוה[ר
303 1,1	שׁמע	]מבינים שמעו ו◦[
303 1,5	תֹּהוּ	או]ר במקום תהווב[הו

4Q**304** MEDITATION ON CREATION B

Ref.	Word	Context
304 1,1	אֶרֶץ	/ ואת הארץ וכו]ל צבאם
304 1,1	אֵת	/ ואת הארץ וכו]ל צבאם
304 1,2	חֹשֶׁךְ	/ החשך על כן נ◦]
304 1,1	כֹּל	/ ואת הארץ וכו]ל צבאם
304 1,2	כֵּן	/ החשך על כן נ◦]
304 1,2	עַל	/ החשך על כן נ◦]
304 1,3	עשה	/ עשה ◦◦◦]

4Q**305** MEDITATION ON CREATION C

Ref.	Word	Context
305 1ii2	אָדָם	/ נתן לאדם דע]ת
305 1ii1	ברא	/ ויברא בו חיות]
305 1ii2	דַּעַת	/ נתן לאדם דע]ת
305 1ii3	דַּעַת	/ ורׄעׄ]]לדׄעׄתׄ]
305 1ii1	חַיָּה	/ ויברא בו חיות]
305 1ii2	נתן	/ נתן לאדם דע]ת
305 1ii3	רַע	/ ורׄעׄ]]לדׄעׄתׄ]

4Q**411** SAPIENTIAL HYMN

Ref.	Word	Context
411 1ii5	אָדָם	לאדם והוא בׄ]
411 1ii10	אֹהֶל	/ בׄאהל לש]בת
411 1ii3	אֶחָד	טוב יום אחדׄ]
411 1ii6	אֵת	ידעתי את]
411 1ii8	בִּצָּה	וגאל בׄצה ◦]
411 1ii12	ברא	יהוה ברא הׄ]
411 1ii13	ברא	יהוה ברא שׄ]מים
411 1ii11	בָּשָׂר	בׄשרׄ יהו]ה ברא
411 1ii8	גאל	וגאל בׄצה ◦]
411 1ii5	הוא	לאדם והוא בׄ]
411 1ii4	הֵנָּה	הנא החלתי לׄ]
411 1ii7	חָכָם	מי חכם וׄ◦]
411 1iii1	חָכְמָה	[ו]תשמח בחכׄ]מה/ת
411 1ii4	חלל	הנא החלתי לׄ]
411 1ii3	טוֹב	טוב יום אחדׄ]
411 1ii6	ידע	ידעתי את]
411 1ii2	יהוה	יׄהׄוה פן יסׄח]ר
411 1ii11	יהוה	בׄשרׄ יהו]ה ברא
411 1ii12	יהוה	יהוה ברא הׄ]
411 1ii13	יהוה	יהוה ברא שׄ]מים
411 1ii17	יהוה	[י]הוהׄ]
411 1ii3	יוֹם	טוב יום אחדׄ]
411 1ii14	יפע	הופיעו לאׄ]
411 1ii10	ישב	/ בׄאהל לש]בת
411 1ii7	מִי	מי חכם וׄ◦]
411 1ii9	מִי	ותבונתו מי]
411 1ii2	סחר	יׄהׄוה פן יסׄח]ר
411 1ii2	פֶּן	יׄהׄוה פן יסׄח]ר
411 1ii15	ראה	להרׄאותׄ]
411 1iii1	שׂמח	[ו]תשמח בחכׄ]מה/ת
411 1ii13	שָׁמַיִם	יהוה ברא שׄ]מים
411 1ii16	שַׁעֲשׁוּעַ	לשעשׄ[וע]ים)
411 1ii9	תְּבוּנָה	ותבונתו מי]

4Q**412** SAPIENTIAL-DIDACTIC WORK A

Ref.	Word	Context
412 1,1	אַל	/ [ואת]הׄ אל תפעׄ[ל
412 1,2	אַל	אל תפעׄ[ל
412 2,2	אַל	]◦ורׄתׄי אל ת]
412 1,4	אֵמֶר	/ [ו]תׄבׄוׄך באמרי יׄוׄ]
412 4,5	אֱנוֹשׁ	]◦תׄ אנוׄש]
412 1,1	אַתָּה	/ [ואת]הׄ אל תפעׄ[ל
412 1,4	בוך	/ [ו]תׄבׄוׄך באמרי יׄוׄ]
412 1,4	בִּינָה	]בׄיׄנׄה הוציא מליׄםׄ]
412 1,6	בקש	צ]דׄיׄקׄ(?) למבקשי] בינה
412 4,2	ברא	כ]רׄצונו ברא]
412 1,3	גַּם	וׄגׄם מעוון לדׄעׄתׄיׄ]
412 1,3	דבב	הוציא] / [עלי]כׄה דבתדבוב *vacat*
412 1,3	דבוב	הוציא] / [עלי]כׄה דבתדבוב *vacat*
412 1,5	דֶּלֶת	[*vacat*?] וללשונכה דלתי מ[גן *vacat*

Context	Word	Reference
ו֯ג֯ם מעוון לד֯ע֯ת֯י֯]	דַּעַת	**412** 1,3
צדק הגה בהמה֯]	הגה	**412** 1,6
/ תן הדות לשמו֯]	הוֹדָה	**412** 1,8
/ בכול פיכה הלל ◦]	הלל	**412** 1,7
מ]ל֯י֯ ו֯י֯דעים א]	ידע	**412** 4,4
/ יומם וליל]ה	יוֹמָם	**412** 1,10
]ב֯י֯נ֯ה הוציא מל֯י֯ם֯]	יצא	**412** 1,4
/ בכול פיכה הלל ◦]	כֹּל	**412** 1,7
/ יומם וליל]ה	לַיְלָה	**412** 1,10
[*vacat?*] וללשונכה דלתי מ]גן *vacat*	לָשׁוֹן	**412** 1,5
[*vacat?*] וללשונכה דלתי מ]גן *vacat*	מָגֵן	**412** 1,5
מ]שלח֯ מ֯דנים ◦]	מָדוֹן	**412** 2,4
/ [ש]י֯ם מוסר על ש֯פ֯ת֯י֯כה֯[?*vacat*]	מוּסָר	**412** 1,5
]ב֯י֯נ֯ה הוציא מל֯י֯ם֯]	מִלָּה	**412** 1,4
] על מלי כ֯]	מִלָּה	**412** 3,2
מ]ל֯י֯ ו֯י֯דעים א]	מִלָּה	**412** 4,4
ו֯ג֯ם מעוון לד֯ע֯ת֯י֯]	מִן	**412** 1,3
מ]שפטי צד֯]ק	מִשְׁפָּט	**412** 3,1
]ע֯שר֯י֯ ו֯נח֯י֯ל]	נחל	**412** 4,1
/ תן הדות לשמו֯]	נתן	**412** 1,8
ו֯ג֯ם מעוון לד֯ע֯ת֯י֯]	עָוֹן	**412** 1,3
/ [ש]י֯ם מוסר על ש֯פ֯ת֯י֯כה֯[?*vacat*]	עַל	**412** 1,5
] על מלי כ֯]	עַל	**412** 3,2
]ע֯שר֯י֯ ו֯נח֯י֯ל]	עֹשֶׁר	**412** 4,1
/ בכול פיכה הלל ◦]	פֶּה	**412** 1,7
] על מלי כ֯]	פֶּה	**412** 3,2
/ [ואת]ה֯ אל תפע֯]ל	פעל	**412** 1,1
אל תפע֯]ל	פעל	**412** 1,2
צ]ד֯י֯ק֯(?) למבקשי] בינה	צַדִּיק	**412** 1,6
צדק הגה בהמה֯]	צֶדֶק	**412** 1,6
מ]שפטי צד֯]ק	צֶדֶק	**412** 3,1
/ [קה(?)]לר֯בים	קָהָל	**412** 1,2
/ בקהל רב֯י֯ם֯ מ֯]	קָהָל	**412** 1,9
]ם אקרא ו֯ק֯]ולי	קוֹל	**412** 4,3
]ם אקרא ו֯ק֯]ולי	קרא	**412** 4,3
/ [קה(?)]לר֯בים	רַב	**412** 1,2
/ בקהל רב֯י֯ם֯ מ֯]	רַב	**412** 1,9
]ר֯עשכה]	רַעַשׁ	**412** 1,7
כ]ר֯צונו ברא [	רָצוֹן	**412** 4,2
/ [ש]י֯ם מוסר על ש֯פ֯ת֯י֯כה֯[?*vacat*]	שׂים	**412** 1,5
]◦◦ן֯ שלוש֯]	שָׁלוֹשׁ	**412** 2,3
מ]שלח֯ מ֯דנים ◦]	שׁלח	**412** 2,4
/ תן הדות לשמו֯]	שֵׁם	**412** 1,8
/ [ש]י֯ם מוסר על ש֯פ֯ת֯י֯כה֯[?*vacat*]	שָׂפָה	**412** 1,5

4Q**413** COMPOSITION CONCERNING DIVINE PROVIDENCE

Context	Word	Reference
והתבוננו בדרכי אנוש ובפועלות / בני אד֯]ם	אָדָם	**413** 2
[ההולך אחר מ]ש֯מע אוזניו ומראה עינו	אֹזֶן	**413** 3
כי באהבת]א֯ל֯ את איש	אִישׁ	**413** 2
כי באהבת]א֯ל֯ את איש	אֵל	**413** 2
כאשר גלה א֯ל֯ /	אֵל	**413** 4
הרבה לו נחלה ב֯דעת אמתו	אֱמֶת	**413** 2
והתבוננו בדרכי אנוש ובפועלות / בני אד֯]ם	אֱנוֹשׁ	**413** 1
כי באהבת]א֯ל֯ את איש	אֵת	**413** 2
והתבוננו בדרכי אנוש ובפועלות / בני אד֯]ם	בין	**413** 1
ובינו ב֯ש֯ני ד]ור ו]ד֯ור	בין	**413** 4
ב֯ל֯ יחיה *vacat*	בַּל	**413** 3
והתבוננו בדרכי אנוש ובפועלות / בני אד֯]ם	בֵּן	**413** 2
כאשר גלה א֯ל֯ /	גלה	**413** 4
וכפי גועלו / כל רע֯]	געל	**413** 2
ובינו ב֯ש֯ני ד]ור ו]ד֯ור	דּוֹר	**413** 4
ובינו ב֯ש֯ני ד]ור ו]ד֯ור	דּוֹר	**413** 4
מ֯ז֯מ֯ת֯ ד]עת מצאו] וחוכמה אלמדכמה	דַּעַת	**413** 1
הרבה לו נחלה ב֯דעת אמתו	דַּעַת	**413** 2
והתבוננו בדרכי אנוש ובפועלות / בני אד֯]ם	דֶּרֶךְ	**413** 1
ב֯ל֯ יחיה *vacat*	חיה	**413** 3
מ֯ז֯מ֯ת֯ ד]עת מצאו] וחוכמה אלמדכמה	חָכְמָה	**413** 1
ועתה / חסד [	חֶסֶד	**413** 4
כאשר גלה א֯ל֯ /	כַּאֲשֶׁר	**413** 4
וכפי גועלו / כל רע֯]	כֹּל	**413** 3
מ֯ז֯מ֯ת֯ ד]עת מצאו] וחוכמה אלמדכמה	למד	**413** 1
מ֯ז֯מ֯ת֯ ד]עת מצאו] וחוכמה אלמדכמה	מְזִמָּה	**413** 1
[ההולך אחר מ]ש֯מע אוזניו ומראה עינו	מַרְאֶה	**413** 3
[ההולך אחר מ]ש֯מע אוזניו ומראה עינו	מִשְׁמַע	**413** 3
הרבה לו נחלה ב֯דעת אמתו	נַחֲלָה	**413** 2
[ההולך אחר מ]ש֯מע אוזניו ומראה עינו	עַיִן	**413** 3
ועתה / חסד [	עַתָּה	**413** 3
וכפי גועלו / כל רע֯]	פֶּה	**413** 2
והתבוננו בדרכי אנוש ובפועלות / בני אד֯]ם	פְּעֻלָּה	**413** 1
]ר֯י֯א֯שונים	רִאשׁוֹן	**413** 4
הרבה לו נחלה ב֯דעת אמתו	רבה	**413** 2
וכפי גועלו / כל רע֯]	רַע	**413** 3
ובינו ב֯ש֯ני ד]ור ו]ד֯ור	שָׁנָה	**413** 4

4Q420–421 WAYS OF RIGHTEOUSNESS[a–b]

Reference	Word	Context
421 12,5	אוֹ	]מה אוׄ בׄ[
420 1a ii-b,4	אָחוֹר	ל[ו]א ישוב א[חור] / עד
421 1a ii-b,15	אָחוֹר	לוא ישו]ב אחור עד
421 1a i,1	אֵיבָה	]םׄ באיבת עׄ[ולם
421 6,3	אַיִן	]אשר איננו ◦[
421 1a i,3	אִישׁ	]ל◦ לסרך הכול איש לפני רע[הו]
421 1a ii-b,10	אִישׁ	אי]שׁׄ משכיל ונבון / ידלם
421 1a ii-b,12	אִישׁ	איש ◦[
421 1a ii-b,15	אִישׁ	אׄ[יש עניו ונכי שכלו
421 2,3	אִישׁ	כו]לׄ[א]יׄש לפנׄ[י רעהו
421 3,2	אִישׁ	]◦ איש ושומרׄ[
421 6,4	אִישׁ	]רׄ אׄישׁ כׄ◦[
421 10,1	אִישׁ	אי]ש נאמן בכוׄ[ל דרכו(?)
421 11,5	אִישׁ	]ואיש בחדׄ[
421 13,5	אִישׁ	] אל יער איש אׄ[
421 11,2	אכל	ב]טוח לאכול ולשתות ממנו כׄוׄל ◦[
421 12,2	אכל	וכול עבד ואמה לוא יוכל במׄ[קדש אל(?)
421 11,3	אַל	אל ישאב ממנו ◦[
421 11,4	אַל	אל יׄחל[
421 12,3	אַל	]אׄ ואל יבא בשער חצרו ובשעׄ[ר
421 13,3	אַל	]ם אל יחשבׄ[לו
421 13,5	אַל	] אל יער איש אׄ[
420 1a i,5	אֵל	]◦ות אל /
421 1a ii-b,12	אֵל	]ללכת בדרכי אל / לעשות צדקהׄ[
420 1a i,5	אֵל	]◦ות אל /
421 5,1	אִם	א]ם ישיבׄ[
421 12,4	אִם	ואם בא כׄ[ו]ל[
421 13,1	אִם	]כׄיא אם אלפׄ[ני]המהׄ[יפלו(?)
421 12,2	אָמָה	וכול עבד ואמה לוא יוכל במׄ[קדש אל(?)
420 1a ii-b,5	אמן	איש]נאמן
421 9,1	אמץ	]◦ יאמץ לנ◦[
421 1a i,5	אֹמֶר	י]תישרו אמרינו
420 1a ii-b,3	אֱמֶת	ידר]ש אמת משפט
420 4,2	אֱמֶת	א]מתׄ נ◦◦[
420 6,3	אֱמֶת	]◦ אמת דׄ[
421 3,3	אֱמֶת	ע]ל אמתו יוׄצׄי[א דברו
420 1a ii-b,2	אַף	]בארוך אפים ישיב פתגם ושׄ[
420 2,1	אַף	ארך] אפים [
421 1a ii-b,14	אַף	בארך אׄ[פים ישיב פתגם
420 1a ii-b,2	אֹרֶךְ	]בארוך אפים ישיב פתגם ושׄ[
421 1a ii-b,14	אֹרֶךְ	בארך אׄ[פים ישיב פתגם
420 2,6	אֲשֶׁר	]◦ות אשר דברׄ[
421 1a ii-b,8	אֲשֶׁר	]אשר / אשר דבר[
421 1a ii-b,9	אֲשֶׁר	]אשר / אשר דבר[

Reference	Word	Context
421 6,3	אֲשֶׁר	]אשר איננו ◦[
421 1a i,6	אֵת	א]וׄתו ליסרו
421 12,3	בוא	]אׄ ואל יבא בשער חצרו ובשעׄ[ר
421 12,4	בוא	אל יבי]אׄ ממקומו חנםׄ
421 12,4	בוא	ואם בא כׄ[ו]ל[
421 11,2	בָּטוּחַ	ב]טוח לאכול ולשתות ממנו כׄוׄל ◦[
421 1a ii-b,10	בין	אי]שׁׄ משכיל ונבון / ידלם
421 1a ii-b,14	בין	ולוא ידבר בטרם / יבין
420 1a ii-b,7	בִּינָה	/ בבינה כׄלׄ[
421 1a i,2	בִּינָה	ח]כׄמתו ודעתו ובינׄתו וטׄובׄוׄ [ביחד
421 1a ii-b,17	בִּינָה	בצדק נׄגאׄל בבינ[ה כול
421 1a i,14	בַּל	]בׄל
421 2,2	ברך	] דבר לברך ◦[
420 1a ii-b,6	גאל	בצדק נׄגאׄ[ל]
420 1a ii-b,7	גְּבוּל	]שׄדותיו גבולו [
421 1a i,4	גּוֹרָל	יצ]א הגוׄרׄל הרישון וכן יצׄאׄו
420 2,10	גְּעָרָה	]לׄגערתו וׄ◦[
420 2,7	גרד	]לכול גורדיוׄ ◦[
420 1a ii-b,2	דבר	/ וׄ[לוא ידב]רׄ בׄ[טרם יבין]
420 2,6	דבר	]◦ות אשר דברׄ[
420 4,1	דבר	]ותדׄ[בר
421 1a ii-b,9	דבר	]אשר / אשר דבר[
421 1a ii-b,13	דבר	ולוא ידבר בטרם / יבין
421 2,2	דבר	] דבר לברך ◦[
420 1a ii-b,3	דָּבָר	/ יוציא דבׄרׄ[
420 6,1	דָּבָר	ע]ל כול דׄבׄ[ר
421 13,4	דָּבָר	]דברי קודש כחוק [
420 6,2	דּוֹר	]לדרו[תם(?)
421 1a ii-b,11	דלה	אי]שׁׄ משכיל ונבון / ידלם
421 1a i,2	דַּעַת	ח]כׄמתו ודעתו ובינׄתו וטׄובׄוׄ [ביחד
420 1a ii-b,5	דֶּרֶךְ	לוא יסור מדרכי צדק[
421 1a ii-b,12	דֶּרֶךְ	]ללכת בדרכי אל / לעשות צדקהׄ[
420 1a ii-b,3	דרש	ידר]ש אמת משפט
421 11,4	הִיא	]כׄיא מלאכת צׄ[דק]היאה
420 1a i,4	הוֹן	ה]וׄן רשעים /
420 3,2	היה	]◦◦ היה משקׄ[ל צדק
421 11,3	היה	והיה חינםׄ
421 1a ii-b,12	הלך	]ללכת בדרכי אל / לעשות צדקהׄ[
420 1a ii-b,1	זֹאת	[בדרכי אל לעשות צדקהׄ]בׄזׄות
421 13,2	זֶבַח	כ]וׄל העולות והזבחים אׄ[
420 2,5	זֶרַע	]וׄםׄ וזרעם על תנחומׄ[ים
421 9,2	חָבֵר	ח]בׄריו
421 9,2	חזק	לחזק לבבׄ נׄגׄ[ועים(?)
421 1a i,2	חָכְמָה	ח]כׄמתו ודעתו ובינׄתו וטׄובׄוׄ [ביחד

Reference	Lemma	Context
421 1a ii-b,10	חָכְמָה	]◦נט[ ]לשאת / עול חכמ]ה
421 11,3	חִנָּם	והיה חינם
421 12,4	חִנָּם	אל יבי]א ממקומו חנם
421 12,3	חָצֵר	]א ואל יבא בשער חצרו ובשע]ר
421 13,4	חֹק	]דברי קודש כחוק [
420 2,8	חרש	]ובתלמיה יחרוש ותמיד[
421 13,3	חשב	]ם אל יחשב[לו
421 1a i,2	טוב	ח]כמתו ודעתו ובינתו וטובו [ביחד
420 1a ii-b,1	טֶרֶם	לוא ישיב בטרם ישמ]ע[
421 1a ii-b,13	טֶרֶם	ולוא ידבר בטרם / יבין
421 5,2	ידע	]עשר לדעת ו◦[
421 11,4	יחל	אל יחל[
421 1a ii-b,11	יכח	י]וכח תוכחת / משכיל
420 2,3	יסף	להו]סיף? מדתם [
421 1a i,6	יסר	א]ותו ליסרו
420 1a ii-b,3	יצא	/ יוציא דבר[
421 1a i,4	יצא	יצ]א הגורל הרישון וכן יצאו
421 1a i,4	יצא	יצ]א הגורל הרישון וכן יצאו
421 3,3	יצא	ע]ל אמתו יוצי]א דברו
421 1a i,5	ישר	י]תישרו אמרינו
421 11,4	כִּי	]כיא מלאכת צ]דק]היאה
421 13,1	כִּי	]כיא אם אלפ]ני]המה[יפלו]?[
420 1a ii-b,7	כֹּל	/ בבינה כל[
420 2,7	כֹּל	]לכול גורדיו ◦[
420 6,1	כֹּל	ע]ל כול דב]ר
421 1a i,3	כֹּל	]ל◦ לסרך הכול איש לפני רע]הו[
421 1a ii-b,17	כֹּל	בצדק נגאל בבינ]ה כול
421 2,3	כֹּל	כו]ל[א]יש לפני[רעהו
421 9,3	כֹּל	]ל[כ]לות כל עבדי ר]שע]?[
421 10,1	כֹּל	אי]ש נאמן בכו]ל דרכו]?[
421 11,2	כֹּל	ב]טוח לאכול ולשתות ממנו כול ◦[
421 11,6	כֹּל	כ]ול ◦[
421 12,2	כֹּל	וכול עבד ואמה לוא יוכל במ]קדש אל]?[
421 12,4	כֹּל	ואם בא כ]ו[ל[
421 13,2	כֹּל	כ]ול העולות והזבחים א[
421 13,6	כֹּל	]ש בכ]ו[ל הקר]בנות
421 9,3	כלה	]ל[כ]לות כל עבדי ר]שע]?[
421 1a i,4	כֵּן	יצ]א הגורל הרישון וכן יצאו
420 1a ii-b,6	כַּף	עצ]מותיו וכפיו
420 1a ii-b,1	לא	לוא ישיב בטרם ישמ]ע[
420 1a ii-b,4	לא	ל]ו[א ישוב א]חור[/ עד
420 1a ii-b,5	לא	לוא יסור מדרכי צדק[
421 1a ii-b,13	לא	ולוא ידבר בטרם / יבין
421 12,2	לא	וכול עבד ואמה לוא יוכל במ]קדש אל]?[
421 4,2	לֵב	]ובלבו
420 2,9	לֵבָב	]מה בלבב מ]שכילים]?[
421 9,2	לֵבָב	לחזק לבב נג]ועים]?[
420 2,2	לוה	]תנלוים עד[
421 1a i,3	לִפְנֵי	]ל◦ לסרך הכול איש לפני רע]הו[
421 2,3	לִפְנֵי	כו]ל[א]יש לפני[רעהו
421 8,2	מְגִלָּה	מג]לת ספר לקרוא[
420 2,3	מִדָּה	להו]סיף? מדתם [
420 1a ii-b,3	מֶחְקָר	ובמחקר צדק
421 11,4	מְלָאכָה	]כיא מלאכת צ]דק]היאה
420 1a ii-b,5	מִן	לוא יסור מדרכי צדק[
421 11,2	מִן	ב]טוח לאכול ולשתות ממנו כול ◦[
421 11,3	מִן	אל ישאב ממנו ◦[
421 12,4	מִן	אל יבי]א ממקומו חנם
420 1a ii-b,4	מצא	/ ימצא תוצ]אותיה
421 1a ii-b,14	מצא	ובמחקר צ]דק ימצא / תוצאותיה
421 12,2	מִקְדָּשׁ	וכול עבד ואמה לוא יוכל במ]קדש אל]?[
421 12,4	מָקוֹם	אל יבי]א ממקומו חנם
421 1a ii-b,6	משל	/ מושל ב[
420 1a ii-b,3	מִשְׁפָּט	ידר]ש אמת משפט
420 2,4	מִשְׁפָּט	] על נגועי משפ]ט
420 3,1	מִשְׁפָּט	מ]שפט [
420 3,2	מִשְׁקָל	]◦◦ היה משק]ל צדק
421 10,1	נֶאֱמָן	אי]ש נאמן בכו]ל דרכו]?[
420 2,4	נגע	] על נגועי משפ]ט
421 9,2	נגע	לחזק לבב נג]ועים]?[
420 1a ii-b,4	נכה	איש] עניו ונכי שכלו
421 1a ii-b,9	נשא	]◦נט[ ]לשאת / עול חכמ]ה
420 1a ii-b,5	סור	לוא יסור מדרכי צדק[
421 11,3	ספר	]ספר
421 8,2	סֵפֶר	מג]לת ספר לקרוא[
421 1a i,3	סרך	]ל◦ לסרך הכול איש לפני רע]הו[
421 9,3	עֶבֶד	]ל[כ]לות כל עבדי ר]שע]?[
421 12,2	עֶבֶד	וכול עבד ואמה לוא יוכל במ]קדש אל]?[
420 1a ii-b,5	עַד	ל]ו[א ישוב א]חור[/ עד
420 2,2	עַד	]תנלוים עד[
421 1a ii-b,15	עַד	לוא ישו]ב אחור עד
421 10,2	עַד	]לו עד ל[
421 1a i,1	עוֹלָם	]ם באיבת ע]ולם
420 2,4	עַל	] על נגועי משפ]ט
420 2,5	עַל	]ים וזרעם על תנחומ]ים
420 6,1	עַל	ע]ל כול דב]ר
421 1a ii-b,7	עַל	/ פעמיהם על[
421 1a ii-b,8	עַל	/ הרפאמה על[
421 3,1	עַל	]ד על תוצ]אות
421 3,3	עַל	ע]ל אמתו יוצי]א דברו
421 13,1	עַל	]כיא אם אלפ]ני]המה[יפלו]?[
421 1a ii-b,10	עֹל	]◦נט[ ]לשאת / עול חכמ]ה

כ[ול העולות והזבחים א]	עֹלָה	**421** 13,2
איש[עניו ונכי שכלו	עָנָו	**420** 1a ii-b,4
עצ[מותיו וכפיו	עֶצֶם	**420** 1a ii-b,6
[אל יער איש א]	ערר	**421** 13,5
[ללכת בדרכי אל / לעשות צדקה]	עשה	**421** 1a ii-b,13
[עשר /	עֶשֶׁר	**421** 1a i,15
[עשר /	עֹשֶׁר	**421** 1a i,15
[עשר לדעת ו°]	עֹשֶׁר	**421** 5,2
[ש בפיה]ו	פֶּה	**421** 2,1
[כיא אם אלפ]ני[המה] יפלו(?)	פָּנָה	**421** 13,1
/ פעמיהם על]	פַּעַם	**421** 1a ii-b,7
[בארוך אפים ישיב פתגם וש]	פִּתְגָם	**420** 1a ii-b,2
צ[דיקים]	צַדִּיק	**420** 2,9
ובמחקר צדק	צֶדֶק	**420** 1a ii-b,3
לוא יסור מדרכי צדק]	צֶדֶק	**420** 1a ii-b,5
בצדק נגא[ל]	צֶדֶק	**420** 1a ii-b,6
ובמחקר צ[דק ימצא / תוצאותיה	צֶדֶק	**421** 1a ii-b,14
[כיא מלאכת צ[דק [היאה	צֶדֶק	**421** 11,4
[ל]עשות צ[דקה]	צְדָקָה	**420** 1a ii-b,8
[ללכת בדרכי אל / לעשות צדקה]	צְדָקָה	**421** 1a ii-b,13
[דברי קודש כחוק]	קֹדֶשׁ	**421** 13,4
מג[לת ספר לקרוא]	קרא	**421** 8,2
[ש בכ[ו]ל הקר[בנות	קָרְבָּן	**421** 13,6
יצ[א הגורל הרישון וכן יצאו	רִאשׁוֹן	**421** 1a i,4
[ל° לסרך הכול איש לפני רע[הו]	רֵעַ	**421** 1a i,3
/ הרפאמה על]	רפא	**421** 1a ii-b,8
ה[ון רשעים /	רֶשַׁע	**420** 1a i,4
[ל]כ[לות כל עבדי ר[שע(?)	רֶשַׁע	**421** 9,3

אל ישאב ממנו °]	שאב	**421** 11,3
[שדותיו גבולו]	שָׂדֶה	**420** 1a ii-b,7
לוא ישיב בטרם ישמ[ע]	שוב	**420** 1a ii-b,1
[בארוך אפים ישיב פתגם וש]	שוב	**420** 1a ii-b,2
ל[ו]א ישוב א[חור] / עד	שוב	**420** 1a ii-b,4
לוא ישו[ב אחור עד	שוב	**421** 1a ii-b,15
א[ם ישיב]	שוב	**421** 5,1
[וישם / [לבו ל	שים	**421** 1a ii-b,16
[מה בלבב מ[שכילים(?)	שכל	**420** 2,9
אי[ש משכיל ונבון / ידלם	שכל	**421** 1a ii-b,10
י[וכח תוכחת / משכיל	שכל	**421** 1a ii-b,12
איש[עניו ונכי שכלו	שֶׂכֶל	**420** 1a ii-b,4
לוא ישיב בטרם ישמ[ע]	שמע	**420** 1a ii-b,1
] בזות לוא ישיב בטרם יש[מע	שמע	**421** 1a ii-b,13
[° איש ושומר]	שמר	**421** 3,2
[° ישמור	שמר	**421** 4,1
[א ואל יבא בשער חצרו ובשע]ר	שַׁעַר	**421** 12,3
[א ואל יבא בשער חצרו ובשע]ר	שַׁעַר	**421** 12,3
[° שורר ב]	שרר	**421** 8,1
ב[טוח לאכול ולשתות ממנו כול °]	שתה	**421** 11,2
י[וכח תוכחת / משכיל	תּוֹכַחַת	**421** 1a ii-b,11
/ ימצא תוצ]אותיה	תּוֹצָאָה	**420** 1a ii-b,4
ובמחקר צ[דק ימצא / תוצאותיה	תּוֹצָאָה	**421** 1a ii-b,15
[ר על תוצ]אות	תּוֹצָאָה	**421** 3,1
[ובתלמיה יחרוש ותמיד]	תֶּלֶם	**420** 2,8
[ובתלמיה יחרוש ותמיד]	תָּמִיד	**420** 2,8
[ים וזרעם על תנחומ]ים	תַּנְחוּם	**420** 2,5

4Q425 SAPIENTIAL–DIDACTIC WORK B

[אוילי לב ו[ש]געונו]	אֱוִיל	**425** 1+3,8
[ת איש]	אִישׁ	**425** 1+3,6
[°°° איש בלי[על] איש שוע עינים]	אִישׁ	**425** 1+3,7
[°°° איש בלי[על] איש שוע עינים]	אִישׁ	**425** 1+3,7
[ואל ידב]ר	אַל	**425** 6,2
להלל[/ [ו]להודות לאל על כו[ל	אֵל	**425** 4ii4
[אמת]	אֱמֶת	**425** 2+4i,7
[/ א[ו]מר]	אֹרֶךְ	**425** 4ii6
[°°° איש בלי[על] איש שוע עינים]	בְּלִיַּעַל	**425** 1+3,7
[° בעד לבו לבלתי ה]	בִּלְתִּי	**425** 1+3,2
[° בעד לבו לבלתי ה]	בְּעַד	**425** 1+3,2
[ואל ידב]ר	דבר	**425** 6,2
[ל מוסר תועבה דב[ר [מב]	דָּבָר	**425** 1+3,1

[דרכיו ובמ[ש]קל לוא י[עשה פעלתו	דֶּרֶךְ	**425** 1+3,6
[ל דרכיו]	דֶּרֶךְ	**425** 1+3,11
[°°נה הואה]	הוא	**425** 5,2
[מזהר ל°°°°ט]	זהר	**425** 4ii5
[חוקי °]	חֹק	**425** 5,5
להלל[/ [ו]להודות לאל על כו[ל	ידה	**425** 4ii4
(אל?) [ישפט ביום]	יוֹם	**425** 6,3
[/ [ב]כול מחשבת קוד[ש(ו)	כֹּל	**425** 4ii3
להלל[/ [ו]להודות לאל על כו[ל	כֹּל	**425** 4ii4
[°תנובה לוא ימר°]	לא	**425** 1+3,3
[ולשון ולוא]	לא	**425** 1+3,5
[דרכיו ובמ[ש]קל לוא י[עשה פעלתו	לא	**425** 1+3,6
[° בעד לבו לבלתי ה]	לֵב	**425** 1+3,2
[אוילי לב ו[ש]געונו]	לֵב	**425** 1+3,8

Reference	Lemma	Context
425 2+4i,5	לקח	]ל לוקחי [ר]שף
425 1+3,5	לָשׁוֹן	]ולשון ולוא [
425 2+4i,3	לָשׁוֹן	]ם לשון למכון[
425 6,4	לָשׁוֹן	]יעוה ובלשונו[
425 4ii1	מָה	] / מה נדדת[
425 1+3,1	מוּסָר	]ל מוסר תועבה דב[ר]מב[
425 4ii3	מַחֲשָׁבָה	] / [ב]כול מחשבת קוד[ש(ו)
425 2+4i,3	מָכוֹן	]ם לשון למכון[
425 5,3	משל	]משל ברוחו[
425 1+3,6	מִשְׁקַל	] דרכיו ובמ[ש]קל לוא י[עשה פעלתו
425 4ii1	נדד	] / מה נדדת[
425 4ii1a	נתן	] / תן[
425 2+4i,4	סלה	]עים סולה °[
425 6,4	עוה	]יעוה ובלשונו[
425 1+3,7	עַיִן	]°°° איש בלי[על] איש שוע עינים[
425 4ii4	עַל	להלל] / [ו]להודות לאל על כו[ל
425 1+3,10	פלס	]בים לו לפל[ס
425 4ii3	קֹדֶשׁ	] / [ב]כול מחשבת קוד[ש(ו)
425 1+3,4	קָטָן	]שקר קטן כ°[
425 5,1	קָלוֹן	]ש ק[ל]ון[
425 5,3	רוּחַ	]משל ברוחו[
425 5,4	רֶשַׁע	]רשע ו°[
425 6,5	רֶשַׁע	] רשע °ה°[
425 2+4i,5	רֶשֶׁף	]ל לוקחי [ר]שף
425 1+3,8	שִׁגָּעוֹן	]אוילי לב ו[ש]געונו[
425 1+3,7	שׁוע	]°°° איש בלי[על] איש שוע עינים[
425 6,3	שׁפט	(אל?)]ישפט ביום [
425 1+3,4	שֶׁקֶר	]שקר קטן כ°[
425 1+3,1	תּוֹעֵבָה	]ל מוסר תועבה דב[ר]מב[
425 1+3,3	תְּנוּבָה	]°תנובה לוא ימר°[
425 4ii2	תַּרְדֵּמָה	]תרדמה מ[

4Q**426** SAPIENTIAL-HYMNIC WORK A

Reference	Lemma	Context
426 4,2	אהב	]אוהב ב[
426 7,3	אוֹצָר	]ופתח אוצ[ר(ו) (?)
426 10,1	אוֹצָר	]אוצר[
426 1i6	אַח	א]חיהו
426 1i10	אַיִן	]ל וכול זר אין / [...
426 1ii5	אִישׁ	...] / צעדו איש ידע י°[
426 1ii9	אִישׁ	...] / איש °[
426 2,1	אִישׁ	]איש הבהב ל[וא] ישר[
426 8,3	אִישׁ	א]יש לק °[
426 10,2	אִישׁ	]איש בינה °[
426 1i11	אֹכֶל	]ה ואוכל טוב ענפיה / [...
426 1ii6	אַל	...] / ישר ונחלה ואל[
426 1ii7	אַל	...] / ואל יביאני עד[
426 1i4	אֵל	]נתן אל בלבבי דעה ובינה /
426 6,1	אֵל	ו]עתה אלי[
426 8,1	אֵל	]°תה (כי אלי)[
426 1i5	אֵמֶר	ולנוצר[י אמ]ת אמרי / [
426 1i5	אֱמֶת	ולנוצר[י אמ]ת אמרי / [
426 1ii4	אֱנוֹשׁ	...] / ואתבוננו בפעו̇ל⟦ו⟧ת אנו[ש
426 1i1	אֹרֶךְ	כב]וד ומדת דעת ואורך ימים /
426 12,3	אַרְפַּכְשַׁד	(בני שם) עילם וא]שור וארפכשד ול[וד וארם
426 1i13	אֶרֶץ	]ה °ול למלכי ארץ רוד[ף]
426 12,4	אֶרֶץ	]וכול שוכני[
426 1i14	אִשָּׁה	]ים ונשים
426 12,3	אַשּׁוּר	(בני שם) עילם וא]שור וארפכשד ול[וד וארם
426 5,3	אֲשֶׁר	]ה א[ת] אשר °[
426 11,4	אֲשֶׁר	נ]פשו אש[ר (?)
426 2,3	אֵת	] אותם[
426 5,3	אֵת	]ה א[ת] אשר °[
426 1ii7	בוא	...] / ואל יביאני עד[
426 4,4	בחר	ב]חר בשרים ת[
426 1ii3	בין	...] / יתבונן ואגידה לכמה[
426 1ii4	בין	...] / ואתבוננו בפעו̇ל⟦ו⟧ת אנו[ש
426 1i4	בִּינָה	]נתן אל בלבבי דעה ובינה /
426 10,2	בִּינָה	]איש בינה °[
426 1ii2	בְּכוֹר	...] / בכור ארים ש[
426 1ii8	בְּעַד	...] / תשוך בעדי[
426 1i4	דֵּעָה	]נתן אל בלבבי דעה ובינה /
426 12,2	דרשׁ	]דרשו ומשפחות[
426 1i8	היה	]לה לוא יהיו / [...
426 11,2	הפך?	]הפכה⟦נ⟧ ישכון ל[
426 11,2	הֲפֵכָה?	]הפכה⟦נ⟧ ישכון ל[
426 1i10	זָר	]ל וכול זר אין / [...
426 1i2	זֶרַע	וזרע רשעים / [...
426 5,1	חֶדֶר	]חדרי שא[ול
426 1i6	חיה	י]חיהו
426 9,2	חרץ	]°ו נחרצה[
426 7,2	חשׁב	]שכל יחש[ב
426 1i11	טוֹב	]ה ואוכל טוב ענפיה / [...
426 1ii10	טוֹב	...] / טוב[
426 4,5	טָמֵא	]ם טמא(ה)

426 1i1	ידע	כב]וֹד ומדת דעת ואורך ימים /
426 1ii5	ידע	...] / צעדו איש ידע י◦[
426 2,1	יהב	]איש הבהֹב ל[וא] יֹשרֹ[
426 1i1	יוֹם	כב]וֹד ומדת דעת ואורך ימים /
426 1i12	יוֹם	]ת בסתרֹ מלפני{{ו}} הֹיֹוֹם /
426 1ii6	יָשָׁר	...] / ישר ונחלה ואלֹ[
426 2,1	יָשָׁר	]איש הבהֹב ל[וא] יֹשרֹ[
426 1i1	כָּבוֹד	כב]וֹד ומדת דעת ואורך ימים /
426 8,1	כִּי	]◦תה {כי אלֹיֹ}[
426 1i2	כֹּל	שו]מֹרי כול מצוותיו
426 1i9	כֹּל	]כול תאר בתבל / [
426 1i10	כֹּל	]לֹ וֹכול זר אֹיןֹ / [...
426 10,3	כֹּל	ל/י]תעב כול עובדֹיֹ[
426 10,4	כֹּל	כו]ל[ ]מֹלכֹיֹם א◦[
426 12,4	כֹּל	]וֹכול שוכני[
426 1i8	לא	]להֹ לוא יהיו / [...
426 2,1	לא	]איש הבהֹב ל[וא] יֹשרֹ[
426 2,2	לא	]◦ ולוֹ[א] יֹפֹלגֹ[
426 4,3	לא	לו]אֹ ישג יהו◦[
426 5,5	לא	]אֹ מֹיֹ משולחֹ לֹוֹאֹ[
426 5,6	לא	]לוֹאֹ ישוֹבֹ[
426 11,3	לא	]לרוֹחֹו לוא יש[
426 12,1	לא	]◦יה לוא ה[
426 1i4	לֵבָב	]נתן אל בלבבי דֹעֹה ובינה /
426 12,3	לוד	]בני שם{ עילם וא[שור וארפכשד ול[וד וארם
426 1i12	לִפְנֵי	]ת בסתרֹ מלפני{{ו}} הֹיֹוֹם /
426 8,3	לֵץ	א]יש לץ ◦[
426 9,1	מאר	]תו נמארֹ[
426 1i1	מִדָּה	כב]וֹד ומדת דעת ואורך ימים /
426 5,5	מִי	]אֹ מֹיֹ משולחֹ לֹוֹאֹ[
426 1i13	מֶלֶךְ	]ה ◦ול למלכי ארץ רוד[ף]
426 10,4	מֶלֶךְ	כו]ל[ ]מֹלכֹיֹם א◦[
426 1i12	מִן	]ת בסתרֹ מלפני{{ו}} הֹיֹוֹם /
426 1i2	מִצְוָה	שו]מֹרי כול מצוותיו
426 12,2	מִשְׁפָּחָה	]דרֹשו ומשפחותֹ[
426 1ii3	נגד	...] / יתבונן ואגידה לכמהֹ[
426 1ii6	נַחֲלָה	...] / ישר ונחלה ואלֹ[
426 11,1	נַחֲלָה	]נֹחֹלתו *vacat* {◦}[
426 11,4	נֶפֶשׁ	נ]פשוֹ אש[ר (?)
426 1i5	נצר	וֹלנֹוֹצֹרֹ[י אמ]תֹ אמרי / [
426 4,3	נשׂג	לו]אֹ ישג יהו◦[
426 1i4	נתן	]נתן אל בלבבי דֹעֹה ובינה /
426 1i12	סֵתֶר	]ת בסתרֹ מלפני{{ו}} הֹיֹוֹם /
426 10,3	עבד	ל/י]תעב כול עובדֹיֹ[
426 1ii7	עַד	...] / ואל יביאני עד[
426 1i11	עָנָף	]הֹ ואֹוכל טוב ענפיה / [...
426 6,1	עַתָּה	ו]עתהֹ אֹלי[
426 2,2	פלג	]◦ ולוֹ[א] יֹפֹלגֹ[
426 1ii11	פלס	...] / יפלסֹ[
426 1ii4	פְּעֻלָּה	...] / ואתבוננו בפעוֹל{{ו}}ת אנֹוֹ[ש
426 7,3	פתח	]יֹפתח אֹוֹצֹ[רו] (?)
426 1ii5	צַעַד	...] / צעדו איש ידע י◦[
426 1i13	רדף	]ה ◦ול למלכי ארץ רוד[ף]
426 11,3	רוּחַ	]לרוֹחֹו לוא יש[
426 1ii2	רום	...] / בכור ארים ש[
426 9,3	רחב	]ירחיב[
426 1i2	רֶשַׁע	וזרע רשעים / [...
426 5,1	שְׁאוֹל	]חֹדרי שא[ול
426 8,2	שְׁאוֹל	]◦ שאוֹלה[
426 5,6	שׁוב	]לוֹאֹ ישוֹבֹ[
426 1ii8	שׁוּךְ	...] / תשוך בעדוֹ[
426 7,2	שֶׂכֶל	]שכל יחשֹ[ב
426 11,2	שׁכן	]הֹפכה{{נ}} ישכון לֹ[
426 12,4	שׁכן	]וֹכול שוכני[
426 4,3a	שָׁלוֹשׁ	]◦ ושלושה [
426 5,5	שׁלח	]אֹ מֹיֹ משולחֹ לֹוֹאֹ[
426 1i2	שׁמר	שו]מֹרי כול מצוותיו
426 5,2	שִׁקּוּץ	]◦פ שקוצים[
426 4,4	שַׂר	ב]חֹר בשריֹםֹ תֹ[
426 1i9	תֹּאַר	]כול תאר בתבל / [
426 1i9	תֵּבֵל	]כול תאר בתבל / [
426 7,1	תּוֹצָאָה	]◦ ותוֹצאתֹ[
426 10,3	תעב	ל/י]תעב כול עובדֹיֹ[

PLATES

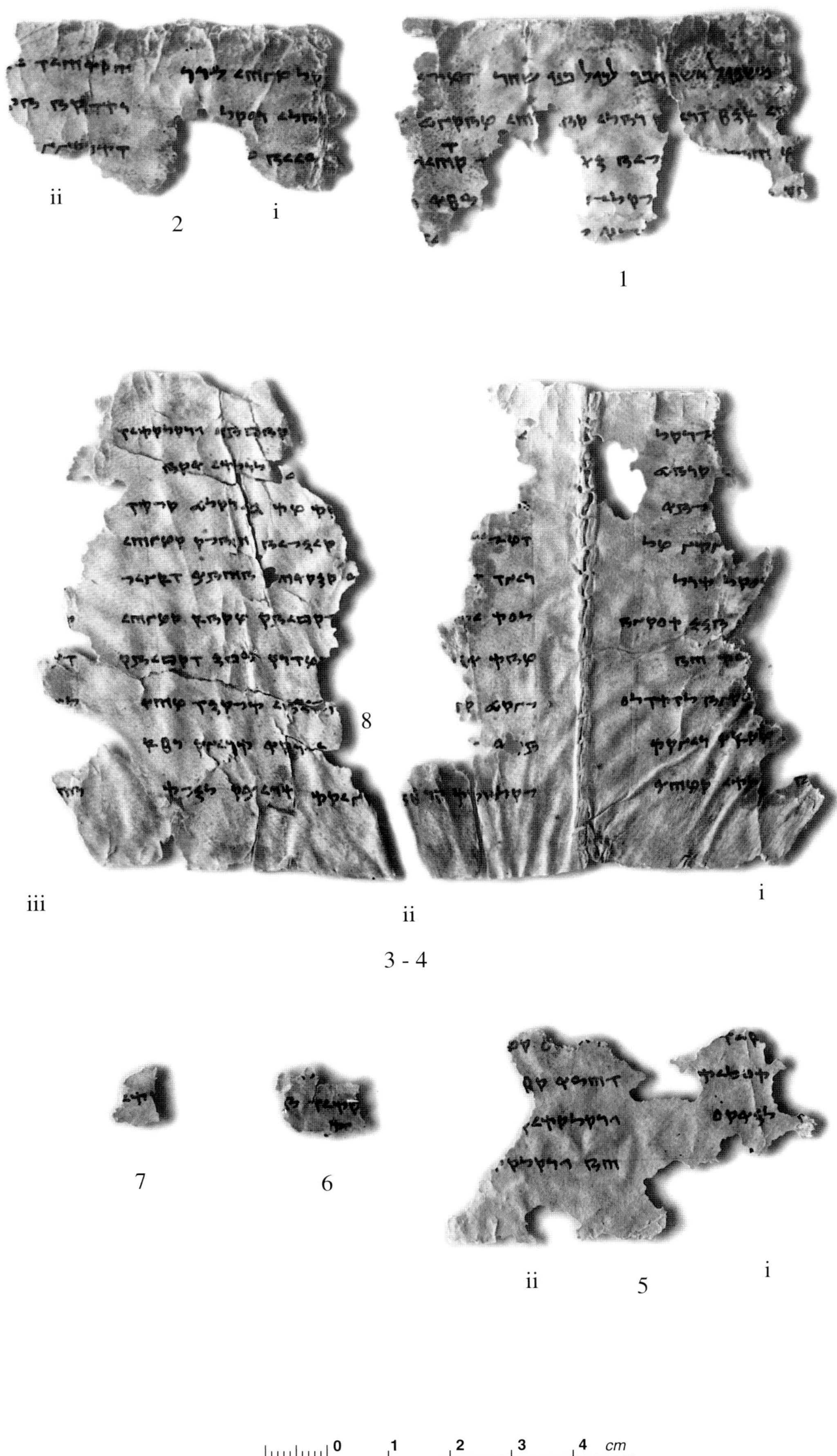

298. 4QcryptA Words of the Maskil to All Sons of Dawn
PAM 43.384; Mus. Inv. 898

Back of reconstructed wad with frg. 3 positioned on top of frg. 4. Note line of cracking caused by shrinkage of leather tie.

Reconstructed wad with frgs. 1, 2, and 5 positioned on top of frg. 3. (Frg. 4 lies under frg. 3; frg. 2 under frg. 1; frg. 5 under frg. 9.)

298. 4QcryptA Words of the Maskil to All Sons of Dawn
Photos: S. Pfann

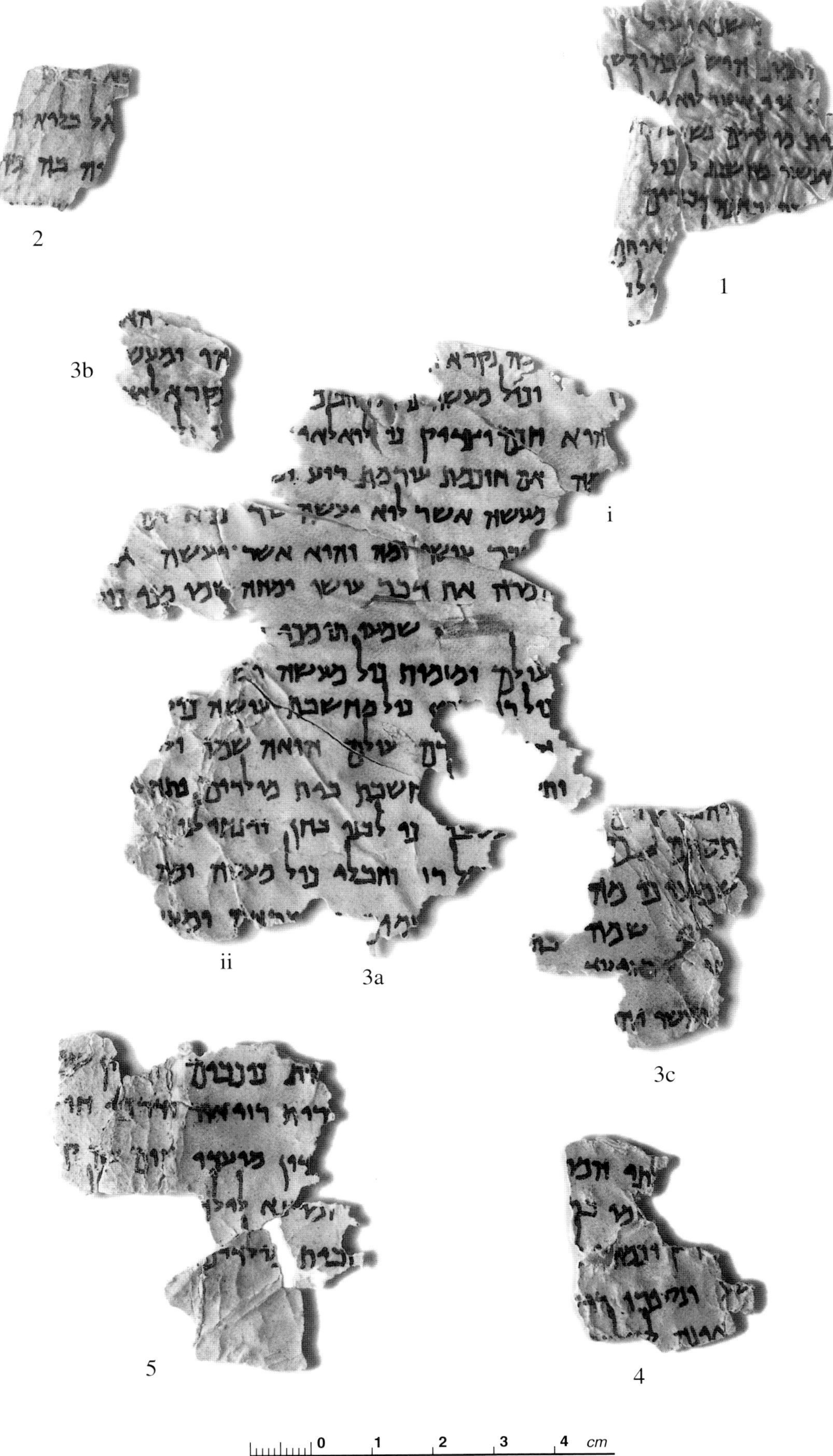

299. 4QMysteries[a]
PAM 43.389; Mus. Inv. 605

299. 4QMysteries[a]
PAM 43.390; Mus. Inv. 604

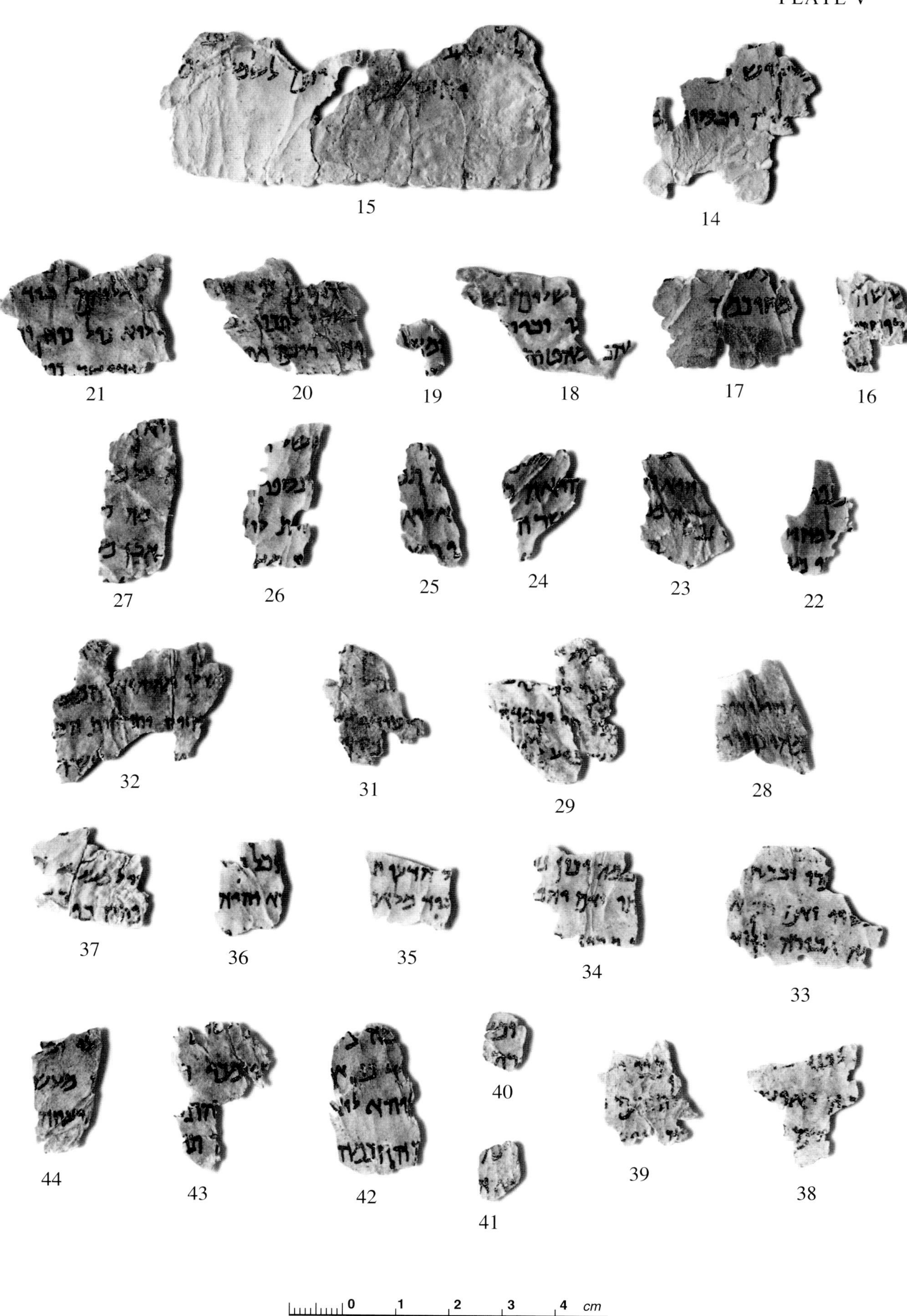

299. 4QMysteries[a]
PAM 43.391; Mus. Inv. 594

299. 4QMysteries[a]
PAM 41.321, 43.392; Mus. Inv. 595

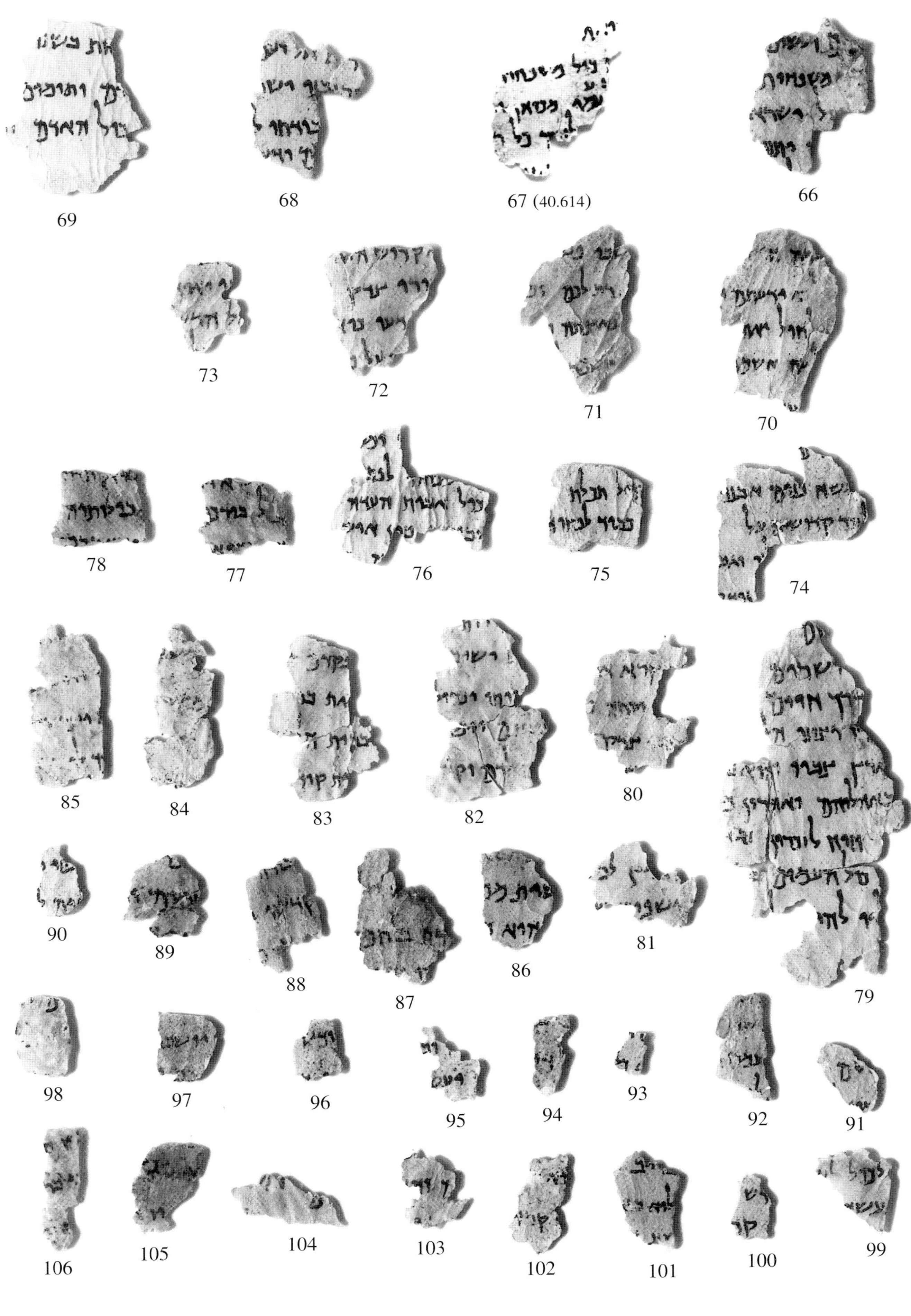

69 68 67 (40.614) 66

73 72 71 70

78 77 76 75 74

85 84 83 82 80 79

90 89 88 87 86 81

98 97 96 95 94 93 92 91

106 105 104 103 102 101 100 99

0 1 2 3 4 cm

299. 4QMysteries[a]
PAM 40.614, 43.393; Mus. Inv. 592

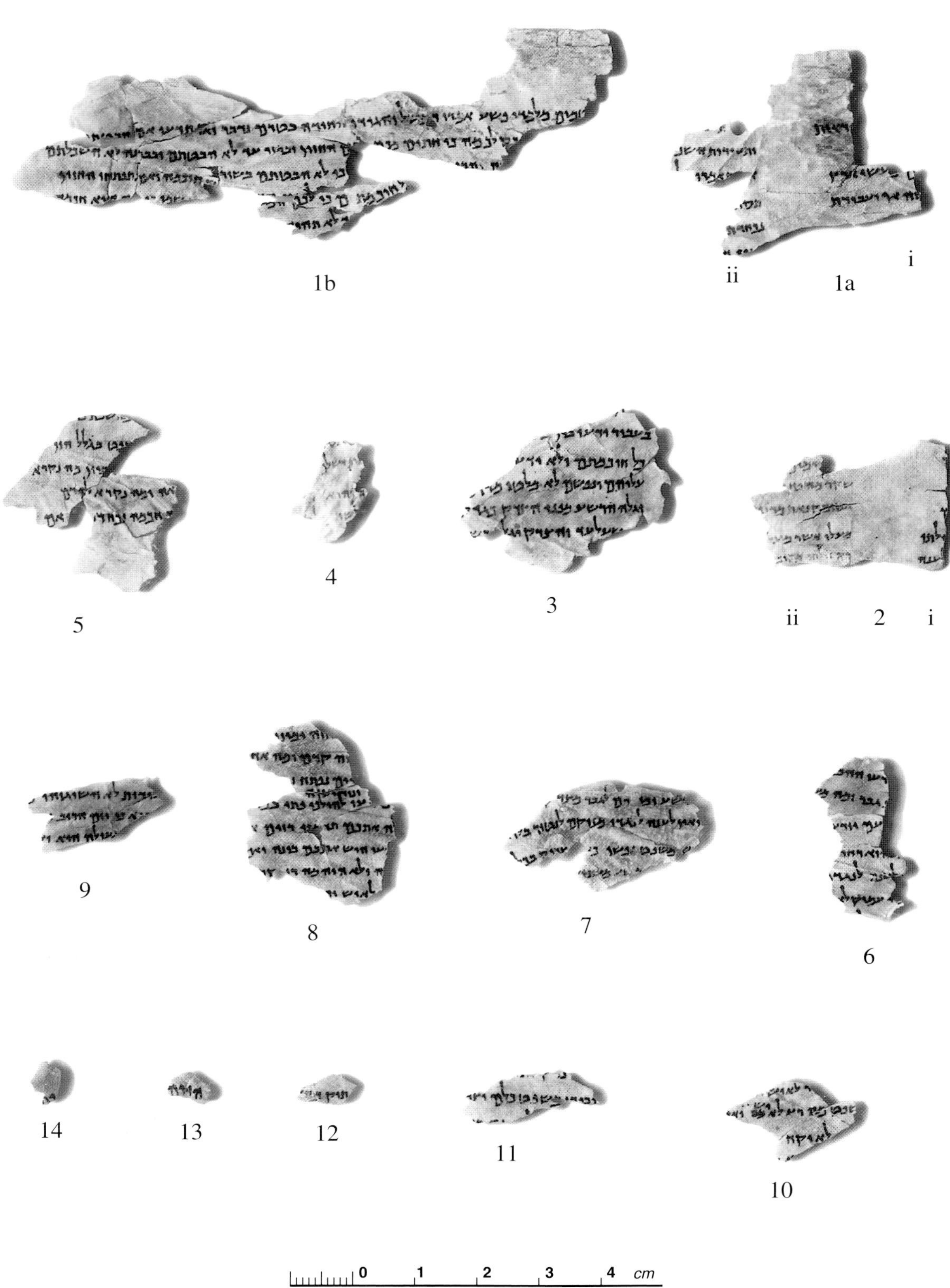

300. 4QMysteries[b]
PAM 43.388; Mus. Inv. 591

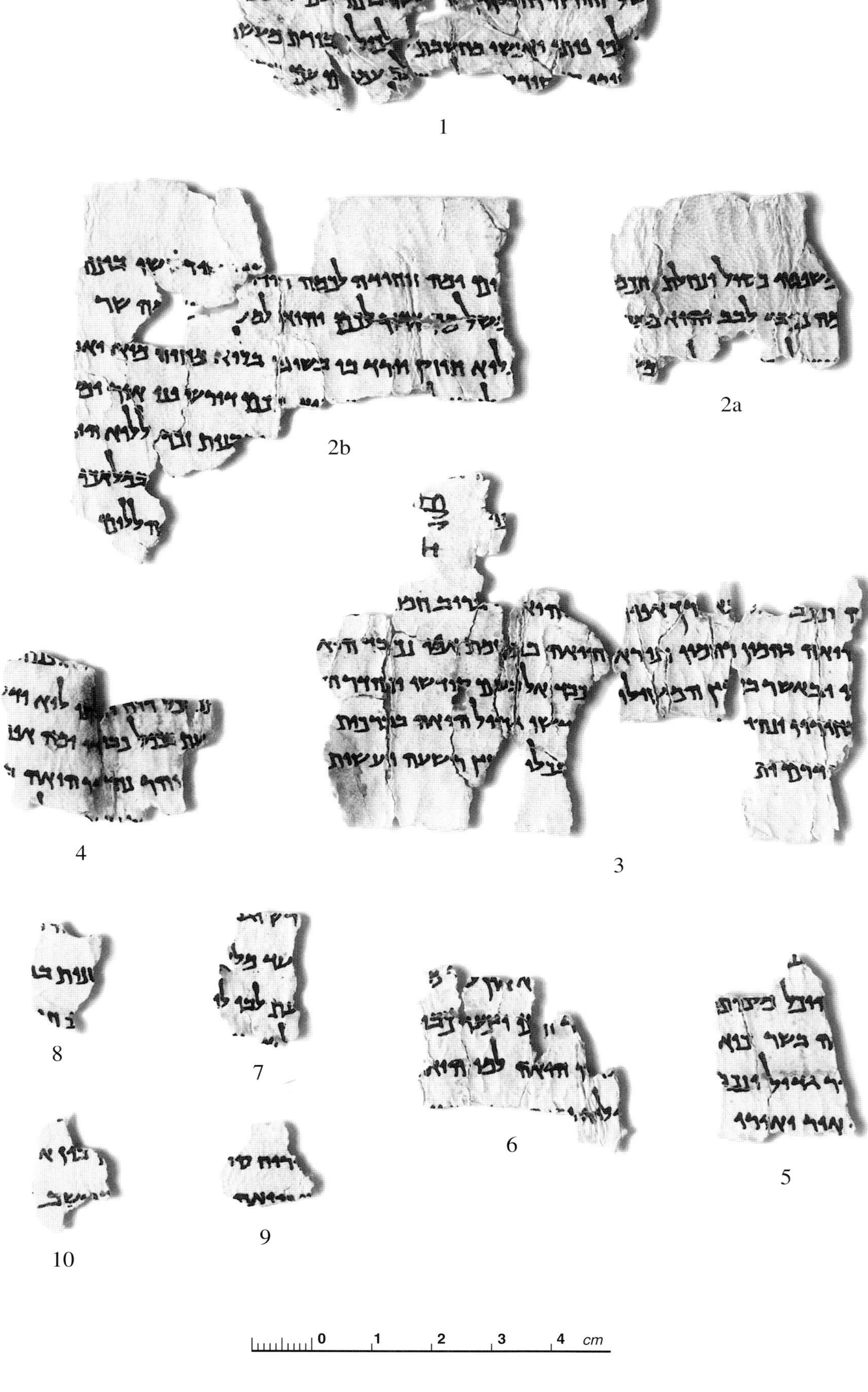

301. 4QMysteries[c]?
PAM 43.394; Mus. Inv. 582

302. 4QpapAdmonitory Parable
PAM 43.395, 43.396; Mus. Inv. 333, 356

iii ii i

3

3c 3b 3a

302. 4QpapAdmonitory Parable
PAM 43.395; Mus. Inv. 356

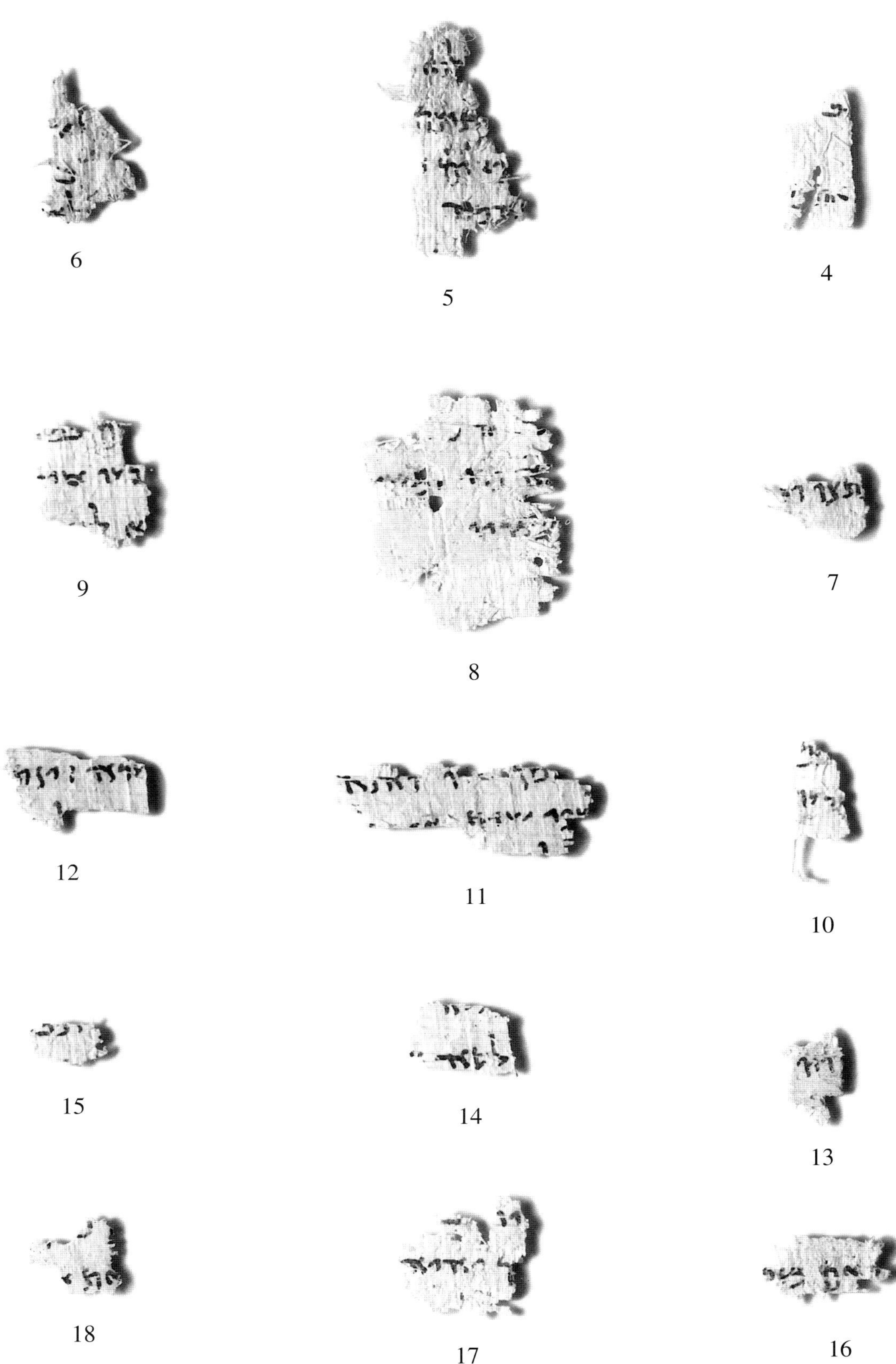

302. 4QpapAdmonitory Parable
PAM 43.396; Mus. Inv. 333

303

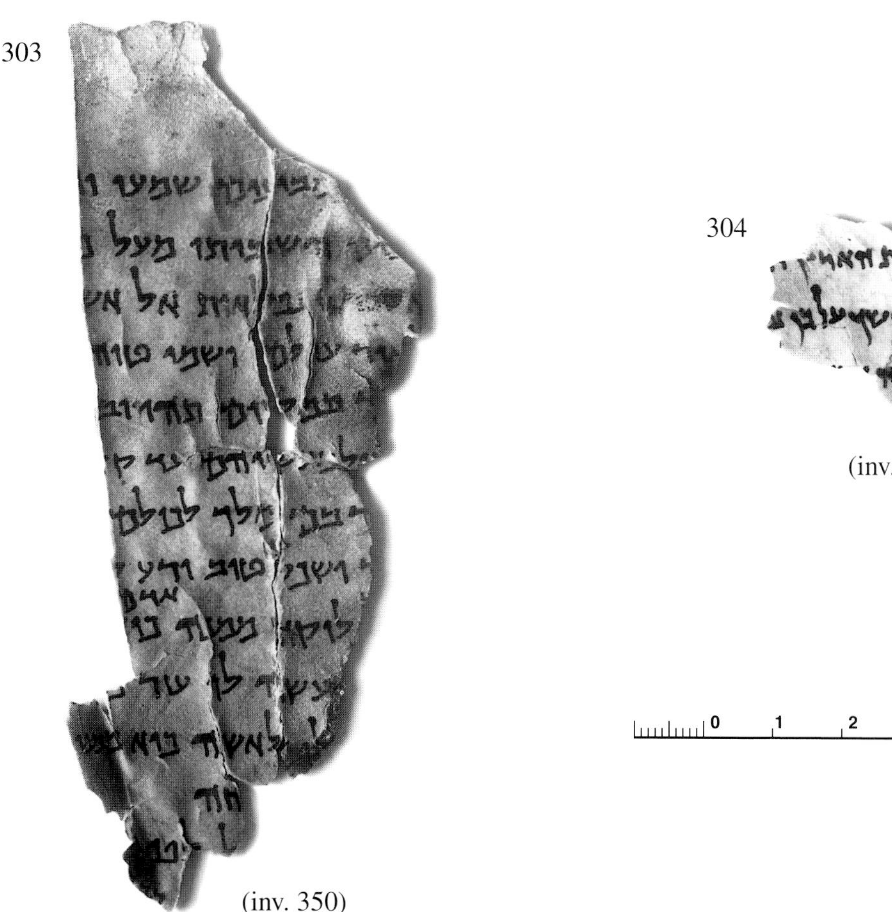

(inv. 350)

304

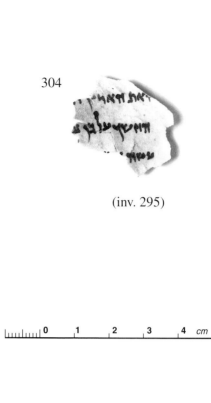

(inv. 295)

0 1 2 3 4 cm

305

(inv. 295)

ii

i

303. 4QMeditation on Creation A
304. 4QMeditation on Creation B
305. 4QMeditation on Creation C
PAM 43.397; Mus. Inv. 295, 350

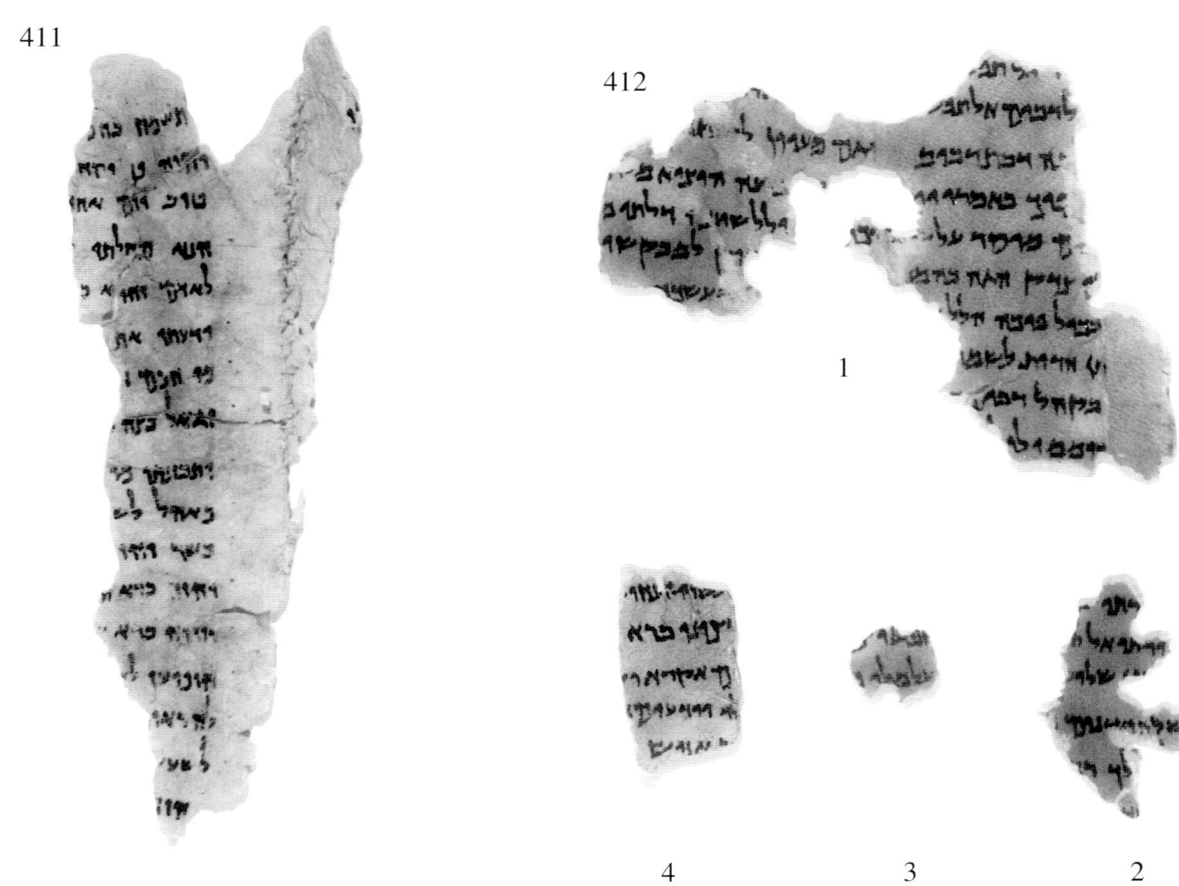

411. 4QSapiential Hymn
412. 4QSapiential–Didactic Work A
PAM 42.916; Mus. Inv. 292

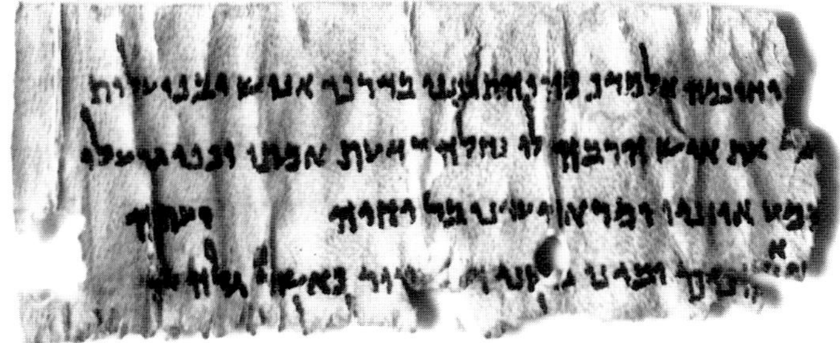

413. 4QWork concerning Divine Providence
PAM 43.499; Mus. Inv. 127

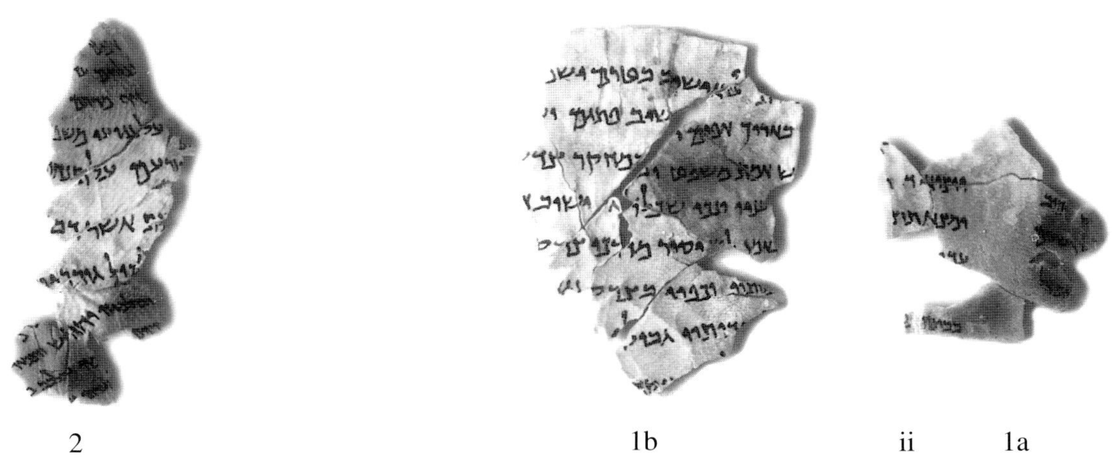

2 1b ii 1a

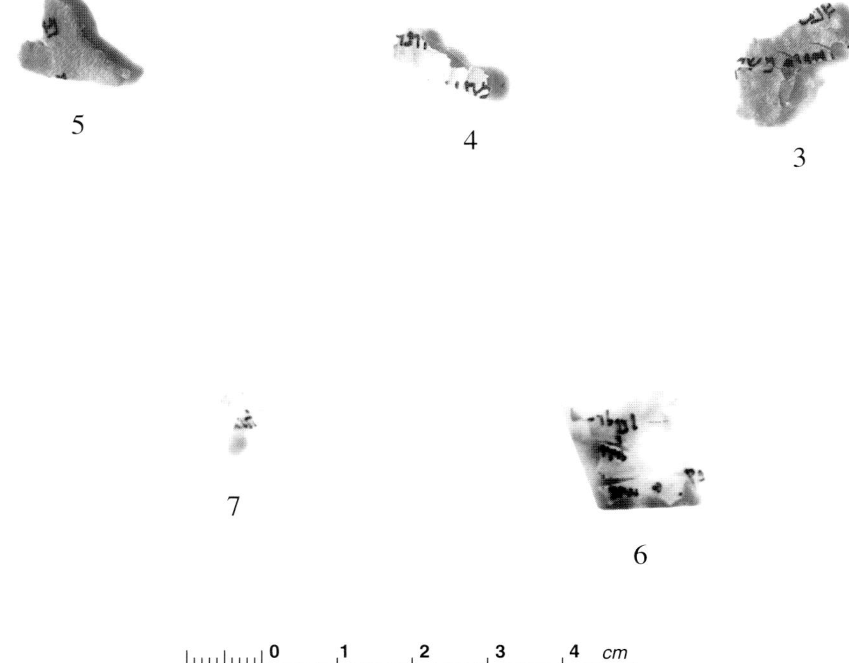

5 4 3

7 6

420. 4QWays of Righteousness[a]
PAM 43.534; Mus. Inv. 509

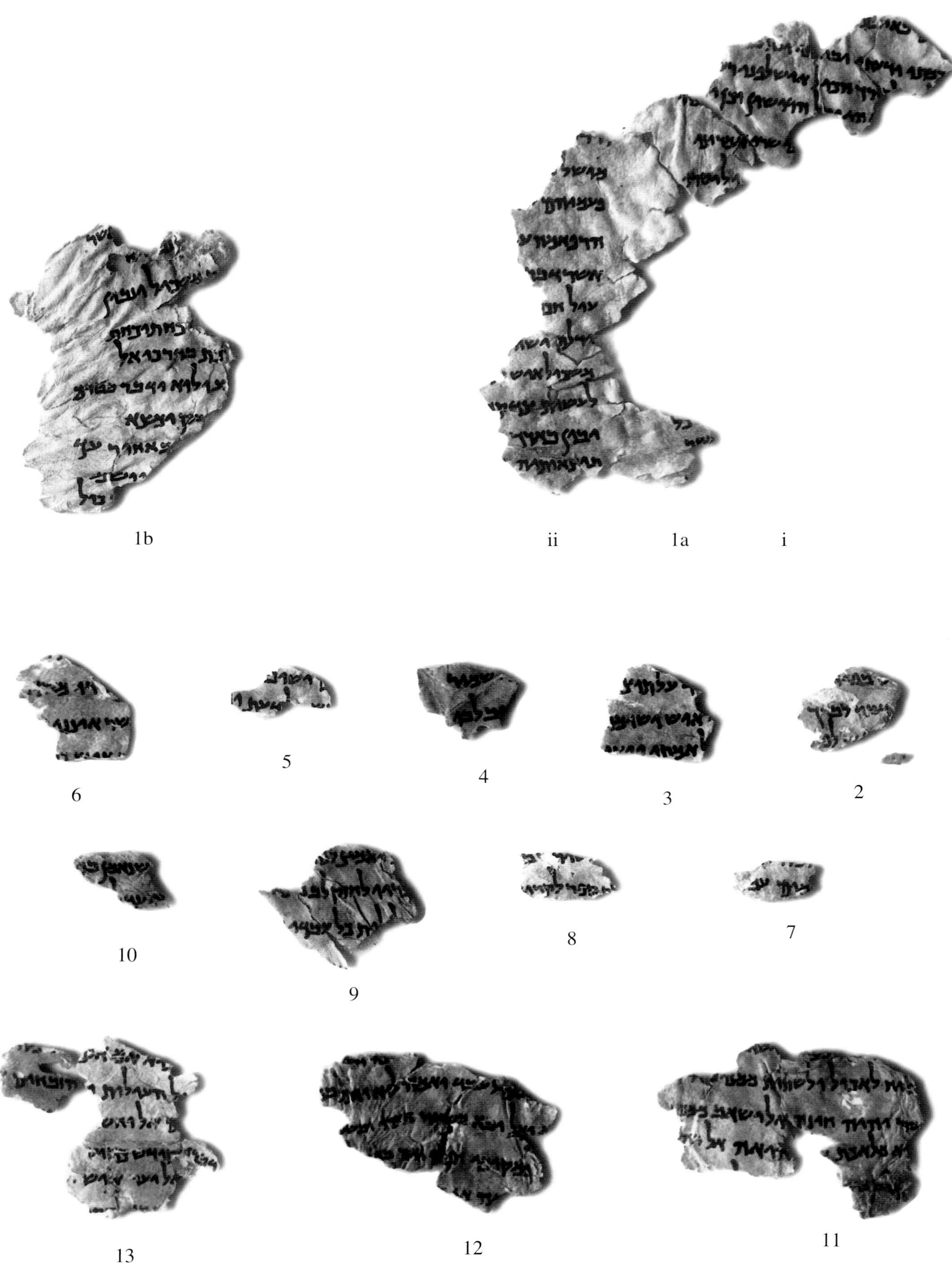

1b ii 1a i

6 5 4 3 2

10 9 8 7

13 12 11

421. 4QWays of Righteousness[b]
PAM 43.537; Mus. Inv. 512

3

1

2

ii i

4

6 5

425. 4QSapiential–Didactic Work B
PAM 43.541; Mus. Inv. 501

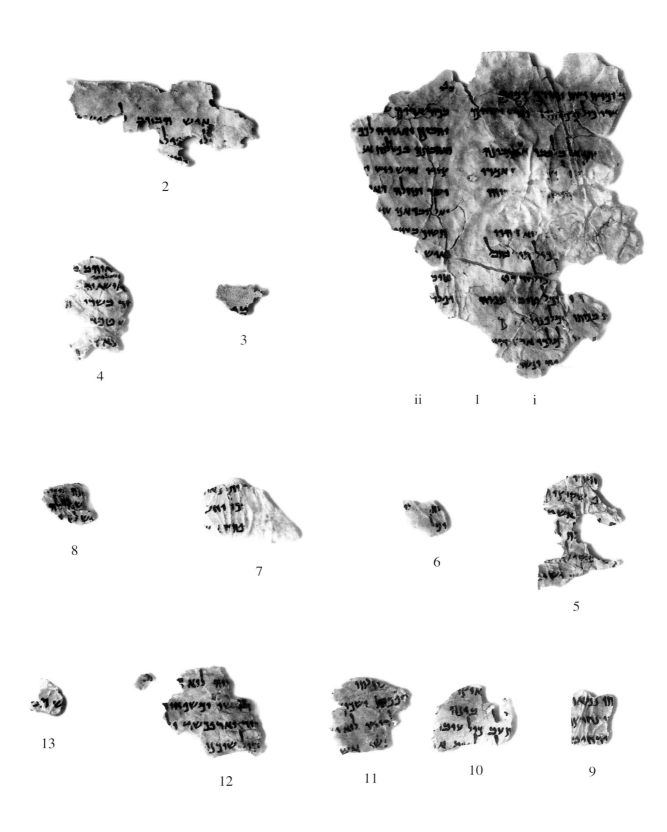

426. 4QSapiential–Hymnic Work A
PAM 43.541; Mus. Inv. 276